The Orphaned Imagination

THE

ORPHANED

IMAGINATION

Melancholy and Commodity Culture

in English Romanticism

Guinn Batten

Duke University Press Durham and London

1998

© 1998 Duke University Press
All rights reserved
Printed in the United States of America on acid-free paper ∞
Typeset in Adobe Garamond with Copperplate display
by Keystone Typesetting, Inc.
Library of Congress Cataloging-in-Publication Data appear
on the last printed page of this book.

For my parents,
Mary and Jim

Contents

Acknowledgments

A book that has in its title the word "orphan" can only evoke, and be grateful for, those who helped it come into the world. *The Orphaned Imagination* began as a dissertation at Duke University. Robert Gleckner's inspired teaching of Romanticism sparked my interest in that field, and the intellectual intensity and generosity that he brings to poetry and its critics have made him an ideal mentor. Through his encouragement of cooperative scholarship emerged the Duke Romanticists Collective. These compatriots—especially Nigel Alderman, Ghislaine McDayter, John Waters, and Mandy Berry—challenged and strengthened my work on melancholy and Romanticism in its earliest stages, and they remain valued readers and friends. Eve Sedgwick and Toril Moi gave me invaluable tools for reading poems as extensions of the body, Fred Jameson for reading in the materials of history a politics of compassion and hope. I thank Barbara Herrnstein Smith and Jan Radway for encouraging me to begin the process that led to this book and Stanley Fish—whose demanding, rewarding Milton I cannot erase from the fleshly tables of the heart—for asking me to transform the dissertation into a book. At Duke Press I am also indebted to Reynolds Smith, whose deft editing of the Introduction helped sharpen the book's focus; and to both Pam Morrison and my copyeditor Estelle Silbermann for their tactful improvements.

My colleagues and graduate students at Washington University have welcomed me into a special community where poetry and theory help each other thrive. Two colleagues have read and commented on versions of *The Orphaned Imagination*: Naomi Lebowitz, whose enthusiasm picks us up when fallen, and Joe Loewenstein, who as chair brought me into a department for which he gave me high expectations. I am fortunate in having colleagues in Romanticism and nineteenth-century studies whose opinions and friendships I have valued highly: Miriam Bailin, the late John Morris, and Judy Weissman. Mary Bly and Erin Mackie, who share and support my interest in a poetics of embodiment, have, with Kevin Ray, Steven Meyer, Amy Pawl, and Paul Rosenzweig, offered encouragement when it has been needed most. I have learned much from my graduate students, and have a special debt to John Griffin. And I am grateful to Dan Shea for supporting requests for leave that ensured the timely completion of this manuscript.

Much of my research took place at Wake Forest University. Isabel Zuber and her colleagues at Z. Smith Reynolds Library helped me find the books I needed and keep them long enough to make the search worthwhile. Among many friends in the Wake Forest community, five deserve special thanks: John Archer Carter, who introduced me to metacritical approaches to nineteenth-century literature; Edwin Wilson, the Romanticist and godfather of the Wake Forest University Press, which I managed for three years; Candide Jones, the press's current manager; Germaine Brée, who introduced me to French feminism and with whom it was a pleasure to work on the press's expansion into French poetry; and Philip Kuberski, my theoretical debts to whom will appear in the pages that follow. I especially thank Phil for the care with which he read various drafts of this book and for opening doors into alternative ways of thinking about ghosts in the machinery of the imagination.

I must also thank colleagues within the extended family of Irish studies, especially Tony Bradley and James Olney, who provided early opportunities for me to try out ideas on the family romances of poetry. Declan Kiberd, Eileen Cahill, Adrian Frazier, Bill Wilson, and Edna Longley have also encouraged me in various ways. The poets published by Wake Forest have in their different ways inspired and furthered the ideas in this book. I am especially grateful to Paul Muldoon, who asks the right questions about Yeats and who long ago took me into the underworld of words. Nuala Ní Dhomhnaill and C. K. Williams kindly offered their beautifully phrased responses to a draft of the introduction and afterword. John Montague has kept me true to my thesis by offering himself as a model for the orphaned imagination.

My other extended family lives, seasonally, at Stoots Mountain, Virginia. My thanks to Rick Mashburn, Ken Frazelle, and Lee and Edith Potter for sharing music, books, and vegetables through the long days of peace there. And to Iris Hill, a gifted publisher who helped me find my way in the world of bookmaking, and George Entenman.

But a book on orphans must finally give credit to the author's own family. Jim and Mary Batten, who first taught me the value of books and the possibilities of self-education, offer the best reasons for challenging a culture that hurries us into orphanhood. Julia and

David have given so much encouragement. Kathleen and Devin
Johnston have, since they were children, shown me how capacious
can be our inclusiveness, whether we extend our sympathy to a
foster child who is blind and deaf or to a poet whom we have not yet
learned to hear or see.

Finally, I am grateful for the two decades that I have shared with
Dillon Johnston. He is the best reader of poets, living and dead, I
will ever know. It is he who taught me that metaphors carry, and the
value of engaging in carriage.

Introduction: Romantic Melancholy

and Commodity Culture

> But words are things, and a small drop of ink,
>   Falling like dew upon a thought, produces
> That which makes thousands, perhaps millions, think.
>   'Tis strange, the shortest letter which man uses
> Instead of speech, may form a lasting link
>   Of ages. To what straits old Time reduces
> Frail man, when paper, even a rag like this,
> Survives himself, his tomb, and all that's his.
>   LORD BYRON, *Don Juan,* canto 3

The English Romantic poets were born in the era that unlocked many of the secrets of nature and of money, discoveries that would make England the country that entered early, and energetically, the age of industry. Witnesses of that industrious but tumultuous transition to a commodity culture, these poets, because of their early experiences as, in one sense or another, orphans, could not help but observe that England's accelerated exchange of labor and things for cash, and of things for words, created not only capital, not only markets, and not only a proliferation of print for Byron's "millions." Commodity culture also cultivates melancholia. While the Romantic poets embraced in their youth a radicalism fostered by social and economic injustices made more visible by the unprecedented speed of economic change, they also recognized that the individual freedom advocated by Adam Smith no less than by Thomas Paine could not alone solve the systemic problems of a free-market economy. Such economies alienate workers from their products, efface for consumers the origins of their fetishized purchases, convert desire itself into an exchangeable commodity, and estrange human intelligence from a "Nature" that at the close of the eighteenth century receded even as the mind mastered so many of its mysteries.

Words, as Byron acknowledges, reproduce the invisible ideology that leads millions to believe—with a faith once devoted to the church—in the efficacy (and perhaps even in the inevitability) of the modern systems of exchange that unite us as a society even as they isolate us as subjects. Ideology is engendered, as Byron playfully suggests, in the very locus of sexual desire and bodily reproduction. To restrict words to their place in exchange is to resign ourselves not only to the success of ideology but also to a condition of orphanhood, believing that we have only words to designate the flesh and blood we are no longer allowed to possess. Yet words, as Byron concludes, may yet metamorphose back into such possessions, not only mimicking but *becoming* the "shortest letter that man uses." The "small drop of ink" that disseminates by serving the "think" of ideology may also both spawn and change thinking. But if poetic words are to do so without making of art simply another fetishized and uniformly produced commodity that leaves unaltered how we think, they must constantly question their own presence at the foundations of linguistic and economic exchange. In the procreative poetics of the Romantics, we may witness a resistance to forms of thinking, whether idealist or empiricist, shaped increasingly, like production and consumption, by standardization and specialization. For as an orphan especially understands, the living body is itself a medium, one that links the past and the future, and one whose sexuality and linguistic fertility are interdependent. Yet the orphan also may intuit, more keenly than others, how ideology may co-opt that fertility, shaping a culture in which the two-parent, heterosexual family becomes the standard form of sexual, and reproductive, expression.

That standard bears little resemblance to the family arrangements most of the Romantic poets grew up in, or those they subsequently chose. Wordsworth, Coleridge, Byron, and Keats all lost at least one parent early in life and had lost both before entering fully into manhood. Blake and Shelley, famous for their insights into modern forms of patriarchy, came close to emotional collapse at key moments in their respective careers because they could not, finally, work through their melancholic attachment to dead fathers. While the grief that hurt them into poetry took no single form, their second home in the materials of verse—materials that for these poets were inseparable from the materials of the body—offered to them a genuine position from which to critique the orphanage of culture. The Romantic poets who are the focus of this study remind us of the cost of resigning one's self to early, not-quite forgotten losses. Hearing what Wordsworth called a "ghostly language," calculating what Blake called the "price of experience," they remain unreconciled to the compensatory strategies of their culture. In questioning the value of a modernity purchased through the ostensible surrender of origins, however, these poets are neither nostalgic nor engaged in wishful thinking. What appears to have been lost, they tell us, in fact persists. At the margins of our systems of symbolic exchange, of the Lacanian "Law of the Father" that could only come into being through the exclusion of "the Real," dwell the banished objects whom these poets evoke. We may find them in the Wordsworthian and Shelleyan sublime, the gothic and negative predilections of Coleridge and Keats, Byron's ruined empires and liminal, prolific revisions of stanzas, and Blake's gonadal forges and looms.

As the example of Blake suggests most clearly, the Romantic poets, in challenging the principle of exchange that founds capitalist economies, also question its twin injunctions of sublimation and work. They further recognize that both injunctions are intimately linked to sexual prohibitions. To earn the right to be free, whether that freedom is to participate in democratic governance or in the marketplace, the subject is required by society to surpass what Freud in "Mourning and Melancholia" articulates as the "regressiveness" of melancholia. Following a centuries-old precedent for the cure of melancholia through astral, dietary, and exercise regimens, Freud adapts the panacea of work to what he calls the necessity of "working through" sexually unhealthy attachments until one has achieved a "mourning" that is "healthy." No less than linguistic and economic exchange, the compensatory logic of sexual substitution or of sublimation structures the horizon of consciousness that separates the "healthy" subject from the past. Such logic seems itself to have neither a beginning nor an end, for the incest taboo, as Freud argues in *Totem and Taboo,* similarly structures the horizon of law-abiding cultures. Inseparably linked to that taboo, as Freud concluded, is the totem. In the place of the absent father-tyrant (murdered, Freud speculates, by an Oedipal band of brothers) stands an impersonal, universally accepted rule of law, one that is founded on prohibition and substitution.

Whatever freedom is promised by the law, the law cannot free itself from its origins in prohibited desire. Even as the ideology of capital urges modern subjects to work, to defer, and to save, it also and in open contradiction urges them to desire, to spend, and to consume. Yet we may be sure that the consumer ultimately may anticipate neither lasting joy nor final satisfaction in this marginal utility. The free market, which depends upon desire, is no less dependent on need: it cannot operate without the presence of the working poor and "acceptable" levels of unemployment. While most consumers recognize, on some level, the two faces of a "want" that fissures a culture that claims to be built by work, such recognition can lead only to cynicism in a society where economic inequity seems the inevitable price of freedom. Cynicism, as Slavoj Žižek has persuasively argued, while keen in its analysis of the overdetermined contexts of its own (and others') ideologically constructed subjectivity, can neither efface the unconscious bases of the thinking self's illogical consumption nor escape the ideological structures to which that self accedes, most abjectly, at the very moment of its cynical analysis.[1] But if our cynicism brands us as postmodern, like the Romantics we live in a culture that denies its origins even as its desires bespeak its unconscious attachment to what it claims to have relinquished.

The Oedipal model, which endorses the necessity of such denial and underwrites systems of symbolic as well as sexual exchange, in fact misrepresents the Romantic poets' subtle and in many ways quite contemporary understanding of the crucial nexus between desire, language, and ideology. Yet studies of the canonical Romantic poets (even those that are not explicitly psychoanalytic) have, with remarkable consistency, employed explicitly or implicitly Oedipal models of intellectual, no less than sexual, development. Likewise, these studies have supposed that the Romantic poets wrote in order to establish their freedom and their individuality. These presumptions unite scholars whether their approaches are liberal or Marxist, humanist or poststructuralist or deconstructionist, and whether they are sympathetic to poets who allegedly are seeking to improve culture through a self-development that surpasses the past, or suspicious of poets who they claim impede radical change either by aesthetically ratifying a hegemonic culture's free-market ideology or by regressively persisting in the archaic modes of a residual aristocracy. "Develop" is a key word in such debates, for to develop requires, in a culture founded on the Oedipal injunction no less than on systems of symbolic exchange, that the maturing subject accept the terms of an orphan's exile: to work, to sublimate, to substitute, and to forget. In liberal and humanist terms, one must lose what is remembered as paradise, put words in the place of loss, and then call that exchange not only equitable, not only inevitable, but, indeed, a fall into personhood that is fortunate. While liberal humanism has been increasingly vilified by the current generation of Romanticists, many of our own theoretical alternatives (as I will argue throughout this study) are no less committed to the abandonment of origins that is endorsed by poststructuralism as well as by liberalism's teleologies of personal and cultural progress.

Yet scholars of English Romanticism, in their fretful anticipation of the poet's maturation, are only echoing the larger anxieties of our culture, anxieties that are also apparent in the research and recommendations of psychologists who work with orphans. To read the results of their investigations of childhood loss and grief is to learn quickly that these psychologists' leading concern is to enable the orphan to surrender his attachment to the lost parent(s) so that this child may grow up as a "healthy" adult. In the words of the author of what is perhaps the most impressive twentieth-century study of loss and its aftermath, John Bowlby's three-volume series *Attachment and Loss,* the mission of the psychoanalyst is to help orphans grow up to be adults whose health is measurable according to the following criteria: "They were living in an intact home, their marriage appeared to be satisfactory, relationships with their children seemed adequate, and their scores on a brief test of social adaptation were confirmatory" (Vol. 3, p. 313). The multitude of studies of the failures and achievements of orphans conducted by British and American psychoanalysts since World War II attests, in fact, to the strength of related fears that coexist with a genuine concern for the happiness and welfare of orphaned children. The more obvious fear is that, because orphans experience greater trauma in the movement from home into the world that *all* children are asked, in fact, to make *symbolically,* orphans will fail to develop into hardworking adults with "normal" outlets for pleasure—they will become melancholic, which means that they will grow up to be "idle" burdens on society or, worse, criminals, psychopaths, or poets (or all of the above).[2] But the larger and more subtle fear underlying these studies may be expressed as follows: because orphans cannot follow what has come to seem, within the past two centuries, not only the normal but also the natural model for the child's life and development in the family home, the very existence of a child without two parents puts that model to the test.

The literary scholar who seeks to understand the influence of early orphaning on the life and writings of a Romantic poet will find insufficient guidance either from contemporary scholars of Romantic literature (who presume that it is normal and natural for a poet to have two parents, one whom he desires and one whom he resents) or from contemporary theorists of childhood loss (who presume that every normal child grows up in a stable, twentieth-century, middle-class home, with two "healthily" heterosexual parents, and that any other childhood setting would lead to "un-healthy" development).[3] It is no coincidence that the era that produced Blake's *Songs* and Wordsworth's "Michael" invented our now commonplace ideal of the family as an intimate, private, and loving space where two heterosexual, married adults delay the child's fall into the world.[4] Yet the family then as now, we may learn by reading those poems, served as the site for the child's instruction in experience and for the interpellation of ideology as often as it offered the child its shelter.

Fortunately, we may find sophisticated appraisals of ideology and its logic of exchange in four relatively recent investigations, specifically, of melancholia. Julia Kristeva explicitly investigates depression in two works—*Powers of Horror* and *Black Sun*—and, in two others, offers alternative paradigms for understanding the oppressiveness of symbolic exchange: *Tales of Love* and, most important, *Revolution in Poetic Language*. Kristeva seeks to understand how the symbolic order denies the material processes of the body (the semiotic process) upon which all speech, in fact, depends. "Poetic language" and what she calls the "signifiable sadness" of melancholic writing deliberately employ the negative drives of the body in order to disrupt the acts of denial and negation that characterize linguistic exchange. Judith Butler, in *Gender Trouble* and, more recently, *Bodies That Matter*, offers a different but no less useful account of how the earliest prohibition the child encounters—the homosexual incest taboo—leads to the melancholic encryption of that early, same-sex desire *as* "normal" and "healthy" identification with the sexual identity of the now-taboo object of the negative Oedipus. Both Kristeva and Butler acknowledge their indebtedness to studies that I, too, have found indispensable in approaching the language of poetry no less than that of melancholy: the work of Nicolas Abraham and Maria Torok on what they came to call "cryptonymy," a linguistic resistance to the work of mourning that takes advantage of the child's earliest (and most regressive) form of dealing with loss: "incorporation,"[5] the ingestion (and the preservation) of the dead at the very locus of speech acquisition. And Slavoj Žižek, whose other works will be cited often in this text, suggests in *The Metastases of Enjoyment* that masculine violence has its origins in an urge to "awaken" a depressive body from which it is estranged and that is gendered as feminine. All of these theorists will figure importantly in *The Orphaned Imagination*.[6]

To examine Western European culture through its long history of commentaries on melancholia is to discover that melancholia, while it becomes more visible during times of economic expansion, may be as constitutive of Western civilization as is the incest taboo and the totem of law. Those who have provided subsequent generations with those commentaries were themselves released, either by personal wealth or by a society's economic surplus, from physical toil. Yet to be free *not* to work physically, as these writers acknowledge, can make the intellectual particularly susceptible to the melancholia that he may, in turn, seek to study. Robert Burton, who wrote *The Anatomy of Melancholy* in order to recover from the disease through the "work" of reading, thinking, and writing, concluded by establishing principles of psychic hygiene not only for himself or for fellow scholars but for society as a whole. For, as he argues, entire societies may be melancholy.

Burton, fully aware that his melancholic ailment was a consequence of his scholarly mode of living, concluded that the mind "penned up" (as he calls it) in solitude is both unlikely to challenge the public authority of a "royal and ample" patronage and all too likely to "rove," "for want of good method," from its tasks. Boasting, nevertheless, that his "unconfined thoughts" resist the slavery of self-interest (including the impediments of family), Burton claims to watch as a "spectator" the absurdities of the world below his ivory tower, for he has no financial stake in that world: "I have little, I want nothing: all my treasure is in Minerva's tower."[7] Yet like other philosophers of economy, Burton did not feel obliged to restrict his views on economy to the treasures of Minerva. He urged his countrymen to regulate the "free" market that he recognized was transforming England into the most melancholy of nations, yet he insisted that regulation must begin not with trade but with self-discipline. Calling for individual restraint, Burton urged the English to work harder and control consumption, panaceas that he urged the rich and powerful to adopt first. The "idleness" of rich and poor alike, Burton continued, is "the malus genius of our country" (57). Using diction that becomes as unbridled as the marketplace he describes (and that anticipates Marx's own, often gothic descriptions of commodities and capital),[8] Burton describes the economic woes of his country before he envisions an alternative: a utopia in which the melancholic English would become as hard-working and well ordered as the Dutch.[9] Here, those who cannot work would be allowed charity, but the able-bodied malingerer would not be tolerated: "Wherefore I will suffer no beggars, rogues, vagabonds, or idle persons at all, that cannot give an account of how they maintain themselves" (67). Vacations, like work, would be closely regulated. Without such rules, Burton concludes, a melancholic society cannot be transformed into a society of healthy workers.

Shifting from Burton's early modern melancholia to the eighteenth-century Age of Reason, we may note that when discipline can no longer be a matter of (to borrow Blake's epithet for Urizen) a "Work master's" external force, then the workmaster must be installed within the mind itself.[10] The modern, free, and self-disciplined subject is driven by the work ethic of Milton's Protestant and internalized "Taskmaster" God, except that only an abstract law has survived the banishment of that deity. Orphaned by reason from the Father, governing desire through constant self-surveillance, the modern subject believes she or he has "earned" through self-reliance the surplus time and space called "leisure." Such a worker feels, unreasonably but perhaps understandably, threatened by signs of a visible and growing unemployed populace.

Michel Foucault offers evidence in *Madness and Civilization* that widespread concerns with monitoring work in the Age of Reason were directly related to a fear of madness—specifically, of melancholia—as a "disease" of the undisciplined that infects "reason."[11] Combined with a near-hysterical resentment of those who do not work but who benefit from the work of others, such anxieties were directly related to the increasing visibility both of leisured genius and of the unemployed poor who arrived in great numbers to seek work in cities.[12] In *Melancholy and Society*,[13] Wolf Lepenies defines melancholia historically as an enforced impotence in public life disguised as privileged leisure, a nonthreatening critique of social and political authority that emerged at key periods in modern European history: the aestheticization (and political demobilization) of the aristocrats of the Fronde; the rise of an academic and artistic class among the bourgeoisie in the late eighteenth century that earned aesthetic but not aristocratic status or political power; the creation of such readers as Madame Bovary within the leisure classes in the nineteenth century.

Anxieties about the melancholic's leisurely consumption of art are seemingly inseparable from fears concerning the melancholic's sexuality. Both concerns arise in societies that, because they are rapidly developing new means of production and avenues of trade, are no longer certain where "natural" production—including sexual reproduction—begins or where, in the marketplace of mass and uniform production and widespread distribution, it will end. Such anxieties, I would argue, are exacerbated when the melancholic who provokes that anxiety is an artist. Even though sales of more tangible products than poetry can grow only when consumers desire, more than most products the work of art, which begins and ends in acts of imagination, both elicits and baffles regulation. Perhaps that is because the work of art, and the labor of the artist, exposes the unconscious mechanisms of an economy in which not work but pleasure, not need but desire, *is* the impetus—literally, the seemingly unending "surplus"—that, combined with the underpayment for labor, generates economic "development." Haunted by the figure of the melancholic, whose very sloth—fueled by concupiscence—may nevertheless engender art, those who promote the "healthy development" of an individual or a society might well fear that beneath the demands and satisfactions of communal forms of symbolic exchange, beneath the free market's self-regulating system, lurk unmet needs that may easily find expression as private perversion, whether the site for its enjoyment is the bedroom or the study.

To investigate the relationship between literature, desire, melancholia, and "freedom," one need not turn to studies, specifically, of melancholia in order to discover that in our own age anxieties about work continue to establish and enforce strict standards of cultural value that poetry (and the figure of the poet) may fail to meet. Those standards in turn have promoted fears that, should culture cease to move forward, it will (like the unhealthy melancholic) dangerously regress. The academic work ethic has made strange bedfellows of late-twentieth-century critics of English Romantic poetry. The approaches they espouse may differ but they agree in their presumption that poetry should be "work"; the work of poetry should be an advancement of culture that meliorates a society's problems; and the work of poetry must include the "working through" of loss that concludes in the poet's psychic health, that is to say, in the mental independence we call maturity. If the critic presumes that Romantic poetry continues to have value in the present age, that critic is likely to presume that it does so either because

Romantic poetry "transcends" the "merely" material operations of ordinary labor and the everyday exchanges of the marketplace or because poetry, since it encourages more than most literary forms open-ended freedom of interpretation, educates consumers of literature. Alternatively, if the critic presumes that Romantic poetry is of only questionable or, at best, carefully qualified value in our age, that critic is likely to presume that Romantic poets have obscured, denied, or simply ignored the material history that motivates exchange, offering freedom to a leisured minority at the expense of the laboring poor. If the reader of Romantic poetry wishes to seek an alternative basis for recognizing the value of such poetry that neither sequesters the cultural from the economic nor presumes that poetry (even canonical poetry) is invariably complicit with capitalist ideology, then that reader cannot ignore the vexed relationship, during and after the Romantic Age, between work, subjectivity, and the melancholic's reluctance to enter into modern sites of exchange.

Geoffrey Hartman has asked a question that clearly defines the importance of that relationship: "Romantic lyricism, pensiveness, and melancholy are interrelated, even if the exact nature of the relation has remained obscure. We know that surmise expresses the freedom of a mind aware of itself, aware and not afraid of its moods or potentialities—what darker burden, then, is expressed by this 'dewy' melancholy?"[14] *"Dewy," languid, lonely, despondent:* such adjectives not only have come to characterize Romantic melancholy but even, arguably, have made "Romantic" and "melancholic" synonymous. Perhaps for this reason there has been, to my knowledge, only one book-length investigation of Romantic poetry and its English melancholic forebears, Eleanor Sickels's 1932 study, *The Gloomy Egoist.*[15] While Sickels's efforts to assign blame (or is it gratitude?) for the sinking mood of art in eighteenth-century England are as plausible as the (not surprisingly) similar explanations provided by standard studies of the "rise" of "Romanticism"—the "tightening grasp of the Industrial Revolution," the failure of the French Revolution to shake up politics at home, the faltering consolations of religious faith in an Age of Reason, the alienation of urban dwellers from nature, the feeling of literary belatedness in relation to Shakespeare and Milton—such explanations finally do not illuminate the obscurity that Hartman calls to our attention. If "melancholic" and "Romantic" are near-synonyms, then we might ask why "self-discipline" and "Romantic" are nearly antonymic. For, as stated earlier, discipline is merely the other face of desire in an economy that depends as fully on consumption as it does on a reliable workforce. If self-discipline requires that we restrict desire "for our own good," then freedom may well be the ambivalent bequest of a reason that taxes the recipient with depression. Indeed, there is no better reminder that the force of law in democratic cultures lies, as Freud discovered, not in "reason" or in "consciousness" but rather in "conscience," the irrationally punitive superego. Yet, as I hope to show, if melancholia begins in the loneliness of a freedom that both serves and is constructed by the systemic needs of economic exchange, even recent studies of its "gift" to genius typically do not look beyond the self for its cure.

On the one hand, a scholar such as Kay Redfield Jamison may be sympathetic to the suffering of the depressive artist but disinterested in the cyclical mood swings of free-market economies that can, like depression, only be treated symptomatically. Indeed, Jamison's findings in *Touched with Fire* could lead the reader to conclude that the inexplicable eruption of art out of the misery of the unfettered mind and the unregulated market is itself just compensation for the anxiety and pain that we do not know how to eliminate from either site without radically reconceiving what it means for them to be free. In this well-documented study of manic-depressiveness and "the artistic temperament," Jamison raises interesting questions about the price a society pays for art: "Would one want to get rid of this illness if one could? . . . Does psychiatric treatment have to result in happier but blander and less imaginative artists?"[16] Yet Jamison, like Burton, does not move from her fascinating diagnosis of her patients to a consideration of how melancholia is itself a symptom of the systems of exchange that we refuse to regulate except through therapies for the individual: work, exercise, diet, and—now—Prozac.

Approaching the price of poetry from a very different angle, Kurt Heinzelman concludes that poetry offers a compensatory freedom to those who participate as hardworking consumers in the marketplace of ideas and words. In the most sophisticated study to date of English poetry and capitalist economics, Heinzelman in *The Economics of the Imagination* proposes that we "seek to understand 'labor' as it applies both to the productions of the artist and the 'consumer' role of the reader. By emphasizing the subjective actions of the reader in making a text an object of labor, we may get beyond the rather constrictive question of whether the writer is a worker and address the more significant topic: how does literature itself *work?*"[17] Heinzelman offers a model of poetic "value" that is market driven, for poetry yields an instructive and compensatory freedom to the consumer who democratically "participates directly in the poem's creation of value" (195), reminding us that discussions of poetic labor are inseparable from those of poetic value.

A less explicitly therapeutic or economic but more familiar model for the creation of poetic value in a free market might be summarized as the following: poetry "transcends" the valuations of the marketplace, even as the poet is praised for a labor that is not merely strenuous but, indeed, heroic. Among modern critics of Romanticism, M. H. Abrams is perhaps the most successful exponent of this view. No limpid victim of *acedie,* Abrams's Romantic poet never takes a vacation from vocation for, in Abrams's muscular terms, the poet yearns in order to earn:

It is only by an extreme historical injustice that Romanticism has been identified with the cult of the noble savage and the cultural idea of a return to an early stage of simple and easeful "nature" which lacks conflict because it lacks differentiation and complexity. On the contrary, all the major Romantic writers, and Blake most emphatically, set as the goal for mankind the reachievement of a unity which has been *earned* by unceasing effort and which is, in Blake's term, an "organized" unity, an equilibrium of opponent forces which preserves all the products and powers of intellection and culture. Like his contemporaries, Blake recognized the strength of civilized man's yearning for the simple self-unity of the life of infants and of instinctual creatures, and he made a place for it in his geography of the mind: the state he called "Beulah." . . . its inhabitants enjoy only such primitive security as the "beloved infant in his mother's bosom round incircled / With arms of love & pity & sweet compassion." This mental state has value to the Sons of Eden as a *vacation resort* which they can visit for "a mild and pleasant rest"; but it is dangerous, in its languor and sterility, because it can become an habitual refuge from *"intellectual war," that creative strife of contraries in the strenuous life of intellect and of imagination.*[18] (my emphases)

Later in this subsection titled "Unity Lost and Integrity Earned," Abrams enlists in his war on indolence the German contemporaries of the Romantics, who share, he argues, the poets' faith in a "return which is also a 'progression'" (260). Poetry, according to Abrams, must indeed earn its place in an intellectual regimen that will resist regressing to an earlier "state" of pleasure or of nature in which Nature—if we read the larger text by Schiller that Abrams cites—is, incestuously, both the poet's sister and his mother. Here Abrams paraphrases the philosopher: "Schiller, we recall, had said that the 'nature which you envy in the nonrational is unworthy of your respect and longing,' that our only possible road is not 'back to Arcadia' but 'onward to Elysium,' and that we must struggle on until we 'restore by means of a higher Art'—the imaginative creations of poetry and the fine arts—'this wholeness in our nature which Art has destroyed'" (261). According to Abrams, poetry proves that it really does "serious work" only when it gives birth to the orphaned, freely creative "self," repudiating the poet's material (and, by implication, maternal and natural) origins. As he argues throughout *Natural Supernaturalism*, the "moral *man*" is, in other words, by definition the *man* (and the gender, of course, is restrictive) who has forsaken the "sensuous" (and—by implication—the feminine and incestuous) beckoning of Nature so that he may commit himself to the life of the mind, abiding within the structures of culture.[19] Only after such an exchange of allegiances, only after a fall that, paradoxically, claims to make the higher life of the mind possible *because* it makes it impossible for the son to regress from the Law of the Father to the bosom of Nature, can the grown-up son contemplate a poetic marriage with Nature that obviates incest, keeping the bride firmly in her place and the sister and mother safely at a distance. The "discipline" of Blake's Los-like art is both "consummation" and "sublimation," a "marital embrace" in which the "conflicts" that have alienated Albion from Vala are "sublimated into the creative and life-enhancing 'Wars of Love'" (264). Citing approvingly Northrop Frye, Abrams concludes that "'Golgonooza . . . the total form of all human culture and civilization'" (261) is the transcendent home to which the Romantic poet seeks to return, now that it is safe for a law-abiding son to do so.

Abrams's conception of poetry's role in preparing free-world students for the battles of the Cold War has proved to be an easy target for Marxist critics, yet even those critics leave unchallenged the presumptions regarding work that ground ideologies promoting individualism and freedom. These critics believe, as Abrams does, that poetry works (*if* it works at all) in complicity with "the total form" of cultural authority. In the works of two critics who explicitly employ Marxist critiques of ideology—the groundbreaking investigations of Romanticism and ideology undertaken two decades ago by Jerome McGann and the more recent work of Terry Eagleton on Romantic aesthetics—we can see how the persistence of conventional assumptions concerning work, philosophy, and poetry have hindered a more urgent project for scholars who find that poetry and economics may be mutually illuminating.

Employing the "socio-historical focus of Marxist criticism," McGann in *The Romantic Ideology* finds Romantic poetry to be "everywhere marked by extreme forms of displacement and poetic conceptualization whereby the actual human issues with which the poetry is concerned are resituated in a variety of idealized localities."[20] Although McGann reassures the reader that his historical materialist approach is not meant to "debunk" or "deconstruct" the poetry—that his analyses "aid in elucidating the actual work of Romantic artists" by disqualifying the erroneous conclusions reached by such humanist scholars as Abrams—in fact McGann shares Abrams's sense that the measure of poetic value is its hard-working "seriousness" and its ability to remain faithful to a universal, political "Truth" two centuries after it was written: "Poetry's first obligation is to reveal the contradictory forces which human beings at once generate and live through, and its second is to provide the reader, both the contemporary and future alike, with the basis for a sympathetic and critical assessment of those forces" (121). McGann differs from Abrams in finding that poetry shirks its work, a failure that Romanticists have failed to notice, he claims, because they themselves have not worked hard enough: "I can only say that some severity seems called for since criticism has, of late, increasingly allowed its rigor and clarity—its scholarly obligations—to lapse into disuse" (18). The serious scholar, McGann chides, must orphan herself from poetry; she should not expect to find in poetry a political truth equivalent to her own but, rather, the now-historical mistakes—that is, the errors of an ideologically contaminated "imagination"—that can only become apparent through the distance of time and of hard-earned scholarly objectivity: "We may take it as a rule, then, that any criticism which abolishes the distance between its own (present) setting and its (removed) subject matter—any criticism which argues an unhistorical symmetry between the practicing critic and the descending work—will be, to that extent, undermined as criticism. In such cases criticism becomes important in the history of ideology rather than in the history of criticism" (30). McGann decries the misguided work of the academy's ideology "industry": "Poetry like Wordsworth's belongs to what Hans Enzensberger has called 'The Consciousness Industry'—a light industry, if the pun be permitted, which Wordsworth and the other Romantics helped to found, and which they sought to preserve free of cultural contamination" (91). Finally, he proposes that an ignorance of ideology leads to "the grand illusion of every Romantic poet":

". . . an ideology is made out of what it does not mention; it exists because there are things which must not be spoken of." These remarks are a latter-day version of a recurrent truth. From Wordsworth's vantage, an ideology is born out of things which (literally) *cannot* be spoken of. . . . If Wordsworth's poetry elides history, we observe in this "escapist" or "reactionary" move its own self-revelation. It is a rare, original, and comprehensive record of the birth and character of a particular ideology—in this case, one that has been incorporated into our academic programs. The idea that poetry, or even consciousness, can set one free of the ruins of history and culture is the grand illusion of every Romantic poet. This idea continues as one of the most important shibboleths of our culture, especially—and naturally—at its higher levels. (91)

Terry Eagleton, in *The Ideology of the Aesthetic*,[21] explores just how the "aesthetic" has created the illusion that art may lead to freedom. The aesthetic, he argues, only appears to restore to our lives a material plenitude that capitalist cultures have lost in an increasingly rational and alienated age. Eagleton opens boldly with the statement "Aesthetics is born as a discourse of the body," an assertion that might have challenged a metaphysics that, like capitalism, is founded not only on the alienation of labor and product but also on the foundational difference between "regressive" gratifications and sublimatory cultural progress, and between aesthetic play and political work. Sadly, such oppositions remain, for Eagleton, firmly in place, as we may see in the summary of the book's argument presented in its final pages:

Work, sexuality and sociality all bring with them the possibility of gratification. The pleasure of the small baby is at first inseparable from the satisfaction of biological need. But just as, for Freud, sexual desire is born as a kind of swerving away from such instinctual need, so in the course of social development the processes of pleasure and fantasy come to separate themselves out to a certain extent from the fulfilling of material wants, in the phenomenon we know as culture. Once the economic surplus permits, a minority can be released from labour to enjoy such culture as an end in itself, in dissociation from the exigencies of labour, sexual reproduction and political regulation. "Value," in this sense, comes to distinguish itself from "fact," and finally comes to deny its roots in material practice altogether. This culture is often enough employed as an escape from or sublimation of unpalatable necessity, and as a means of mystifying and legitimating it; but it can also offer a prefigurative image of a social condition in which such pleasurable creativity might become available in principle to all. The political struggle which arises at this point is between those who wish to divert the forces of production to the end of allowing social life to become a gratifying end in itself, and those who, having much to lose from the prospect, resist it by violence and manipulation. (411)

While Eagleton unnecessarily blames the aesthetic for problems that are in fact systemic in an economy founded on the exclusion of the artist, no less than the worker, from its rewards, he justly indicts capitalist ideology (and the idealist philosophies it has spawned) for estranging philosophy and art from life, and, more important, from each other. Ideology accomplished that estrangement (as Eagleton describes with admirable clarity) by, first, removing philosophy itself from the everyday world of workers. In a second stage, ideology made art the pleasure-giving but subordinate handmaiden to both the disinterested philosopher and the materially interested bourgeoisie.

Yet Eagleton's conclusion need not have followed from these premises. Arguing that poetry is merely "play" rather than the arduous work of praxis, Eagleton concludes that poetry lacks the mind and muscle required to challenge the exploitative logic of capitalist exchange. Thus to the "ludic and poetic" he opposes what he endorses as the "labour of inquiry" of Marx's utilitarian or "instrumental" mind in pursuit of universal "Truth": "That final aestheticization of human existence which we call communism cannot be prematurely anticipated by a reason which surrenders itself wholly to the ludic and poetic, to image and intuition. Instead, a rigorously analytical rationality is needed, to help unlock the contradictions which prevent us from attaining the condition in which instrumentalism may lose its unwelcome dominance" (227–28).

The instrumentalism of rationality is precisely the source of a melancholia in which the more the mind labors, the more it disciplines itself into a denial of the ludic and the poetic, and the more susceptible does it find itself to the tyranny of the modern taskmaster. It acquires what Hartman calls the "freedom" of a mind "aware of itself" that is, nevertheless, seemingly unable to alter the conditions that literally "subject" the self to freedom.

"The origin of poetry," Thomas Love Peacock begins in his "The Four Ages of Poetry," lies in violence and a kind of backwardness. "Like all other trades," he writes in this heavily ironic essay, poetry "takes its rise in the demand for the commodity, and flourishes in proportion to the extent of the market" (491). Baiting Percy Shelley to come to the "defense" of poetry, Peacock proclaims that it has never ceased to be the other face of a tyrant's self-interest, whether the tyrant is openly bellicose or coldly utilitarian. The market for poetry opened in the age of chieftains, as Peacock reminds us, when Law had not yet clothed naked aggression with "neutral" symbols: "In these days the only three trades flourishing (besides that of the priest which flourishes always) are those of king, thief, and beggar."[22] As the rule of law (joined with a philosophy of "progress" and an economy of industry) ascended, poets (with God and King) fell from power and (as Peacock suggests) into darkness: "A poet in our times is a semibarbarian in a civilized community. He lives in the days that are past. His ideas, thoughts, feelings, associations, are all with barbarous manners, obsolete customs, and exploded superstitions. The march of his intellect is like the crab, backward. The brighter the light diffused around him by the progress of reason, the thicker is the darkness of antiquated barbarism, in which he buries himself like a mole, to throw up the barren hillocks of his Cimmerian labors" (513).

In our own day, whatever unpaid and invisible labor poets themselves perform (and typically they do so well beyond the walls of the academic institutions that claim to enlighten their works), finally theirs is a labor that cannot be measured. Or, in the words of Derrida, their work may look to outsiders like both a sexual perversion (unprocreative pleasure enjoyed in private) and a labor that seems "incapable of engendering anything."[23] When we, as scholars, are engaged only in the reasonable work of a mourning—whether it is that of psychoanalytic science, rhetorical analysis, material history, or other forms of literary scholarship—that sets itself apart from what I will describe in the chapters that follow as the productive melancholia of poets who bring to life (in the dark, in secrecy, perhaps in bed) those matters we have denied or negated, then we may delude ourselves that we are able to resist whatever fetishism, or whatever ideology, we may accuse these white, male, dead poets of believing and promoting. But if there is, indeed, any difference between today's literary scholar and today's poet in America, it is in a real sense economic. Regardless of gender or race, scholars who are tenured get paid reasonably well for their work; poets rarely do. Unless a poet has a creative writing position in one of our institutions, he or she is likely to exist, in a real and painful sense, among the outcast lumpen proletariat of our late-capitalist society: perhaps unemployable, perhaps queer, perhaps clinically neurotic, nearly inevitably impoverished by the standards of our affluence.

That scholars no longer leave unquestioned a moribund poetics of Romantic "Imagination" that had masculinized, reified, and even apotheosized poetry's place in everyday life is a tribute to the continuing value of approaches to poetry that care about the material conditions out of which poems emerge and that do not take for granted the universal or transcendent value of canonical poetry from (and for) any period in literary history. Nevertheless, three recent studies of Romantic literature and melancholia lead me to conclude that the full resourcefulness of poetic melancholia may remain unacknowledged by scholars if we presume that the male and canonical poet has no access to what Kristeva calls the "semiotic processes" of an embodied, and emotional, poetics. Our academic culture continues to find the body of the poet who is gendered as male difficult to locate in a poststructuralist psychic economy. While we have learned to question difference and to deposit into the account(s) of the other the virtues of marginality, subversion, and embodied thought, it seems that we cannot yet altogether conceive of male creativity as disruptive, rather than dependent upon, the edifices of our culture.

Tilottama Rajan, in her two far-reaching essays on abjection and Romanticism, assumes that Kristevan melancholia clearly may be a linguistic resource for the female writer (Mary Shelley). It may be so for the male poet (Coleridge), she concludes, only insofar as his dejection imitates feminine depression in its abjection of an originary maternal object and in contributing to the production of a fragmentary art that imitates the fragmented (nonphallic) body.[24] Esther Schor, in *Bearing the Dead,* an impressive, book-length study of mourning practices and the consolidation of community in Romantic and Victorian English culture, concludes that the poetry of loss written by Wordsworth served finally not to enlarge but rather to commodify his readers' sympathy for the other, a poetic project that endorsed a larger cultural effort to masculinize, and to introduce into Adam Smith's marketplace of self-interested symbolic exchange, a merely meliorating sentimentality.[25]

Contrary to these recent readings of Romantic poetry, *The Orphaned Imagination* proposes that the poetry of Wordsworth, Blake, Coleridge, Byron, Shelley, and Keats is neither complicit with an economy founded on the work of mourning nor ignorant of that economy's operations and questionable compensations. Rather, the poetry of the four poets who receive full chapters in this book (and of the two whose critical reception are the occasion for an afterword) emerges from a profound awareness of the *significance* of a fundamental but forgotten loss, a loss that persists *as* a "nothingness" or absence that is in fact replete with irrecoverable but nevertheless emotionally charged presence. The poetry of the Romantic period returns, repeatedly, to the site of a fall into univalenced language and sexually differentiated "experience." A vocation—literally, a parental *voice*—either is heard by the homesick, inconsolable orphan, or it frustrates the orphan by refusing his invocations.[26]

In the chapters that follow, I begin with Byron, an orphan who blamed his Father for failing to call him, and conclude with Wordsworth, an orphaned but chosen son. While Wordsworth has become the Romantic poet to whom scholars are most likely to attribute a middle-class eagerness for professional and commercial success, I argue to the contrary that Wordsworth's growing sense of "vocation" derives from his hearing of a calling during different periods of depression, a calling that led him to subvert the demands of exchange in language, in sexual and psychic development, and in the conversion of the self's hidden treasures into the commodity of the book. Byron, too, while he masterfully exploited the commodification not only of his poetry but also of his person, in fact understood keenly the ways in which writing poetry enabled him both to profit and to hoard. Making of what he called his "ennui" a powerful mode of literary production, transforming the borderline disorders of abjection into an art that exploits, in various senses, the in-between, Byron serves as a fitting subject for a chapter that continues the Introduction's discussion of leisure, desire, and melancholy in commodity culture. Few scholars would associate libidinal lassitude with Blake, whose opposition to tyranny has led scholars to identify this poet and artist with Los, the muscular laborer at the forge of liberation. Yet Blake in fact describes the state in which he produced *The Four Zoas* as a depressive failure of "perseverence." In any case this work, itself resurrected from Blake's illustrated *Night Thoughts*, requires us to reconceive the erotic, and indeed the homoerotic, dimension of a labor that generates life as well as art, and that regenerated, for Blake, the dead. Both Blake and Shelley would seem exemplary of Harold Bloom's creative and Oedipal self-orphaning. Yet in their different identifications of and with paternal tyranny, they wrote poetry capable of critiquing an Enlightenment faith in the Law that takes the place of an absent Father. While Blake learned to construct from the loss of his father a bodily Golgonooza, Shelley encountered in parental vacancy the sublime and obscene "want" on which the Law founds its authority. That the ambivalent identifications of melancholia darken the discipline of academic readers no less than the desires of poets is the subject of a brief afterword on Keats, Coleridge, and the problem of poetic "pleasure." The orphaned poet who seems in many ways exempt from melancholy, Keats is nevertheless the orphan whose death haunts his detractors as much as his admirers. *The Eve of St. Agnes,* a poem whose eroticism has elicited chastisement from its first to its most recent readers, also invites the reader to look into the mirror of an artwork that exposes nothingness as the basis for ideological, as well as for sexual, identification.

If the heterosexual family is itself a romance, then we might learn from these orphaned poets that we may not know in advance what is meant by family, and what books, bodies, and imaginations we might come to inhabit as home. We need not endorse the term "family values" co-opted by forces of reaction in our culture to recognize that both "family" and "home" must assume more creative forms in the face of an economy that, more than ever, demands daily our disavowals of the objects—and the selves—who remain, however unconscious, in fact most important to us. *The Orphaned Imagination* begins with the confidence that the imagination of its readers, two hundred years after the births, and the deaths, of the poets whom they still read, remains, in the most creative sense, Romantic.

1

Byron's In-Between Art of Ennui:
"The World Is Full of Orphans"

What is the reason that I have been, all my lifetime, more or less *ennuyé?* . . . I do not know how to answer this, but presume that it is constitutional. . . . Temperance and exercise . . . made little or no difference. Violent passions did;—when under their immediate influence—it is odd, but—I was in agitated, but *not* in depressed spirits. . . . in general they are low, and get daily lower. That is *hopeless:* for I do not think I am so much *ennuyé* as I was at nineteen. The proof is, that then I must game, or drink, or be in motion of some kind, or I was miserable. At present, I can mope in quietness. . . .

LORD BYRON, Ravenna journal, January 6, 1821

Byron's great strength as a writer, in the words of W. H. Auden, is that he understands that a friend—and a writer—must never be boring, however profound his thought or deep his lassitude. Afflicted by ennui (an illness that encourages dalliance and retrospection) even during periods of intense, worldly activity, Byron in fact labored more vigorously, more regularly, and more productively than any other English Romantic poet from *within* the dark lacunae of loss, silence, and boredom that threaten the horizon of hope. "That awful yawn which sleep cannot abate" Byron says in describing the suffocating void of "*ennui* . . . a growth of English root / Though nameless in our language" (*Don Juan*, 13.101).[1]

A poet for whom prospects seem less before him than behind may relieve the palpable weight and jaded flight of *time* that is characteristic of ennui with the word it echoes, *rhyme:*

> The world is all before me or behind,
>> For I have seen a portion of that same,

And quite enough for me to keep in mind.
  Of passions too I have proved enough to blame,
To the great pleasure of our friends, mankind,
  Who like to mix some slight alloy with fame,
For I was rather famous in my time,
Until I fairly knocked it up with rhyme.
(14.9)

Rhyme extends "time," echoing it across the space of silence and using that moment in the dark to seduce (and reproduce) time, disseminating (illegitimately) other, rhyming words ("chyme" is a favorite) that will extend time by filling its yawning mouth, even though these rhymes may, in turn, like chyme imitate Chronos's digestion of his progeny. Desire and ennui, as Byron keenly understood, are virtually indistinguishable "vacancies" for both sexes; although he refers, specifically, to the female in the lines that follow (in line endings that are, of course, feminine), in the most important sense the male no less than the female may, in Byron's poetry, generate from some inner space of "want" new life, or new desires, either of which leads from self to others:

A something all-sufficient for the heart
  Is that for which the sex are always seeking,
But how to fill up that same vacant part?
  There lies the rub, and this they are but weak in.
(14.74)

In the spacious stanza of the Italian ottava rima, Byron could wander leisurely before returning home to a reunion (or, more typically, a parody of a reunion) in the final, rhyming couplet. What Auden identifies as Byron's disrespect for the integrity of words served him technically, enabling him to yoke outrageous rhymes for this stanzaic form. Further, it led him to transgress both the Word of the Father and the words of any son who claimed to be a recipient of paternal favors: Plato, preachers, and Lakers.[2]

Haunting the spurious boundaries between two fraudulent English paradises—one of active, commercial "hops and high production,"[3] another of static, aristocratic "pleasure and *ennui*"[4]—Byron was at home in neither. He pitched his tent and his timbre in the spacious distance " 'twixt life and death."[5] He made a home for himself in verse, straying *between* a home country whose language he could not abandon and the fecund foreignness of other languages and their verse forms; idling in the moment of anticipation and fear that suspends narration *between* a hero's promise and his disappointment or even his death; sounding the echoing abyss *between* two preexisting poetic stanzas; and exploiting the invisible productivity of poetic labor that exists *between* the inspiration that beckons from ennui and the publication that generates readers and cash.

Byron is not, like Plato, a go-between for divine Truth and erring ("controlless") humanity, one who tells earnest and gullible truth seekers that they may make their outer lives—through systematic, intellectual rigor—metaphors for metaphysical, phosphorescent inner light:

> Oh Plato, Plato, you have paved the way
>   With your confounded fantasies to more
> Immoral conduct by the fancied sway
>   Your system feigns o'er the controlless core
> Of human hearts than all the long array
>   Of poets and romancers. You're a bore,
> A charlatan, a coxcomb, and have been
> At best no better than a go-between.
> (1.116)

More Hermes (who is himself, of course, a go-between) than Apollo, Byron thrives, in the dark, on seemingly "inconceivable" couplings and absorptions that prove to be outrageously, uncontrollably, metonymically procreative. No intellectual idealist, neither is he—despite his sophisticated understanding of finance and of the marketplace of poetry—one of "your men of business," a go-between who spends his life and his substance circulating goods and generating gold:

> Eureka! I have found it! What I mean
>   To say is not that love is idleness,
> But that in love such idleness has been
>   An accessory, as I have cause to guess.
> Hard labour's an indifferent go-between;
>   Your men of business are not apt to express
> Much passion, since the merchant ship, the *Argo*,
> Conveyed Medea as her supercargo.
> (14.76)

Byron refused to accept as elusive the alternatives of sublimation through work or satisfaction through sex, defining his art as productive idleness, or reproductive ennui. Hence the bad bargain that he blames his forebears for accepting in exchanging "enjoying" for "employing":

> Adam exchanged his Paradise for ploughing,
>   Eve made up millinery with fig leaves,
> The earliest knowledge from the tree so knowing,
>   As far as I know, that the Church receives;
> And since that time it need not cost much showing
>   That many of the ills o'er which man grieves,
> And still more women, spring from not employing
> Some hours to make the remnant worth enjoying.
> (14.78)

Willing to rhyme but not to oppose "enjoy" and "employ," Byron similarly confounds relationships of blood and ink. He cannot think of one without the other, as in these lines on his hero, Harold, inspired by thoughts of his daughter:

> 'Tis to create, and in creating live
> A being more intense, that we endow
> With form our fancy, gaining as we give
> The life we image, even as I do now.
> What am I? Nothing: but not so art thou,
> Soul of my thought! with whom I traverse earth,
> Invisible but gazing, as I glow
> Mix'd with thy spirit, blended with thy birth,
> And feeling still with thee in my crush'd feelings' dearth.
> (*Childe Harold*, 3.6)[6]

But despite such descriptions of his poetry as leisurely and biologically reproductive, Byron, like the poet Yeats describes in "Adam's Curse," labored privately and intensively *between* the lines he produced to make his hard-won poetry seem "a moment's thought." Indeed, he sometimes openly feigns a disclosure of the seams, the processes, and even the (allegedly) market-driven impulses of his poems, as we may witness in two examples:

> My way is to begin with the beginning.
> The regularity of my design
>   Forbids all wandering as the worst of sinning,
> And therefore I shall open with a line
>   (Although it cost me half an hour in spinning)

Narrating somewhat of Don Juan's father
And also of his mother, if you'd rather.
(*Don Juan*, 1.7)

In the mean time, without proceeding more
　　In this anatomy, I've finish'd now
Two hundred and odd stanzas as before,
　　That being about the number I'll allow
Each canto of the twelve or twenty-four;
　　And laying down my pen, I make my bow,
Leaving Don Juan and Haidée to plead
For them and theirs with all who deign to read.
(2.216)

Such feigned, digressive disclosures, even though they teach the reader to be wary of the poet's seductions, nevertheless endow Byron's productions with the erotic, conversational, and affectionate qualities that he believes the earnest "go-between," whether he inhabits the world of ideals or the world of commerce, is unlikely to value or to possess, even as he investigates "the Good" or inventories his goods. For unlike the merchant, a writer cannot dun the reader to whom he turns over his merchandise: "I can't oblige you, reader, to read on; / That's your affair, not mine. A real spirit / Should neither court neglect nor dread to bear it" (12.87). The writer's success, as he moves between his offspring and his audience, depends on his skill in convincing the reader that he has not yet surrendered (and may *never* surrender) *all*.[7] The reader must come to want the author's "hero," and to want that hero to live, as much as the author does himself. The writer who, like the Argo merchant, would sacrifice the living cargo that he carries for a stranger's money could never earn that which cannot be procured so coldly or possessed so absolutely.

Throughout his career, Byron located the place of poetry in a fallen world, and in a mature age, not only in the in-between spaces of mediation just identified but also within what he recognized as a terrifying and exhilarating moment of suspense and suspension: the boundary—the moment of almost falling—that lies between innocence and experience.[8] Sustaining simultaneously a rational skepticism toward, and an irrational belief in, a Calvinist God, Byron was resigned to the uncertain state (and estate) called "preterition," even as he refused to accept the absence of the Father who had (like his own father) abandoned him. Hating, exaggerating, and willfully reenacting his own fallenness, Byron wrote to cast beyond himself both the irrational sinner and his irresponsible Creator and judge. In doing so he both bested and resurrected the Father (and father) who bestowed life before leaving the world. To write, for Byron, was in some sense to provoke the return of both fathers. Indeed, he wrote in order to restore some notion of familial love (even, mischievously, incestuous love) to a commercial world of exchange that is lubricated by the sacrifice of blood (in both senses). To write was to exfoliate, ridding Byron of the impoverished, depleted, and rejected self that suffered from ennui, and allowing the poet to begin life anew, with replenished reserves of affection.[9]

If the Lord, as Lucifer remarks to Cain, created mankind in order to flee the lonely, restless ennui of perfection, Byron's adversarial creativity derived from the ennui of preterition, a terrifying inversion of Calvinist election in which sons are damned as a consequence not of paternal rejection but of paternal neglect: God failed to name (or to call) as explicitly "damned" those who are *not* positively elected for salvation. Living between grace and perdition, neither one thing nor the other, the preterite son—precociously "fallen" even before he is allowed to lose "freely" his innocence—is marked not by the Father's presence but by the invisible sign of his absence. In *Byron: A Portrait* Leslie Marchand stresses the importance of Calvinism in shaping both Byron's early childhood experiences—marked by poverty and by his profligate father's absence—and, more important, his lifelong need to resist the unforgiving theology he imbibed informally through his nurses. While Byron may joke in *Don Juan* that he is worldly and tolerant about religious matters because he was "born a moderate Presbyterian," his life—even at its most prodigal—betrayed the ineradicable guilt instilled by that church's teachings.[10]

To believe in the Calvinist God without believing one is saved is to install, within the sanctuary of the self, both a judging and a condemned "self." The son who is not chosen will value himself, ultimately, according to God's Law, even as he protests the fairness of that Law and seeks to defend its victims. Such feelings of betrayal, anger, and inadequacy are, according to Marchand, the source of Byron's "Satanic pose": "[D]eeply ingrained in his unconscious mind, a gloomy Calvinism made him feel that the majority of men and he in particular had the mark of Cain on them and were slated for damnation. After exhausting his powers of reason, wit, and ridicule in trying to refute the arguments of religion, he would often say with violence: 'The worst of it is, I *do believe'* " (194).

Related to the absence that marks the preterite son's place in Creation is the inner experience of absence, or emptiness, called ennui. Etymologically derived from the Latin *odium,* as in *"esse in odio,"* "ennui" literally means "object of hate." In an age of reason that has supplanted a loving, judging, but nevertheless living God with the abstract Law of the Father, to be hated by God is to be hated by the tyrannical, implacable, and irrational superego, a ghostly paternal presence that thrives on the hatred of the death drive but cannot love. Ennui, according to the single major study of the subject, is a state that is the opposite of grace.[11] The victim of ennui does not hear the call of a loving Father; rather, he possesses an uncomfortable, illogical certainty that such a Father both does not exist *and* that He has excluded this son from the family (the elect) whom he *does* continue to love, a family of sons who manifest their "election" (in circular logic) through their faith in His existence, and their freedom from ennui. A poetry such as Byron's that recoils from the rejected self earns strength, delight, and self-distinction—"laurels"—in opposing, "with blood or ink," whatever appears to spring from grace, metaphysical health, and a smug certainty of salvation: " 'Tis sweet to win, no matter how, one's laurels / By blood or ink. 'Tis sweet to put an end / To strife; 'tis sometimes sweet to have our quarrels" (1.126). To be certain of damnation—to bear openly God's mark into exile—is better than to be the in-between "nothing" called "preterite." It is to *do* something, rather than to *be* the nothing evoked by ennui.

Byron, like his self-styled Cain, digressively and obsessively returned as a poet to the scene of his parents' fall into mortality, to ruined estates and squandered legacies for whose loss Byron and Cain blame their antecedents, but especially their Father.[12] A poet who haunted forbidden and forbidding spaces, Byron is himself haunted throughout his career by the ghost of a first Being, both parental and divine, who, in abandoning him, convinced the grieving son that salvation—Paradise—could never be his, for reasons he would never be old enough to understand. Orphaned by his father at the age of three, by God even as he learned that He existed, by the Earl of Carlisle in seeking to establish his legitimacy before Parliament, and by his mother just after he had returned home to claim the fruits of his majority, Byron would find failed recognition, abandonment, and death not only painful, recurring realities throughout his short life but also a fecund source for a poetry that refused to recognize the boundaries of genre, gender, class, and decorum. Eschewing or incapable of the response to death through the aesthetic work that Peter Sacks has defined as "elegiac,"[13] the healthy work of mourning, Byron is spurred to his unfalteringly prolific production of poetry by the death instinct of melancholia. Byron's term for the "rage" to write that came over him—often in his bedroom and contiguous to more conventional expressions of emotional release— was, simply, "estrus." A word that crosses the border of gender, it also challenges the opposition of activity to idleness and aggressiveness to passiveness, evoking the frenzied receptivity of that first step toward the creation of new life. Byron anticipated Freud's *Beyond the Pleasure Principle* in understanding intuitively that the drive to produce poems, no less than the drive to reproduce, owes as much to the aggressive and destructive force of death (Thanatos) as to the binding and healing energies of Eros. Both death and love inhabit the idleness of seduction, writing, and ennui.

To understand why and how writing was for Byron an aggressive activity, we must first possess a clearer understanding of its parallel or originating state in the paralysis of ennui. Reinhard Kuhn in *The Demon at Noontide* defines ennui as a kind of melancholia that is also characterized by the following conditions: "the state of emptiness that the soul feels when it is deprived of interest in action, life, and the world (be it this world or another), a condition that is the immediate consequence of the encounter with nothingness, and has as an immediate effect a disaffection with reality" (13). In reaction to ennui's paradoxical condition of "satiated" emptiness, the sufferer may seek its cessation in the plenitude of worldly activity or in the asceticism of sainthood; he may also, or alternatively, write. As Christian acedia gradually metamorphosed into modern ennui, St. Augustine became Petrarch, for whom "writing is no longer a mere recording of an already existing reality but the bringing into being of reality. It is an existential act whose product, the book, is no longer just a transcription of an intellectual and emotional case history but the very arena of the spiritual struggle that is life, whose inevitable outcome is death" (69). According to Kuhn, literary creation became for modern sufferers of ennui, as it had for Donne, something to fill the " 'hollowness' " of the self's " 'rotten walls' " (122), or, as for Goethe, an escape from a boredom haunted by the hidden centrality of death: " 'Thus the poet,' " Kuhn cites Goethe,

" 'is lost and trapped in the labyrinth of ennui, at the center of which lurks the inescapable Minotaur of death. . . . The poet sings to keep the monster at bay' " (133). Or, as Kuhn himself declares in his concluding comments, poets engage in creative work simply in order to fill the empty space of loss.

Yet Kuhn's explanation, bolstered by compelling and exhaustive examples of literary ennui, does not really answer the question Byron himself poses in the citation that opens this chapter: Why do certain victims of a certain kind of melancholy called ennui—a disease that is spawned by solitude, idleness, and a lessening of faith—shun more likely (more socially sanctioned and more visibly active) ways of filling the bored hours in order to engage in the lonely and often painful activity of writing? For if writing relieves ennui, it is not itself an unrelieved pleasure. "As to that regular, uninterrupted love of writing, which you describe in your friend," Byron once wrote to Thomas Moore, "I do not understand it. I feel it as a torture, which I must get rid of, but never as a pleasure."[14] Insofar as there is pleasure in such elimination, it is for Byron somehow uneasily contiguous to the ennui that generates what he calls in his journal the "vicious pleasures" of "the gloomy sequestration and old age of the tyrant."[15] Byron follows that observation, seemingly without transition, with a definition of poetry that links its practice to nostalgia and to hope, twin passages from the jaded ennui of the present: "What is Poetry?—The feeling of a Former world and Future." Writing and hope are united in Byron's mind in opposition to the tyranny of pleasure itself, and to the ennui that both generates and results from such pleasure.

Byron makes these speculations just a few weeks after writing, in January 1821, the comments on "*ennuyé*" that open this chapter. They appear in a journal entry that begins with his declaration to write four tragedies on the topic of tyranny and its resistance: on Sardanapalus, Cain, Francesca of Rimini, and Tiberius. These observations proceed to a more general reflection on the fear of falling that suggests that Byron is not, like Milton's Jesus, a son who can count on his Father to save him from Satan's final temptation: "Why, at the very height of desire and human pleasure,—worldly, social, amorous, ambitious, or even avaricious,—does there mingle a certain sense of doubt and sorrow—a fear of what is to come—a doubt of what *is*—a retrospect to the past, leading to a prognostication of the future? (The best of Prophets of the future is the Past.) Why is this? or these?—I know not, except that on a pinnacle we are most susceptible of giddiness, and that we never fear falling except from a precipice—the higher, the more awful, and the more sublime." To live the life of the rich and famous, as Byron well knew, is not only to fear falling but also to know that even success's pinnacle can become an habitual station from which one may willingly plummet (into "vicious pleasures," real or vicarious) as an escape. Yet the more—and more varied—pleasures or possessions one may acquire with wealth, the shorter the duration of their enjoyment:[16] "and, therefore, I am not sure Fear is not a pleasurable sensation; at least, *Hope* is; and *what Hope* is there without a deep leaven of Fear? and what sensation is so delightful as Hope? and, if it were not for Hope, where would the Future be?—in hell. It is useless to say *where* the Present is, for most of us know; and as for the past, *what* predominates in memory?—*Hope baffled.* Ergo, in all human affairs, it is Hope—Hope—Hope. I allow sixteen minutes, though I never counted them, to any given or supposed possession. . . . It is all a mystery. I feel most things, but I know nothing except" [here, according to the entry's editor, Thomas Moore, Byron slashed several lines across the page].

> *Thought for a Speech of Lucifer, in the Tragedy of Cain:*
>
> Were *Death* an *evil,* would *I* let thee *live?*
> Fool! live as I live—as thy father lives,
> And thy son's sons shall live for evermore
> Ravenna journal, January 28, 1821

To be a victim of ennui is to abandon hope, to suffer with Lucifer and God's preterite sons a single legacy, whatever one's rank: the daily, endless, deadliness called life.[17]

Those who are most privileged and powerful—those who may command (tyrannically, if they like, in the manner of God or Satan) pleasures of all kinds—are, according to Kuhn, European culture's earliest and most profound sufferers of ennui. They are (like Prince Hamlet) its exemplary practitioners of verbal creativity—a keen insight even though Kuhn does not offer an explanation as to why this would be true. In *Melancholy and Society,* Wolf Lepenies does. He defines as "resignative behavior" the high-toned ennui characteristic of the French court during the reign of Louis XIII, a verbally fruitful despondency associated with the excessive leisure forcibly imposed on a disempowered aristocracy: " 'ennui' meant a loss of opportunities for development . . . and the gradual realization of this loss. If no wars were being waged that shifted internal conflicts outside society and thus reduced internal tensions, then a high degree of reflection was provoked among the aristocracy, who now had nothing to do.[18] Fredric Jameson, in "The Vanishing Mediator, or, Max Weber as Storyteller,"[19] observes that literary ennui in the second half of the nineteenth century is a legacy of impotent and affluent boredom inherited by the ascendant bourgeoisie from such devolutionary aristocrats as Byron. Jameson terms as "melancholia" rather than "ennui" the "Romantic despair of the early years of the century," in which the afflicted person "withdraws completely from the world, to sit apart in a post of Byronic malediction or to return in the guise of the Satanic outcast and enemy of society." Such melancholia, Jameson continues, conforms to Freud's own definition of that condition, "the essential gesture of which is *refusal,* either heroic or dejected," (6) and has, at its roots, the ambivalence characteristic of parricidal guilt: "We may perhaps overhastily suggest that the object thus mourned by the Romantics was the aristocratic world itself, which even the Restoration was unable to bring back to life." By mid-century, Jameson contends, heroic melancholia had declined into the bathos of ennui, which in turn would be replaced in our own century by existential "anxiety." That these two centuries of bustling human activity and commercial, technological expansion may be characterized by three terms that suggest an impeded spirit may seem paradoxical, Jameson acknowledges, but in fact that paradox is consistent with Kuhn's observations on the correlations that exist between unhappy privilege and active, verbal expressiveness. The very success of abstract systems of symbolic exchange in the commercial, bourgeois world—which extend to so many the formerly aristocratic privileges of buying pleasure on credit, of finding oneself with time on one's hands, of commanding words in order to acquire things—"goes hand in hand with a spreading philosophic and existential despair" (10). While Jameson's argument for the distinction between melancholy and ennui is founded on terms that are crucial for understanding Byron's position as a poet who both is and is not a member of the murdered class for which he is supposed to be grieving, the term Byron preferred for the predicament of his in-betweenness—and of his writing's—is Kuhn's: ennui.

Byron, like England's aging aristocracy but also like the infant Eros of Plato's *Symposium,* entered the world on the uncertain edge of privilege and of poverty in what is today called a "single-parent household." His body and his bank account bore the scars of the condition that Jerome Christensen in *Lord Byron's Strength* has characterized as "interstitial," afflicting the adult aristocrat with his well-documented alternation of profligacy (including binge eating) and penury (including anorexia). He learned, like Eros and like Hermes, Eros's tricky father, to exploit his vacillating, unstable status, moving in the dark between heaven and Psyche, pandering between two imaginary lovers, and trafficking between the worlds of the living and the dead.[20] Christensen establishes, through a dazzling (and inimitable) exercise of erudition, Byron's lordly appropriation of (and disdain for) the bourgeoisie's economics of symbolic exchange, finding in the poet's interstitial state a class position, and a poetry, whose status fluctuates: "It has ever been and will always be this symbolic mobility—between the general system called Byronism and the writer who signs his name, between the body of the debauchee and the bulimic, between the love of women and of men, between narrative flow and digressive blockage—that makes Lord Byron fascinating. It is the task of a biographical criticism to plot those vicissitudes, to map the interstitial career."[21] Yet to understand Byron's uncomfortable and ambivalent relationship to the commerce of publishing and to the "lordship" he inherited only after an early childhood spent without expectations—to understand what Christensen rightly terms the "symbolic mobility" of his "interstitial career"—requires that we do precisely what Christensen argues that we *cannot* do: we may not, he argues, define our task as biographical critics to be the study of the "referent for the biographical subject-form of the writer of *Juan*" (354).[22] Contrary to Christensen's conclusion, I will argue that to "perform lordship" as a poetic act required of Byron more than the strength of class prestige, more than an intuitive exploitation of an archaic class position that is somehow analogous to an archaic, pre-Oedipal drive, more than an appreciation and exploitation of how symbolic exchange (literally) works. Indeed, as I will argue, Byron's boast that his "best Canto" will "turn upon Political Economy" is fulfilled throughout a poem that simultaneously exploits and refutes the status of such analogical thinking, even as his ambivalent anger toward what Christensen calls the "abdication of fathers" (18) took the form of a poetry that both challenges (like the god of Love) and exploits (like the god of the underworld) the commercial resources of a symbolic exchange founded on the death of the Father.

Such poetry emerged from a need to gain distance from *and* to liberate a self (and, sometimes, selves), a self that was often, literally, beside itself with a loathing conferred by the judgment of the Father's Law (the superego) and by the irreparable loss of the Father's (and father's) *love*. The impoverishment of love, according to Freud, is the condition of melancholy, an illness that returns love itself to its forgotten origins in parental criticism and childish resentment. "To withdraw *myself* from *myself* (oh that cursed selfishness!) has ever been my sole, my entire, my sincere motive in scribbling at all," Byron wrote during that moment in his young career when he awoke and found himself famous, not as a lord but as a lordly poet (Journal, Nov. 27, 1813). He would never be fully at home with any of the multiple selves he would create from such aversion, but he mastered the advantages of living, through them, life astray.[23]

In relating poetry to the larger scheme of human endeavor, Byron claimed not to appraise highly his creativity or his mastery. A few days earlier in his 1813 journal the suddenly famous young lord made the following comment: "I do think . . . the mighty stir made about scribbling and scribes, by themselves and others—a sign of effeminacy, degeneracy, and weakness. Who would write, who had any thing better to do?" A city-bred aristocrat, one might answer, with tastes his own culture defined as effeminate, degenerate, and weak. Such a member of British society lives not on his land but on its earnings. He is an admired parasite distinguished by his ability, and his willingness, to do nothing, to do it for money, and to do it with such style that the "lower orders" will gladly pay for the pleasure of reading about it. From the day that Byron learned of his inheritance, he was given an improved education in letters (partly at his own request), but he was nevertheless trained for no work in life except, perhaps, for the speechmaking role in Parliament that he ultimately declined to fulfill. While infatuated with the romance of Newstead Abbey, he knew little and cared less about the work that went on in the entailed estates that he inherited.

Byron became a lord precociously, as he acquired early so many other adult privileges, pleasures, and expressions of guilt. He learned before he could read that he had acquired a legacy that his forefathers had willfully (if not insanely) squandered, and his mother reminded him repeatedly that he had inherited not only his paternal ancestors' titles and land but also their debts and bad characters. An orphan, he would have been keenly aware that the price of his lordship was the death of his father (and grandfather, and uncle). A lord who borrowed to the hilt on his expectations before he had reached his majority, Byron at last had to orphan himself from his native land, recognizing that his most graceful and gainful (and least socially parasitic) occupation, until he came into possession of his inheritance, was idleness in the relative anonymity (and distance from creditors) that life abroad provides. (England, as the narrator reminds us in *Don Juan,* is "a country in all senses the most dear" [10.77].) At such a time in a young lord's life, his single, approved position in society (if he has no benefactors) is that of "absence." That occupation only became second best for the peripatetic Lord Byron when he found a more lucrative and more celebrated way to do nothing: to write about it.

A case study of *ennuyé, Childe Harold* became, to the author's astonishment, not only unexpectedly profitable but also prophetic. A hero who is prematurely both sated and disappointed, Byron's Harold ameliorates his "moping fits" and "bloated Ease" with "toilsome" travel. If the victim of ennui suffers a self-loathing that infects (or has been infected by) the too-familiar surroundings that Kuhn terms *horror loci* (including being surrounded by the family and friends whom Harold left "without a sigh" but with whom his author left, nevertheless, sizable debts to be paid), then wandering in the world, witnessing the consequences of tyrants' vanities in the genuine sufferings of the victims of the Napoleonic wars, becomes a strong antidote to the "vicious pleasure" to which he had become too early accustomed: "With pleasure drugg'd he almost longed for woe / And e'en for change of scene would seek the shades below" (1.6).

However compelling (and self-distracting) Harold's confrontations with death, bloodshed, and moldering antiquity on his travels in the first two cantos, none of these experiences prepared his author for the series of personal losses he faced almost as soon as he again set foot on native soil: the deaths of his mother, of his close friend at Cambridge Charles Matthews, of a Harrow schoolmate John Wingfield, and of the choirboy he loved "innocently"—and who came to represent for Byron innocence personified—John Edleston.[24] Whatever the reasons that led Byron to seek the solace of writing in addition to the medicine of travel while he was abroad, he returned to the manuscript of *Childe Harold* in October 1811, after learning of Edleston's death in May, to express in the second (and then final) canto the shock of a more personal encounter with sadness than the inexplicable ennui of the previous ninety stanzas. In the letters Byron wrote that fall, no less than in the (then) concluding stanza of *Childe Harold,* canto 2, Byron intuited that he, like his hero, would be "doom'd to go" away once more from a home where he was, more than ever, an orphan.

When Byron next resumed *Childe Harold* in 1816, less than a month after he had set sail from England for the final time, his disappointments—and Harold's—could no longer be classed with the vague or unspecifiable unease of *ennuyé*. The "gloomy wanderer," "the world's tired denizen" in canto 2, Byron/Harold found society increasingly athwart his often-promiscuous search for love in the intervening years of fame and notoriety that occurred between that canto and the third: his marriage was broken (in part by Byron's abusive, saturnine behavior toward his wife), his reputation was blemished by rumors of incest with his half-sister Augusta, his daughter Ada was estranged from him, and—most devastating of all—his relationship with Augusta had become, at a distance, exclusively epistolary. Even more than in 1809, the only role that would be open to this orphaned, scapegrace aristocrat in English society would be that of absence. In the *Childe Harold* that he turned to once again, in exile, Byron made increasingly explicit the close connections he perceived between the melancholic loss of those from whom he was estranged (by death or by law), the survival of memory, and the relief of writing. Anger, or "hatred," for Byron, coexisted with love in the barren void of loss and of prohibition; writing, which "replaces what we hate," also "replenishes" the void opened by death "with a fresher growth":

> The beings of the mind are not of clay;
> Essentially immortal, they create
> And multiply in us a brighter ray
> And more beloved existence. That which Fate
> Prohibits to dull life in this our state
> Of mortal bondage, by these spirits supplied,
> First exiles, then replaces what we hate:
> Watering the heart whose early flowers have died,
> And with a fresher growth replenishing the void.
> (*Childe Harold,* 4.5)

For Byron, poetic writing "can re-people with the past," but it nevertheless weighs fully the loss of "beings" of "clay" that it cannot restore to the poet except (as in the lines that follow) as "spectres." Such poetry seeks recourse not merely in a writing that "creates," that "peoples" (to use one of Byron's frequent verbs) through Eros's gentle, healing tears, "watering the heart," but also in a death-driven labor of incurable, stormy, "blackening" rage:

> And how and why we know not, nor can trace
> Home to its cloud this lightning of the mind,
> But feel the shock renew'd, or can efface
> The blight and blackening which it leaves behind,
> Which out of things familiar, undesign'd,
> When least we deem of such, calls up to view
> The spectres whom no exorcism can bind,
> The cold—the changed—perchance the dead—anew,
> The mourn'd, the loved the lost—too many!—yet how few!
>
> But my soul wanders; I demand it back
> To meditate amongst decay, and stand
> A ruin amidst ruins; there to track
> Fall'n states and buried greatness. . . .
>
> (4.24, 25)

The poems that Byron wrote during his first years abroad powerfully illuminate a darkened imagination that cannot surrender its losses (the most important of which will be the loss of Augusta and Ada) or its anger with its own and the world's fallenness; they include, of course, the Augusta poems, "Darkness," "A Fragment," *The Prisoner of Chillon,* and *Manfred.* In these poems of often apocalyptic despair, the world itself becomes a barren, dead object, a prison abandoned by its jailors. In "Darkness," "a dream that was not all a dream,"

> The bright sun was extinguish'd, and the stars
> Did wander darkling in the eternal space,
> Rayless, and pathless, and the icy earth
> Swung blind and blackening in the moonless air;
> Morn came and went—and came, and brought no day,
> And men forgot their passions in the dread
> Of this their desolation; . . .

In "A Fragment," the poet who knows he cannot look behind— "remount the river of my years / To the first fountain of our smiles and tears"—looks forward, but only to death:

> What is this Death?—a quiet of the heart?
> The whole of that of which we are a part?
> For life is but a vision—what I see

> Of all which lives, alone is life to me;
> And being so—the absent are the dead,
> Who haunt us from tranquillity, and spread
> A dreary shroud around us, and invest
> With sad remembrancers our hours of rest.
> The absent are the dead—for they are cold,
> And ne-er can be what once we did behold.

In this poem, the necropolis beneath the surface of the earth is more alive than the spirit of the melancholic poet. The image he chooses here to express life's fragile passage—a *bubble*—will, in *Don Juan*, restore life. But the poet who writes "A Fragment" sees and hears only death:

> Or do they in their silent cities dwell
> Each in his incommunicative cell?
> Or have they their own language? and a sense
> Of breathless being?—darken'd and intense
> As midnight in her solitude?—O earth!
> Where are the past?—and wherefore had they birth?
> The dead are thy inheritors—and we
> But bubbles on their surface; and the key
> Of thy profundity is in the grave,
> The ebon portal of thy peopled cave,
> Where I would walk in spirit, and behold
> Our elements resolved to things untold . . .

Cain: A "Hideous Heritage" and the Abject Heir

The poem that delineates most clearly Byronic preterition—and the relationship of that particular version of fettered fallenness and melancholic loss to the activity of writing as Byron defines it in his journals and letters—does not emerge until his fifth year in exile, 1821. *Cain,* the poem Byron almost always cites in his letters in conjunction with the proud but (for him) ironic adjective "metaphysical," was begun in Ravenna after Byron had already completed five cantos of *Don Juan* and during the weeks when he was describing in his journal the *ennuyé* of his personal state and his participation in the turmoil of the Papal States. By the time that he had begun *Cain,* he had learned as an author the difficulty of losing a son: the hero Juan, whom the poet has pulled from near-death at sea (and perhaps, subsequently, from the death of too-perfect love), and *Don Juan*, the prodigy he does not yet want to end but that he will reluctantly promise Teresa Guiccioli to cease writing, in July. Playing the part of Lambro in that poem, Byron had performed the tyranny of a father who lives his life by trade but who refuses to surrender his daughter in the exchange called marriage. Byron, now in real life an estranged father, knew intimately the unrelieved sorrow of losing the immediacy of a child's love. *Cain*, a drama about a demanding father, blood sacrifice, and fratricide, took shape only a month after Byron witnessed the murder of a military officer on the threshold of his home (a trauma he described vividly in his letters and in canto 5 of *Don Juan*). But in many ways, he had been preparing for this poem of entailed estates and inadvertent sin since early childhood.

In 1794, the same year that Byron learned (not without the usual difficulties of six-year-olds) how to read, he also learned that he was "heir presumptive" to his grandfather Byron's title and estates. The young aristocrat would not be introduced to poetry, the legacy that would provide him with a still larger share of fame and fortune, until the following year. Through the same Presbyterian nursemaid who would initiate him, precociously, into sexual experience at the age of nine, Byron learned at the age of seven to enjoy reading the Bible, particularly the poetry of Psalms. But the Old Testament scripture that most compelled the imagination of the boy who read voraciously *all* of its books before he was eight was the story of Cain and Abel.[25] That same year he read Gessner's *Death of Abel* with, according to Leslie Marchand, "delight": young Byron was struck with "the fascinating idea that he was predestined to evil,"[26] an idea no doubt confirmed by the "mark" of his destiny as a disobedient son: his lame foot.[27] Like Cain—and like Manfred—Byron understood that

> . . . grief should be the instructor of the wise;
> Sorrow is knowledge: they who know the most
> Must mourn the deepest o'er the fatal truth,
> The Tree of Knowledge is not that of Life.
> (*Manfred*, 1.1.9–12)

The sorrow of experience, the presence of death, and the hypocrisy of Calvinist libertinage would share a fixed place in the boy's imagination by the time he became the sixth Baron Byron of Rochdale at the age of ten in January 1798.

Like the young Byron whose inheritance is only a promise, the hero of Byron's *Cain* inherits his parents' memories of the nobility that might have been his birthright (indeed, that of the human race). Angry with Adam who (in Cain's eyes) foolishly failed to pluck the fruit from the Tree of Life after eating that of Knowledge, Cain grumbles about the hard labor of the fields—"the earth yields nothing to us without sweat" (1.182)—and "lingers" at twilight at the gates of the "Gardens which are my just inheritance" (1.85). Seeming almost to summon Lucifer by dawdling where he does not belong, Cain confesses to Satan, God's other unhappy son, his dissatisfaction with man's curtailed estate, a condition that sounds remarkably like Byron's description of his own *ennuyé* in the month when he began this poem:

> I live,
> But live to die: and, living, see no thing
> To make death hateful, save an innate clinging,
> A loathsome, and yet all invincible
> Instinct of life, which I abhor, as I
> Despise myself, yet cannot overcome—
> And so I live. Would I had never lived.
> (Act I, ll. 105–11)

Lucifer responds by defining God as himself a victim of ennui, a melancholic tyrant who could have summoned any pleasure to fill the empty hours of eternity. Instead (as Lucifer tells the story), God created in his own image not a perfected life but its failure—*death:* "let him reign on, / And multiply himself in misery!"[28] Cain's obsession with the ruined Eden coexists with his obsessive desire for knowledge of a condition that he cannot yet know except in the abstract—*death:*

> But thou canst not
> Speak aught of knowledge which I would not know,
> And do not thirst to know, and bear a mind
> To know.
> (1.244–47)

Transported by Lucifer through the abyss of space and time that is God's failed Creation, Cain finds (as did Childe Harold) that the past opens its vistas spatially.[29] Like Harold's tour of ancient civilizations, Cain's journey through this galactic ruin is peopled by ghosts and fossils. To witness such divine abortions, Lucifer argues, is to understand the unalterable disparity between the failed piece of work that is man (including his Malthusian capacity to spawn that failure) and the magnitude of his ideals, hopes, and desires. Yet to *see* the evidence of death amid the ruins of God's earlier creations—literal representations of the "Destroyer's" death drive—is nevertheless, as Cain realizes, not yet to *know* either death or its links to a human reproductivity in which he and his sister Adah are already participants:

> Cain:　　　　　　　　Spirit! I
> Know nought of death, save as a dreadful thing
> Of which I have heard my parents speak, as of
> A hideous heritage I owe to them
> No less than life; . . .
>
> . . . .
>
> Here let me die: for to give birth to those
> Who can but suffer many years, and die,
> Methinks is merely propagating death,
> And multiplying murder.
> (2.1.52 ff.)

Cain at least understands that, while he does not wish to imitate a melancholic Destroyer, neither does he want to identify with God's melancholic son, Lucifer. He fears that, like Lucifer, his restless ennui will lead him (as, of course, it does) to become a wanderer who "canst range / Nature and immortality—and yet / Seem'st sorrowful" (2.1.82). In fact, however, Cain is not given leisure either to enjoy or to be bored with Creation, for his melancholic Father is a taskmaster who deprives the fallen laborer not only, ultimately, of his own days on Earth but also of the living fruits produced by his hours of labor:

> Cain:　　It is not with the earth, though I must till it,
> I feel at war, but that I may not profit
> By what it bears of beautiful, untoiling,
> Nor gratify my thousand swelling thoughts
> With knowledge, nor allay my thousand fears
> Of death and life. (2.2.330ff.)

Cain has begun to understand that to identify with a Creator who is (in Lucifer's terms) in fact a Destroyer is itself life-destroying. Indeed, he half-suspects that Lucifer has himself *created* such a God in a misrecognition of his image; yet, even knowing that Lucifer's creation of such a God has brought him only the loneliness and unhappiness that he attributes to God, Cain cannot help but imitate Lucifer in misrecognizing in God's unhappy image his own, miserable self:

> Cain: Why do I exist?
>   Why art *thou* wretched? why are all things so?
>   Ev'n he who made us must be, as the maker
>   Of things unhappy! To produce destruction
>   Can surely never be the task of joy,
>   And yet my sire says he's omnipotent:
>   . . . .
> Lucifer: What does thy God love?
> Cain: All things, my father says; but I confess
>   I see it not in their allotment here.
>   (2.2.485 ff., 518 ff.)

That question—"What does thy God love?"—will, in the end, be the crucial one for us to answer in relation to Byron's art and the absent Father's systems of symbolic exchange.

Cain's final refusal of the required "bribe / To the Creator" has two components: first, he and his siblings are innocent of the guilt for which they are to atone; and, second, they have sufficiently fulfilled God's curse through labor:

>   By sacrificing
> The harmless for the guilty? what atonement
> Were there? Why, *we* are innocent: what have we
> Done, that we must be victims for a deed
> Before our birth, or need have victims to
> Atone for this mysterious, nameless sin—
> If it be such a sin to seek for knowledge?
>   . . . .
> I have toil'd, and till'd, and sweaten in the sun
> According to the curse:—must I do more?
> For what should I be gentle? for a war
> With all elements ere they will yield
> The bread we eat? For what must I be grateful?
> For being dust, and grovelling in the dust,
> Till I return to dust? If I am nothing—
> For nothing shall I be an hypocrite,
> And seem well-pleased with pain? For what should I

Be contrite? for my father's sin, already
Expiate with what we all have undergone,
And to be more than expiated by
The ages prophesied, upon our seed.
(3.1.87 ff., 109 ff.)[30]

In writing as Cain's son rather than the Father's, Byron reenacted, repeatedly, the banishment of a son who, having lost faith in the Father, nevertheless cannot transfer faith to the Law of the Father, a Law whose "Father" refuses to dwell in the fallen family of man that He created. Like Cain, Byron by definition strays from the immediacy of the Father because he is a disseminator, fragmenting and scattering the immediacy—the voice or presence—of the Word across pages of written words. Writing, Derrida writes in *Dissemination,* is "a son abandoned by his father. . . . His impotence is truly that of an orphan as much as that of a justly or unjustly persecuted patricide."[31] On the other hand, Derrida continues, Plato, the philosopher, is a master of sincere speech, a noble son who inherits his father's (Socrates') truths, in whose home (and near whose voice) metaphor permits him to stay (and to live) forever. Writing introduces the possibility of death into that relationship: "As a living thing, *logos* issues from a father. There is thus for Plato no such thing as a written thing. There is only a *logos* more or less alive, more or less distant from itself. Writing is not an independent order of signification; it is weakened speech, something not completely dead: a living-dead, a reprieved corpse, a deferred life, a semblance of breath. The phantom, the phantasm, the simulacrum . . . of living discourse is not inanimate; it is not insignificant; it simply signifies little, and always the same thing" (143). The philosopher accuses the writer of introducing the discord of difference into the Father's Creation; the writer, however, perceives (like Cain, tutored by Lucifer) that the absent Creator is the absent Destroyer; the God of Love has become the Father of the Law. The writer knows—like Cain—that he owes not only his unhappiness but also whatever wisdom he may possess to his awareness of a death that troubles him (but not his community) and to his anger both at the inexplicable loss, and ongoing demands, of a dead, or at least melancholic and reclusive, Father. Socrates, like Christ, is himself a good son, for he willingly sacrifices his life in obedience to that Father's Law.[32] Cain, like Byron a disobedient son, questions the authorization for such systems of exchange, perceiving that a Creation that is marred by death and that exacts repeated acts of death in exchange for "salvation" expresses not a *living* but a *dead* (and, in turn, deadly) Creator. The fall into language—a symbolic exchange dependent on sacrifice—whether that language is expressed in speech or in writing, has already required that sons sacrifice the living Father (thereby establishing Him as different and apart from themselves) so that his Name and his Law may rule universally. Difference, in other words, by no means originates with writing, or even with sin.[33]

To disrupt the hypocrisy of the Father's Law, and to expose the sacrifices that it demands, requires a kind of writing that transgresses established taboos, that haunts or even invades the so-called living Word,[34] so that the seed of Creation may be sown and allowed to thrive far from home in unexpected or even forbidden places.[35] The good son who is saved—who claims to speak God's truth, to sow his seed in the production of more obedient sons, and to die willingly as a martyr to God's "love"—fears contamination of his seed with the bad that has been proscribed. But the exiled son who persists in writing in preterition—"by blood or ink," in Byron's words—is able to write openly and even outrageously without fear of greater punishment, whatever the trials and tribulations to be faced by his publishers. Paradoxically, as we will see in *Don Juan,* the preterite poet may both broadcast and hoard his seed-capital—and his objects of love—in the act that Byron mischievously called "philogenitiveness." Those who claim to speak for the Father—the philosopher and the chosen son—may accuse the preterite writer of parricide, but Byron and Cain believe they know better: *they* are the sons who challenge the Father to a better Creation, to return materially a son's love, and—simply—to return.

We do not know whether Byron as a child ever conjectured that he was somehow responsible for his father's death. It would, of course, be a likely mistake for a boy who must have served prematurely as his mother's confidant (as we are told that he served as scapegoat for her anger toward the absent father). Even the best-behaved children who lose a parent through separation or death experience such feelings, as we may learn by reading studies of orphans, the phenomenally popular self-help books for children of "dysfunctional" families, or Julia Kristeva's important work on victims of melancholic "borderline disorders," *Powers of Horror: An Essay on Abjection.* In the absence of a responsible father (or Father) to admire and to emulate, a son (according to Kristeva) may internalize that very absence at the place where he would normally be "cathecting" an increasingly confident, stable, and self-respecting (self-loving) ego. Into that void moves prematurely, first, words (used almost as incantations to ward off the phobias associated with that dark emptiness) and, second, a terrifying ghost: the Law, that harsh, judgmental, and destructive aspect of the paternal parent who has been lost (or, in the child's guilty imagination, killed) before he might have served as the loving, paternal presence who, through his voice, would call encouragingly to the son struggling to establish—through language—a sense of himself and of self-worth. What also threatens to enter that internal space is, in Julia Kristeva's terms, the "abject": the no less terrifying presence of the "archaic mother" at the border of the self (between "inside" and "outside") from whom the son must begin to separate in order to establish any boundaries at all between "self" (or ego) and "world."[36] In the psychodrama that Kristeva terms abjection, a kind of writer emerges who will restage, again and again, Cain's encounter with a God who signifies not love or life but death,[37] a Father who expects him to engage in an exchange that involves a ritual of bodily purification,[38] which is in fact a murder (blood sacrifice and/or matricide):

> Two seemingly contradictory causes bring about the narcissistic crisis that provides . . . a view of the abject. *Too much strictness on the part of the Other,* confused with the One and the Law. The *lapse of the Other. . . .* The abject is the violence of mourning for an "object" that has always already been lost. The abject shatters the wall of repression and its judgments. It takes the ego back to its source on the abominable limits from which, in order to be, the ego has broken away—it assigns it a source in the non-ego, drive, and death. Abjection is a resurrection that has gone through death (of the ego). It is an alchemy that transforms death drive into a start of life, of new significance. (*Powers of Horror,* p. 17)

If, as Byron suggests in his various writings of January 1821, *ennuyé* is the disease of a jaded, tyrannical half-dead God who will make a son the scapegoat for his failure, then "abject" writing may itself be the punishment that forces such doomed sons, on the one hand, both to repeat the Father's failed creativity (and failed love) and to fulfill his expectations of the sinner he has unintentionally made. Alternatively, through writing such a son may forestall his sentence, using the time between condemnation and execution to rewrite his Word, and—through dissemination—to conceive a different, not-yet fallen self for himself, one that does not yet know that the preterite, in God's book, have never been innocent. Through writing the preterite poet may revive, at once, an adventurous and philandering dead father—dun "John" Byron, "Don Juan"—the youthful love that remained throughout his life the most innocent ideal ("John" Edleston) and the dead Father behind the abstract Law that governs symbolic exchange. The dejected writer (one who is subjected *to* the abject) may succeed in such ambitious revivals precisely because, as Kristeva states, he does not "respect borders, position, rules," because he is "in-between, the ambiguous, the composite" (*Powers of Horror,* p. 4): "A deviser of territories, languages, words, the *deject* never stops demarcating his universe whose fluid confines . . . constantly question his solidity and impel him to start afresh. A tireless builder, the deject is in short a *stray. . . .* And the more he strays, the more he is saved" (8). Such a writer may, as Peter Manning suggests in *Byron and His Fictions,* "assert identity only through a perpetual re-establishment of his difference, yet another digression. He must at every moment perform himself anew" (243). Through such performance, he is assured that he is not (yet) dead.

Don Juan: "Between the Gaping Heir and Gnawing Gout"

To read the photocopies of Byron's *Don Juan* manuscripts is to witness the visceral vitality of that performance of self-renewal, an active creativity that is comparable to the impudent aggression and generous affection that by turns drive the poet's voluminous correspondence. Byron once suggested to his estranged wife that he wrote in order to retain in exile the English language; in reading his word-strewn manuscripts, one may see that that loss, at least, he was spared. Spaces between stanzas spawn new stanzas; the margins bloom with revisions. One can almost hear Byron stuttering explosively successive attempts at rhyme until he gets what he wants. Truman Guy Steffan reminds us that, while Byron often made light of his "idling," he labored obsessively to produce the effect of facility and speed in his finished art, of a gracious, leisurely writing that is all pleasure and no work.[39] Steffan proposes a number of motives for these additions, but perhaps most useful is his relation of Byron's "fertile" productivity to the "negative, skeptical, destructive forces of his mind" (85): "Accretion is usually not tame and neutral; not really addition, but eruption. . . . Byron's was a temperament under almost constant strain, much of it self-imposed and self-aggravated ('I was born for opposition'). His writing has a mental tenseness,

an emotional excitement, a jumping restlessness and waywardness" (96).

The dynamic relationship between fertility and destructiveness in
Don Juan, played out in the progression (and digression) of narration, the uses (and abuses) of metaphor, and in representations of
getting and spending and getting-with-child, drives a poem that is
characterized—if a single word must be chosen—by *movement.* Auden in his essay "Don Juan" suggests that Byron's poetry cannot be
read slowly without losing its appeal, whereas "at the description of
things in motion or the way in which the mind wanders from one
thought to another he is a great master" (405). A poet who understood that life does not stand still for the living, the dead, or the
living dead who inhabit ennui, Byron, when faced with the consequences of his own creation—the death of the creatures in whom he
has invested so much life—learned to summon as a poet strategies
either for their survival or their renewal. The pleasure that he derived in such creative salvation may be summarized in Manning's
affectionate portrait: "Living in a foreign land, hearing all day a
foreign language, Byron elaborated his inner life in those solitary
hours of composition often mellowed by gin and water. 'Donny
Johnny' became his most intimate companion, and what he found
in its writing he gave liberally to his readers. . . . [It is] the victory of
self-consciousness over its own divisions (264)."

Narrative digressions are Byron's most celebrated technique for
such pleasurable, poetic procreation. As we have learned from
Steffan, digressions were often in fact what he calls "accretions,"
added interstitially between stanzas after the primary or "matrix"
text of a canto was completed. The earliest accretions, in canto 1,
suggest how Byron works "on" and "in" the boundaries between
things, words, lines, and stanzas to make the void "matter," to fall
into the middle of a middle and therefore to forestall the inevitable
end of a narrative drive that—as he so often reminds himself and his
readers in his conclusions to such digressions—must itself end (ultimately with the writer himself) in death.

In a poem in which a creator's love either forestalls an inevitable
death or sows the seeds for a new life to rise from its ruins, it
is perhaps appropriate that the narrator introduce himself by con-
fessing a desire that a writer would seem uniquely able to satisfy
through the process of composition: "I want a hero." Yet the narrator immediately remembers—by stanza's end—that this particular,
legendary hero will inevitably die. Originally that stanza was fol-

lowed by one that recalls the brevity of history's memory of the dead. In revision, Byron inserted new stanzas between the two, generating a memorial roll call of heroes. What leads the narrator from one version with one hero to another in which heroes literally seem to reproduce each other? In this canto concerned with bringing a dead legend back to life—and sustaining that life through the duration of narration—we also find later a digression that itself spawns a digressive accretion that concerns dead things that seem to come, uncannily, to life.

That digression occurs with a forestalling at a boundary of sorts, one that may bring forth human life: Juan and Julia are just on the verge of their fall into adultery (it would be Juan's fall into sexual experience). "I'm almost sorry that I e'er begun," the narrator concludes, in mock apology (1.115). And yet the irresistible happens to the couple (and, poetically speaking, also to the couplet) as the go-between narrator coyly panders to our prurience: in stanza 117 the poet rhymes "repented," "I will ne'er consent," and "consented." At that very moment the narrator turns aside from whatever pleasure (and whatever else) is being generated offstage to distract us with a later addition (an accretion) that is a digression on the various ways to construe "pleasure," a word that he immediately rhymes with "treasure" and then—that word associated with ennui—"leisure":

> 'Tis said that Xerxes offered a reward
>   To those who could invent him a new pleasure.
> Methinks the requisition's rather hard,
>   And must have cost His Majesty a treasure:
> For my part I'm a moderate-minded bard,
>   Fond of a little love (which I call leisure);
> I care not for new pleasures, as the old
> Are quite enough for me, so they but hold.
>
> Oh Pleasure you're indeed a pleasant thing,
>   Although one must be damned for you, no doubt
> I make a resolution every spring
>   Of reformation, ere the year run out,
> But somehow this my vestal vow takes wing;
>   Yet still I trust it may be kept throughout.
> I'm very sorry, very much ashamed,
> And mean next winter to be quite reclaimed.
> (1.118–19)

In the original stanzas on pleasure (" 'Tis sweet to . . .") that follow in the final version (as st. 122–27) the above accretion, one delight seems to evoke another and another, suggesting a kind of mnemonic in which remembered desires metonymically evoke desires that do not seem, on first reading, contiguous, rendering for the reader the sensation of a tyrant's restless quest for "new pleasures" that may indeed be (as Byron once said) "vicious":

> Sweet is the vintage, when the showering grapes
>> In bacchanal profusion reel to earth,
> Purple and gushing. Sweet are our escapes
>> From civic revelry to rural mirth.
> Sweet to the miser are his glittering heaps.
>> Sweet to the father is his first-born's birth.
> Sweet is revenge, especially to women,
> Pillage to soldiers, prize-money to seamen.
>
> Sweet is a legacy, and passing sweet
>> The unexpected death of some old lady
> Or gentleman of seventy years complete,
>> Who've made "us youth" wait too, too long already
> For an estate or cash or country-seat,
>> Still breaking, but with stamina so steady
> That all the Israelites are fit to mob its
> Next owner for their double-damned post-obits.
>
> 'Tis sweet to win, no matter how, one's laurels
>> By blood or ink. 'Tis sweet to put an end
> To strife; 'tis sometimes sweet to have our quarrels,
>> Particularly with a tiresome friend.
> Sweet is old wine in bottles, ale in barrels.
>> Dear is the helpless creature we defend
> Against the world; and dear the schoolboy spot
> We ne'er forget, though there we are forgot.
> (1.124–26)

In the space of this fertile recall, boundaries are elided between the accrual of gold, the reproduction of children, the inheritance of estates, and the production of writing. Such suggestive proliferation, a kind of teasing seduction between "chaste Muse" and "chaste reader"—with the (unchaste) narrator as the "medium" writing in between—seems almost to defy the reader's foreknowledge that to experience pleasure is to *be* "experienced." For Juan, the fall from innocence looms, just as the comic poet has become serious in the defense of innocence—"Dear is the helpless creature we defend / Against the world":

> But sweeter still than this, than these, than all
>   Is first and passionate love. It stands alone,
> Like Adam's recollection of his fall.
>   The tree of knowledge has been plucked; all's known,
> And life yields nothing further to recall
>   Worthy of this ambrosial sin, so shown
> No doubt in fable as the unforgiven
> Fire which Prometheus filched for us from heaven.
> (1.127)

Notably, it is not to innocence but to the precise moment of the Fall that Adam, like Byron, returns. There are no fruits of postlapsarian sin equal to the taste of the "ambrosial" apple that transforms innocent love into the erotic pleasure of lust, introducing the stain of the destructive drive of Thanatos that cannot, henceforth, be removed from Eros. That first moment when ambrosia has not yet separated into sin is likened by the narrator to the first *creative* spark borne with suffering and great labor by the productive writer's progenitor, Prometheus. Neither love's pleasure nor the pleasure that a writer derives can, in an impure age, be free of the death Adam incurred with knowledge. The "vicious pleasures" of a tyrant are sought, to some degree, by all.

The stanza that follows, stanza 128, begins another accretion (it continues through st. 132 before returning us to an original stanza, st. 133). In it Byron seeks to account for the perversion of Adam's fruit and Prometheus's fire in appropriations by the modern marketplace:

> Man's a strange animal, and makes strange use
>   Of his own nature and the various arts,
> And likes particularly to produce
>   Some new experiment to show his parts.
> This is the age of oddities let loose,
>   Where different talents find their different marts.
> You'd best begin with truth, and when you've lost your
> Labour, there's a sure market for imposture.
>
> What opposite discoveries we have seen . . .
> (1.128, 129.1)

In Byron's strange new world, where honest "labour" has been replaced by a "sure market for imposture," where useless commodities and venereal diseases proliferate, where technology succeeds only in entertaining the short-lived dead ("to set some corpses grinning" in st. 130), and where "new inventions / For killing bodies and for saving souls" may be "All propagated with the best intentions" (132), science cannot restore innocence to pleasure, or remove the tincture of death that characterizes the ennui of routine, sanctioned love. The digression ends and we arrive at an original stanza (133):

> Man's a phenomenon, one knows not what,
> >And wonderful beyond all wondrous measure.
> 'Tis pity though in this sublime world that
> >Pleasure's a sin and sometimes sin's a pleasure.
> Few mortals know what end they would be at,
> >But whether glory, power or love or treasure,
> The path is through perplexing ways, and when
> The goal is gained, we die you know—and then?
>
> What then? I do not know, no more do you,
> >And so good night. Return we to our story.
> (1.133, 134.1–2)

Death drives this digression (spurred by deadly diversions) forward to its own "end," "and then" all that the narrator can do is continue to tell a tale that he has just realized all over again can have only one certain and sad goal for the preterite poet: "we die you know." With a brief wink at "Lycidas" (there are many such flirtations in *Don Juan* with Milton's oddly anti-elegiac elegy) and a nod toward the "greater" pox, November's frost on the mountaintops has been time-"lapsed" forward to "clap a white cape on their mantles blue" (134). We are again with Juan and Julia, who we now know surely have fallen in the interval, between the stanzas, "between" being the only time that "matters": between having the world all before one, and after.

"This sin" of poetry, as young Byron calls it in his preface to the second edition of *Hours of Idleness,* is contiguous for the poet throughout his career with his association of last things and first kisses; one often summons the other. Two weeks before he wrote in his 1813 journal, "I am *ennuyé* beyond my usual tense of that yawning verb, which I am always conjugating" (Dec. 10), he devoted almost a page to reflections on his first infatuation, at the age of seven, with Mary Duff. (We may recall that this is also the year in which Byron was taken with the story of Cain and with the poetry of the Old Testament.) Of Mary Duff he writes, "How very odd that I should have been so utterly, devotedly fond of that girl, at an age when I could neither feel passion, nor know the meaning of the word": "How the deuce did all this occur so early? where could it originate? I certainly had no sexual ideas for years afterwards; and yet my misery, my love for that girl were so violent, that I sometimes doubt if I have ever been really attached since. . . . it is a phenomenon in my existence (for I was not eight years old) which has puzzled, and will puzzle me to the latest hour of it. . . . Next to the beginning, the conclusion has often occupied my reflections, in the way of investigations" (Nov. 26, 1813). Literally the boundary between innocence and experience, between Adam's prelapsarian lovemaking and his experience of first lust, "kiss," as a more jaded Byronic narrator will observe in *Don Juan* "rhymes to 'bliss' in fact as well as verse; / I wish it never led to something worse" (6.59).[40]

The conclusion of things that Byron claims in his letter fascinates him almost as much as the beginning is evoked in a second series of images in the early poems: the ruins of Newstead Abbey. In the early poems, as Gleckner observes, "one of Byron's favorite image patterns, that of the ruin, . . . parallels that of memory": "The ruin is at once the reminder of past greatness, glory, even a kind of Eden on earth, and an assertion, all the more powerful for its immortal associations, that the paradisaical past is irretrievable. Further, in contrast to those splendid ruins, the structures of the modern world are dwarfed and awry, the flawed products of postlapsarian man" (31). Indeed, in "On Leaving Newstead Abbey," the young poet finally comes to define his noble legacy as that which was born, and is borne, within his own person. The abbey is itself a kind of decaying corpse: "Thou, the hall of my fathers, art gone to decay." Neither the poem nor the pile can efface the violence of his "mail-cover'd" ancestors' lives and deaths or the visible presence of death's own ongoing ruination in the present abbey. Yet the heir lives, and so long as he goes about, "abroad, or at home, your remembrance imparting," so "lives" Newstead and, by extension, so does the reputation of his ancestors. Paradoxically, Byron *must* leave the ancestral seat so that he may propagate materially (in various senses) the family legacy. He early anticipated the abbey's fate: Byron at last liquidated his inherited assets so that he could live the life of not merely a comfortable but indeed a profligate poet of literary repute and social notoriety.[41] Not only in verse but also in fact, he converted the estate into "paper." Even in this early poem, however, Byron understands the overlapping borders of these economies and that his personal, material existence begins (and ends) at the border of his family ruins: "When decay'd, may he mingle his dust with your own!"

Byron returns to those ruins in *Don Juan,* not to bury his hero in the family sarcophagus of Newstead/Amundeville but to sustain him in an English "Paradise of Pleasure and *Ennui.*" Significantly, by the time Byron has reached the English cantos his accretions and revisions are rare. The ease of these magnificent, concluding cantos has everything to do with Byron's increasing skill at incorporating the seeming contradictions of our culture—pleasure, leisure, and treasure—into a poetry that radically exposes their overlapping relationships: erotic desire and material consumption; the consumption of the commodity called poetry and the stagnation of the corpse (or "post-obit") of poetic reputation; the paper of poetry that is to be "ingested" by the reader and the paper called "debt" that the poet may exchange for further (perhaps vicious) pleasures; the pleasures of misers and the pleasures of poets. Byron's art in the later cantos has become almost entirely a kind of digression that ingests (and perhaps, digests) the world, item by item, as one thing reminds him of another and another that he wants. As Stuart Curran concludes in *Poetic Form and British Romanticism,* the form of *Don Juan,* an extravagant exercise in aggression toward multiple genres, itself enacts incorporation, leading us to perceive that "the inconclusive and the inclusive are ore and the same" (197): "What accrues in this desultory fashion is truly encyclopedic . . . , enveloping Western culture even as it refuses to systematize it" (198).[42] Or, in the terms of "incorporation" (or of abjection) that Byron himself favors, "one system eats another up," with parricidal sons imitating their voracious, tyrannical fathers:

> If from great Nature's or our own abyss
>   Of thought we could but snatch a certainty,
> Perhaps mankind might find the path they miss,
>   But then 'twould spoil much good philosophy.
> One system eats another up, and this
>   Much as old Saturn ate his progeny,
> For when his pious consort gave him stones
> In lieu of sons, of these he made no bones.

But System doth reverse the Titan's breakfast,
    And eats her parents, albeit the digestion
Is difficult. Pray tell me, can you make fast
    After due search your faith to any question?
Look back o'er ages ere unto the stake fast
    You bind yourself and call some mode the best one.
Nothing more true than not to trust your senses,
And yet what are your other evidences?
(14.1, 2)

Byron's quarrel with philosophy does not begin in these cantos, but in them the metaphysician acquires an interesting fellow traveler: the tradesman, whose appetites turn out to be equally large and equally abstract. For Byron, "things"—which for him includes, as Auden reminds us, *words*—exist in physical, metonymical contiguity and contingency to each other, yet the mind has so succeeded in estranging itself from matter that it can perceive the world only through metaphysical, metaphorical leaps of identification across an in-between "void," an absent "presence" that performs an indispensable but ghostly function in linguistic signification. The hole in language that Derrida calls "dead time" and that Slavoj Žižek calls the *Real*ity of language's own death that eludes the synchronic Law of the Father,[43] this void is a hidden, resonant "place" between signifying word and signified thing, a place not unlike that which exists between two words for whom rhyme serves both to evoke and to deny identity. That void is a blank monument to the fall into the (fatherless) Law that breaks apart son and parent, words and things, desire and its fulfillment, labor and its products. Our culture's founding and gendered fissure between mind and matter, as Jean-Joseph Goux demonstrates in *Symbolic Economies: After Marx and Freud,* transforms those things that were once deemed most "real"—before that fall—into supernatural ghosts that haunt the empty spaces of loss, silence, and boredom.[44]

Goux, like Foucault, is fascinated by the change in perspective that altered human beings and their culture as Western Europe entered the Age of Reason, a change in which a single system (Goux follows Marx in calling it the system of the "general equivalent") defeated the others by installing itself in the subject's superego (through that subject's unconscious "introjection" or "swallowing" of the Law's self-regulating system). The Law stands in for the God that this system has murdered. As Marx himself defines it in *Capi-*

tal, the "general equivalent" that is the basis for the rule of this system of Law was originally (like Freud's totem animal that stands in for the Father) one ordinary, material object among many others circulating and competing for value (typically, in the case of economics, a mineral). Like Freud's "band of brothers," the Protestant bourgeoisie that was at this time re-forming the community around capital had consigned the Father to a metaphysical, abstract existence. Thus He became a reified, transcendental signifier of value in its most general sense, one that, like the gold standard or, sexually speaking, the phallus in Freud's libidinal economy, bestows in turn "value" upon the "saved" who *recognize* His symbolic value. Indeed, such reified objects can *only* become deified if a culture (or an individual) "sacrifices" the immediate gratification of their use for their symbolic (or exchange) value. Neither capitalist economies nor idealist philosophies (and Goux painstakingly establishes the intimate interdependence of the two) can exist without such transcendent values; neither, just as crucially, can they exist without the suppression or repression of what they choose to signify as "stubborn matter" in contradistinction to these "free" and mobile abstractions.

Notably, the elements that constitute this repressed materiality (and here Goux continues to foreground analogies between libidinal and labor-driven economies) include the polymorphous and perverse pleasures of the unconscious libido and the pain (or *sacrifice*) of labor that drives the machinery of capitalist exchange. The immaterial yet omnivorous consumption of one system by another, the metaphoric/introjective conversion of goods into the Good and then back again into other, circulating goods, may be alternatively and euphemistically called free trade or symbolic exchange. But it is always founded not only on the sacrifice of Cain's labor in the fields but also, subsequently, on the son's surrender of his physical (and incestuous) desire of an Adah/Augusta/(Ada), and of his physical (and incestuous) desire for the absent father/Father whom he may emulate but whom he cannot have.[45] Goux concludes that the sacrificial basis of the Law of the Father (politically, economically, and psychically) underwrites not only our culture's "dominant form of value," but, indeed, "the very concept of value" (4), a term that our fallen condition has divided misleadingly along the lines of matter and mind (or to use Byron's rhymes, the "phthisical" of the body and the "metaphysical" of the spirit).[46]

Goux's insights into the modern subject's peculiar readiness to view the world through the operations of metaphor—"as though" the world were composed entirely of reified objects that may be endlessly substituted for one another—suggests the central weakness of what is otherwise the most persuasive study of Byron's poetic preoccupation with work, leisure, and symbolic exchange. In "Byron's Poetry of Politics," Kurt Heinzelman defines Byron's view of the relation of poetry to politics (and, by implication, to economics) in terms of a "metaphorical exchange": "To focus on the poetry of (not in or for) politics is to imagine the two neither as form and content nor as cause and effect; it is, rather, to see them as modeling one another, as involved in a dynamic metaphorical exchange."[47] Such, Heinzelman continues, has been his own method, which he defines as "the economics of the imagination: " 'As if' is the key phrase, for in speaking of metaphor in this (Romantic) way we are also speaking of the public, political status (and value) of the private imagination itself" (373). In other words, Heinzelman is describing a world that is dominated by metaphorical (that is, exchange) value; neither he—nor the Byron that he reconstructs—critiques the ideological bases of a culture that installs such exchange value at the cost of denying its basis in material (or use) value. As a consequence, Heinzelman cannot help us to perceive (as Byron does) in a political and economic context the hidden, repressed "matters" that such an economy of "general equivalence" (or metaphor) fails itself to perceive, to literally "take into account": libido and labor, pleasure and pain. If, like Heinzelman, we restrict our conception of either economy or language to metaphors, then we may never recognize the importance of the in-between, the gap that founds the possibility of metaphors that seem to cross, even as they divide, the public and the private, the economic and the aesthetic, signs and objects. That gap beckons most urgently when Heinzelman ignores it in his exploration of the ways in which a poet such as Byron perceives the "economic modelling of our very language" or, conversely, how the "troping of economics" in language generates in turn an awareness that *some* kind of relationship exists between "political 'facts,' " and "the context of the artist's private needs and public aspirations" (374).

Ultimately, Heinzelman concludes that Byron must settle *either* for the "public role" *or* the "private need" of the poet. He may either put poetry on the market where he will receive cash for it in exchange for making it available as a commodity, or he may hoard it in private: "In *Don Juan* the question is reconstituted so that Byron *must* ask, and by means of his art, how publicly useful the work of imagination is" (384). The answer: "[T]he commoditization of his labor into the system of production and exchange" is precisely what the "poem attempted to represent. . . . Byron has shown himself able to understand the amassing irony of such vulnerability but without being able to do anything about it" (384–85). What Byron nevertheless retains in the private sphere with which he is left, Heinzelman proposes, is the aesthetic consolation of "sublimation": the "sublimation of the young Byron's fear that his character as an author and as a man of rank would bankrupt one another, that the 'fact' of composing would dispossess him of his reputation and feelings" (385). Byron may console himself with "the *value* affirmed here": "the moment of composition, which Byron calls his 'dream.' This moment is a kind of spot of time, caught between the precompositionary act of turning one's regard back to the past and the postcompositionary act of casting one's pages on the stream of an uncertain futurity" (385; my emphasis).

Such an in-between moment, as Heinzelman keenly perceives, is indeed Byron's particular space of poetic productivity, one that may well be private, but it is also a space of pleasure and labor that in fact has no value assigned for it in the system of production and exchange and the aesthetics it engenders. Indeed, as Marx himself writes in *Capital,* something produced by human labor (or by, to use Heinzelman's phrase, "the moment of composition") may have use value without being converted into a commodity through its entry into public exchange: "Whoever directly satisfies his wants with the produce of his own labour, creates, indeed, use-values, but not commodities."[48] Such produce may remain, in other words, captive within the poetic (and Lacanian) imaginary. On the other hand, something produced can indeed be simply "useless," in which case "so is the labour contained in it; the labour does not count as labour, and therefore creates no value" (7). The narrator of *Don Juan,* constantly depreciating the seriousness of his enterprise even while he makes manifest the labor hours invested, exposes this logic of value on which his poetry is based ("I can't oblige you reader to read on," "although it cost me half an hour in spinning"). Indeed, Byron enables us to see the paradoxical place that poetry—and poetic laborers—hold in our interlocking and homologous signifying and monetary economies. And in so doing he effectively subverts the intentions of an economy and an aesthetics founded on the operation of general equivalence, or the sublimation of pleasure in work and the sacrifice of sexual love to the demands of the Law. In two mock efforts to describe analogously the most ephemeral and whimsical of pleasures—the *bubbles* of champagne—Byron veers unexpectedly toward the viciousness of "tyrants" before declaring the futility of metaphorical thought—and of sublimation. As he says of poetry, it is a "paper kite, which flies 'twixt life and death, / A shadow which the onward soul behind throws" (14.8). His is "a *bubble* not blown up for praise, / But just to play with, as an infant plays" (14.8; my emphasis).[49]

In a canto that opens with spectral speculations, the narrator proposes that some crucial pleasures in life seem—like "spirits"—to elude description, conversion, or (paradoxically) distillation altogether, such as the dying of a day spent in "pleasure and ennui," that is, first, like spiritless champagne and then like "a system coupled with a doubt":

> The evaporation of a joyous day
>   Is like the last glass of champagne without
> The foam which made its virgin bumper gay,
>   Or like a system coupled with a doubt,
> Or like a soda bottle when its spray
>   Has sparkled and let half its spirit out,
> Or like a billow left by storms behind
> Without the animation of the wind . . .
>   (16.9)

In the stanza that follows, the poet concludes that the pleasure of the evaporation of a joyous day is "like nothing that I know / Except itself":

> Or like an opiate which brings troubled rest
>   Or none, or like—like nothing that I know
> Except itself. Such is the human breast,
>   A thing of which similitudes can show
> No real likeness. Like the old Tyrian vest
>   Dyed purple, none at present can tell how,
> If from a shell-fish or from cochineal.
> So perish every tyrant's robe piecemeal.
>   (16.10)

"Nothing" is precisely what characterizes all of the processes the poet has just carried us through: from loss to loss we move from the evaporation of a day, to evaporation of "champagne without /

The foam," to the evaporation of a metaphysics that rhymes "without" with "doubt," and, finally, to a comically serious effort to try one more time for a likeness: the vestments of a tyrant, dyed the color of blood. "Nothing"—the in-between place of the preterite poet in God's kingdom or of the insecure aristocrat in England's—is precisely, as Byron perceives in these lines, what drives the endless exchanges that are ruled by the similitudes of "general equivalency": almost anything could be substituted within the ellipses of "like . . . like . . . like." Yet Byron turns wittily on his own philosophy in the final line: just as words cannot cease to be substituted in our daily lives for the things that they clothe, however keenly we may be aware of the cost of symbolic exchange, no tyrant's robe will cease to represent the tyrant's power simply because we know it derives its hue from commercial processes (or, perhaps, from bloodshed). That does not stop Byron from robing, disrobing, and then disassembling the erstwhile ruler of a disappearing day (a day that cannot be monumentalized, elegized, possessed forever in "amber"):

> But next to dressing for a rout or ball,
> 　　Undressing is a woe. Our *robe de chambre*
> May sit like that of Nessus and recall
> 　　Thoughts quite as yellow, but less clear than amber.
> Titus exclaimed, "I've lost a day!" Of all
> 　　The nights and days most people can remember,
> (I have had of both, some not to be disdained),
> I wish they'd state how many they have gained.
> (16.11)

This "undressing" of the operations of similitude in symbolic exchange is more fully elaborated in yet another, earlier use of champagne in canto 13. In five stanzas on how metaphor provides the illusion of immediate transport (also as in "rapture," or "letting go"), Byron's play with those meanings leads to a deferred explosion, to champagne, and to frozen (or blocked metaphorical) passages. He teasingly explodes the confident and insentient crossings of metaphor, exploring at leisure the shoals and dangers within that space that metaphor heedlessly passes over (or through) in its flight toward identity:

> But Adeline was not indifferent, for—
> 　　Now for a common place—beneath the snow,
> As a volcano holds the lava more

Within, et cetera. Shall I go on? No.
I hate to hunt down a tired metaphor,
    So let the often used volcano go.
Poor thing. How frequently by me and others
It hath been stirred up till its smoke quite smothers.

I'll have another figure in a trice.
    What say you to a bottle of champagne,
Frozen into a very vinous ice,
    Which leaves few drops of that immortal rain.
Yet in the very centre, past all price,
    About a liquid glassful will remain,
And this is stronger than the strongest grape
Could e'er express in its expanded shape.

'Tis the whole spirit brought to a quintessence,
    And thus the chilliest aspects may concentre
A hidden nectar under a cold presence.
    And such are many, though I only meant her,
From whom I now deduce these moral lessons,
    On which the Muse has always sought to enter.
And your cold people are beyond all price,
When once you have broken their confounded ice.
    (13.36–38)

A frozen passage leads—inevitably—not only to the "grey signal flag" and "dreary '*fuimus*'" (or dreary "passing") of a (metaphorical) mission that has been thwarted but also (again, via "Lycidas") to death, when "life's thin thread's spun out":

But after all they are a Northwest Passage
    Unto the glowing India of the soul,
And as the good ships sent upon that message
    Have not exactly ascertained the pole
(Though Parry's efforts look a lucky presage)
    Thus gentlemen may run upon a shoal,
For if the pole's not open, but all frost
(A chance still), 'tis a voyage or vessel lost.

And young beginners may as well commence
    With quiet cruising o'er the ocean woman,
While those who are not beginners should have sense
    Enough to make for port, ere Time shall summon

With his grey signal flag, and the past tense,
    The dreary *fuimus* of all things human
Must be declined, while life's thin thread's spun out
Between the gaping heir and gnawing gout.
    (13.39, 40)

"Between" the hungry heir and the gout that is his destiny (that old age when "tedium / Make some prefer the circulating medium" [10.22]) lies "that horrid equinox" of middle age toward which Juan, commanded by his two "sovereigns," Catherine and Death, is now hurrying:

He lived (not Death, but Juan) in a hurry
    Of waste and haste and glare and gloss and glitter

. . . .

And this same state we won't describe. We could
    Perhaps from hearsay or from recollection;
But getting nigh grim Dante's "obscure wood",
    That horrid equinox, that hateful section
Of human years, that half-way house, that rude
    Hut, whence wise travellers drive with circumspection
Life's sad post-horses o'er the dreary frontier
Of age, and looking back to youth, give one tear—

I won't describe, that is, if I can help
    Description; and I won't reflect, that is
If I can stave off thought, which, as a whelp
    Clings to its teat, sticks to me through the abyss
Of this odd labyrinth; or as the kelp
    Holds by the rock; or as a lover's kiss
Drains its first draught of lips. But as I said,
I won't philosophize and will be read.
    (10.26–28)

The narrator of *Don Juan* who wants (and gets) a newly minted hero in the first stanza of canto 1 finds himself stuck in the later cantos with one who (unlike coinage) is growing older by the stanza (and one whose approaching death reminds the narrator, as ever, of first kisses and last things). While the author has aged only five years during the duration, the Don has grown from infant to adult. If Don Juan has not seen Death in the specter-lined gallery in canto 16, he certainly looks closer to it by the morning light of the final canto in *Don Juan:* just how, exactly, are we to distinguish the "ghosts" from the wan-faced "guests" that we witness at such a gathering? How much longer has Juan to live if, having been summoned originally by the narrator's "desire" for a new beginning, this new beginning has now grown old and even repetitive? And, finally, why does the final canto that begins on the subject of orphans and "lost parents"—"beginnings" that were too-soon "ended"—conclude with a ghost who is not dead and an ending that is reluctant to end?

As I have suggested earlier, Byron's accretions seem often to arise from a reluctance to move the narrative forward to its natural end. Digressions enlarge both the space and time of *Don Juan*, but typically as a consequence of these narrative strategies time grows backward, to enlarge a past that the narrator—from the "distance" of his "middle-age" of the present—may at first seem to mourn "elegiacally," with a graceful acceptance of his "loss." "No more—no more—oh never more, my heart": the refrain ("no more") in canto I, stanzas 214–15, and the general tone of mature and gentle mourning in the accretion that begins with stanza 201, may lead us at first to speculate that the man who regrets his lost youth did well to bury it by imaginatively summoning another "Don(e)": "Whate'er it was, 'twas mine. I've paid, in truth, / . . . . / But have not learned to wish it any less" (12.17). Following Freud's investigations of the work of mourning, Peter Sacks defines the creative process as sublimation, the task of finding a substitute "object" through art for the object that must be surrendered. The elegiac poem that results compensates the poet for his loss, as it will compensate those readers who have suffered similar losses. Yet Byron's narrator violates the rules of such compensation before he has even begun: he has already "spent my life, both interest and principal, / And deem not, what I deemed, my soul invincible" (1.213). Byron uneasily confounds the aesthetic exchanges performed by metaphor and the public exchange-values performed by money.

By the time we reach stanza 216, the tone has decidedly shifted toward the parodic, and the "compensation" becomes more aggressively monetary: "My days of love are over, me no more / The charms of maid, wife, and still less of widow / . . . I think I must take up with avarice." We are again witnessing Byron's fascination with the vicious tastes of the cochineal-cloaked tyrant to which the leisured victim of ennui may turn. Yet, in a manner typical of the digressions in *Don Juan*, the trajectory of the stanzas that follow fail to rise (as we might expect of champagne) onward and upward through satire to the sheer levity of unalloyed pleasure. The poet passes from love, to its loss, to its substitutes (its "general equivalents" in our fallen age) in fortune, avarice, and ambition. By stanza 217, personal ambition (perhaps the Byronism on which the poet has already fully capitalized) is an "idol" that has fallen like an exhausted market; the "pleasure" of youth declines to "leisure," which falls, ineluctably, to "treasure" in this stanza: the "chymic treasure" of a "glittering youth, which I have spent betimes, / My heart in passion and my head on rhymes." In stanza 218, the paper that bears poetry itself rhymes with "vapour":

> For this men write, speak, preach, and heroes kill,
>   And bards burn what they call their midnight taper,
> To have, when the original is dust,
> A name, a wretched picture, and worse bust.
>
> What are the hopes of man? Old Egypt's King
>   Cheops erected the first pyramid,
> And largest, thinking it was just the thing
>   To keep his memory whole and mummy hid;
> But somebody or other rummaging,
>   Burglariously broke his coffin's lid.
> Let not a monument give you or me hopes,
> Since not a pinch of dust remains of Cheops.
>   (1.218–19)

But this is not yet the end of this digression's descent into the sepulchral. "Philosophy" leads the poet to the anti-idealist conclusion that "All things that have been born were born to die," including the corpse-flesh that will nourish the second birth of "grass"; "And flesh (which Death mows down to hay) is grass" (220). That stanza concludes with the scarcely consoling thought that even if he had a second youth (Don Juan's perhaps?), that one, also, " 'twould pass" to a similar end. As we reach the original ending of the canto— what is now stanza 221—we realize that this digressive progress toward death was "born" between a canto that ends with the image of a "panoramic view of hell" and a canto that begins by jokingly imploring the "gentle reader, and / Still gentler purchaser" to extend the life of this new commodity (or still-fresh hero), this speculation on paper.

Yet another stanza was added to canto 1: stanza 222, a satire on Southey that begins simperingly (and commercially) "Go, little book, from this my solitude!" An accretion of related intention is added to the end of a later canto, stanza 90 of canto II ("go forth, thou lay, which I will back / Against the same given quantity of rhyme"). By this time, the narrative has moved far forward; indeed, the narrator has just digressively observed how much has happened with so little change that is "new" in the narrator's life. He warns an aging Juan—and, of course, the engaged reader who, in an effort to avoid ennui, wants both to consume and to prolong the "time" during which to consume (and prolong) this commodity—not to take for granted a single day that's left: "But *carpe diem,* Juan, *carpe, carpe!* / Tomorrow sees another race as gay / And transient and devoured by the same harpy" (II.86). The harpy may, of course, be the reader to whom the book was sent forth, or it may be, simply, time. Juan's fate, we are told in the added stanza 90, "Is yet within the unread events of time. / Thus far go forth, thou lay, . . ." That the narrator will "back" his speculation in Juan's futures with "the same given quantity of rhyme" is an appropriate (added) transition into the canto that follows on misers, poets, and the miseries of ennui:

> Too old for youth, too young at thirty-five
>> To herd with boys or hoard with good threescore.
> I wonder people should be left alive,
>> But since they are, that epoch is a bore.
> Love lingers still, although 'twere late to wive,
>> And as for other love, the illusion's o'er;
> And money, that most pure imagination,
> Gleams only through the dawn of its creation.
>
> Oh gold! Why call we misers miserable?
>> Theirs is the pleasure that can never pall.
> Theirs is the best bower-anchor, the chain cable
>> Which holds fast other pleasures great and small.
> Ye who but see the saving man at table
>> And scorn his temperate board as none at all
> And wonder how the wealthy can be sparing
> Know not what visions spring from each cheese-paring.
>
> Love or lust makes man sick, and wine much sicker.
>> Ambition rends, and gaming gains a loss.
> But making money, slowly first, then quicker,
>> And adding still a little through each cross

(Which *will* come over things) beats love or liquor,
The gamester's counter, or the statesman's dross.
Oh gold! I still prefer thee unto paper,
Which makes bank credit like a bark of vapour.
(12.2–4)

Heinzelman contends that in these and related passages Byron carefully instates an "ironic distance between the miser who is 'your only poet' and Byron's poetic project" (381), noting Byron's punning "speculation" on "paper" in stanza 21 ("I'm serious—so are all men upon paper"). Heinzelman also argues that Byron's own skeptical attitude toward "cash" is revealed in the cynical movement from "Love" to "Cash" in stanza 14: "the base term that defines" "capitalized abstractions" (383), including the "Poetry" that the poet cannot help "capitalizing" by putting before the reader, in the marketplace: "Since poetry's utility cannot be willed by the poet but must depend upon the willingness of the reader to profit from it, it must become, lacking such response, merely a form of self-serving private capitalism, like the miser's. But even *with* such a response, the poet risks selling out to such approbation—he risks becoming a mere entertainer" (384). Even the poetic labor that seems least tainted by such capitalization and commodification—what Heinzelman calls the "spot of time" "moment of composition" (385)— "degenerates" the poet's "self" that had seemed to exist, during the labor of composition, in an unmediated "transaction" with "time." Byron now understands, Heinzelman concludes, that he is unable

to stop the process of composition from being reified, from acquiring a commodity status. Answering the question "why publish" with the question "why read," Don Juan confronts its own imaginative economics head-on, yielding a kind of fictive coinage that deflates at the moment of issue its own self-inflationary tendencies. What the poet possesses, then, is not his own. The poem, cast upon the platitudinous stream of time, invites us to recall here its opening line: "I want a hero." In time, however, this desire has become, like the poem itself, the property of its readers, if they want it. Even more perversely, the lack of that hero is precisely what continues to authorize desire and to authenticate this whole poetic/proprietary exchange. (385–86)

Yet in fact Byron uses every strategy at hand to avoid giving up that hero, withholding (as the narrator implies) certain matters from the marketplace and extending the narrative, again and again, to save Juan from death. He uses his "desire" for a hero—his as well as the reader's desire for Juan/ *Don Juan*—to profit, like a miser, without surrendering his reserves. In letters that Byron wrote four years and more before beginning work on the twelfth canto of *Don Juan*, we can already see his playful manipulation of the reader's (and the publisher's) expectation that poetic creation, publishing profits, and the carnal pleasures that such profits may purchase do not mix in polite company:

P.S. Whatever Brain-money—you get on my account from Murray—pray remit me—I will never consent to pay away what I *earn*—that is *mine*—& what I get by my brains—I will spend on my b- -ks—as long as I have a tester or a testicle remaining. . . . — My balance—also—my balance & a Copyright—I have another Canto—too—ready—& then there will be my half year in June—recollect—*I* care for nothing but "monies."

> Letter to Hobhouse and Kinnaird, January 19, 1819
>   (this postscript dated January 20)

My dear Douglas—I have received a very clever letter from Hobhouse against the publication of Don Juan—in which I understand you have acquiesced (you be damned)—I acquiesce too—but reluctantly.—this acquiescence is some thousands of pounds out of my pocket—the very thought of which brings tears into my eyes—I have imbibed such a love for money that I keep some Sequins in a drawer to count, & cry over them once a week—and if it was not for a turn for women—(which I hope will be soon worn out)—I think in time that I should be able not only to clear off but to accumulate. . . . I say—that as for fame and all that—it is for such persons as Fortune chooses—and so is money.

> Letter to Douglas Kinnaird, January 27, 1819

In such letters and in *Don Juan* itself, Byron hints at the existence of a space for the "passion" of poetry that in our fallen age is even more sequestered ("bower-anchored") from the fall into symbolic exchange than the "private" pleasure that Heinzelman defines as Byron's spot of time: "And what I write I cast upon the stream / To swim or sink. I have had at least my dream." In imitation of the miser, he keeps that dream, which he establishes as both in his possession and in the past, to himself.

In the opening stanza of the twelfth canto, Byron prepares us to understand that the "monetary" rewards of the middle-aged, while their exchange-value may be calculated in order to make present-day investments in pleasure or treasure, cannot be converted into the lost passions once experienced, in youth, and in flesh and blood. In the stanza that opens this canto, Byron almost pursues another version of the "anti-simile" disappearing act that we examined earlier: middle age is "—I really scarce know what." In fact, being in the middle of life is a condition of "hovering," like a predatory bird, a phantom, or signification itself, between two worlds or two identities:

> But when we hover between fool and sage
> And don't know justly what we would be at,
> A period something like a printed page,
> Black letter upon foolscap, while our hair
> Grows grizzled and we are not what we were,
> (12.1)

Even stanza endings (observe the comma) in the middle-aged ennui of the English Cantos have come to hesitate between going forward and coming to full stop. To observe such details hardly constitutes overreading in a stanza that instructs us to perceive a second simile for middle age: the rhyming "printed page." In the stanzas that follow, Byron will show us just how print, "Black letter upon foolscap," stands in relation to poetry, but more immediately we should observe that it is in the same relation as middle age stands to youth and—in the second stanza—as money relates to gold.

Money, Byron writes, is "that most pure imagination," yet beyond the now-vanished "dawn" in which it originated, it exists only as one of the properties (it "gleams") of the now-vanished gold that fathered it. It may be generated as paper wealth through the printing of paper money, the acquisition of paper debt, or the printing (publication) of a commodity—poetry—which earns money for both publisher and poet. Poetry can likewise only gleam beyond its first creation, even though it is created anew through exchange (when a reader tenders cash for its acquisition) and consumption (literally, when the reader converts the words of the poem into a gleam in her imagination). Publication, a public act of exchange that converts the labor of imagination into a paper commodity, lies well beyond whatever suffering or joy initially inspired the creative act in the "dawn" of solitary composition.[50] In this sense the poem is like the circulating medium of money. It accrues, like money, "magic," for, as Marx writes of money in *Capital*, the circulating medium can exist only because it has effaced its origins. Both commodities were once substances mined by a labor that has become invisible in a society where people are used like objects and the goods they produce are worshiped as gods.[51] And poetry, even when it is no longer widely read, and even for those who are not consumers of poems, continues to serve, like money (even when it no longer requires a gold standard), as a general equivalent or universal value. A still-gleaming but buried object lies behind money and poetry, whether it is the glittering mineral that has been mined and then stored in vaults or the libidinal wealth of the mind, hauled through poetic labor from unsunned recesses. Those origins, whether or not they actually exist, must be hoarded—kept out of circulation—if they are to sustain the confidence of the public in paper. For only such faith in "reserves," in matters and mysteries yet to be brought forth, carries forward the futures trading of a capital economy, one that will sustain the poetic reputation that survives the poet's death. Not only through the circulation of a tangible good but also through the seduction of investors and readers who are willing to speculate can that economy, like poetic reputation, authorize itself. Byron, having witnessed the depreciations and inflations of laureates and Lakers, knows all too well the liquidity of aesthetic holdings, and how easily a poet's integrity may drown in fame. Never comfortable with investments (in his letters he repeatedly urges his gents to sell his "Funds"), Byron in canto 1 has the narrator remind himself to "read your Bible, sir, and mind your purse" (st. 220), even as he seduces the "gentle reader" (and "still gentler purchaser"). For the "quantity of rhyme" that he rhymes with "time" in canto 11 is as likely to be bought by readers to provoke "attack / As ever yet was any work sublime."[52]

In the miser who provokes the criticism of others, Byron recognizes a fellow skeptic of financial and metaphysical speculations, a man who is unlikely to invest in useless commodities or futile wars. To hoard and to accumulate, "adding still a little through each cross" of misfortune and through each pen stroke of poetic revision, is to keep before one's eyes, whether miser or poet, what the "middle age" of Western man, a fallen yet "advancing" civilization, would have one ignored: that "old Europe's" bankrupt politics are a consequence not of hoardings but of debts and loans, of "speculations on paper" (including letters of seduction), and of expenditures on worthless commodities: "Wars, revels, loves" (st. 11) are the enterprises that circulate misfortune. At worst, the miser, like the poet, may be trapped in imaginary, specular possessions and delusions:

He is your only poet. Passion, pure
  and sparkling on from heap to heap, displays,
Possessed, the ore, of which mere hopes allure
  Nations athwart the deep. The golden rays
Flash up in ingots from the mine obscure.
  On him the diamond pours its brilliant blaze,
While the mild emerald's beam shades down the dyes
Of other stones, to soothe the miser's eyes.
  (12.8)

Given a preference, the miser (like Byron) would have his fortune (which is equivalent to his desire) kept—incestuously—in the family: "I say, methinks that philo-genitiveness / Might meet from men a little more forgiveness" (12.22). His fortune passes, with his genetic code, directly to his heirs, reproductions of "his likeness" that are not unlike the mintings alluded to in stanza 12: "Lean miser, / Let spendthrifts' heirs inquire of yours—who's wiser?" (st. 11). These heirs may even keep the genius confined at home ("Yes! ready money is Aladdin's lamp" [st. 12]). In any case love, the narrator concludes, beyond the miser's persistence in pre-Oedipal incest and hoarding, no longer exists in a capitalist culture. What does? "Cash does, and cash alone. / . . . . / . . . cash rules love the ruler, on his own" (st. 14). Money is, like Death (as Byron reminds us in Juan's sexually depreciative relation to Queen Catherine), "the Sovereign's sovereign."

From the moment that Juan sets foot on English soil death, money, and commerce will haunt his quests, first, for the much-vaunted English "freedom,"[53] and, second, for (more or less) love. Juan's ability to retrain his youthful freshness has been tarnished by his own participation in Catherine's economy of sexual payoffs, for his trip abroad (to improve his health) was laboriously earned. While Juan admires the cliffs of Dover, "Albion's chalky belt"—that (money) belt evokes an ironic chain of associations that move from nostalgia, to Adam Smith, to alchemy:

At the first sight of Albion's chalky belt—
A kind of pride that he should be among
  Those haughty shopkeepers, who sternly dealt
Their goods and edicts out from pole to pole
And made the very billows pay them toll.
  (10.65)

> But Juan saw not this. Each wreath of smoke
>> Appeared to him but as the magic vapour
> Of some alchemic furnace, from whence broke
>> The wealth of worlds (a wealth of tax and paper).
> The gloomy clouds, which o'er it as a yoke
>> Are bowed and put the sun out like a taper . . .

(10.83)

At the threshold of a nation that distills imperial wealth through acts of sublimatory, symbolic exchange, an economy that—like "chyme"—consumes raw materials and raw labor in the production of wealth, Juan is robbed by hoteliers and is taken in (like the Berkeley to whom Byron alludes) by his "speculations" before he is (almost) held up by a highwayman:

> "Here are chaste wives, pure lives. Here people pay
>> But what they please, and if that things be dear,
> 'Tis only that they love to throw away
>> Their cash, to show how much they have a year.
> Here laws are all inviolate; none lay
>> Traps for the traveller; every highway's clear.
> Here"—he was interrupted by a knife,
> With "Damn your eyes! your money or your life!"

(11.10)

But if life for the rich is perilous in the "Paradise of hops and high production," it turns out to be no less so among the aristocratic pleasure seekers whom Juan is about to join. Death does not rob these victims; it simply hovers and lingers along the long corridors and longer hours of Amundeville (or "worldly village") Abbey. In such "dull" and "dreary" emptiness speculation (both philosophical and financial) and poetry (which is, as the poet knows, no less a matter of paper, dreams, and a faith in flotation) thrive:

> In youth I wrote, because my mind was full,
> And now because I feel it growing dull.
>
> But "why then publish?" There are no rewards
>> Of fame or profit when the world grows weary.
> I ask in turn why do you play at cards?
>> Why drink? Why read? To make the hour less dreary.
> It occupies me to turn back regards
>> On what I've seen or pondered, sad or cheery,

And what I write I cast upon the stream
To swim or sink. I have had at least my dream.
(14.10, 11)

In canto 12 the narrator promised that his introduction was over and his hundred-canto book was about to begin: "The plan at present's simply in concoction" (st. 87). But neither the introduction of Aurora, who extends the possibility of yet another dawn of life for Juan (and a wealth, equated to gold, to be hoarded philogenitively for the author), nor the promise of more supernatural suspense can finally extend the living hell of Amundeville or the lives of its spectral aristocrats.

"The world is full of orphans": this line that begins the final, unfinished canto of *Don Juan* will be fulfilled by an author who leaves his creatures in suspense, to be "too soon" the "parents to themselves" (17.4). Juan, himself an orphan, discovered early—like his author—that a pleasure even greater than his many falls into "first kisses of love" or miserly saving could be found in an act that combined the two: saving the innocent. Leila, whom he has rescued from another death, in another narrative, and Aurora, who sits, like a gentle version of Cain by Eden's door, do not at last become the incestuous lovers for Juan that Augusta became for Byron. Juan's relationship to them suggests that the author has come to appreciate the value of a love that, without falling altogether into sin, nevertheless flirts with the laws of marital exchange and the taboo against incest. Byron may enjoy parodying "The noblest kind of Love," "love platonical / To end or to begin with" (9.76), observing that the "purest platonism" lay "at bottom" of Juan's feelings, "only he forgot 'em" (10.54). Yet in fact he explores with rare sincerity Juan's protective affection for Leila. "He was not an ancient debauchee" (st. 54), for he "loved the infant orphan he had saved, / As patriots (now and then) may love a nation" (st. 55).

Byron hoarded his earnings in the final year of his life so that he could spend them in an attempt to save a country whose citizens he never fully trusted with his money, or with the freedom he sought for them. His campaign in Greece brought to a premature end his own life and *Don Juan*'s. A stanza that resurrects the "bubbles" of poetry and of champagne introduced in earlier stanzas originally began with the line, "Between two worlds I hover like a star":

Between two worlds life hovers like a star
'Twixt night and morn upon the horizon's verge.

How little do we know that which we are!
   How less what we may be! The eternal surge
Of time and tide rolls on and bears afar
   Our bubbles. As the old burst, new emerge,
Lashed from the foam of ages; while the graves
Of empires heave but like some passing waves.
   (15.99)

Such bubbles, like seeds and like hope, are fragile but self-renewing. Before Byron resumed writing *Don Juan* in 1822, he wrote in his "Detached Thoughts" the following entry:[54] "What a strange thing is the propagation of life!—A bubble of Seed which may be split in a whore's lap—or in the Orgasm of a voluptuous dream—might (for aught we know) have formed a Caesar or a Buonaparte—there is nothing remarkable recorded of their Sires—that I know of—" (No. 102). A bubble, the very image of nothingness, may stray and even survive to lead, as Byron hoped himself to do, a nation into freedom, but it may also vanish or go astray and (like a Caesar or a Buonaparte) become tyrannical. While Byron never failed to anticipate such disappointments, he also never ceased to create—by blood *and* ink—reasons, and creatures, to love beyond the horizon of hope or the limits of the law:

   But words are things, and a small drop of ink,
     Falling like dew upon a thought, produces
   That which makes thousands, perhaps millions, think;
     'Tis strange, the shortest letter which man uses
   Instead of speech, may form a lasting link
     Of ages. To what straits old Time reduces
   Frail man, when paper—even a rag like this,
   Survives himself, his tomb, and all that's his.
   (3.88)

2

Spectral Generation in *The Four Zoas:*

"Indolence and Mourning Sit Hovring"

Writers of course are considered to be mavens of Sloth. They are approached all the time on the subject. . . . The stereotype arises in part from our conspicuous presence in jobs where pay is by the word. . . .

But Sloth's offspring, though bad—to paraphrase the Shangri-Las—are not always evil. . . . It is of course precisely in such episodes of mental traveling that writers are known to do good work, sometimes even their best, solving formal problems, getting advice from beyond, having hypnagogic adventures that with luck can be recovered later on. Idle dreaming is often of the essence of what we do. We sell our dreams. So real money actually proceeds from Sloth. . . .

  THOMAS PYNCHON, "Nearer, My Couch, to Thee"

O weakness & O weariness O war within my members
. . . .
O weary life why sit I here & give up all my powers
To indolence to the night of death when indolence & mourning
Sit hovring over my dark threshold.

  WILLIAM BLAKE, *The Four Zoas*

In a letter Blake wrote to Butts in 1801, during the protracted gestation of *The Four Zoas,* he apologized for what he called his "want of steady perseverance," by which want, he says, "I am still so much your debtor & you so much my Credit-er. . . . I labour incessantly & accomplish not one half of what I intend because my Abstract folly hurries me often away while I am at work, carrying me over Mountains & Valleys which are not Real in a Land of Abstraction where Spectres of the Dead wander. This I endeavour to prevent & with my whole might chain my feet to the world of Duty & Reality. but in vain!. . . . Alas wretched happy ineffectual labourer of times moments that I am! . . . Mr Hayley is now Labouring with all his matchless industry."[1] Blake's ambivalent portrayal of an artist's happy ineffectuality is echoed, two centuries later, in Thomas Pynchon's defense of indolence and critique of the hidden tyrannies of the conscience that is engendered by late capitalism.[2] The novelist who correlates Slothrop's erections and Hitler's ballistics in *Gravity's Rainbow* argues that melancholic "sloth" in fact not only produces the "work" we call "art" but also that such work constitutes a revolutionary act against ideology's Foucauldian overseers in more conventional workplaces. The writer who appreciates the productivity of indolence challenges equally humanist models of creativity that believe in the transcendence (and sequestration) of the imagination's mental work and more contemporary theoretical approaches that narrowly restrict to the factory and the marketplace issues of historical materialism, labor, and economic productivity.[3]

Melancholia in modern cultures emerges explicitly at the troubled nexus of an increasingly interiorized and leisured self and a society that promotes the freedom of that self by colonizing (through ideology) the self's most private spaces of appetite and remorse. Blake, so often himself melancholic and yet cognizant that melancholia is a symptom of the larger problems of capital and modernity, could not ignore the famished exiles—Enion, Urthona, Ahania—who haunt, spectrally, the permeable margins of a fortressed and fearful self no less than society's public palaces of power. And because these revenants are often difficult to distinguish from the ghostly agents that modern and capitalist structures of power themselves deploy in urging us to engage in both consumption and discipline, within the modern self (as within the modern state) the voices of deprivation coexist with the depravity of despotic desire, competing for the attention of the visionary poet who may hear the calling of divine voices even while being lured by ideology's invocations to work, to desire, and to forget the dead.

Before turning to Blake's work on the *Zoas,* it may be helpful to suggest how my discussion of ideology and aesthetic labor departs from two recent discussions of those topics by Blake scholars. Mark Bracher, in an approach that combines Lacan and Althusser, offers a sympathetic reading of Blake's opposition to (and appropriation of) ideological interpellation in "Rouzing the Faculties: Lacanian Psychoanalysis and the Marriage of Heaven and Hell in the Reader."[4] Blake, Bracher argues, deploys his own version of interpellation in order to challenge, linguistically, the hegemony of the Law of the Father, constructing, in effect, an alternative (and, Bracher argues, less phallocentric) Symbolic Order. For Bracher, Blake's intention is psychoanalytically therapeutic: he seeks to substitute for the sickness of repressed speech the health of symbolic expression. Blake writes, therefore, in order to help the reader—through acts that Bracher distinguishes as "desire" and "interpretation"—displace "hellish" desire for (bad) partial objects (which are by implication regressive) toward the "heavenly" goal desire truly seeks: "being" in and through language. Ceasing to identify melancholically with the dead ("non-being"), the reader submits to the inevitability of Oedipal castration, a process that may lead the enlightened subject to reconfigure the Other as "feminine": "this (provisional) alteration of the Other displaces the phallic fantasy, directing desire away from this particular metonym of being and toward the metonym of the female position" (193). In "recovering" from our castration, Bracher alleges, we are able (with Blake's help) to integrate desire into the Law, producing a kinder, gentler code by which to live.

Absent from Bracher's position on the revolutionary potential of poetry is Lacan's recognition, in his later work, that the hegemonic success of the Law of the Father ultimately depends not upon masculine (as opposed to feminine) configurations of the Symbolic Order (or even of the imaginary) but rather on the banishment of what Lacan labels the Real, the unsignifiable, unassimilable domain of God, the noncategory of woman, and death itself. As Slavoj Žižek argues in *The Sublime Object of Ideology* the Law, far from being divorced from desire, interpellates *through* desire. The subject, who originates in the substitution of a Law for the Father cannot help but be haunted by that Law's secret "want," its desire no less than its "lack." To Bracher's claim that Blake issued his proverbs as an "admonishment for individuals and society at large not to remain subservient to the past but to use the remains of the past as a road to the future, or as a material to be broken up and assimilated into the soil that nourishes new growth" (194), one could counter that Blake believes we cannot give birth to a future, and more just, society so long as we repudiate the past by refusing to incorporate—into the very fabric of our being—the dead whom we will, through art, in turn regenerate as "new growth." To Bracher's teleology of healthy self-improvement, in which, he proposes, we "rise up 'over the bones of the dead' in a much more substantial way than that imagined by the original Oedipal fantasy," and to his urging that we "rise above the power that death possesses when it is identified with non-being" (196), I will propose in this chapter an alternative art of insurrection. Blake resurrects spectral "non-being" in order to produce, in Julia Kristeva's words, a poetry of melancholy that transgresses a Law founded on both matricide and parricide.

In a less sympathetic reading of Blake than Bracher's, David Aers in "Representations of Revolution" seeks to discredit Blake's reputation as a heroic, proletarian artist. Arguing that the poet's representations of labor through the "arts of death" in the *Zoas* are "unrealistic," Aers claims that Blake's poetry is incapable of comprehending the "sphere of work." Aers, in limiting the political expressiveness of poetry to its portrayal of an oppressed class that is victimized by hegemony (but, in Aers's view, not so victimized that it cannot find a "realistic" way out of its predicament), cannot reconcile the poem's violent acts of "incorporation" with the liberation of the oppressed that is to follow from the *Zoas'* final apocalypse:[5]

> Nor does the poem present the sphere of work as prefiguring human liberation, whether in development of material forces promising an end to the reign of scarcity over the majority of people or in the forms of organization working people might evolve in the face of their employers. Unlike many pre-Marxist and Marxist radical traditions, Blake's poem does not see the forces and relations of production as decisive areas in the desired transformation of the social formation and the forms of human life it makes possible. Night II does, of course, concentrate on the labor processes with the kinds of pain and domination they incorporate. But they are represented in a way that denies the significant working-class struggles and their potential for change. . . .
>
> Characteristic of Blake's writing about labor in the prophetic books, this offers no grounds for cultivating ideas about a revolutionary working class, the privileged bearers of human emancipatory potential. Far from it, the vision here is of a working class assimilated to evolving production processes. . . . The production processes become "arts of death" (foreshadowing our own industrial-military fusion), but such is the workers' assimilation that they can be persuaded to abandon all concern with the nature of the products they themselves make. (255)

Unable to account for the simultaneous presence in the poem of agricultural and urban labor, Aers is further troubled that Blake's "language fails to engage with the immense diversity of social situations and experiences in Blake's England—let alone the 'Universe,' which the poet and his rather Eurocentric critics assume to be involved in this revolution" (261). Praising the "parent-laborers" in the *Songs,* which Los and Enitharmon become in the seventh night, Aers nevertheless cannot, after all, explain their constructive presence in the context of Blake's otherwise "one-dimensional" writing during the nineties, with its "despairing sense of Urizenic hegemony and mass passivization" that shape the prophecies (268, 269), a "passivization" that he characterizes as the proletariat's willing "assimilation" and "incorporation" into "evolving capitalist production processes" (255).

As I will demonstrate, Blake's workshop of melancholic incorporation and procreation—produced from his crisis in the nineties—indeed defies critical expectations that are generated by the conventions of narrative realism no less than by masculinist assumptions about where work—and change—may occur. For Blake recognizes, as Aers does not, that the materials of history (and of hegemony) are not only forged but woven, in the manner of Enion's art, out of and within a body at rest as well as at work, and by a body that has been excluded from "public" sites of production and consumption precisely because it confounds these two categories that such Marxists (no less than capitalists) seek to segregate.[6]

If melancholia is a consequence of ideology's success, it is also a resource for the artist who refuses the consolations of its promises of freedom and knowledge in exchange for the unexchangeable. In the words that Blake speaks through the "Voice of the Ancient Mother":

> What is the price of Experience do men buy it for a song
> Or wisdom for a dance in the street? No it is bought with the price
> Of all that a man hath his house his wife his children
> Wisdom is sold in the desolate market where none come to buy
> And in the witherd field where the farmer plows for bread in vain[7]
> (2.35.11–15 E325)

The visionary may see and hear what remains unconscious to others not because of a quest to transcend history but, rather, because for the visionary the past and the future are as immediate as the present. In the mental life of the visionary, as in the psyche of the melancholic or the paranoid, the necropolis of the unconscious teems with those who have been sacrificed to the dreams of bellicose Work masters. They clamor for rebirth in the forms that emerge from the productive interiors of the creative self. It is a commonplace of

Blake criticism that, like Los, Blake takes charge, in artisanal fashion, of such resurrection in his visionary representations (linguistic and pictorial), reproducing them mechanically but demiurgically in his own and solitary workshop so that he may control how his visions are to be consumed by readers who will themselves serve as agents of political revolution. It has also become commonplace, in an academic climate made cynical by the belatedness, or "post"-ness, of its various enterprises, to conclude that such labor can only be futile in states where hegemonic surveillance reaches deep into the structures of desire, decision making, and "difference."[8] In fact, however, Blake's poetic production is politically resourceful, not despite but because of its emergence from the workshop of what Kristeva in *Black Sun* has called "nameable melancholia," a "signified sadness" that (like the process that she calls "signifiation" in *Revolution in Poetic Language*) is a process that dialectically employs both the drives of the body and the structure of language to bring back, rather than to repress, the dead who are our origins but also our ends, whose sufferings are the seeds, as Walter Benjamin has suggested, of a revolutionary sowing of utopia.[9] A resource that generates Blake's sexually explicit drawings in the *Zoas* as well as the poet's strategies for signifying absence, such melancholia beckons, nevertheless, from innocence, from the body's expressive potential before language (the Law of the Father) has fully colonized the self's spacious and sexually charged interiors. As such, a poet's or artist's melancholia may resist the fall into a world where difference (including the difference between play and work) and deferral (not only of meaning but also of pleasure) govern desire.

Two Blake scholars, Robert Gleckner and Thomas Vogler, offer radical readings of innocence that recognize Blake's resources and strategies for resisting ideology, providing models for a criticism that seeks to understand how Blake, as an advocate of revolutionary progress, also looked (regressively) backward, to the origins of language in a "realm" or proto-sexualized "space" before signification (and its strategies of absence and of difference) colonized once-replete sites of bodily pleasure and parental presence.

In *The Piper and the Bard*,[10] Gleckner writes that for Blake "the child is the symbol of primal unity . . . an unconscious self; or, in other words, innocence is the Eternal Family united in God by common participation in eternal life." Blake recognized that innocence is eroded by "the man-made law of father, priest, and king," who create "the individual self" in order to "reach the individual soul," persuading that "self" that the languages of body and mind are distinct from one another. Only through "an improvement in sensual enjoyment, by thwarting law, by cleansing the windows of perception" can innocence be restored (47), a restoration through a reconceived sexuality that is in fact a "'redemption of instinct'" (49).[11] In his later essay "Most Holy Forms of Thought," Gleckner explicitly addresses the paradox that "words," the instruments of our fallenness, may nevertheless be used creatively to challenge the hegemony that has perverted innocence by blinding (or, more accurately, *deafening*) the linguistically competent self to the presence of Eternity—which is to say, to the *Word*—that exists within as well as beyond the self. Blake conceived of such signifiable innocence, Gleckner argues in this essay and elsewhere,[12] as a refusal to recognize the differences upon which language is founded (including, of course, the difference between innocence and experience). When we, as linguistically competent speakers, writers, and readers, are again able to hear (through Blake's words) that revolutionary and *embodied* "Word," we will be able to restore to sexual experience (that is, to desire) a phenomenon—"love"—that unites sexual, spiritual, and intellectual regeneration. In that restoration, and regeneration, begins community.[13]

Thomas Vogler shares Gleckner's recognition that Blake makes of language a resource that resists Urizenic Workmastery if we are willing to reclaim, within the "mediating space" of the text, our engraved (and embodied) "Emanations":

The realm of the absence of the signified, as the realm of *play,* is the realm both of labor and of rest, the contraries that need each other for the full engagement in Mental Fight. As such the realm is a mediating space, like that of Barthes' pleasure of the text. If it is to be found and entered, and the Emanation reclaimed, it must be on the level of experience rather than of abstract thought, a textural as well as a textual Beulah. What this means is that if Blake "found" it, it would be in the *writing* of his text, as a writing not yet inscribed in the book "of" Urizen, not as the spectral representation of something always already absent, but as a "sourcing" component of his writing, the rest before labor and the rest during labor.[14]

Citing Blake's comment in *A Vision of the Last Judgment* that the "Spectator" would "arise from his Grave" if he "could enter into these Images in his Imagination," Vogler concludes that contemporary criticism has failed to take Blake's advice that revolutionary writing, in anticipating a future utopia, is also (like the melancholic) refusing to leave home:

I am convinced that the main tendencies brought to the reading of Blake are among those tendencies in literature—and in his own artistic efforts— that he was struggling to overcome in the only way he could imagine overcoming them; not through a writing as allegoresis, a writing that pointed away from itself toward "an allegorical abode where existence hath never come" (*Eur* 6.7) but a writing as mode of praxis, the writing of a full word rather than a univocal word. The goal is not to escape "Albions land: / Which is this earth of vegetation on which now I write" (*M* 14.40– 41) but to experience it as a home, to be at home in it, to be human in it—which means to be creative, to be an artist, to labor in a material medium.[15] (175)

As Gleckner and Vogler suggest, Blake, in supervising the invasion of words and images—spectral extensions of his own haunted interiors—into the inner recesses of his readers, may seem to be imitating the ideological apparatuses of the Urizenic (and melancholic) Law when, in fact, he is planting seeds for its resistance, planting them in the very ground—the sites, in and on the body— where sexual longing and unappeasable sorrow supersede the original occupancy of *both* parental objects of need and of identification, reversing (in Blake's words) "all the order of delight" and hiding "wonders allegoric of the Generations" (7b.88[96].2 and 4 E361).[16] As Nelson Hilton argues in *Literal Imagination,* the most useful study to date of Blake's lifelong and linguistically procreative preoccupation with graves, shrouds, specters, vampires, and other manifestations of melancholy, words for Blake exist materially in a "polysemous" medium, one that is as physical as flesh and blood, or as semen and ovum. In extending Hilton's conclusions, we will see that poetic language for Blake revives, repeatedly, the regrets and dreams of the dead in the human places of germination, an act that itself preserves whatever seeds of hope lie hidden within the darkness of the melancholic imagination. Such seed can resurrect from the "night of death," from "indolence and mourning," the Fallen Man, restoring to life the Eternal "Man of future times" (9.120.7 and 5 E389).[17] But to germinate, this seed must physically engage, as the erotic illustrations of the *Zoas* suggest, in a life-and-death, dialectical struggle with the equally potent seed of the sullen and splenetic Work master. For Urizen's armies have besieged, illegitimately, the heart and loins (that is, the "warring members") of

Blake's libidinous, indolent, and melancholic Fallen Man.[18] In the *Zoas'* nightmarish and postpastoral world, the stricken Man has fallen away not only from Vala but also from the progeny they jointly brought to life before humankind was alienated from Nature, and before labor was alienated from its sources and its products. Yet even as they fall repeatedly from innocence into experience, from sameness into difference, and from "Days & nights of revolving joy" (1.3.11 E301) into "Wheel without wheel / . . . labours / Of day & night" (7b.92.26–28 E364), Blake's various creators resurrect, through their melancholic art, their lost origins as recovered offspring.

"Lost! Lost! Lost!" are the first words spoken by a Zoa. While loss begets not only "Los" but also further loss in the reiterative narratives that Donald Ault has helpfully identified as "embedded," out of the Zoas' (and their partners') refusals to surrender what they claim to have already lost emerge new beginnings that, in turn, are succeeded by new hauntings and melancholic relapse:[19]

> Begin with Tharmas Parent power. darkning in the West
>
> Lost! Lost! Lost! are my Emanations   Enion O Enion
> We are become a Victim to the Living We hide in secret
> I have hidden Jerusalem in Silent Contrition   O Pity Me
> I will build thee a Labyrinth also O pity me   O Enion
> Why has thou taken sweet Jerusalem from my inmost Soul
> Let her Lay secret in the Soft recess of darkness & silence
> It is not Love I bear to [Jerusalem] It is Pity
> She hath taken refuge in my bosom & I cannot cast her out.
>
> The Men have received their death wounds & their Emanations
>   are fled
> To me for refuge & I cannot turn them out for Pitys sake
>
> Enion said—Thy fear has made me tremble thy terrors have
>   surrounded me
> All Love is lost Terror succeeds & Hatred instead of Love
> And stern demands of Right & Duty instead of Liberty.
> (1.4.6–19 E301)

Out of loss, feeling a need to make a home for the dead (or is it for the not-yet-living?) within his "bosom," Tharmas overcomes his fear of a succubus that could as easily be fetal or neonatal as spectral.[20] In a gesture of "Pity," Tharmas recognizes that even though he is male, he in fact possesses a generative and nutritive "innerness"—"the Soft recess of darkness & silence." That space appears here to be already occupied (in an inversion of the hermaphroditic "Mystery" of Night the Eighth) by a female being. Named Enitharmon in the earlier drafts, in this nonsequential (and nonteleological) narrative the emanation that Tharmas claims already to have "lost" will in fact come into existence *through* loss and through the consequence of loss: the jealous hiding and seeking (or paranoia) that estranges Tharmas from Enion.[21] Such prying (or *spec*ulation) into one another's interiors, places of absence once occupied by a "presence," not only *generates* innerness but may also in fact reinforce (indeed, it may en*gender*) the sexual discord that ensues. Mutual suspicion will bring forth—out of guilt, resentment, and remorse—a sexually reproductive *spec*ter who mirrors the melancholic's compelling sense of worthlessness. Tharmas's fear of the surveillance through which Enion governs him inspires her own fears, and the secrecy that she requests in turn evokes—for both partners—the energy and the emptiness of undirected sexual desire, twin symptoms of a "Melancholy" in which preoccupation with unconscious loss may lead not only to suspicion but also to the concupiscence that each suspects:

> I have lookd into the secret soul of him I lovd
> And in the Dark recesses found Sin & cannot return
>
> Trembling & pale sat Tharmas weeping in his clouds
> Why wilt thou Examine every little fibre of my soul
> Spreading them out before the Sun like Stalks of flax to dry
> The infant joy is beautiful but its anatomy
> Horrible Ghast & Deadly nought shalt thou find in it
> But Death Despair & Everlasting brooding Melancholy
> (1.4.26–33 E301–2)

Each partner's effort to hide from the speculative and judgmental eyes of the other leads,[22] in this our first introduction to Tharmas and Enion, the ancient and innocent father and mother, to mutual shame, loneliness, despair, and self-destruction. Yet such hiding leads also to creative (indeed, anticipatory) encryption of the not-yet-alive, which, in turn, lead to the (re)birth of specters *from* Tharmas's corpse through (and in) Enion's loom/womb:[23]

Enion said Farewell I die   I hide from thy searching eyes

So saying—From her bosom weaving soft in Sinewy threads
A tabernacle for Jerusalem she sat among the Rocks
Singing her lamentation. Tharmas groand among his Clouds
Weeping, then bending from his Clouds he stoopd his innocent
  head
And stretching out his holy hand in the vast Deep sublime
Turnd round the circle of Destiny with tears & bitter sighs
And said.   Return O Wanderer when the Day of Clouds is oer

So saying he sunk down into the sea a pale white corse
In torment he sunk down & flowd among her filmy Woof
His Spectre issuing from his feet in flames of fire
In gnawing pain drawn out by her lovd fingers every nerve
She counted. every vein & lacteal threading them among
Her woof of terror. Terrified & drinking tears of woe
Shuddering she wove—nine days & nights Sleepless her food was
  tears
Wondring she saw her woof begin to animate. & not
As Garments woven subservient to her hands but having a will
Of its own perverse & wayward Enion lovd & wept

Nine days she labourd at her work. & nine dark sleepless nights
But on the tenth trembling morn the Circle of Destiny Complete
Round rolld the Sea Englobing in a watry Globe self balancd
A Frowning Continent appeard Where Enion in the Desart
Terrified in her own Creation   viewing her woven shadow
Sat in a dread intoxication of Repentence & Contrition
(1.5.5–28 E302–3)

Blake scholars have disparaged such labor *in* the tomb and *at* the
womb/loom, if they have not, indeed, failed to recognize it as, in
any sense, labor. An art such as Enion's, one that derives from the
body's sites of death, desire, and reproductivity, is judged to be
regressive in its narcissism. Harold Bloom, in his commentary on
the *Zoas* in Erdman's edition, presumes in several statements that
the women in this text impede creation in its "highest" expression.[24]
Vala represents secrecy only in its negative sense: "Her name is
presumably founded on the word 'veil,' since in one aspect she
represents the veil of illusion interposed by the phenomenal world"
(948). Enion, Bloom claims, in her "jealousy" of Jerusalem, is responsible for Albion's fall (in which the body revolts against man

and fragments the self). In re-creating Tharmas, Bloom continues, Enion in fact "weaves chaotic Tharmas into the cycle of 'nine days & nights' which complete the first fall, and which constitute on another level the nine nightmares that together form the poem. The terror of Enion at her own creation (5.27) is founded on her consciousness that the physical ruin of Tharmas was caused by her withdrawal, which rendered him indefinite" (E949).

The Daughters of Beulah would seem to share Bloom's disapproval of Enion's resurrection of the dead, for they intervene in Enion's demiurgic work by themselves creating "Spaces lest they [sleepers] fall into Eternal Death" (1.5.35 E303). They shut "the Gate of the Tongue"—Tharmas's realm—"in trembling fear." Through such encryption and censorship, the Daughters collude in confining Enion's melancholic creation (like her experience of melancholic loss) to silence and secrecy within her own expanding and yet inaccessible innerness:[25]

> What have I done! said Enion accursed wretch! What deed.
> Is this a deed of Love I know what I have done. I know
> Too late now to repent. Love is changed to deadly Hate
> A[ll] life is blotted out & I alone remain possessd with Fears
> I see the Shadow of the dead within my Soul wandering
> In darkness & solitude forming Seas of Doubt & rocks of
>   Repentence
> Already are my Eyes reverted. all that I behold
> Within my Soul has lost its splendor & a brooding Fear
> Shadows me oer & drives me outward to a world of woe
> So waild she trembling before her own Created Phantasm
> (1.5.44–53 E303)

Yet in fact Enion, like Blake, "draws" from "life"; she works during nine days, even as Blake works during nine nights. Her productivity is one of Blake's paradigms for an imagination, whether it belongs to a male or female, that celebrates even a creation that must be endlessly repeated, reincorporated, and revived, one that may not, at last, be reproduced in final and book form and one that erodes, rather than ratifies, any sense of a self unified by the imagination's confident transcendence of birth, death, and life. Out of a labor that was inspired by loss and accompanied by tears, woe, and lamentation, a creativity that Blake characterizes as "perverse & wayward," Enion might understandably experience—initially— chagrin.[26] More simply, it may not be surprising that the artist experiences a kind of postpartum depression. "Brooding," she repudiates the artwork bred from the materials of death for she perceives there "the Shadow of the dead," "Seas of Doubt & rocks of Repentence."[27] Yet Enion, in the next moment, sufficiently forgets her remorse both to defer to the authority of "her own Created Phantasm" (asking him to narrate her *own* origins) and to yield to its/his sexual advances. In so fetishizing her own creation, she transforms ambivalence ("Love is changd to deadly Hate") into appetite. Out of the artist's, and artwork's, now mutual desire, out of a consuming need that is consummated in their union, are born (as secondary creations) Los and Enitharmon,[28] progeny who will reject their creator (Enion), scorn the ensuing melancholy of their putative father (Tharmas), and generally torment every other character (including each other) until, at last, the Spectre of Urthona in Night the Seventh reconciles the sibling-lovers to each other and to their necessary identification with a mother who creates works of art that are also resurrections of the dead.

Enion's interrogation of the specter she has created from Tharmas's "death" is only one of many speculations into the mystery of human origins that seem to accompany nearly every exercise of labor, whether private or public, in the *Zoas*. These self-contradicting and often confusing accounts of a creation and primordial paradise of indivisible work and play are "embedded" throughout the nine nights at the innermost (or most secret) sites of other narratives, narrations that often confusingly interrelate public and catastrophic forms of destruction (war, famine, civil disobedience) with those of private jealousy, sexual impotence, and antipathy. But one such origin actually straddles the public and private worlds of these nights. This origin—Urthona's blinded interruption of labor at the demiurgic and primal forge—mediates Enion's procreation (through the Phantom) of Los and Enitharmon and their subsequent banishment of their mother;[29] Urizen's usurpation of power and the arts of generation under the cloak of darkness (and perhaps of intoxication) but in the name of Reason, Enlightenment, and accelerated productivity; Tharmas's assumption, as a resurrected and "bad" father, of the law-giving and tyrannical function once fulfilled by Urizen; and the liberation of Los and Enitharmon from the Parent power of Tharmas and from Urizen's Law through their creative embodiment of the ancestral dead. As I will suggest, in my final interpretation of Urthona's forge and its narrative contexts in the

Zoas, Blake's representations in the *Zoas* of Workmastery, paranoia, and a pleasure that is suspect because it is sexually "regressive" are paradigmatic of a melancholic culture that exists as the darker side of an age of reason, a culture that has Oedipally and totemistically murdered the Father (whether God or King) and installed in that vacancy the Law of the Father, a culture that fears not only death but also impotence, weakness, and (therefore?) any act of creativity that evokes homoerotic or female sexuality. That these symptoms of melancholia are also signs of social adjustment (or self-discipline) should remind us that the invisible and universal laws that police self-governing societies reproduce, as a condition of the Law's authority, a melancholia that (like the sexual perversions it finds suspect) it henceforth must vigorously (and for the most part unsuccessfully) suspect. But at the carefully patrolled margins of melancholic selfhood may be heard Enion's now-spectral voice. While her son and daughter thrive in her absence by "Ingrate . . . scorning her drawing her Spectrous Life / Repelling her away & away by a dread repulsive power / Into Non Entity revolving round in dark despair. / And drawing in the Spectrous life in pride and haughty joy" (1.9.4–8), Enion hovers at the edge of their "golden" heavens and feasts, decrying the stolen labor of the weaver, the stolen food of the poor who themselves feed desperately upon each other, and denouncing the lawgiver and schoolmaster who offer poison rather than nourishment:

> The Spider sits in his labourd Web, eager watching for the Fly
> Presently comes a famishd Bird & takes away the Spider
> His Web is left all desolate, that his little anxious heart
> So careful wove; & spread it out with sighs and weariness
> (1.18.4–7 E310)

"It is an easy thing to rejoice in the tents of prosperity," proclaims Enion, herself a weaver who has lost her home (2.36.12 E325). When Enion returns in the final night of the *Zoas,* consumption and consummation are confounded in an apocalyptic feast day that is also, nearly unthinkably, itself a return to the pastoral, a pastoral in which Urthona, the happy shepherd and good father, is not elegized but, rather, brought forth from the specter he became when stricken at the forge. In the apocalypse in which "evil is all consumd"—literally, through a consumption of seed sown and harvested by a renewed Urizen, the grain baked as bread by Dark Urthona—when the divine "have walkd thro fires & yet are not consumed," "the stars consumd like a lamp blown out," Urthona is "arisen in his strength no longer now / Divided from Enitharmon no longer the Spectre of Los" (9.138.22–39 E406–7; 139.4–5 E407). Melancholic speculation succeeds to a different, and brighter, vision as "the depths of wondrous worlds" are uncovered (the root meaning, after all, of "apocalypse") before "The Expanding Eyes of Man" (9.138.25 E406). Yet such revelation, such resurrections from crypts of the incorporated dead, may occur only after the "works" of Dark Urthona—in which "Men are bound to sullen contemplations in the night / . . . / Feeling the crushing Wheels they rise they write the bitter words / Of Stern Philosophy & knead the bread of knowledge with tears & groans"— succeed to his "Bread of Ages" (9.138.11–17 E406).

"My Spectre Around Me Night & Day"

Blake, broken and impoverished, confronted during his production of *The Four Zoas* what he called his own "Deep pit of Melancholy, Melancholy without any real reason for it" (E706). As Blake discovered in the closing years of the eighteenth century—the years during which he shifted from the public (and published) labor of illustrating Young's *Night Thoughts* to the nocturnal, secretive labor of the *Zoas*—the indolence and despair with which he had been afflicted was in part correlative with his "glum" resistance to the uninspired, daytime tasks assigned by his patron William Hayley. He resisted that Workmastery by engaging in a crepuscular creativity, keeping alive the artist and poet who might have figuratively perished (as did his fortune and reputation) with the commercial failure of *Night Thoughts*. Dependent upon but also resistant to Hayley's efforts to serve as a patron and mentor—in both senses, a substitute father—Blake also at this time began to recognize the disabling persistence of the paternal loss that he had not successfully (in Freud's terms) "worked through." Nearly twenty years earlier, the death of Blake's father had, in a real sense, inaugurated the son's career. Blake, transforming Young's chastened, consolatory, and elegiac acceptance of death's terrors into an art that aggressively and erotically eschews consolation, turned a graveyard poetry into an exploration of the pockets within the self out of which the dead are reborn. Incorporating (a charged term to which I will return) the engravings for *Night Thoughts* into *The Four Zoas,* Blake produced this highly unconventional manuscript in darkness, indolence, and passivity, which is to say in a state not of freedom, of self-awareness, but rather (in his own words) of "dictation."

In October 1800 he wrote to Thomas Butts from Felpham that he hoped "now I have commenced a new life of industry to do credit to the new life by Improved Works" (E712). By September of the following year he continued to express confidence, but he now sought forgiveness for his "want of steady perseverence."[30] But by November 1802 Blake presented a very different picture of Hayley's workshop:

I have been very Unhappy & could not think of troubling you about it or any of my real Friends. . . .

. . . Tho I have been very unhappy I am now so no longer I am again Emerged into the light of Day I still & shall to Eternity Embrace Christianity and Adore him who is the Express image of God but I have traveld thro Perils & Darkness not unlike a Champion . . . & in the Abysses of the Accuser My Enthusiasm is still what it was only Enlarged and confirmd (E719–20)

Blake is more forthcoming about that unhappiness in his letter of January 10, 1803, and he discusses explicitly how the "drudgery" of Hayley's business contributed to his depression:

I will divide my griefs with you that I cannot hide what it is now become my duty to explain—My unhappiness has arisen from a source which if explord too narrowly might hurt my pecuniary circumstances. As my dependence is on Engraving at present & particularly on the Engravings I have in hand for Mr H. & I find on all hands great objections to my doing any thing but the meer drudgery of business & intimations that if I do not confine myself to this I shall not live. this has always pursud me. You will understand by this the source of all my uneasiness. . . . that I cannot live without doing my duty to lay up treasures in heaven is Certain & Determined & to this I have long made up my mind & why this should be made an objection to Me while Drunkenness Lewdness Gluttony & even Idleness itself does not hurt other men let Satan himself Explain—The Thing I have most at Heart! more than life or all that seems to make life comfortable without. Is the Interest of True Religion & Science & whenever any thing appears to affect that Interest (Especially if I myself omit any duty to my [*self*] <Station> as a Soldier of Christ) It gives me the greatest of torments,

Blake's "emergence" from "Darkness," he claims, was enabled by "Messengers from Heaven":[31]

I am not ashamed afraid or averse to tell You what Ought to be Told. That I am under the direction of Messengers from Heaven Daily & Nightly but the nature of such things is not as some suppose. without trouble or care. . . . But if we fear to do the dictates of our Angels & tremble at the Tasks set before us. if we refuse to do Spiritual Acts. because of Natural Fears or Natural Desires! Who can describe the dismal torments of such a state!—I too well remember the Threats I heard!—If you who are organized by Divine Providence for Spiritual communion. Refuse & bury your Talent in the Earth even tho you should want Natural Bread. Sorrow & Desperation pursues you thro life! . . . But I am now no longer in That State & now go on again with my Task Fearless. (E724–25)

In a letter he wrote to Butts on April 25 Blake continues his discussion of his previous depression (subsequently called, as though he were Tharmas or Albion, "my three years Slumber on the banks of the Ocean") and the "Dictation" that has reawakened him. He has decided to leave Hayley:

I can alone carry on my visionary studies in London unannoyd & that I may converse with my friends in Eternity. See Visions, Dream Dreams, & prophecy & speak Parables unobserv'd & at liberty from the Doubts of other Mortals. . . . "He who is Not With Me is Against Me" There is no Medium or Middle state . . .

. . . .

But none can know the Spiritual Acts of my three years Slumber on the banks of the Ocean unless he has seen them in the Spirit or unless he should read My long Poem descriptive of those Acts for I have in these three years composed an immense number of verses on One Grand Theme Similar to Homers Iliad or Miltons Paradise Lost the Persons & Machinery intirely new to the Inhabitants of Earth (some of the Persons Excepted) I have written this Poem from immediate Dictation twelve or sometimes twenty or thirty lines at a time without Premeditation & even against my Will. the Time it has taken in writing was thus renderd Non Existent. & an immense Poem Exists which seems to be the Labour of a long Life all producd without Labour or Study. . . .

. . . I see the face of my Heavenly Father he lays his Hand upon my Head & gives a blessing to all my works. . . . I sing forth his Praises. that the Dragons of the Deep may praise him & that those who dwell in darkness

& on the Sea coasts may be gatherd into his Kingdom. Excuse my perhaps too great Enthusiasm. (E728–29)

Critics have sought, perhaps understandably, to explain the psychic behavior that Blake recounts, and enacts, in these passages as paranoia ("He who is Not with Me is Against Me") and auditory hallucination ("Dictation"). Judith Weissman, in her provocative, compelling, and wide-ranging investigation of "poets who hear voices," concludes that Blake—like Virgil, Dante, Milton, and other visionary poets—received messages from an archaic part of the brain that also inscribed the commandments of law on the tablets of the imagination.[32] In their own explorations of the psychic dimensions of Blake's voices and visions, Nelson Hilton and Paul Youngquist conclude from their quite different arguments that, nearly two decades after his father's death, Blake at last reintegrated (which is to say, *submitted* to) the internalized ghost of his father: the superego.[33] To use Youngquist's more explicitly psychoanalytic paradigm, Blake, through the linguistic resources of poetry, overcame a schizophrenic failure of articulation, finding in poetry a psychic discipline and a reasonable voice, one capable of communication (that is, of acts of verbal exchange performed under the Name of the Father) with others because it no longer warred against a second (and superegoistic) self. Hilton and Youngquist find support for their speculations on Blake's relationship to paternal authority in evidence available in the letters previously cited, in Blake's changing figuration of paternal figures in *The Book of Urizen* and the *Zoas,* in the odd poem he sent to Butts in November 1802 (E720–22), in the Notebook poem that begins "My Spectre around me night & day," and in a letter Blake wrote not to Butts but to Hayley on October 23, 1804:

O Glory! and O Delight! I have entirely reduced that spectrous Fiend to his station, whose annoyance has been the ruin of my labours for the last passed twenty years of my life. He is the enemy of conjugal love and is the Jupiter of the Greeks, an iron-hearted tyrant. . . . Nebuchadnezzar had seven times passed over him; I have had twenty; thank God I was not altogether a beast as he was; but I was a slave bound in a mill among beasts and devils . . . [who] are now, together with myself, become children of light and liberty, and my feet and my wife's feet are free from fetters. O lovely Felpham, parent of Immortal Friendship, to thee I am eternally indebted for my three years' rest from perturbation and the strength I now enjoy. (E756)

We might well wonder at Blake's inconsistency at, or on, this point: while in the letters to Butts he blames Felpham (or Hayley) for the tyranny of drudgery, in writing to Hayley he praises Felpham for providing "three years' rest" and, implicitly, for "liberating" him from the specter's "mill." In the letter's remaining lines, Blake concludes that "he is become my servant who domineered over me, he is even as a brother who was my enemy" (E757). As a consequence, "I take a pencil or graver into my hand, even as I used to be in my youth, and as I have not been for twenty dark, but very profitable years. . . . In short, I am now satisfied and proud of my work, which I have not been for the above long period" (E757).

The enemy who has been converted into a colleague is, in Hilton's view, Blake's father, who died twenty years earlier and thereby brought into being both "profit" and superegoistical dissatisfaction. By the time he wrote this letter, Hilton argues, Blake had at last come to recognize that rivalry with the father is a battle the son can only lose. In resigning himself to Parent power by identifying with it rather than resisting it, Blake ensured that the paternal specter could be laid at last to rest. Indeed, Blake's morbid fascination with the "grave" could now be directed to the creative (and instructive) productions of "engraving," so that nocturnal "mourning" could at last become (in a fashion suitable to the polysemous creator) its redemptive homonym: "morning."[34] Arguing that Blake's father was the "Work master" who "in good bourgeois tradition" urged his son to work hard in order to earn worldly success ("proofs of industry in my success"), Hilton concludes that Blake could be reconciled with the paternal superego only by "positively reidentifying himself with his father—never an easy task, since the spectral image can be most cruel in its demands" (*Literal Imagination*, p. 154). Hilton correctly notes that his argument is shared by most interpreters of Blake's specter: "Critics generally agree in finding in the spectre 'a repressive father figure, a selfish old man who moralistically restrains, judges and punishes.' It is under this sign (in the name of the father and the holy spectre) that Blake's conception takes shape—from the tension of inhibited, shadowy desires emerges a picture of the inhibiting censorious spectre whose attributes open the path for its later assimilation of rationing 'rational power' " (154). Hilton also recognizes that *where* Blake locates the haunting— in the "loins"—is significant: "The connection of the spectre with the physically dead explains their unincarnate state as they await woven vegetable bodies (hence their dwelling place in the 'loins'), and also their vicarious existence in the present, in the spirit and imagination of each of us" (154). Just as important, Hilton acknowledges the "dialectical" relationship between "rational spectre" and "craving lust—the two, like Bromion and Oothoon, are bound 'back to back' and feed off one another" (170).

There is, however, in *The Four Zoas* an alternative explanation for Blake's relationship to the spectral voices that seem to emerge from within the "private" self—indeed, from within the self's "privates." Blake learned through his sufferance of Hayley's uninspired industry, from his diurnal enslavement to Hayley's patronage, but also from his attraction to Hayley's persistent charm, to reconceive the raw materials and processes of a nocturnal, poetic labor that takes place in the earliest home from which not the son but the father is evicted: the loins, literally, as Judith Butler has argued in *Gender Trouble*,[35] the son's testament (as in swearing on one's testicles) to the Parent power that prevails not only as Oedipal antagonism but also, in what Freud configured as the negative, homosexual Oedipus, as desire. That Blake should manifest ambivalence toward a second father (Hayley) even as he approached the twentieth anniversary of the death of his first suggests the endurance of Parent power *as* the experience of desire that haunts the locus of an originary and paternal presence.[36] While the productivity that emerges where such melancholic seed lies buried may seem "the Labour of a long Life," it may be, through the guidance of the nightly voices Blake called "Messengers," in fact a poetic vocation—as he declared in an 1803 letter—"without Labour or Study" (E728–29). In the voice of the Messengers who called Blake from his secular drudgery to a new avowal of allegiance to—through identification *with* and incorporation *of*—a heavenly, self-sacrificing Father-as-Son, Blake heard a poetic vocation that derived its power from the very origins of modernity's division of laborer and consumer, or (to use the terms that open Blake's letter to Butts) "debtor" and "Credit-er": the unwritten, unspoken law—or ideology—of the Oedipal injunction that requires fathers to surrender sons, sons to surrender fathers, and each (as they become untouchable, disembodied specters to each other) to disavow the other in the name of the ghostly Law. "Eternals," Blake responds in 1794, "I hear your call gladly" (*The Book of Urizen*, E70). But he cannot put their words into his own mouth without, first, incorporating the spirits he will thereby revive.

Incorporation is the poetic theme or strategy that Blake's most important scholars have identified as distinctively Blakean. As Robert Essick persuasively argues in *William Blake and the Language of Adam,* incorporation characterizes the vocal nature of Blake's written words, a visual art that paradoxically recalls the presence of speech in the graphic absences of writing. It further describes a creative process in which Blake's revisions typically subsume and elaborate earlier versions of his own work (including his visual art).[37] Donald Ault has instructively diagrammed the embedded (or, as I would argue, encrypted) structures of Blake's nonrepresentative and antiteleological narrative.[38] Hilton has mapped the intertextual and autobiographical connections of Blake's polysemous productivity, describing Blake's construction of a verbal medium that is both inspired by the losses of difference and deferral and, in the face of loss, protective as well as procreative. And Youngquist, who has characterized Blake's writing in Foucauldian terms as both paranoid and liberatory, recognizes that a cryptic process—one of "hiding" and "seeking"—both threatens and engenders characters in the *Zoas.* In each case, Blake's incorporative strategies enable him to develop a visual context that, while it is explicitly preoccupied with matters our culture considers private (sexual temptation, sensual expressiveness, and human reproduction), nevertheless contributes to a verbal narrative that concerns war, famine, and pestilence. A political reading of Blake must not only take into account the private as well as the public scope of the *Zoas,* but also recognize that ideology itself succeeds by creating, and then colonizing—indeed, feeding upon—the most private (and pleasurably sexualized) places on and in the self.

In order to "identify" with the Law that stands in for fathers, the son, according to Freud, must first "introject" his own father, thereby putting ideology in the father's former place. The son, in effect, reproduces ideology even as he himself is interpellated by ideology as biologically reproductive—which is to say, in this model, heterosexual. Incorporation, which Freud characterizes as a "regressive" resolution of such separation from the father, prolongs the son's melancholic attachment, for it slows the son's ability to put words in the place of unspeakable loss. Yet Freud's explanation alone does not help us to understand how the various weavings of wombs, comminglings of specters and shadows, and enclosures within hermaphrodites may in *The Four Zoas* represent, depending upon context, either Urizenic hegemony or the liberation of Los. Judith Butler's model is more helpful, for she suggests that melancholic incorporation enables (1) the encryption of the father *in* the space opened by his evacuation in the son's psyche, and (2) the literalization of the son's "loss" of the father on and in the body. In other words, the primordial loss of the parent of the same sex is manifested, paradoxically, in the development of sexual difference and of heterosexual desire. Because the father is banished by the incest taboo even before the Oedipal injunction puts in place the Law, the subsequent "real" death of the son's actual father can only exacerbate a haunting that begins with the very origins of selfhood: "If the identifications sustained through melancholy are 'incorporated,' then the question remains: Where is this incorporated space? If it is not literally within the body, perhaps it is *on* the body as its surface signification such that the body must itself be understood *as* an incorporated space" (67). Incorporation, the expression of loss that takes place through a figurative consumption of the banished object of former need, desire, and/or love, is both antimetaphorical and libidinous: "[I]ncorporation *literalizes* the loss *on* or *in* the body and so appears as the facticity of the body, the means by which the body comes to bear 'sex' as its literal truth. The localization and/or prohibition of pleasures and desires in given 'erotogenic' zones is precisely the kind of gender-differentiating melancholy that suffuses the body's surface. The loss of the pleasurable object is resolved through the incorporation of that very pleasure with the result that pleasure is both determined and prohibited through the compulsory effects of the gender-differentiating law" (68–69). Earlier even than the taboo against heterosexual incest that Freud tied to the Oedipus complex, Butler continues, is the taboo against homosexual incest: "[The] refusal of the homosexual cathexis, desire and aim together, a refusal both compelled by social taboo and appropriated through developmental stages, results in a melancholic structure which effectively encloses that aim and object within the corporeal space or 'crypt' established through an abiding denial. If the heterosexual denial of homosexuality results in melancholia and if melancholia operates through incorporation, then the disavowed homosexual love is preserved through the cultivation of an oppositionally defined gender identity" (69).

Heterosexual denial may also be preserved in such socially sanctioned outlets for homosocial aggression as rivalry and warfare. War, in *The Four Zoas,* which ghosts inexplicably the quarrels of lovers and enemies alike, may actually represent not only the political conflicts of Europe's reactionary powers—or the struggles within the

Enlightenment self between Reason and Passion—but also a contest at the very locus of sexual difference between hatred and love.

In what E. P. Thompson in *Witness against the Beast* calls the "doctrine of Two Seeds" (74), a dialectical contest of demonic and divine origins takes place in each human being that, in defiance of reason, derives from, even as it engenders, two alternatives: either sexual strife, shame, and sin, or secular *and* divine union and redemption.[39] It begins with Eve's eating of the fruit, an act of incorporation that is also a kind of copulation with the serpent/Satan. Indeed, according to Muggletonian creed, the Tree of Knowledge *is* Satan: "Entering within Eve's womb the Serpent transmuted himself 'into Flesh, Blood and Bone' and the offspring of this intercourse was Cain, whereas Abel and his young brother Seth (in whose generation the Devil had no part) were the offspring of the divine principle in which God had created Adam. But from the moment of the Fall, Satan disappears from the rest of the cosmos, having dissolved himself in Eve's womb and perpetuated himself in Cain and Cain's seed and only there. Hence there was implanted within the human race, at the moment of the Fall, two contrary principles, diabolic and divine: the offspring of Cain and the offspring of Seth" (73). Salvation, no less than damnation, begins and ends in the womb of creation: "It was now God, and not the Serpent, who entered Mary's womb and dissolved into her conception" (77). Using language that is explicitly associated both with sexual reproduction and with the art of weaving, the following Muggletonian creed expresses the sect's belief that God as well as Jesus entered the grave before being resurrected from the womb/tomb:[40] "I believe in God the Man Christ Jeasus, in Glory who was a Spiritual Body from all Eternity Who by Virtue of his Godhead Power Entered into the narrow passage of the Blessed Virgin Mary's Womb And so Dissolved Himself into Seed and Nature as Clothed Himself with Flesh Blood and Bone as with a Garment; thereby made Capable to Suffer Death who made himself man, the Express Image of his Father's Person And so become a Son to his own God power. He absolutely poured out His Soul unto Death; and lay three Days Dead in the Womb of the Earth . . ." (77; Thompson's ellipses). In *The Four Zoas,* this seed warfare, which is waged within an inner space that belongs, by turns, to a male or a female creator, thrives at the expense of the starved laborer. Urizen, the Work master, has orphaned himself from "Parent power," governing the self through law, reason, and discipline and waging war against the creative aspects of the self that labor to produce art, or children, through pleasure. Like the Muggletonians' seed warfare, Urizen's struggle with the forces of life evokes, as Thompson implies, competing conceptions of the Creator as a loving and heavenly Father and as the hegemonic, ideological Law of the Father.[41]

In a struggle in which the dead and the living feed upon each other (as in the actual war in Europe between reactionary rulers), the warmongering Zoas create famine, extract labor, inflict pain, and exclude the poor from the songs and banquets of the wealthy. Yet, in an inversion of Plato's *Symposium,* the banquet in which Socratic self-denial ratifies the untouchable, unspeakable purity of the beautiful god who lives within the ugly and libidinous satyr, Blake does not finally exalt innerness at the expense of the matter (or *mater*) in which living beings are encrypted. Indeed, Blake figures Vala in the later books as Mystery to remind us that the consequence of denying the maternal (and the material) results in her return as the deadly (and dead, or "corrupted") Mystery, licentious counterpart (and *embodiment*) of the Reason (Socratic or Urizenic) that lurks within her savage and seductive loins. Specters haunt precisely those sites, and those settings, where the Enlightenment self feels least bound by matter and most inner, most "orphaned," and most "free," as we may learn through Blake's various representations of philosophical and poetic labor: writing, reading, and working in private. As in the case of Milton's Satan, such encounters follow the son's perceived loss of power or esteem in relation to the Father, an experience of loss and of envy that summons a corresponding need to aggrandize the self that in fact originates in the introjection of fathers. The specter originates, in other words, in loci where the self itself originates, where the child (like Milton's Satan or his dreaming Eve) falls from the innocence of parental proximity into an experience where he or she may acquire knowledge alone, hidden by night, hearing voices, discovering secrets, soaring in Godlike fashion. Blake's specters, as both Ault and Hilton have suggested, remind us that the roots of the word "specter" lie in the "specular": a specter is (to use Freud's definition for the "uncanny") that which should be kept hidden but which comes to light. Indeed, it becomes visible as an entity that itself looks back at (and speculates upon) the spectator and the spectator's origins.[42]

In this, Blake's parody of an Age of Enlightenment, a Newtonian and Godwinian age characterized by the near-paranoid pursuit of the hidden secrets of the natural world, the Prince of Light (Urizen) and the solar Los are, for reasons I will explore in the final section that follows, as afflicted by the innervation of damp darkness as Tharmas, the god of gloom in this cosmos of loss. The natural world, the *mater* and matter who is Vala, becomes in this empirical and utilitarian age first a female slave (as in Night II) and then (as in Night VIII) Mystery, a life-threatening ur-mother of darkness, a maw that incorporates human sacrifices, a crypt that hides and protects Satan *as* Urizen. Yet Vala, whether she shares attributes with Enion, Enitharmon, or the Shadowy Female, is inevitably complicit with the presences whom she devours, mourns, once again brings into being, and hides. Like such presences enshrined or enbalmed within the hermaphroditic Mystery, or enwombed or enbalmed within both Tharmas and Enion, the specter derives its authority through its deployment—and violation—of visibility, which is to say, through its challenge to a metaphysics that depends upon absolute distinctions between absence and presence, the dead and the living, the internal and the external. Like Mystery, who hermaphroditically houses a male presence within her sacred shrine, the specter is, in a sense, a parody of the Son whom Milton describes as existing in heaven at the center of the "orbs within orbs" of angels, "embosom'd" in God's embrace. Indeed, Blake twice cites passages from the Gospel of John as opening epigraphs for the *Zoas* both to distinguish the divine Word from the ordinary, symbolic exchanges transacted in the world and to reiterate the Son's place *as* the Father's place within each human breast:

That they all may be one; as thou, Father, art in me, and I in thee, that they also may be one in us: that the world may believe that thou hast sent me.

And the glory which thou gavest me I have given them; that they may be One, even as we are one . . .

In Night the Seventh, the Spectre of Urthona remembers unfallen Albion in terms that suggest not only the mutual encryption of man and God but also a mutual interpenetration that evokes this line from John: "I in them, and thou in me, that they may be made perfect in one, and that the world may know that thou hast sent me, and hast loved them, as thou hast loved me."[43]

But in the melancholic Age of Enlightenment, which establishes the sensation of innerness by evicting from the subject such inner beings, the Urizen who rises to power out of the void left by the Eternals can only, as a consequence of his denial of their now hidden presence, see Death: "No more Exulting for he saw Eternal Death beneath / Pale he beheld futurity; pale he beheld the Abyss" (2.23.14–15 E313). Haunted by a mortality that cannot see the immortal Parent powers within, Urizen thereby fortifies an allegedly unified self that appears to itself to be both self-authoring and private. Urizen personifies the modern, Foucauldian subject who, through self-discipline (and self-surveillance) becomes capable of entering productively into systems of symbolic exchange as both worker and consumer, exercising (or so he mistakenly believes) the will required to consume responsibly. In such a culture (and in such an economy) the Urizen who not only exploits the labor of others but who also writes and reads remains a troubling figure precisely to the extent that his own, real labors seem to involve the production of private pleasure as well as public law, the fetishization as well as the generation of texts.

We must make a seeming digression at this point and ask why Urizen's secret reading, and his furtive writing, elicit such scholarly chastisement. David Simpson, in "Reading Blake and Derrida," at one moment gestures with obvious glee toward the obviously "onanistic" pleasure that Urizen takes with texts, only to condemn in the next (with obvious and equal pleasure) what he calls the political failure of Urizen's intellectual pursuits, an "oscillation between omnipotence and impotence" that he labels (and indicts) as "deconstructive," implying that Blake's own pleasure in the texts that he kept mostly to himself was politically, sexually, and morally suspect.[44] Perhaps Urizen summons such responses as Simpson's because Blake's readers intuit that the hidden, the mysterious, and the secretive in Blake's texts are inevitably associated also with a particular kind of absence, a "nothingness" incorporated and encrypted at the very center of the self. Reading evokes the origins of the self in a pleasure—desire—taught by books that supplant the child's first need for paternal, as well as maternal, nurture. In such art, as in the Law-inscribing writings of Urizen in *The Book of Urizen,* inevitably the Eternals will retreat, a*ghast* (because they are made *ghosts*) by the private act upon which they are spying.[45] Yet if the Eternals (or God) can exist only (as Blake believed) within man, then even Urizenic reading—and writing—can be redemptive, as indeed it will be by the end of the *Zoas.* Paul Mann, in "*The Book of Urizen* and the Horizon of the Book," is correct in suggesting that *The Book of Urizen* is about how the world—and how we ourselves—are books. Yet to limit that trope to the reification of the body as an entity constructed by the Law of the Father ignores the claims of that statement's inversion: the book is inevitably an investment not only of paper and ink but also of flesh and blood, tears and sweat, pleasure and pain. To enter a book is to enter a body haunted by many specters at multiple sites of pleasure, and by "torment" (to use Blake's term in his invocation to the Eternals). To read, no less than to write, is to resurrect the dead Father (the Eternals), and our dead fathers and mothers, however we seek to obey the linguistic Law. It is to give (as does the writer and/or artist) the paternal ghost a body.

Blake himself moved beyond the pleasure—and the despair—of Urizenic bookmaking-as-selfmaking that he portrays in *The Book of Urizen* to offer, in *The Four Zoas,* an enlarged—and internalized— context for the fall of the Creator into Workmastery. The mournfulness of the managerial Urizen, the gloom of the despotic Tharmas, the impotence of the laboring Los, and the destructive desire of the rebellious Luvah/Orc are all manifestations of a body— Albion's—that, in denying a banished presence, denies also the body's "Dictates," and its resources. The crisis of Oedipal resistance and obedience that Hayley (or Urizen), as a son who seeks to possess the authority of the dying father (Albion), provoked in Blake (or Los) enabled the visionary poet, with the assistance of his "Messengers," to transform his trade into a labor that does not alienate one generation—or one *form* of generation—from another.

"United with Thy Spectre Consummating"

In the first description of Urthona's failure at the forge, the Messengers from Beulah address the Council of Eternity, describing Urizen's surrender of the sun's light—"the chariots of morning"—to Luvah while the Work master sought to establish his cold authority through the "clouds opake" of his bribery ("every tenth man / Is bought & sold & in dim night my Word shall be their law") and "silent brooding death" (1.21.26–35 E311; 22.12 E312). Luvah recognized, however, that Urizen, in cloaking his "morning" in "mourning," his enlightenment in night, has enacted a division of labor and power with Luvah that in fact "dictates" not only by inscribing the authority ("Word") of the now-enshrouded Law but also by gaining an alliance with its lawless, libidinous, opponent (Luvah), seeking to make an ally of the desire that Urizen will in turn repress and enslave. In a scene indebted to Milton's transformation of an envious, light-bearing, and brooding Lucifer into the divisive Prince of Darkness, Urizen feigns partnership with Luvah. Buying and selling "each tenth man," Urizen masters through symbolic as well as monetary exchange: "my Word shall be their law" (1.21.35 E311). As bloodshed and "Discord begin" within the unconscious, melancholic Man ("dark sleeper"), Urizen successfully deploys the "opake" arts of melancholy against the open bellicosity of Luvah, described (like Urthona's forge) as "fiery": "While thus he [Luvah] spoke his fires reddend oer the holy tent / Urizen cast deep darkness round him silent brooding death / Eternal death to Luvah" (1.22.11– 13 E312). As war escalates between these rebellious sons, Urthona's peacetime labor at the forge is halted. He hears an "Eternal voice" and then his own sons and emanation divide from him. Urthona becomes a falling and Satanic serpent to Urizen's fallen Lucifer, his emanation transformed into a buried, embalmed "corse":

> Beside his anvil stood Urthona dark. a mass of iron
> Glowd furious on the anvil prepard for spades & coulters All
> His sons fled from his side to join the conflict pale he heard
> The Eternal voice he stood the sweat chilld on his mighty limbs
> He dropd his hammer. dividing from his aking bosom fled
> A portion of his life shrieking upon the wind she fled
> And Tharmas took her in pitying Then Enion in jealous fear
> Murderd her & hid her in her bosom embalming her for fear
> She should arise again to life Embalmd in Enions bosom
> Enitharmon remains a corse such thing was never known
> In Eden that one died a death never to be revivd
> Urthona stood in terror but not long his spectre fled
> To Enion & his body fell. Tharmas beheld him fall
> Endlong a raging serpent rolling round the holy tent
> The sons of war astonishd at the Glittring monster drove
> Him far into the world of Tharmas into a cavernd rock
> (1.22.16–31 E312)

This first narration of Urthona's falling hammer/falling serpent/ dying emanation anticipates the final struggle between the seed of the serpent and the voice of the Saviour in the final night. Henceforth the *Zoas* will be confined to (or will seek confinement *in*) various cavernous places where secrets (and libidinal energy) may both originate and be hidden. Urizen himself immediately and in secret falls, in Satanic fashion, into the very void that he had feared ("a-voided" or denied), a "Space" that, in being both "unknown" and hellishly "horrible without End," may be related to the origination of desire, guilt, and "opake" powers of repression within a now experienced (or sinful) self. That self's newly spacious interiors, voided of the Eternals, are "opend to pain" and to a melancholic rage. Refuge there is withheld from Jerusalem and her "little ones":

> Mustring together in thick clouds leaving the rage of Luvah
> To pour its fury on himself & on the Eternal Man
> Sudden down fell they all together into an unknown Space
> Deep horrible without End. Separated from Beulah far beneath
> The Mans exteriors are become indefinite opend to pain
> In a fierce hungring void & none can visit his regions
>
> Jerusalem his Emanation is become a ruin
> Her little ones are slain on the top of every street
> And she herself le[d] captive & scatterd into the indefinite
> (1.22.36–41; 21[19].1–3 E312)

Of course, the war between good and evil is itself a struggle within the various interiors of the Fallen Man, interiors that have become "opake" to him. As Night the First comes to a close, the Daughters of Beulah seek to protect Jerusalem within Enitharmon's "fine wrought brain" and "bowels within her loins / Three gates within Glorious & bright open into Beulah / From Enitharmon's inward parts," but Enitharmon "barrd them fast," reluctant to engage in creative regeneration because she fears that Los might also enter (21[19].3–6 E313). Without such merciful, and bodily, acts of "enwombing," without such transformations of the bellicose death drive into a creative renewal of life, Night the First closes with an inversion of the image of a son embosomed in the Father—and vice versa—that opened the *Zoas*: wheels that (in an act of incorporation) murderously "consume":

> Terrific ragd the Eternal Wheels of intellect terrific ragd
> The living creatures of the wheels in the Wars of Eternal life
> But perverse rolld the wheels of Urizen & Luvah back reversd
> Downwards & outwards consuming in the wars of Eternal Death
> (1.22[20].12–15 E313)

Albion at this point explicitly surrenders authority to Urizen, ensuring his own descent into the melancholic "dark sleep of Death."

Urizen, hearing the "call" of the Man to assume new authority, recoils from the "body of Man pale, cold, the horrors of death" even as he glimpses the "Abyss" opened by the Man's submission to Urizen where "Enion blind & age bent wept in direful hunger craving / All rav'ning like the hungry worm, & like the silent grave / Mighty was the draft of Voidness to draw Existence in" (2.23.1–18 E313–14). Urizen responds to these melancholic behaviors by, first, banishing Luvah "into the Furnaces of affliction . . . seald," which Luvah's lover "Vala fed in cruel delight," although she, too, is enslaved to this Work master's womb/loom/forge that creates alternative, but petrifying, spaces in reaction to the abyss he has abjected (2.25.40–41 E317):

> Luvah & Vala trembling & shrinking, beheld the great Work master
> And heard his Word! Divide ye bands influence by influence
> Build we a Bower for heavens darling in the grizly deep
> Build we the Mundane Shell around the Rock of Albion
>
> The Bands of Heaven flew thro the air singing & shouting to Urizen
> Some fix'd the anvil, some the loom erected, some the plow
> And harrow formd & framd the harness of silver & ivory
> The golden compasses, the quadrant & the rule & balance
> They erected the furnaces, they formd the anvils of gold beaten in
>   mills
> Where winter beats incessant, fixing them firm on their base
> The bellows began to blow & the Lions of Urizen stood round the
>   anvil
> (2.24.5–15 E314)

In fact, Urizen succeeds in the enormous labor of apportioning and dividing space into a hellish pleasure palace ("Heaven walled round" [2.33.8 E321], "a Golden World" [2.32.8]) because the victims he must coerce have themselves already turned away from "visions in the air" as they stand on an "infinite earth" in order to seek, to labor on behalf of, the confinements of Urizenic law and order.[46] Yet Urizen, recognizing that his construction is founded on division, that his wife, Ahania, a spectral prisoner in this bower, has become estranged from him, and that Vala (who is both a laborer and Nature) is hostage to his "flames incessant labouring" (2.31.5 E320), is made only more melancholic by the imposition of his Law and his Word. He discovers that profits accrued through the labor of others do not bring him happiness:

When Urizen returnd from his immense labours & travels
Descending She reposd beside him folding him around
In her bright skirts. Astonishd & Confounded he beheld
Her shadowy form now Separate he shudderd & was silent
Till her caresses & her tears revivd him to life & joy
Two wills they had two intellects & not as in times of old
This Urizen percievd & silent brooded in darkning Clouds
To him his Labour was but Sorrow & his Kingdom was Repentence
He drave the Male Spirits all away from Ahania
And she drave all the Females from him away
(2.30.43–52 E320)

Vala, now an enslaved laborer, is, like the Nature she also represents, alienated from the Work master who has commanded her to resist the entreaties of Luvah, her lover and a fellow laborer upon her materials:

And Vala like a shadow oft appeard to Urizen

The King of Light beheld her mourning among the Brick kilns
    compelld
To labour night & day among the fires, her lamenting voice
Is heard when silent night returns & the labourers take their rest
(2.30.56; 31.1–3 E320)

"Sorrowing went the Planters forth to plant, the Sowers to sow" (2.32.16 E321) in the Urizenic empire imposed in the Parent power's absence.

Urizen ultimately falls from this "paradise" because, like Tharmas (who is, as Ault has demonstrated, in so many ways Urizen's other), he spurns his female counterpart. A gesture that expresses insecurities about patriarchal authority in bed and in the home no less than it manifests Urizen's anxieties concerning the public authority of his Law, this act of sexual divisiveness in turn initiates a sequence of Oedipal, mournful acts that will open still other chasms, caverns, and crypts, both within and beyond the self. Ahania, who seeks to tell Urizen what he in fact has already intuited—that the power he has usurped from his father will in turn be usurped by another son (Orc)—is described by the melancholic Urizen in terms that he projects from his own abjection a *re*jection of an "indolent bliss" he calls "feminine." He describes her as having existed, once, within the cave of *his* breast, even as, paradoxically, she provided for him *her* body as comfort when work had wearied her lover. As Urizen recounts their past together, he invokes also the rural (and, he implies, regressive and narcissistic) origins that his melancholic and masculinist Workmastery now occludes and condemns:

> Saying Art thou also become like Vala. thus I cast thee out
> Shall the feminine indolent bliss. the indulgent self of weariness
> The passive idle sleep the enormous night & darkness of Death
> Set herself up to give her laws to the active masculine virtue
> Thou little diminutive portion that darst be a counterpart
> . . . .
> And thou hast risen with thy moist locks into a watry image
> Reflecting all my indolence my weakness & my death
> To weigh me down beneath the grave into non Entity
> Where Luvah strives scorned by Vala age after age wandering
> Shrinking & shrinking from her Lord & calling him the Tempter
> And art thou also become like Vala thus I cast thee out.
> (3.43.5–22 E328–29)

With the expulsion of Ahania, the warfare between embattled sons and fathers escalates in earnest. As Ault has observed, the fall of Urizen coincides with the rising power of Tharmas, an archaic authority who depends upon the abjection of Enion no less than upon the subjection of Urizen, Los, and Enitharmon. Night the Fourth opens with Tharmas's acknowledged ambivalence toward his wife and children, continues with Los's Oedipal resistance to the efforts of Tharmas to aggrandize an archaic and dynastic authority, and reaches a climax as Tharmas reasserts his primitive authority by raping his daughter, thereby dividing (and conquering) the incestuous Los and Enitharmon. When it is abused, watery, archaic Parent power in the Zoas is as effective as the hard, Urizenic Law in originating divisions of labor and of gender that themselves evoke "Dolor":

> For if I will I urge these waters. If I will they sleep
> In peace beneath my awful frown my will shall be my Law
>
> So Saying in a Wave he rap'd bright Enitharmon far
> Apart from Los. but covered her with softest brooding care
> On a broad wave in the warm west. balming her bleeding wound
>
> O how Los howld at the rending asunder all the fibres rent
> Where Enitharmon joind to his left side in griding pain
> He falling on the rocks bellowd his Dolor. till the blood
> Stanch'd, then in ululation waild his woes upon the wind
> (4.49.2–10 E332)

While the "rap'd" Enitharmon is now "wrapped" (or hidden)
from Los ("Enitharmon wrapd in clouds waild loud" [4.53.5 E335]),
Los's experience of sexual loss and submission to an archaic, paternal will that has the force of Law nearly miraculously materializes
the previously hidden Dark Spectre of Urthona who has "falln"
"upon the Shores / With dislocated Limbs" (4.49.11–12 E333).
Tharmas enslaves the Spectre, who in turn provides an account of
the day of Tharmas's flight from battle—"a dread vortex." On the
day of Urthona's falling hammer his sons divided from his side,
leading to "loss": bloodshed, dividing limbs, and falling bodies. Yet
such signs may also designate the labor of bringing new life (a
"vortex" of "animation" or birth) from the cave (and through the
canal) of generation. In a related narrative the Spectre tells Tharmas
that when Enitharmon was born, the Spectre came into being as an
exhalation of depleted breath (or spirit) through the "Nostrils":

I slumber here in weak repose. I well remember the Day
The day of terror & abhorrence
When fleeing from the battle thou fleeting like the raven
Of dawn outstretching an expanse where neer expanse had been
Drewst all the Sons of Beulah into thy dread vortex following
Thy Eddying spirit down the hills of Beulah. All my sons
Stood round me at the anvil where new heated the wedge
Of iron glowd furious prepard for spades & mattocks
Hearing the symphonies of war loud sounding All my sons
Fled from my side then pangs smote me unknown before. I saw
My loins begin to break forth into veiny pipes & writhe
Before me in the wind englobing trembling with strong vibrations
The bloody mass began to animate. I bending over
Wept bitter tears incessant. Still beholding how the piteous form
Dividing & dividing from my loins a weak & piteous
Soft cloud of snow a female pale & weak I soft embracd
My counter part & calld it Love I named her Enitharmon
But found myself & her together issuing down the tide
Which now our rivers were become delving thro caverns huge
Of goary blood strugg[l]ing to be deliverd from our bonds
She strove in vain not so Urthona strove for breaking forth,
A shadow blue obscure & dismal from the breathing Nostrils
Of Enion I issued into the air divided from Enitharmon
I howld in sorrow I beheld thee rotting upon the Rocks
I pitying hoverd over thee I protected thy ghastly corse

From Vultures of the deep then wherefore shouldst thou rage
Against me who thee guarded in the night of death from harm
(4.50.1–27 E333–34)

Tharmas's succinct reply to the narration of the Spectre who saved him—"Thou knowest not what Tharmas knows" (4.50.31 E334)—realigns the various manifestations of melancholia in the Zoas: the paranoid pursuit of (parental) secrets, the simultaneous protection and dispossession of a Parent power, and the association of the end of life with its origins. Tharmas reminds the Spectre that "Urthona is My Son O Los thou art Urthona" (4.51.14 E334). Yet Tharmas, once a father, has now made himself a lawgiver, declaring he "Is God" (4.51.15 E334). He is a "God," however, unhappy with his own Creation for he has banished "A portion of my life / That in Eternal fields in comfort wanderd with my flocks / At noon & laid her head upon my wearied bosom at night / She is divided" (4.51.20–23 E334). His obsession with controlling the Chaos of "monstrous forms" that his desire for power in fact "breeds" makes Tharmas merely a more nostalgic, and morose, version of Urizen. Indeed, the Word (now the *Will* of the Law) of Tharmas leads (as it also does for Urizen) ultimately both to despair and to divine departure, to the solipsism of subjectivity and the dejection of a mind that divides (not altogether successfully) Creation into subjects and objects. This lachrymose (and Jehovah-like) Tharmas, now a Master, requires a Slave:

> And I what can I now behold but an Eternal Death
> Before my Eyes & an Eternal weary work to strive
> Against the monstrous forms that breed among my silent waves
> Is this to be A God far rather would I be a Man
> To know sweet Science & to do with simple companions
> Sitting beneath a tent & viewing sheepfolds & soft pastures
> Take thou the hammer of Urthona rebuild these furnaces
> Dost thou refuse mind I the sparks that issue from thy hair
>
> I will compell thee to rebuild by these my furious waves
> Death choose or life thou strugglest in my waters, now choose life
> . . . .
>
> So saying Tharmas on his furious chariots of the Deep
> Departed far into the Unknown & left a wondrous void
> Round Los. afar his waters bore on all sides round. . . .
> (4.51.26–33; 52.1–9 E334–35)

In the wake of this departing God, all that Los can do—even with the able assistance of the Spectre—is rebuild "the Ruind Furnaces / Of Urizen. Enormous work: he builded them anew / Labour of Ages in the Darkness & the war of Tharmas / And Los formd Anvils of Iron petrific" (4.52.16–18 E335). Such labor, even with the stolen hammer of Urthona, can neither destroy nor revive Urizen; it can neither free Creation from Urizen's (and from Tharmas's) melancholia nor liberate a son victimized equally by Tharmas, the father-God, and by Urizen, the father-God's object of unappeasable hatred and of ineluctable identification. Urizen, who in "stoned stupor" is the petrific and silent monument to, and of, "brooding contemplation," "grey oblivio(n)" and still "mighty power," has himself been hardened by labor at Urthona's "Anvils of Iron petrific." Like Los, whose behavior will become increasingly sadomasochistic, and like the enervated Enitharmon, Urizen is bound in a "stoned stupor" by mills and chains.

Just as Urizen, the rebellious son who once ruled the sun became, earlier in the *Zoas,* the gloomy authority he sought to overthrow, and just as the archaic and despotic Tharmas resumed his reign by imitating the modern Work master whom he had expelled, Los now becomes the slave over whom he is Work master.[47] In one of several passages that Blake borrows from *The Book of Urizen* for Night the Fourth, Los "became what he beheld," or Urizen-like, "bound in a deadly sleep," even as "woman" (or sexual difference) at the end of this night, labors into life "imbodied" as that which is different from what man beholds and becomes. Los halts in his melancholy labor:

> In terrors Los shrunk from his task. his great hammer
> Fell from his hand his fires hid their strong limbs in smoke
> For with noises ruinous hurtlings & clashings & groans
> The immortal endur'd. tho bound in a deadly sleep
> Pale terror siezd the Eyes of Los as he beat round
> The hurtling Demon. terrifd at the shapes
> Enslavd humanity put on he became what he beheld
> He became what he was doing he was himself transformd
>
> [The globe of life blood trembled Branching out into roots;
> Fibrous, writhing upon the winds; Fibres of blood, milk and tears;
> In pangs, eternity on eternity. At length in tears & cries imbodied
> A female form trembling and pale Waves before his deathy face]
> (4.55 [second portion].16–27 E338)

Parent power takes many forms in the succeeding nights: Enitharmon gives birth to Orc, who is in turn chained by Los and kept
imprisoned in a cave; Urizen escapes Tharmas's power only to disavow his own daughters; Tharmas proposes that he and Urizen
starve themselves into nonexistence; Los "brood[s] on the darkness"
(6.70.1 E346) while he spurns and envies the son he bred; Urizen,
exploring the "dark world of Urthona" (6.69.29 E346), a "pathless
world of death" (6.70.2 E346) and "regions of the grave" (6.70.15
E347), resumes his passion for writing but only "in bitter tears &
groans in books of iron & brass / The enormous wonders of the
Abysses once his brightest joy" (6.70.3–4 E347) for now he finds in
the Abyss "wandring among / The ruind spirits" specters who were
"once his children & the children of Luvah" (6.70.5–6 E347). Unable to disavow, this time, what he has procreated, Urizen "knew
they were his Children ruind in his ruind world" (6.70.45 E347). Yet
in Blake's cosmos even this reprobate "falling falling falling / Into
the Eastern vacuity the empty world of Luvah" (6.71 [second por-
tion].23–24 E348) is rescued by a savior—a Father who is also a
Son—who, because he is unlike Urizen in being unwilling to allow
any of His creatures to fall absolutely into ruin, allows Urizen to be
reborn, repeatedly, even if only to resume, almost compulsively,
writing books. While these books may well be deadly (in their
"adamantine" or monumental aspect), they nevertheless survive his
own repeated deaths and revivals so that he may forestall the end of
his "journey" (that is, his final death) by resuming his writing:

> The ever pitying one who seeth all things saw his fall
> And in the dark vacuity created a bosom of clay
> When wearied dead he fell his limbs reposd in the bosom of slime
> As the seed falls from the sowers hand so Urizen fell & death
> Shut up his powers in oblivion. then as the seed shoots forth
> In pain & sorrow. So the slimy bed his limbs renewd
> At first an infant weakness. periods passd he gatherd strength
> But still in solitude he sat then rising threw his flight
> Onward tho falling thro the waste of night & ending in death
> And in another resurrection to sorrow & weary travel
> But still his books he bore in his strong hands & his iron pen
> For when he died they lay beside his grave & when he rose
> He siezd them with a gloomy smile for wrapd in his death clothes
> He hid them when he slept in death when he revivd the clothes
> Were rotted by the winds the books remain still unconsumd

Still to be written & interleavd with brass & iron & gold
Time after time for such a journey none but iron pens
Can write And adamantine leaves recieve nor can the man who goes

The journey obstinate refuse to write time after time
(6.71 [second portion].25–42; 72.1 E348–49)

This act of merciful regeneration, of seed bearing, birth, and nurture, must become the model not only for Urizen, who will eventually metamorphose the "iron pen" of engraving into plow and harrow, but also for Los and Enitharmon, who will learn that Urthona's forge cannot serve, alone, as a prototype for poetic production. For neither act is final; if either was absolute, it would lead only to petrifaction.

Los and Enitharmon learn the arts of revival from the Spectre, who, although jealous of the lovers, also helps Los to understand how strife between males leads not only to the loss of love between the sexes but also to the "between-ness" of sexual difference itself. In Night the Seventh, while Urizen "envious brooding" (7.80.49 E356) watches Orc (the son whom Los, in Oedipal fear, has enchained), Los's own "broodings rush down to his feet producing Eggs that hatching / Burst forth upon the winds above the tree of Mystery" (7.81.8–9 E356). The broodings of these Zoas, at this point, come to worse than nothing. For Los, Enitharmon, who "lay on his knees," has become a remote shadow, seduced by the ominous tree above which Los's "eggs" scatter; Urizen, fearing the rebellious Orc, "tracd his Verses / In the dark deep the dark tree grew" (7.81.10). Down into the roots of that Tree of Knowledge and of Mystery, the Shadow of the languishing Enitharmon undertakes her own nocturnal explorations, during which she encounters the Spectre of Urthona. She feels compelled, in his presence, to "tell / Thee Secrets of Eternity" (7.83.4–5 E358). The story of her own origins, it begins with Urizen's birth to Vala and the Fallen Man, involves a hermaphroditic Vala (both sign of and motive for the Fallen Man's alienation), and concludes with a labor (a birth) that is also a bloody melee:

Vala was pregnant & brought forth Urizen Prince of Light
First born of Generation. Then behold a wonder to the Eyes
Of the now fallen Man a double form Vala appeard. A Male
And female shuddring pale the Fallen Man recoild
From the Enormity & called them Luvah & Vala. turning down

The vales to find his way back into Heaven but found none
For his frail eyes were faded & his ears heavy & dull

Urizen grew up in the plains of Beulah Many Sons
And many daughters flourishd round the holy Tent of Man
Till he forgot Eternity delighted in his sweet joy
Among his family his flocks & herds & tents & pastures

But Luvah close conferrd with Urizen in darksome night
To bind the father & enslave the brethren Nought he knew
Of sweet Eternity the blood flowd round the holy tent & rivn
From its hinges uttering its final groan all Beulah fell
In dark confusion mean time Los was born & Enitharmon
But how I know not then forgetfulness quite wrapd me up
A period nor do I more remember till I stood
Beside Los in the Cavern dark enslavd to vegetative forms
(7.83.12–30 E358–59)

After listening to Enitharmon, the Spectre then narrates a related, but different, account of paradise and the fall, one that began before the Spectre, Los, and Enitharmon were divided aspects of Urthona, and before Urthona's interruption at the forge. While the Spectre clearly is tempting Enitharmon with his tale, he does not metamorphose (Urthona-like) into a serpent. Rather, he seduces her by evoking memories of a state of innocence when body and spirit, humanity and God, were undivided. These passages evoke Milton's description of Adam's talks with God in the Garden and the "orbs within orbs" of angels encircling a Father-Son pietà. As the narrative progresses, the Spectre describes "goar," which may be associated both with war and birth, reminding us that the specular produces sexual division as well as specters. It concludes with a "labor" at the forge that becomes a parthenogenesis:

Where thou & I in undivided Essence walkd about
Imbodied. thou my garden of delight & I the spirit in the garden
Mutual there we dwelt in one anothers joy revolving
Days of Eternity with Tharmas mild & Luvah sweet melodious
Upon our waters. This thou well rememberest listen I will tell
What thou forgettest. They in us & we in them alternate Livd
Drinking the joys of Universal Manhood. One dread morn
Listen O vision of Delight One dread morn of goary blood
The manhood was divided for the gentle passions making way
Thro the infinite labyrinths of the heart & thro the nostrils issuing

In odorous stupefaction stood before the Eyes of Man
A female bright. I stood beside my anvil dark a mass
Of iron glowd bright prepard for spades & plowshares. sudden
    down
I sunk with cries of blood issuing downward in the veins
Which now my rivers were become rolling in tubelike forms
Shut up within themselves descending down I sunk along
The goary tide even to the place of seed & there dividing
I was divided in darkness & oblivion thou an infant woe
And I an infant terror in the womb of Enion
My masculine spirit scorning the frail body issud forth
From Enions brain In this deformed form leaving thee there
Till times passd over thee but still my spirit returning hoverd
And formd a Male to be a counterpart to thee O Love
Darkend & Lost In due time issuing forth from Enions womb
Thou & that demon Los wert born Ah jealousy & woe
Ah poor divided dark Urthona now a Spectre wandering
(7.84.5–30 E359)

The Spectre vows to exacerbate that division, seeking revenge against "Los the Slave of that Creation I created" (7.84.31) in vain belief that should he "destroy / That body I created then shall we unite again in bliss" (7.84.34–35). The Spectre remains, at this point in Night the Seventh, a victim of the "Eyes of Man," enslaved not so much to Los as to the "ravening devouring lust" that originates in seeing and being seen, hiding and seeking:

Thou knowest that the Spectre is in Every Man insane brutish
Deformd that I am thus a ravening devouring lust continually
Craving & devouring but my Eyes are always upon thee O lovely
Delusion & I cannot crave for any thing but thee not so
The spectres of the Dead for I am as the Spectre of the Living
For till these terrors planted round the Gates of Eternal life
Are driven away & annihilated we never can repass the Gates
(7.84.36–42 E360)

Blake critics have often found in this statement (and others like it in Blake's subsequent prophetic works) evidence that Blake advocates Los's aversion to the Spectre. Yet if we recall the earliest presentation of the unfallen Urthona in the *Zoas*, labor at the forge of art is inseparable from the propagation of the heirs of Urthona, into which he first mitotically divided, so that their Golgonoozic art may, in turn, bring the ur-father back from the dead, restored to his "beginnings":

> Los was the fourth immortal starry one, & in the Earth
> Of a bright Universe Empery attended day & night
> Days & nights of revolving joy, Urthona was his name
>
> In Eden; in the Auricular Nerves of Human life
> Which is the Earth of Eden, he his Emanations propagated
> Fairies of Albion afterwards Gods of the Heathen, Daughter of
>   Beulah Sing
> His fall into Division & His Resurrection to Unity
> His fall into the Generation of Decay & Death & his Regeneration
>   by the Resurrection from the dead
>
> Begin with Tharmas Parent power. . . .
> (1.3.9–11; 1.4.1–5 E301)

In order to restore that originary power, thereby overcoming the originary division the Spectre has described to Enitharmon, Los must—as the Spectre in the Seventh Night tells him—himself resist the temptation to annihilate the body that is only a symptom of his melancholy. He must heal the body that has estranged the "Auricular" and the generative. Los must love rather than resist, acknowledge rather than "work through," his loss of the predecessor (Urthona) who haunts him now as a Spectre:

> Thou never canst embrace sweet Enitharmon terrible Demon. Till
> Thou art united with thy Spectre Consummating by pains &
>   labours
> That mortal body & by Self annihilation back returning
> To Life Eternal be assurd I am thy real Self
> Tho thus divided from thee & the Slave of Every passion
> Of thy fierce Soul Unbar the Gates of Memory look upon me
> Not as another but as thy real Self I am thy Spectre
> Thou didst subdue me in old times by thy Immortal Strength
> When I was a ravning hungring & thirsting cruel lust & murder
> Tho horrible & Ghastly to thine Eyes tho buried beneath
> The ruins of the Universe. hear what inspird I speak & be silent
>
> If we unite in one[,] another better world will be
> Opend within your heart & loins & wondrous brain

Threefold as it was in Eternity & this the fourth Universe
Will be Renewd by the three & consummated in Mental fires
But if thou dost refuse Another body will be prepared

For me & thou annihilate evaporate & be no more
For thou art but a form & organ of life & of thyself
Art nothing being Created Continually by Mercy & Love divine
(7.95[87] second portion.32–47; 7.86.1–3 E368)

Los heeds the Spectre's words and a new space—or womb—of creative potential is opened by the love between the (male) Spectre and his (male) successor, transforming the emptiness of revenge—"ravning hungring & thirsting cruel lust & murder"—into a space of nurture and regeneration. Los speaks:

> . . . Even I already feel a World within
> Opening its gates & in it all the real substances
> Of which these in the outward World are shadows which pass away
> Come then into my Bosom & in thy shadowy arms bring with thee
> My lovely Enitharmon. I will quell my fury & teach
> Peace to the Soul of dark revenge & repentance to Cruelty
> (7.86.7–12 E368)

While Los embraces both Enitharmon and the Spectre, he cannot be reconciled with Enitharmon until he imitates (or identifies with) her own act of transgression, and of incorporation: "Then Los plucked the fruit & Eat & sat down in Despair / And must have given himself to death Eternal But / Urthonas spectre in part mingling with him comforted him / Being a medium between him & Enitharmon" (7.87.23–6 E369). Before Los ate the fruit, Enitharmon had talked of his sacrifice in terms of hostage exchange, or "ransom": "I knew / That without a ransom I could not be savd from Eternal death / That Life lives upon Death & by devouring appetite / All things subsist on one another thenceforth in Despair / I spend my glowing time" (7.87.16–20). Yet through his act of love, she too learns to love the specters who "devour" them, and through sacrifice of self learns a melancholic labor in which the living, having failed to incorporate the dead, are now the willing hosts (or hostages) of ghosts who carry their wounds from war into the recuperative interiors of the creators who will give them form:[48]

> Los sat in Golgonooza in the Gate of Luban where
> He had erected many porches where branched the Mysterious Tree

Where the Spectrous dead wail & sighing thus he spoke to
   Enitharmon

Lovely delight of Men Enitharmon shady refuge from furious war
Thy bosom translucent is a soft repose for the weeping souls
Of those piteous victims of battle there they sleep in happy obscurity
They feed upon our life we are their victims. Stern desire
I feel to fabricate embodied semblances in which the dead
May live before us in our palaces & in our gardens of labour
Which now opend within the Center we behold spread abroad
To form a world of Sacrifice of brothers & sons & daughters
To comfort Orc in his dire sufferings [;] look [!] my fires enlume
   afresh
Before my face ascending with delight as in ancient times

Enitharmon spread her beaming locks upon the wind & said
O Lovely terrible Los wonder of Eternity O Los my defence & guide
Thy works are all my joy. & in thy fires my soul delights
If mild they burn in just proportion & in secret night
And silence build their day in shadow of soft clouds & dews
Then I can sigh forth on the winds of Golgonooza piteous forms
That vanish again into my bosom but if thou my Los
Wilt in sweet moderated fury. fabricate forms sublime
Such as the piteous spectres may assimilate themselves into
They shall be ransoms for our Souls that we may live

So Enitharmon spoke & Los his hands divine inspired began
To modulate his fires studious the loud roaring flames
He vanquishd with the strength of Art bending their iron points
And drawing them forth delighted upon the winds of Golgonooza
From out the ranks of Urizens war & from the fiery lake
Of Orc bending down as the binder of the Sheaves follows
The reaper in both arms embracing the furious raging flames
Los drew them forth out of the deeps planting his right foot firm
Upon the Iron crag of Urizen thence springing up aloft
Into the heavens of Enitharmon in a mighty circle
(7.98[90].2–34 E370)

In such labor, Los and Enitharmon not only synthesize metallurgy
with biological and aesthetic reproduction (illuminated painting)
but also become, at last, parents worthy to be themselves reproduced: through their offspring's imitation of their good parenting, through their father Tharmas's imitation of their love in his

renewed longing for his wife (their mother), and through their enemy's—Urizen's—imitation of the beloved son that Los "beheld" and thus also "becomes":

> And first he drew a line upon the walls of shining heaven
> And Enitharmon tinctured it with beams of blushing love
> It remaind permanent a lovely form inspird divinely human
> Dividing into just proportions Los unwearied labourd
> The immortal lines upon the heavens till with sighs of love
> Sweet Enitharmon mild Entrancd breathd forth upon the wind
> The spectrous dead Weeping the Spectres viewd the immortal works
> Of Los Assimilating to those forms Embodied & Lovely
> In youth & beauty in the arms of Enitharmon mild reposing
>
> First Rintrah & then Palamabron drawn from out the ranks of war
> In infant innocence reposd on Enitharmons bosom
> Orc was comforted in the deeps his soul revivd in them
> As the Eldest brother is the fathers image So Orc became
> As Los a father to his brethren & he joyd in the dark lake
> Tho bound with chains of Jealousy & in scales of iron & brass
>
> But Los loved them & refused to Sacrifice their infant limbs
> And Enitharmons smiles & tears prevaild over self protection
> They rather chose to meet Eternal death than to destroy
> The offspring of their Care & Pity Urthonas spectre was comforted
> But Tharmas most rejoicd in hope of Enions return
> For he beheld new Female forms born forth upon the air
> . . . .
> Startled was Los he found his Enemy Urizen now
> In his hands. he wonderd that he felt love & not hate
> His whole soul loved him he beheld him an infant
> Lovely breathd from Enitharmon he trembled within himself
> (7.98[90].35–67 E370–71)

The reproductive labors of Los and Enitharmon, however, cannot alone save Urizen. He must himself discover a model for a regenerative art, but he can do so only when the Fallen Man (now the "Eternal Man") in Night the Ninth finally banishes the mournful Work master from his despotism of the heart. The Man, calling out to Urizen "with awful voice," risks becoming in this final night once again both Urizenic ("I will sieze & regulate all my members / In stern severity" [9.120.35–36 E390]) and like Luvah in his rage against the "Schoolmaster of souls":

O Prince of Light where art thou I behold thee not as once
In those Eternal fields in clouds of morning stepping forth
With harps & songs where bright Ahania sang before thy face
And all thy sons & daughters gatherd round my ample table
See you not all this wracking furious confusion
Come forth from slumbers of thy cold abstraction come forth
Arise to Eternal births shake off thy cold repose
Schoolmaster of souls great opposer of change arise
(9.120.14–21 E389)

Urizen, who has by now become the serpent into which his rebellion earlier transformed Urthona, heeds this call from the Man;
he repents, releases the drives of his enemies, and in so doing, frees
his words of the Law's restraint:

. . . O that I had never drank the wine nor eat the bread
Of dark mortality nor cast my view into futurity nor turnd
My back darkning the present clouding with a cloud
And building arches high & cities turrets & towers & domes
Whose smoke destroyd the pleasant gardens & whose running
    Kennels
Chokd the bright rivers burdning with my Ships the angry deep
Thro Chaos seeking for delight & in spaces remote
Seeking the Eternal which is always present to the wise
Seeking for pleasure which unsought falls round the infants path
And on the fleeces of mild flocks who neither care nor labour
But I the labourer of ages whose unwearied hands
Are thus deformd with hardness with the sword & with the spear
And with the Chisel & the mallet I whose labours vast
Order the nations separating family by family
Alone enjoy not I alone in misery supreme
Ungratified give all my joy unto this Luvah & Vala
Then Go O dark futurity I will cast thee forth from these
Heavens of my brain nor will I look upon futurity more
I cast futurity away & turn my back upon that void
Which I have made for lo futurity is in this moment
Let Orc consume let Tharmas rage let dark Urthona give
All strength to Los & Enitharmon & let Los self-cursd
Rend down this fabric as a wall ruind & family extinct
Rage Orc Rage Tharmas Urizen no longer curbs your rage
(9.121.3–26 E390)

Urizen has learned at last a melancholic art that does not discipline but rather disrupts the Law. Invoking it, at first, he summons Ahania to his side, only to kill her with "Excess of Joy" (9.121.35–36). With like excess, his Word now "explodes / All things" in a reversal of Creation that is itself, also, a new beginning: "shaking convulsd the shivering clay breathes / Each speck of dust to the Earths center nestles round & round / In pangs of an Eternal Birth in torment & awe & fear / All spirits deceasd let loose from reptile prisons" (9.122.26–31 E392). In his destructive but also regenerative deployment of the Parent power of language, Urizen practices an art that scatters, upon the dark earth, words that are not only like the spectral dead but that are also, in their turbulent and competitive and futile scattering, like seeds. They are compared to "naked warriors" in battle, to a pastoral father's "wintry flocks," to the food of those flocks—"leaves" "stripd" from "forests." It is a power that harnesses the force of the death drive to the urge to propagate in the very face of death. Because Urizen, like Los and Enitharmon, has learned the generative uses of that power, feasts may follow the Work master's famines in an apocalyptic celebration of creation and its endless revivals. As secret labor becomes a shared product, joy supplants the doleful despotism of the Law's working cure for melancholics. Those who feed upon the dead, ingesting the sacramental host and wine, bring them back:

> Then Urizen commanded & they brought the Seed of Men
> The trembling souls of All the Dead stood before Urizen
> Weak wailing in the troubled air East west & north & south
>
> He turnd the horses loose & laid his Plow in the northern corner
> Of the wide Universal field. then Stepd forth into the immense
>
> Then he began to sow the seed he girded round his loins
> With a bright girdle & his skirt filld with immortal souls
> Howling & Wailing fly the souls from Urizens strong hand
>
> For from the hand of Urizen the myriads fall like stars
> Into their own appointed places driven back by the winds
> The naked warriors rush together down to the sea shores
> They are become like wintry flocks like forests stripd of leaves
> The Kings & Princes of the Earth cry with a feeble cry
> Driven on the unproducing sands & on the hardend rocks
>
> . . . .
> Then follows the golden harrow in the midst of Mental fires
> To ravishing melody of flutes & harps & softest voice

The seed is harrowd in while flames heat the black mould & cause
The human harvest to begin Towards the south first sprang
The myriads & in silent fear they look out from their graves

Then Urizen sits down to rest & all his wearied Sons
Take their repose on beds they drink they sing they view the flames
Of Orc in joy they view the human harvest springing up
A time they give to sweet repose till all the harvest is ripe
(9.124.30–32; 9.125.1–25 E394)

In this renovated pastoral poetry, the banished and feminine other
may be returned to the melancholic Urizen who could not, finally,
surrender his attachment to her. "And Lo like the harvest Moon
Ahania cast off her death clothes" (9.125.26), "And bright Ahania
took her seat by Urizen in songs & joy" (125.35).

Yet not even the arts of death and revival that Urizen, Los, and
Enitharmon now practice are sufficient to bring back the archaic
mother. Rather, it is Vala who, in a narcissistic act that looks back to
Ahania's "watery image," restores Enion, the *Zoas*'s original and
maternal demiurge. Vala, as she "stood in the river & viewd herself
within the watry glass," watches Tharmas as he complains, with
"mournful voice" that the watery "weeds of death" have "wrappd"
him, in her absence, in "the dismal night of Tharmas" (9.129.14; 21–
23). As he sinks into darkness, Vala calls out to Enion; hearing only
an "Eccho of her voice returned" (32), she—unlike Milton's Eve—
persists in recognizing, and recovering, a maternal absence in the
Nature that is her echoing monument. In so doing Vala not only
restores Enion to Tharmas but also regenerates her parents as "two
little children playing" in the "door way" of her own home, an entry
into a space that seems to have given birth to them:

And She arose out of the river & girded on her golden girdle

And now her feet step on the grassy bosom of the ground
Among her flocks & she turnd her eyes toward her pleasant house
And saw in the door way beneath the trees two little children
    playing
She drew near to her house & her flocks followd her footsteps
The Children clung around her knees she embracd them & wept
    over them

Thou little Boy art Tharmas & thou bright Girl Enion
How are ye thus renewd & brought into the Gardens of Vala

She embracd them in tears. till the sun descended the western hills
And then she enterd her bright house leading her mighty children
And when night came the flocks laid round the house beneath the
    trees
She laid the Children on the beds which she saw prepard in the
    house
Then last herself laid down & closd her Eyelids in soft slumbers
    (9.130.1–13 E398–99)

However distant this homely resurrection may seem from the
apocalyptic threshing and winnowing of Urizen, Luvah, and Los, in
fact Blake has prepared us to understand that the poetry of Romantic melancholy recognizes that the humble body itself—the site of
the Law's inscription and of its resistance—reincarnates, in a radically Christian sense, the dead. Even in the "terrible wine presses of
Luvah O caverns of the Grave," the reprobate seed of the Father cry
out "O let us Exist" because "The Pangs of Eternal birth are better
than the Pangs of Eternal Death," of "This dreadful Non Existence"
(9.136.1–15 E404). Even as the sons celebrate the harvest at "the
Golden feast satiated," their counterparts "Enion & Ahania & Vala
& the wife of Dark Urthona / Rose from the feast in joy ascending
to their Golden Looms," preparing for labor, while beyond—or is it
within?—"Nations are gatherd together" in an image that evokes a
final gathering of the hosts (9.137.7–17). For a final consumption, in
which the harvest is consecrated, must consummate the nine nights
of darkness before "The Sun arises" at last, in spring, like a yellow
flower delivered from the "blackness" of melancholia, of winter, and
of the soil that both buries and nurtures.

3

Shelley's Absent Fathers:
"The Awful Shadow of Some Unseen Power"

> While yet a boy I sought for ghosts, and sped
>   Through many a listening chamber, cave and ruin,
>   And starlight wood, with fearful steps pursuing
> Hopes of high talk with the departed dead.
> I called on poisonous names with which our youth is fed;
>   I was not heard—I saw them not—
>   . . . .
>   Sudden, thy shadow fell on me;
> I shrieked, and clasped my hands in ecstasy!
> PERCY BYSSHE SHELLEY, "Hymn to Intellectual Beauty"

> Art mediates . . . between the mutable diversity and division of the human mind on the one hand and the immutable unity of the One Mind, or absolute Existence, on the other . . . shaping diversity into . . . truth, beauty, and goodness.
> EARL WASSERMAN, *Shelley: A Critical Reading*

> In being able to receive the other's words, to assimilate, repeat, and re-produce them, I become like him: one. . . . Through love.
> JULIA KRISTEVA, *Tales of Love*

> If "My Monster, my self" is the slogan of the feminocentric or hysterically-oriented reading of the Gothic, that of the masculocentric or paranoiacally-oriented would have to be, "It takes one to know one." In this latter slogan it is, or is claimed to be, a specifically epistemological project—to know—that motivates the mirroring self-transformation of the male subject.
> EVE KOSOFSKY SEDGWICK, *The Coherence of Gothic Conventions*

A poem is a poet's melancholy at his lack of priority. . . . the poem—unlike
the mind in creation—is a made thing, and as such is an achieved identity.
            HAROLD BLOOM, *The Anxiety of Influence*

No less than a poem, a melancholic poet is a made thing. In the
family romances of a poet, there may be many fathers, dead and
alive, natural and cultural, whose love, tinctured by the ambivalence
of hate, darkens daily the literary ambitions and the personal relationships of the ephebe. As we may learn, especially, from the example of Percy Shelley, a poetic son need not be an actual orphan to
have his life haunted by the shadow of an absent power, a melancholic attachment that one may neither fully surrender nor wholly
surrender *to*. Shelley keenly understood that one cannot re-make
one's self in the image of an admired One that seems to be free of
material attachment without also identifying with the implacable,
hidden, and violent "want" that ghosts the interiors from which
such attachments have been evicted.

   On first acquaintance, Shelley would seem to be the model not
for death-driven, inoedipal melancholy but, rather, for healthy (if
precocious) Oedipal mourning. He broke early and irreparably
with a philistine father, sought in culture and language respected
fathers of the mind with whom to identify, developed a clear sense
of his own special identity and even his mission—through language—within that culture, made (ostensibly) conventional sexual
object choices, and (last but by no means least) wrote "Adonais,"
one of the major nineteenth-century poems in a genre—the elegy—
that is supposed to demonstrate a poet's surpassing of antisocial,
regressive, and indolent melancholia through his successful transformation of sorrow into hardworking, public mourning. Shelley
precociously scorned familial love, abandoning first his parents and
then a wife in pursuit of Intellectual Beauty, or Love.

   In fact, however, it was during a melancholic crisis in 1815 that
Shelley came to recognize that mutability and mortality belie the
polished, reflective, and self-reflexive surface of the One's imaginary
eternity. With insufficient space to discuss fully the achievement of
the poems Shelley wrote after *Alastor* and "Mont Blanc" (notably
Prometheus Unbound and "The Triumph of Life," in which Shelley
harvests the fruits of his crisis in 1815), this chapter will focus on
Shelley's passage, in *Alastor* and "Mont Blanc," from the narcissistic
(and Alastor-like) pursuit of imaginary identification with an ideal
other to a recognition of the ambivalence that haunts such intellec-

tual ardor.[1] Through his keen antipathy toward—and desire *for*—
the various father figures he substituted for his own, weak father,
Shelley came to intuit the nearly invincible ideology of an "unseen
power" that derives from, even as it brings into being, in both senses
"want."

If we compare the quotations that open this chapter, we may see
how the mirroring operations by which "oneness" underpins identification in fact structures the versions of the imaginary denoted by
Earl Wasserman's unsurpassed representation of Shelley and neo-
Platonism, the poetics of influence theorized by Harold Bloom, and
the poststructuralist reconstructions of the embodied imagination
offered, in their different ways, by Eve Sedgwick and Julia Kristeva.
That ideal finds its most compelling expression in the image of a
child and an adult who are constructed by, drawn to, and (nevertheless) separated from each other in a mirroring gaze of loving identity, an image of ocular oneness in which the child is eager to
become like the adult other whom the child (erroneously) presumes
to know everything and to lack nothing.[2] In order to achieve identity with such a figure—which is itself prerequisite to learning a
language in which there must be a subject ("I") that addresses
objects—the prelinguistic son must identify, first, with an adult who
is already (allegedly) a self-contained "one," and, subsequently, with
an absent or distant Father ("One") through whose Law the son
may indeed become that independent entity known as "one," that
is, a subject. To paraphrase Sedgwick's jocular use of the aphorism,
it takes One to know one's self *as* "one."

Yet as Shelley came to know, "the awful shadow of some unseen
power" inevitably introduces into that apparently unblocked passage of identity and transferential love the unexpected sensations of
alienation and repulsion. Between the rapt, metaphorical flight of
the poet and the Intellectual Beauty toward which he soars in pursuit of a mirroring "grace" that is "Dearer, and yet dearer for its
mystery" lies a monstrous and unrecognizable chaos, the uncanny
image and origin of the "dark slavery" that Intellectual Beauty is
supposed to (but cannot) mollify.[3] Beauty (or "loveliness") is itself
whelped by the same, uncanny parent as awful-ness:

(6)

I vowed that I would dedicate my powers
To thee and thine—have I not kept the vow?
With beating heart and streaming eyes, even now

I call the phantoms of a thousand hours
Each from his voiceless grave: they have in visioned bowers
    Of studious zeal or love's delight
    Outwatched with me the envious night—
They know that never joy illumed my brow
    Unlinked with hope that thou wouldst free
    This world from its dark slavery,
    That thou—O awful LOVELINESS,
Wouldst give whate'er these words cannot express.
("Hymn to Intellectual Beauty")[4]

The intellectual roots of Shelley's yearning for a sublime beauty, truth, and love that would complete the soul's unexpressed—and, indeed, inexpressible—inadequacies can be traced to the early years of the Christian millennia. Julia Kristeva argues in *Tales of Love* that neo-Platonism conceived of a spiritual imaginary in order to counter two, more dangerous modes of identification: the dizzying emptiness that lurked beneath Narcissus's self-love, and the fear and pain—associated long before Freud with mortality and mutability—that tincture adult Eros with loss even in its most winged, ecstatic moments of apparent fulfillment.[5] Freud's own models for a psychic health that would substitute shared, progressive cultural ideals for "regressive," death-driven desires in the incestuous family evolved as the psychoanalyst explored the troubled, ambivalent love/hatred of the self that lay at the heart of melancholia and the neuroses associated with failed or "abnormal" identification and transference. The unexpressed fear provoked by the alleged "regression" of narcissism for both the philosopher and the psychoanalyst may be expressed, oversimply, in the following paradox: neither dispassionate reason nor the will to resist the death drive can ever, finally, govern the self so long as the self (the ego) is constructed narcissistically and melancholically through its identification with the moral Law of an absent Father. For his love not only may be missing—indeed, it may metamorphose into desire and/or even hatred.[6] Love for an "Other," whether that love springs from the soul's transferential belief in the neo-Platonic One, from a secular son's effort to enter into the linguistic competence that "subjects" him via (and to) the Law of the Father, or from an analysand's faith in the Freudian analyst, cannot be evacuated of its opposite in these models without endangering—and exposing—the unconscious structures on which they are founded and reproduced. While the Law of the Father may ask its subjects to believe that it is founded *not* on irrational belief but, rather, on the transcendental principles of reason and dispassion that reproduce themselves through the identity of disembodied minds, this Law succeeds, in the last resort, by installing *through* the performative power of transferential love its own dark and irrational violence at the center of the unknowingly violated self.[7]

Shelley, having failed to rid himself fully of his need for some kind of father, came face to face with the unspeakable (and unspeaking) presence of what Slavoj Žižek calls the sublime Real (which Thomas Weiskel defines more narrowly, but still perceptively, as the sublime).[8] This absent, voiceless One, the other and obscene face of Intellectual Beauty, would be memorialized by Shelley in his monuments to the failures (and to the fissures) that sustain an archaic tyranny within the very structures of enlightened Law.[9] In Shelley's most powerful poems, he confronts the unconscious, ambivalent, and melancholic absences on which culture and language are erected and through which poets and sons are made. When Shelley as a poet becomes most "traumatized"—"I shrieked, and clasped my hands in ecstasy"—he is enacting a sublime, ecstatic, and narcissistic union not only with the beauty, intellect, and perfection of the One but also with its "want." Yet even when he transferentially *mis*recognizes in the blank face of the Law the ideal image that he relentlessly pursues, Shelley on some level also understands that, in so "wanting," he is in fact most keenly recognizing—and identifying with—the source of its power. Troubled by the contradictory emotions that the Law aroused in his own psyche, Shelley would come to realize that to be made in the image of one's Maker is to internalize lustful hatred as well as selfless love, to experience both fulfillment in an Other that seems self-sufficient and to internalize, melancholically, the Other's—the One's—actual lack, an aggrieved hunger and an outraged insufficiency that no identificatory act of creation can finally satisfy.[10]

The "made thing" called a poem is, as Bloom claims, indeed an idealized mirror image (an "achieved identity") of its creator.[11] Yet the "made thing" may also bear the visage of an alien image that the creator, and the reader, may protest (in misrecognition) is "not I." A "made thing" that emerges through the invisible processes of the inspired imagination always contains something more than was intended, a "something more" that makes the poet feel fearful and estranged in the presence of the cherished and even fetishized poem. This made thing may in fact mimic the transferential experience of ideological interpellation, the "call" of the Other that produces subjectivity. In such mimicry, the poem talks back to its maker in a sibylline (if not barbarous) tongue, or, to use an image closer to Shelley's preoccupation with the ocular, it returns the eyeless gaze, the condensed codes, of a sphinx. A poem "possesses," in both senses, its maker. So, in a sense, does a subject created by the Law *create* that Law. To "make" is not only to create (and, in turn, to *be* created) but also to "force" and to *be* forced, a lesson in reciprocity for both creators and creatures in transference, identity, love, and violence. That is a lesson, finally, that extends hope as well as fear to the Shelleyan poet who openly battles political tyranny, for if the Law itself is subject to "want," its authority is neither eternal nor absolute.

Shelley, the poet who addresses in "Hymn to Intellectual Beauty" a power that is absent—"Why dost thou pass away, and leave our state, / . . . vacant and desolate"—may discover that the poem he has created simply echoes or reflects the terms of a futile quest for a revolutionary "presence" sufficient to challenge a deceptively "absent" tyranny. "Beauty" responds with a compelling silence to this interrogation. Beauty (an expelled, abstract ideal as vacant as its synonyms: "Demon, Ghost and Heaven") paradoxically can be "made" only in its abiding absence; it can be made to speak only in a silence that is more telling than words. It can inspire worship—manifested as the imitative creation of an aesthetically beautiful object, this poem—only through an awe that is *founded* on that condition of unknowable vacancy, and the corresponding fear that coexists with love's reflection when Beauty is (almost) present as the invisible screen of identity in "lovers' eyes":

(4)

Love, Hope, and Self-esteem, like clouds, depart
And come, for some uncertain moments lent.
Man were immortal and omnipotent,
Didst thou, unknown and awful as thou art,
Keep with thy glorious train firm state within his heart.
Thou messenger of sympathies
That wax and wane in lovers' eyes—
Thou—that to human thought art nourishment,
Like darkness to a dying flame!
Depart not as thy shadow came,

Depart not—lest the grave should be,
Like life and fear, a dark reality.

"Hymn to Intellectual Beauty" closes with an appeal to Beauty to bestow a perhaps immortal "power" upon one for whom Beauty's "spells did bind / To fear himself, and love all humankind."[12] But love and beauty are frail, indeed, in relation to the violence of a "dark reality" that they have succeeded neither in illuminating nor in effacing. Fear, despite the poet's best efforts, triumphs over love: the "messenger of sympathies" apparently cannot deliver love without also bearing anxiety.

Persecution, Paranoia, and the Godwinian Family Romance

Shelley as a troubled adolescent became an atheist and an advocate for political revolution in order to shock and even to injure the figures of authority who had disappointed him, a punitive motive that was exacerbated by Shelley's loss of Harriet Grove and his misguided belief that he had lost her because of his espousal of atheism. At Oxford he had found an ally against the church and its conventions, and a fellow enthusiast for "love," in Thomas Jefferson Hogg, to whom he wrote the following passage on God, Christianity, desperate love, and personal revenge. It begins with the skeptic's impersonal remoteness that characterizes even Shelley's most personal letters but shifts toward an exploration of Shelley's own, personal need for love (a love whose objects are divine as well as human) and his corresponding fear of death. It ends with the uncontrolled fury that so often erupts unexpectedly in Shelley's statements on political philosophy:[13]

Before we doubt or believe the existence of any thing it is necessary that we should have a *tolerably* clear idea of what it is—the word "God" has been [and] will continue to be the source of numberless errors until it is erased from the nomenclature of Philosophy.—it does not imply "the Soul of the Universe the intelligent & *necessarily* beneficent actuating principle"—This *I* believe in; I may not be able to adduce proofs, but I think that the leaf of a tree, the meanest insect on wh. we trample are in themselves arguments more conclusive than any which can be adduced that some vast intellect animates Infinity—If we disbelieve *this,* the strongest argument in support of the existence of a future state instantly becomes annihilated. . . . Love, love *infinite in extent,* eternal in duration, yet (allowing your theory in that point) perfectible should be the reward; but can we suppose that this reward will arise spontaneously as a necessary appendage to our nature, or that our nature itself could be without a cause, a First Cause, a God,—when do we see effects arise without some causes, what causes are there without correspondent effects?—Yet here I swear, and as I break my oath may Infinity Eternity blast me, here I swear that never will I forgive Christianity! it is the only point on which I allow myself to encourage revenge; every moment shall be devoted to my object which I can spare, & let me hope that it will not be a blow which spends itself & leaves the wretch at rest but lasting long revenge! I am convinced too that it is of great disservice to society that it encourages prejudice which strikes at the root of the dearest the tenderest of its ties. Oh how I wish I *were* the Antichrist, that it were *mine* to crush the Demon, to hurl him to his native Hell never to rise again—I expect to gratify some of this insatiable feeling in Poetry. You shall see, you shall hear.—but it has injured me, she [Harriet Grove] is no longer mine, she abhors me as a Deist, as what *she* was before. Oh! Christianity when I pardon this last this severest of thy persecutions may God (if there be a God), blast me! (January 3, 1811)

Reacting against the church's conception of the Father, but also against his father, Timothy Shelley, who could not help him win Harriet's love, could not save him from his consequent expulsion from Oxford, and could not support his demonstrably precocious intellectual development, Shelley increasingly found alternative support for his quasi-atheism in a second father, William Godwin, who believed that an "effect"—progressive human perfectibility (the resistance to irrational tyranny)—may be achieved not through the soul's communion with a loving "First Cause" but through (in his absence) his dispassionate Law, a Law that should govern the self through a disciplined and self-sufficient reason. In a letter Shelley wrote during the early period of his impoverished exile from his family (just after his expulsion) in 1811, addressed to fellow Godwinian and soulmate, Elizabeth Hitchener, he claimed that his personal persecution was merely a manifestation of his society's use of sanctioned terror through its religious institutions:[14]

Poor liberty, even the religionists who cry so much for thee, use thy name but as a mask, that they also may seize the torch, & shew their gratitude by burning their deliverer. *I* should dou[bt] the existence of a God, who if he cann[ot] command our reverence by *Love, surely* can have no demand upon it from Virtue on the score of ter[ror]—It is this empire of terror which is established by Religion, Monarchy is its prototype, Aristocracy may be regarded as symbolising with [*sic*] its very essence. They are mixed—one can now scarce be distinguished from the other, & equality in politics like perfection in morality appears now far removed from even the visionary anticipations of what is called the wildest theorist. *I* then am wilder than the wildest. (July 25, 1811)

Six months later, Shelley boldly wrote to Godwin himself, thereby opening a "free communication of intellect" with the mind he idolized almost too much to approach. While Shelley stiffly imitates Godwin's own latinate, self-rationalizing manner, the effulgence of this fan letter is barely suppressed:

You will be surprised at hearing from a stranger.—No introduction has, nor in all probability ever will authorize that which common thinkers would call a liberty; it is however a liberty which altho' not sanctioned by custom is so far from being reprobated by reason, that the dearest interests of mankind imperiously demand that a certain etiquette of fashion should no longer keep "man at a distance from man" and impose its flimsy fancies between the free communication of intellect. The name of Godwin has been used to excite in me feelings of reverence and admiration, I have been accustomed to consider him a luminary too dazzling for the darkness which surrounds him, and from the earliest period of my knowledge of his principles I have ardently desired to share on the footing of intimacy that intellect which I have delighted to contemplate in its emanations.— Considering then these feelings you will not be surprised at the inconceiv- able emotions with which I learned your existence and your dwelling. I had enrolled your name on the list of the honorable dead. I had felt regret that the glory of your being had passed from this earth of ours.—It is not so—you still live, and I firmly believe are still planning the welfare of humankind.

Having established that his initial relationship with Godwin had been that of a living son for a dead (however revered) father, Shelley represents his own relationship to "humankind" as that of a serious and even messianic adolescent, who, in claiming identity with God- win's "persecutions," aggrandizes his own:

I have but just entered on the scene of human operations, yet my feelings and my reasonings correspond with what yours were.—My course has been short but eventful. I have seen much of human prejudice, suffered much from human persecution; yet I see no reason hence inferable which should alter my wishes for their renovation. The ill-treatment I have met with has more than ever impressed the truth of my principles on my judgment. I am young—I am ardent in the cause of philanthropy and truth. . . . you have gone before me, I doubt not are a veteran to me in the years of persecution. (January 3, 1812)

Shelley's urge to befriend and to learn from this distant, adored, and persecuted father figure closely parallels the central relationship in the book by Godwin that, in many ways, most influenced Shelley: *Caleb Williams.*[15] An orphan who believes his aristocratic employer Mr. Falkland to be a model of erudition, Caleb nevertheless intuits that the powerful, mysterious, and melancholic Falkland has something to hide that he cannot altogether hide, a "something extra" that manifests itself in the silences of his speech and in the visible features of a visage he cannot altogether control. That mysterious, absent presence will, inevitably, make Caleb as melancholic, and as criminal, as the paranoid and hysterical ideal that he, in every sense, pursues:[16]

Mr. Falkland's situation was like that of a fish that plays with the bait employed to entrap him. By my manner he was in a certain degree encouraged to lay aside his usual reserve and relax his stateliness; till some abrupt observation or interrogatory stung him into recollection, and brought back his alarm. Still it was evident that he bore about him a secret wound. Whenever the cause of his sorrows was touched, though in a manner the most indirect and remote, his countenance altered, his distemper returned, and it was with difficulty that he could suppress his emotions, sometimes conquering himself with painful effort, and sometimes bursting into a sort of paroxysm of insanity, and hastening to bury himself in solitude. . . .

. . . Though I was curious, it must not be supposed that I had the object of my enquiry for ever in my mind, or that my questions and innuendoes were perpetually regulated with the cunning of a grey-headed inquisitor. The secret wound of Mr. Falkland's mind was much more uniformly present to his recollection than to mine. (114–15)

Like Caleb, Shelley seemed to have an almost seductive way of provoking moral failure (of opening "secret wounds") in any paternal figure whom he admired. During the course of his short life, Shelley would choose and abandon not one but a succession of ideal fathers, both because he shamed them by rapidly surpassing their achievements and because, inspired by Godwin's *Political Justice,* Shelley drew to his troubled, cathectic spirit not just fathers but entire families whom he would love and then expose, alternative communities based on Godwinian freethinking and free love that

Shelley could not sustain. His early failure to turn the dreams of his most admired, adopted father into a living reality would lead repeatedly to the personal sufferings of those he came to abhor, even while he claimed, still, to love them.

It might have seemed that Shelley had found at last the ideal family that his actual parents and his first wife had failed (in his mind) to provide when he attached himself to William Godwin and his daughter, Mary. In fact, however, Godwin could not serve personally as the intellectually consistent, ideal father and friend that the philosopher (in print) had been; Shelley, in turn, failed the older man by eloping with not one but two of his daughters in July 1814. Their break with Godwin engendered in both Percy and Mary the literary independence and productivity of their annus mirabilis, a year that began in the summer of 1816 with *Frankenstein,* "Hymn to Intellectual Beauty," and "Mont Blanc" and ended in 1817 with their final summer in England, where Mary completed *Frankenstein* while Percy wrote *Laon and Cythna* and gathered materials for a winter's tale of a melancholic idealist and a beloved teacher, *Prince Athanese.* Yet their different responses to a mutual tyrant could not keep the Shelleys from turning, in turn, upon each other. The Shelleys' own early and subsequent disappointments with their relationship, which were sharpened by the death of their son William in 1819, eventually would lead the two writers to produce disturbingly similar works on incest and violence— *The Cenci* and *Mathilda*— even as Percy recovered from (and Mary succumbed to) merely the latest in a long series of family disasters. Slowly, the Shelleys would come to realize that no family or community, however carefully and rationally chosen, could resist a despotic Law that not only invades but *requires* sites within the heart and hearth for its success.

An orphan almost from the day of her birth, Mary Wollstonecraft Godwin Shelley would identify from an early age with both of her distinguished, intellectual, and literary parents.[17] As Godwin's star fell, Mary left his home, turning her admiring gaze to his substitute (or, one might say, his interloper), Percy Shelley, a poet of whose future celebrity Mary was convinced. Shelley, in turn, would call Mary the moon in whose gaze he found the truth of his own identity. Perhaps the most arresting image in *Frankenstein,* that of a ghastly yellow eye staring back at its stricken creator, is a monstrous interpretation of such melancholic identification, an image that Percy himself borrowed originally not only from Milton's "orb within orbs" of angels identifying with the gaze the Father exchanges with the embosomed son, but also from such gothic tales of paranoid pursuit as *Caleb Williams.* It was an image that Percy used frequently and throughout his works: a pair of eyes seeking another in love or in fear, eyes that express the fulfillment or failure of a young man's search for an ideal Maker who will reflect for him an ideal image.

This image of the *process* of imaging is the modest occasion for one of Shelley's earliest poems, "Eyes: A Fragment,"[18] written in 1810, one year before his conversion to atheism and his expulsion from Oxford:

> How eloquent are eyes!
> Not the rapt poet's frenzied lay
> When the soul's wildest feelings stray
> Can speak so well as they.
> How eloquent are eyes!
> Not music's most impassioned note
> On which love's warmest fervors float
> Like them bids rapture rise.
>
> Love, look thus again,—
> That your look may light a waste of years,
> Darting the beam that conquers cares
> Through the cold shower of tears.
> Love, look thus again!

Fixed gazes are no less central in the gothic novel that Shelley published in the same year, *Zastrozzi,* where virtually every element in the plot unfolds for the reader through the cliché of the characters' meaningful (or, to use a word Shelley appropriates there, "un-meaningful") looks: "A pause ensued, during which the eyes of Zastrozzi and Matilda spoke volumes to each guilty soul."[19] In Shelley's juvenilia, as in his more accomplished works, rarely do optical pursuits end favorably for the morbid, depressive personae Shelley creates. At best, these gazing eyes will become, as in *Prometheus Unbound,* "orbs within orbs" of female pupils that foresee and procure redemption for humanity, or they will become, like those of the violet in the succeeding lines, identical with their object: "As a violet's gentle eye / Gazes on the azure sky, / Until its hue grows like what it beholds."[20] At worst such orbs will reflect, as in the subsequent lines of that verse, only emptiness—"As a gray and empty mist / Lies like solid amethyst / Over the western mountain it enfolds"—or, as in *Zastrozzi,* the terror of an infinite regression of images or of an apparently motiveless, paranoid surveillance and pursuit.[21]

Whether such gazes of loving identity and transference return an ideal image, sheer emptiness, or terror, the fascinated gaze of paranoia, as we may learn from Eve Kosofsky Sedgwick, has reason to be as paradigmatic of the writings of Percy as of Mary Shelley, for it is as central to the Age of Romanticism as to the "Age of Frankenstein":

The fate of the family in *Frankenstein* and throughout the paranoid Gothic represents the pared-down nuclear tableau that is seen as embodying primal human essence or originary truth: the tableau of two men chasing one another across a landscape. It is importantly undecidable in this tableau, as in many others like it in Gothic novels, whether the two men represent two consciousnesses or only one; and it is importantly undecidable whether their bond—in the first place, as in *Melmoth* ancestral—is murderous or amorous. I would argue out from the first of these central indecisions that the entire, many-pronged Romantic and nineteenth-century philosophical project of embodiment that centered on the question of solipsism, the question of the very existence of other minds, took its deepest impetus from the crystallization of this paranoid, i.e. specifically homophobic, tableau; surely one could call the nineteenth century, philosophically as well as technologically, the Age of Frankenstein. . . .

. . . The problem here is not simply that paranoia is a form of love, for—in a certain language—what is not? The problem is rather that, of all forms of love, paranoia is the most ascetic, *the love that demands least from its object:* the one . . . that not only bends with the remover to remove but then takes "removal" as its blazon.[22]

The paranoia that Sedgwick elaborates in this quotation and in the quotation opening this chapter is no more or less striking than the father-son (male-male) relationship in the literary family romance established for early-nineteenth-century poets by Harold Bloom or, for that matter, than that of the father and son in the "normal" family that Freud delineates from private life in nineteenth-century bourgeois Vienna. As we may learn from *Caleb Williams,* the love between an almost-adult, aspiring son and a father figure with whom he both competes and seeks to identify can indeed become, in the fearful silence of that unnameable love ("with 'removal' as its blazon"), transformed into a mutually accusatory chase across a wasteland opened by the loss of trust. To call Bloom's "strong" poet engaged in a negative quest across such a landscape "a marvelously articulate, fully paranoid construction"[23] is to understate the Frankensteinian (if not Wagnerian) dimension that Sedgwick helps us to perceive in Bloom's fictions of the haunted, poetic self and its misprisioned fathers.

Identification and the investments of belief that characterize transference, explicitly or implicitly, have been central to scholarly studies of Shelley for several decades. "Transference," as I have already suggested, defines the impulse to seek identity and love in an ideal other and/or Other that motivated Shelley's interest in Platonic and neo-Platonic idealism, an interest well documented and, I would argue, ultimately overstated by Wasserman, who nevertheless remains Shelley's most penetrating modern reader.[24] Bloom, author of the single essay that most astutely locates, appreciates, and contextualizes Shelley's multiple interests ("The Unpastured Sea: An Introduction to Shelley"),[25] claims to sharply distance his own readings from those that argue Shelley's rapt identity with the One, yet Bloom nevertheless defines Shelley as a poet best characterized by "vision" (375). More recently, Shelleyan transference has been defined in Jerrold E. Hogle's theoretically thorough *Shelley's Process: Radical Transference and the Development of His Major Works* as so general a linguistic and social phenomenon—one synonymous with the deconstructionist's injunction against the recovery of origins that inspire desire—as to virtually lose its original force as a charged relationship between the hungering soul (or analysand) and the luminary source (or analyst).[26] "Identification," in Barbara Gelpi's *Shelley's Goddess: Maternity, Language, Subjectivity,* is restricted to her consideration of Shelley's development within (and his understanding of) this mirroring process in the prelinguistic relation to the maternal breast.[27] What is missing from these accounts of the power of loving transference and identification in Shelley's poetry is the commensurable power of transferential *terror,* a power that Shelley, like the Satan whom he defends, came intimately to understand through their identification with objects they feared as well as desired. Laura Claridge in *Romantic Potency: The Paradox of Desire* effectively names that terror as Shelley's recognition of "the male, patriarchal tradition that asserted claims upon him."[28] His awareness of, and rebellion from, that tradition led Shelley to "trumpet," she continues, "his flight from an alienating Law" (129). Claridge concludes that Shelley resisted the "inescapable Name-of-the-Father who desecrated forever the primal place of silence the poet would inhabit" so that as a poet he could, in an ineluctable and

Oedipal reenactment of the terms of patriarchy, "lay claim to be-coming himself the signifier par excellence" (128). In fact, however, what appear to be competing fathers and sons, makers and made things, in contests for linguistic and phallic mastery in Shelley's life and art prove to be subjects and objects that reconstruct each other in relationship to "want."

Alastor: From Imaginary to Symbolic Identification

Whether Shelley pursued an ideal other in a father figure or an ideal Other in some version of idealism, he consistently found that such pursuits left him, literally and palpably, with "nothing."[29] His *Alastor* (1815) portrays vividly a young poet all too familiar with the emptiness that can haunt a youth's ardent pursuit of an ideal, whether it is a mentor, a friend, a lover, or a system of belief (as the poet himself implies, *any* ideal inevitably involves most of these figures). A visionary who believes himself divided from the loving and knowing gaze that could offer direction, the poem's melan-cholic hero does not (like Narcissus) drown in the rivers that he follows and into which he so often peers but, rather, fades into the nothingness that turns out to be the very object of his pursuit. The Poet of *Alastor* seeks the origins of Creation and instead discovers, when his search ends at the birthplace of time, that the absent Creator who awaits him has arranged not for the Poet's rebirth but, rather, for his death.

By 1815 Wordsworth had become for Shelley a loss as powerful as Beauty's absence in the "Hymn": "thou leavest me to grieve / Thus having been, that thou shouldst cease to be" ("To Wordsworth"). Godwin remained an intellectual light for Shelley, even when the poet had clearly superseded his intellectual father's wattage, but Godwin's influence had been diminished by the conventional mo-rality of his outrage that Shelley had entered into an unwedded relationship with Mary and by the unabashed greed that led God-win to pester Shelley for money, even when he refused to extend friendship to the poet. But Shelley in 1815 was, like the visionary in *Alastor,* intellectually adrift for reasons beyond these tarnished fa-ther figures. He had learned firsthand in the Lake District and in Wales how little even Wordsworth and Godwin understood the daily sufferings and political needs of farmers, miners, and other members of the class we now call the working poor. Further, caught between the demands of his estranged wife and his responsibilities for Mary, Shelley could not avoid facing the failure of his efforts to form relationships and families on Godwinian principles—although he did not, it is important to recognize, come to blame such principles for these failures. He had entered his relationship with Mary with the confidence that she, unlike Harriet, would be a more successful student of *his* interpretations of her father's teachings. Yet their gaze of mutual love and instruction was fractured from the first by Godwin's "want"—his needy, inevitable presence (and Shelley's paranoid *attraction* to that presence: in his first months with Mary he reread *Caleb Williams*). Moreover, there was another, equally troubling third party: Godwin's daughter by marriage, Claire Claremont. Although Percy lived more or less in comfortable solitude with Mary in the late spring that followed her miscarriage in February 1815, he became during that period, to use his own words, a "living sepulchre of himself."[30] In the words of Richard Holmes, Shelley, from the beginning of his time alone with Mary, "was assailed by a curious sense of detachment and vacancy, as if suddenly he had seen through life and all it had to offer" (287). "Ghosts, dreams, pursuit, the difficulty of stable human relationships, and the terror and destruction implicit in the solitary 'settled fate' were to be the broad terms within which Shelley worked for the rest of the year" (290).

Depending on one's emphases, Shelley's disappointment with the family romances that had driven him until that year could focus on any one of the alleged fissures in these transferential relationships, all of which became increasingly pronounced during the poet's first full year with Mary: his father's continued stubbornness; Godwin's greed; Wordsworth's decline; Mary's so-called frigidity; Harriet's so-called demands; Hogg's cooperative seduction of Mary. Yet as Shelley himself now recognized, none of the subjects to whom he had addressed his transferential ardor could possibly have supplied all that he thought he needed in order to transform both himself and the world. Indeed, the transference that failed most absolutely in 1815 was Shelley's shattered belief in his own, higher calling, an identity founded on the self-exile and self-reliance of his atheism and elaborated through years of continuous identification with the most celebrated minds of European culture. Shelley confronted, painfully, the limits generally not only of any effort, however well intentioned, to improve one's self through transference and identification but also of any rational, Godwinian effort to perfect human nature. He learned these lessons most powerfully through two relationships that changed in 1815. The bullying paternal grandfather for whom he was named died in early January. During that same period Mary's lunar luminosity was refracted by a comet, Claire, the emotional, easily terrorized "other" of the self-controlled and reasonable Mary.

Claire was officially banished from the home Percy shared with Mary in the spring. A few months later, in *Alastor* Shelley became both child and father to Wordsworth. The young poet, mourning Claire's absence as he had mourned the diminished figure of Wordsworth, would at last come to terms with the hidden, seductive violence of identification and transference when an actual death occurred.

Shelley as a child would intimidate his own father by threatening to repeat, over and over, the words "Bysshe, Bysshe, Bysshe,"[31] the grandfather's name that in itself terrified his father and that, according to Holmes, also reminded Timothy that "Bysshe" was Percy's own name, his "own blunder, his own damnation." Now the elderly bearer of that name had become "nothing"; his grandson and namesake would, through melancholic identification, for a period in 1815, follow suit. Yet the presence of the grandfather persisted in his grandson's own bullying. Shelley learned early in the household *à trois* that had characterized from the beginning his elopement with Mary that, as much as he needed Mary's fond return of his idealism in their mutual, transferential relationship, he needed as well the subliminal stimulation provided by his late-night ghost-story sessions with Claire. An intimacy initiated and elaborated while Mary slept, Shelley's pleasure at frightening Claire probably climaxed, his biographers assume, in some sort of sexual comfort. If Sir Bysshe represented for Shelley the now-dead figure of paternal terror, then Shelley "became" Bysshe's ghost in his relationship with Claire—that is, until he nightly terminated that terror with tenderness.[32] Sir Bysshe and Claire revived for Shelley the gothic qualities in his imagination that had never lain altogether dormant, qualities that persisted, ambivalently, in his imagination with love.

Shelley in this period of crisis, confronting the inner vacancy left by the despotic grandfather's unexpected death and his *own* despotic, insupportable pleasure in arousing Claire's seductive fear—however eager he was to paternally offer loving comfort—appears to have entered into a new and more intimate understanding of the faceless and pervasive tyranny that he had been publicly battling in his politics and his poems for half a decade. Power reproduces itself, he discovered, in the intimacy of the apparently normal, tolerant, two-parent home. It operates not through open claims to absolute authority or through the use of ugly violence but, rather, through its creation of subjects (such as Shelley) who *believe* they are free to choose virtue, beauty, and reason (by identifying with virtuous, beautiful, and reasonable human beings). To perceive, as Shelley now perceived, designs on (and a desire *of*) one's self at the center of the gaze returned by one's ideal other/Other is to recognize within that ocular tableau (as Shelley now recognized) the reflection of an alien power. He came to understand that identification is not simply a transaction between two fixed pairs of eyes, for a third gaze is also watching, invisibly, from beyond the stage on which that imaginary identification transpires. *That* gaze is an occluded part of one's self, the Other, the Law of the Father, that has become internalized as a superegoistical, inner tyrant who judges, punishes, and takes pleasure in identifying with *all* of the various players who are loving, enjoying, and suffering in this illuminated, imaginary theater. Shelley, in reaching this new level of awareness, moved at last from what Žižek calls "imaginary identification," where he truly believed that all he needed was a single, perfect image in which to perfect himself, to "symbolic identification," in which he could look *at* himself as a range of selves who operate from within the enclosure of the group fantasy structured by an absent Real and by the reign of the Symbolic Order.[33] More specifically, Shelley, through his melancholic internalization of the dead Sir Bysshe and through his identification with that dead object in his relationship with Claire, came to perceive within himself not only the qualities of a masochistic savior but also those of a tyrannical sadist.

Shelley does not explicitly address poems to either Sir Bysshe or Claire during that year of profound dejection; indeed, there are few poems or letters that transparently represent any of the household events of 1815. Yet in the poem "To—" ("Oh, there are spirits of the air"),[34] he suggests the relative magnitude of his various disappointments, from Wordsworth and Coleridge (whose "commune" with nature's "ministers" Shelley could no longer believe in or mimic) to Mary ("The glory of the moon is dead") to Claire ("Night's ghosts and dreams have now departed") to his "own soul" that is "true" but only to the fiend—Sir Bysshe—that Shelley now recognizes therein:

To—

Oh! there are spirits of the air,
  And genii of the evening breeze,
And gentle ghosts, with eyes as fair
  As star-beams among twilight trees:—
Such lovely ministers to meet
Oft has thou turned from men thy lonely feet.

. . . .

And thou has sought in starry eyes
  Beams that were never meant for thine,
Another's wealth:—tame sacrifice
  To a fond faith! still dost thou pine?
Still dost thou hope that greeting hands,
Voice, looks, or lips, may answer thy demands?

. . . .

Yes, all the faithless smiles are fled
  Whose falsehood left thee broken-hearted;
The glory of the moon is dead;
  Night's ghosts and dreams have now departed;
Thine own soul still is true to thee,
But changed to a foul fiend through misery.

This fiend, whose ghastly presence ever
  Beside thee like thy shadow hangs,
Dream not to chase;—the mad endeavor
  Would scourge thee to severer pangs.
Be as thou art. Thy settled fate,
Dark as it is, all change would aggravate.

In the nightmare existence evoked by this poem, there is *only* absence with which to identify. "Be as thou art," however, is not the "dark" and resigned advice to himself that Shelley, as a poet, chose to follow. *Alastor,* contrary to most readings, is a poem that refutes not only such settled belief in an ultimate and unifying identification with one's "true" self (however beautiful or loathsome that innermost soul may prove to be) but also any kind of belief in the transcendental, transferential aspirations to identify with the One: at the end of his paranoid pursuit, the visionary of *Alastor* finds neither himself nor an ideal reflection of himself. In an empty (rather than narcissistic) reflection that closes the poem, evacuated of any image and any ideal, he discovers the want that fissures the everyday reality of the Symbolic Order, the Law that desperately seeks to efface all traces of its originary and violent loss of a Father who, himself, "wants." If the Miltonic, transferential, orb-within-orb gaze of a son and a father figure crosses (and ignores) the dark and threatening void that lies between them, *Alastor,* on one level, displaces that uninhabitable, sublime, or uncanny wilderness by shifting it *within* the imaginary tableau, which makes nothingness an object of pursuit, a displacement that disrupts the father-son transference, identification, and reassurance of mutual union. The "daemon of solitude" for which the poem is named materializes that emptiness as a Lacanian imaginary object (*objet petit a*): a "something in it more than itself," to use Žižek's terms, a demonic haunting of the Real, "an objectification of a void, of a discontinuity opened in reality" (97).

More than a poem of failed identification within the narcissistic space of the orb-within-orb imaginary, however, *Alastor* is, finally, a representation of the poetic subject (the visionary Poet) as a performer within a maker's (the nature-poet narrator's) *fantasy* of a visionary whose pursuit of an ideal turns out to be a pursuit of an infinitely receding darkness, or absence. The poem, in other words, itself *performs* what has before been a more or less stationary image for Shelley: identification as the infinite regress of an "orb within orb." The Poet, like the poem, is a "made object," created in the image and in the *imagination* of an other, an older (and different) poet (Wordsworth), but also in the image of an Other, that is, of a tradition, a culture's philosophical and literary ideals. As we learn from Shelley's introduction to the poem, through transference and identification the visionary Poet initially moves from philosophy to the so-called natural world (where love purportedly may seek a "real"—presumably heterosexual—object) into fantasy, where an ideal "Being"—a "prototype"—may be imagined who will return not only ideal love but also an ideal image for the self that "thirsts" not only for sexual union but also for knowledge:

The poem entitled "ALASTOR," may be considered as allegorical of one of the most interesting situations of the human mind. It represents a youth of uncorrupted feelings and adventurous genius led forth by an imagination inflamed and purified through familiarity with all that is excellent and majestic, to the contemplation of the universe. He drinks deep of the fountains of knowledge, and is still insatiate. The magnificence and beauty of the external world sinks profoundly into the frame of his conceptions, and affords to their modifications a variety not to be exhausted. So long as it is possible for his desires to point towards objects thus infinite and unmeasured, he is joyous, and tranquil, and self-possessed. But the period arrives when these objects cease to suffice. His mind is at length suddenly awakened and thirsts for intercourse with an intelligence similar to itself. He images to himself the Being whom he loves.

Shelley, by staging his own autobiographical development, anxieties, and failed dreams within the theater of an older poet's (the narrator's) imagination, attempts several goals simultaneously. First, and most obviously, he takes Wordsworth's Immortality Ode seriously: the child becomes the father of the man, the ephebe turns his maker into a made object, renewing the father-poet's faltering idealism. In *Alastor*, Wordsworth is given the role of a paternal figure (the narrator), who expresses what seems at first to be tender concern for the younger Poet's hopes and disappointments, even if he cannot finally (and this is crucial) help him to succeed. Shelley, by performing—through the transferential and symbolic act of writing a poem—as *both* father and son, poet and poetic subject, can watch from beyond, as well as participate in, the scene of fantasy where he has staged the self-destructive, infinite regress of the Poet's narcissistic gazing, a reflection that finally ends in the dark center of an eye that is empty—the moon's "inwoven darkness" whose "minutest ray" is finally "quenched"—and that therefore, arguably, reflects at last the Real, a gap in the representational regress of reflecting gazes:

> When on the threshold of the green recess
> The wanderer's footsteps fell, he knew that death
> Was on him. Yet a little, ere it fled,
> Did he resign his high and holy soul
> To images of the majestic past,
> That paused within his passive being now . . .
> . . . .
> . . . Hope and despair,
> The torturers, slept; no mortal pain or fear
> Marred his repose, the influxes of sense,
> And his own being unalloyed by pain,
> Yet feebler and more feeble, calmly fed
> The stream of thought, till he lay breathing there
> At peace, and faintly smiling:—his last sight
> Was the great moon, which o'er the western line

Of the wide world her mighty horn suspended,
With whose dun beams inwoven darkness seemed
To mingle. Now upon the jagged hills
It rests, and still as the divided frame
Of the vast meteor sunk, the Poet's blood,
That ever beat in mystic sympathy
With nature's ebb and flow, grew feebler still:
And when two lessening points of light alone
Gleamed through the darkness, the alternate gasp
Of his faint respiration scarce did stir
The stagnate night:—till the minutest ray
Was quenched, the pulse yet lingered in his heart.
It paused—it fluttered. But when heaven remained
Utterly black, the murky shades involved
An image, silent, cold, and motionless,
As their own voiceless earth and vacant air.
(lines 625–30, 639–62)

Through the Wordsworthian narrator, Shelley moves ineluctably from "tenderness" toward the young visionary to what can only be called pleasure in the ephebe's suffering. Only when the ocular, lunar radiance dims may "Hope and despair, the torturers" sleep. Wordsworth's disturbing presence in *Alastor* has become a commonplace of Shelley criticism, usually to the disadvantage of the older poet, deemed excessively "dependent" on Nature and insufficiently respectful of the transferential One.[35] What makes Shelley's "performance" of the Wordsworthian narrator so embarrassing to critics who, in turn, feel called on to defend Shelley *as* the Poet is that Shelley, in *Alastor,* stages poetic influence not as a meeting of souls, or a training of minds, or even as a paranoid, misprisioning relationship between Oedipal son and father, but rather as what Freud calls the sadomasochistic scene of fantasy, where the stage director-maker turns around his sadistic pleasure in an other's suffering into an identification with the sufferer that takes pleasure in suffering.[36] What is missing from such a scene, where one pleasure props on another—an absence that can be much more frightening than anything that visibly happens to the suffering victim within that tableau—is an unexplainable surplus or remainder of pleasure that the powerful, *invisible* father/maker who is "Shelley" (a Shelley identifying with a Wordsworthian narrator) seems to take in *desiring* as well as torturing his "made object" *as* himself. In *Alastor*

Shelley exposes the operation of a "love for love itself" that is not (as Hogle defines it) merely the infinite regress of a receding origin, or absence, but is in fact the originator's obscene and violent interest in the made object. That pleasure, that design on one's creation, violates the decorum of art, of pedagogy, of parenting, and of the Law, yet all of these domains succeed precisely to the extent that beauty and terror are the tools of an ideology excluded (like the creator) from the reality it constructs. This disturbing surplus, or "something extra," will remain in Shelley's accomplished poems (as we will see in "Mont Blanc"), but in them Shelley will have learned how to efface its traces, both veiling and revealing (as in "Hymn to Intellectual Beauty") an unseen, *obscene* power that transforms the "beautiful" into a superegoistical "sublime."[37]

Shelley, in the poems he wrote after his near-drowning that summer in Diodati, in fact continued to gain perspective on the danger—and, nevertheless, the inevitability—of encountering death (like Narcissus) in reflection, particularly when there may be no Providence, or God, to rescue the visionary from the monstrous absence he sees reflected as an infinity in the Other's gaze.[38] In "Mont Blanc," Shelley will so resolutely come to terms with that absence that he will be able to annihilate, in six extraordinary lines, his wavering belief that one *could* find, in the shared identifications of luminous souls and of brilliant minds, an Enlightenment alternative (Law) to the persistence of an authority that is "the secret strength of things" in "governed" "thought":

> . . . The secret strength of things
> Which governs thought, and to the infinite dome
> Of heaven is as a law, inhabits thee!
> And what were thou, and earth, and stars, and sea,
> If to the human mind's imaginings
> Silence and solitude were vacancy?

What if, in other words, there were neither a human mind filled with images nor a natural world filled with things comparable to those images but, rather, two vacant frames of fantasy, reflecting, infinitely, each other's incommensurable, unreadable vacancies through the screen of the Other?[39] In "Mont Blanc" Shelley encounters what Žižek has defined as "radical evil," an "Evil which, as to its form, *coincides with the Good.*"[40] The mountain's "secret strength" is the tyranny of a superego, an obscene Other, that governs thought *and* heaven through a law that is in every sense a sublime vacancy, for it is constituted by our own. An infinite regress of two absences gazing into one another's abysses, transference, as Shelley discovers in his encounter with the "want" that lies behind the sublime object of Mont Blanc, is finally an encounter with a One that is in fact a nothing, a Creator that despoils its creatures, an Other that (like Žižek's portrayal of the Freudian analyst as represented by Lacan) deprives the subject of the very being that it claimed to be able to bestow.[41]

From the beginning of the poem, the process of reflection is by turns "glittering" and melancholic, "gloomy." This exchange between things and self does not clarify or enlighten but rather, literally, clouds the question it raises: is the "everlasting universe of things" or is "mind" the origin reflected in this dynamic exchange? From where *do* the "secret springs" of "human thought" originate, and is the power that demands, like a caesar, from that thought a "tribute" in fact that very source? And if the sound of the tribute bearer is "but half its own," then does the remaining half that it echoes (or identifies with) belong to an Other that is itself divided?[42]

> The everlasting universe of things
> Flows through the mind, and rolls its rapid waves,
> Now dark—now glittering—now reflecting gloom—
> Now lending splendour, where from secret springs
> The source of human thought its tribute brings
> Of waters,—with a sound but half its own.
> Such as a feeble brook will oft assume
> In the wild woods, among the mountains lone,
> Where waterfalls around it leap for ever,
> Where woods and winds contend, and a vast river
> Over its rocks ceaselessly bursts and raves.
> (st. 1)

In this landscape, at once both entirely human (a solipsistic mind reflecting the world) and entirely alien (a nature that is inhuman precisely to the extent that it is inimitably "everlasting," and "ceaseless"), already the reader feels deprived of a place in which to stand and look. In this sense, the reader is no different from the "things" of this landscape, which will simply tumble through and leave the poem's—the mind's—echoing chamber as empty as it began.

The entrance of a place name in the next stanza—"Ravine of Arve"—does not make this frame, as we might expect, more habitable, for it proves to be yet another empty space, despite its many colors, voices, and "homes." A chasm that designates an absent river, the Arve remains inaccessibly frozen into a mere "likeness" of a "Power" that remains commensurately invisible (on "his secret throne"). To the now-frozen breasts of this archaic mother ancient children still cling; indeed, in this place all natural processes, and even all art (like "some unsculptured image") remain suspended. Likewise hypnotized—"in a trance sublime and strange"—by repetitive sound and dizzying stasis, the poet turns inward and finds, in the corresponding abyss of "my own separate phantasy," "some phantom." While the mind "passively" receives *and* renders "the clear universe of things," it also apprehends "shadows," "Ghosts of all things that are," thereby confounding reality and fantasy. The cave of Poesy has become Plato's cave of benighted fantasists:

> . . . the strange sleep
> Which when the voices of the desart fail
> Wraps all in its own deep eternity;—
> Thy caverns echoing to the Arve's commotion,
> A loud, lone sound no other sound can tame;
> Thou art pervaded with that ceaseless motion,
> Thou art the path of that unresting sound—
> Dizzy Ravine! and when I gaze on thee
> I seem as in a trance sublime and strange
> To muse on my own separate phantasy,
> My own, my human mind, which passively
> Now renders and receives fast influencings,
> Holding an unremitting interchange
> With the clear universe of things around;
> One legion of wild thoughts, whose wandering wings
> Now float above thy darkness, and now rest
> Where that or thou art no unbidden guest,
> In the still cave of the witch Poesy,
> Seeking among the shadows that pass by
> Ghosts of all things that are, some shade of thee,
> Some phantom, some faint image; till the breast
> From which they fled recalls them, thou art there!
> (2.27–48)

If the very emptiness of the ravine is, knowably, "*there,*" then the "I" would remain by definition in the elsewhere of "*here.*" The very effort to seek correspondence, transference, or identification at the same time should establish a separateness that would reassure the speaker of his own being ("thou art there," so "I am here"). Yet in fact that effort to establish both identity and distance has already failed. Even as this self ("my own"), this "human mind," "renders" and "receives," it does so in a "phantasy" of "separateness" that begins not in natural "influencings" (suggesting a clear distinction between inside and outside, subject and object) but rather in a trance that begins in a sublime encounter with the very *vide* of a "Dizzy Ravine" that both separates and swallows the emptied self into the yawning, beckoning want of the Other. Orphaned from what seem to be endlessly receding origins in the infinite regress of this sublime exchange, the spirit "fails," "Driven like a homeless cloud from steep to steep / That vanishes among the viewless gales!" (3.57–59). Yet Power's "secret throne," far from receding, persists in the very "vanishing" of this orphaned subjectivity. In Žižek's terms, "the Other's, the dead ancestor's dream" (*Tarrying with the Negative,* 117) survives, in this sublime and transferential encounter, as the ideological delusion that a subject *could* possess a "separate phantasy" within "My own, my human mind," a mind whose independence, whose very being, is only a fantasy (an *objet petit a*) that occludes the sublime nothingness from an "elder time" (line 21) upon which it is—dizzyingly—gazing. "Ghosts of all things" in this Platonic cave of shadows "*are,*" they acquire being through the performative power of prosopopoeia, including the phantom that the poet seeks and encounters ("thou art there!") as the sublime gap—the ravenous Ravine—to which this single-sentence stanza is addressed.

Just at this moment, when the unreality within approaches the unreality without, when the ravine of the self is mirrored by the ravine upon which it gazes and to which it is drawn, "Mont Blanc appears,—still, snowy, and serene," halting the infinite regress of this reflection on (and of) nothingness (3.61). An *objet petit a* that corresponds to the illusion of "my own separate phantasy," Mont Blanc is a powerful and cathectic center in a dissolving tableau that has to this point induced a dissolving subjectivity. A sublime object of desire, by its very presence Mont Blanc establishes subjects who are in turn subject to that object's power precisely to the extent that they seek, transferentially, to have that object's "presence," that is, a presumed innerness or subjectivity. In fact, that object has neither. Almost immediately, the falsely reassured poet realizes that he has emerged as a subject only to discover that he exists alone in a ruined kingdom, one long ago evacuated by an unspecified (or unspeakable) disaster, and that he has been dazzled by an object no longer majestic but hideous in its flagrant survival of what might be construed as its own misused power, hysterical in its frozen (and therefore objectlike) silence:

> A desart peopled by the storms alone,
> Save when the eagle brings some hunter's bone,
> And the wolf tracks her there—how hideously
> Its shapes are heaped around! rude, bare, and high,
> Ghastly, and scarred, and riven.—Is this the scene
> Where the old Earthquake-daemon taught her young
> Ruin? Were these their toys? or did a sea
> Of fire, envelope once this silent snow?
> None can reply—all seems eternal now.
> (3.67–75)

The poet begs this unreplying edifice to employ its "mysterious tongue" to utter clear alternatives—"doubt" or "faith"—or even to "repeal / Large codes of fraud and woe." Yet it only, obdurately, endures like Ozymandias its eternity of ruination, memorializing yet silencing its origins:

> The wilderness has a mysterious tongue
> Which teaches awful doubt, or faith so mild,
> So solemn, so serene, that man may be
> But for such faith with nature reconciled,
> Thou hast a voice, great Mountain, to repeal
> Large codes of fraud and woe; not understood
> By all, but which the wise, and great, and good
> Interpret, or make felt, or deeply feel.
> (3.76–83)

Imitating (but misrecognizing) the Wordsworthian poet who would hear in this wilderness, this landscape deserted by God, nevertheless a "voice" that calls to him in the language of a fraudulent, humanizing Christianity of "mild faith," Shelley next turns with transferential conviction in (and continued misrecognition of) Wordsworthian nature, describing a landscape that consists of "all the living things that dwell / Within the daedal earth," even (or especially) those natural processes that awaken violently "The torpor of the year" (4.85–86, 88). Yet death is smuggled into this pastoral catalog of living things. Coexisting with "hidden buds" and "leaf and flower" are "The works and ways of man, their death and birth / And that of him and all that his may be" (89–90, 92–93). Man, he implies, cannot identify with nature as it manifests its power in the sublime eternity of Mont Blanc because human beings, like all living things in nature, "Are born and die; revolve, subside and swell" (95):

> Power dwells apart in its tranquility
> Remote, serene, and inaccessible:
> And *this,* the naked countenance of earth,
> On which I gaze, even these primaeval mountains
> Teach the adverting mind.
> (4.96–100)

Yet, what may the human observer learn from those objects in nature that, unlike Mont Blanc, appear to be living? Only that they, too, seek nevertheless to identify with death, that is, with Mont Blanc's "apartness" as the power of a Wordsworthian reflection that returns, in the moment of "deeply feeling" in "tranquility," a transferential force so rooted in death that it cannot be overthrown and—more terrifyingly—cannot be resisted:

> . . . The glaciers creep
> Like snakes that watch their prey, from their far fountains,
> Slow rolling on; there, many a precipice,
> Frost and the Sun in scorn of mortal power
> Have piled: dome, pyramid, and pinnacle,
> A city of death, distinct with many a tower
> And wall impregnable of beaming ice.
> (4.100–106)

Such seductive power leads Shelley to speculate that it may lay waste its own progeny, despoil its own resources, and still—and *therefore*—live on in its dream of death and authority, a dream that is, to the contemporary reader, terrifyingly close to the decayed technological, postapocalyptic landscapes of our nightmares:

> Yet not a city, but a flood of ruin
> Is there, that from the boundaries of the sky
> Rolls its perpetual stream; vast pines are strewing
> Its destined path, or in the mangled soil
> Branchless and shattered stand: the rocks, drawn down
> From yon remotest waste, have overthrown

The limits of the dead and living world,
Never to be reclaimed. The dwelling-place
Of insects, beasts, and birds, becomes its spoil;
Their food and their retreat for ever gone,
So much of life and joy is lost. The race
Of man, flies far in dread; his work and dwelling
Vanish, like smoke before the tempest's stream,
And their place is not known. . . .
(4.107–20)

From the waste-place, the empty fantasy of Mont Blanc with whose desolation the poet has begun to identify, whatever "place" where daily human life continues is, literally, unknowable. Quotidian life continues only because its place is itself a fantasy, one that stands in for the death-haunted Real—the violence, the jouissance, and the nothingness—that is Mont Blanc.

"Mont Blanc yet gleams on high:—the power is there." In this poem, which refuses the consolation of human identification and divine transference, finally such power cannot be taken on by, or taken into, the human mind *except* as a recognition that power dwells where the known (or recognizable) self is not. And so the sublime object of this poem remains *blanc*, a blank, white space in what should be an imagination replete with its associations with the things of the external world. There is finally no consolation for Shelley (as there is for Byron) in "peopling" this void, or (as we will discover there is for Wordsworth) in the voices and audible silences that echo across a vast, unpeopled fosterage in the wilderness that is most familiar when it is manifested in the blank desertion of an abyss. There is not even Blake's certainty that the ancestral specter can be co-opted as a partner in a creation that resists the Law. Whatever are the origins of the tyranny in the mind that finds its reflection in the incomprehensible "natural" object that is Mont Blanc, neither the parricide's urge to reform nor the idealist's pursuit of Love, Shelley concludes, can overturn a transferential, uncon-scious misrecognition of authority or make that blankness disap-pear as a symptom of something extra and inexpressible in our-selves. For if Mont Blanc were *not* there, Shelley asks in the most terrifying lines of all, would not the human mind created in (or that creates *itself* in) its image make this made object/Maker all over again, installing yet once more at the very center of its being "want"? Shelley, keen in his understanding of the negativity of authority, perceives that the utter absence of such a Maker, an apocalyptic of death of the Law that now stands in the place of the evicted Father, would be more devastating, even, than the haunting of the murdered, avenging, not-yet-dead ancestor in Mont Blanc's paranoid, hysterical, and melancholic sublimity. Only the Law's "want" leaves open the possibility that ideology is itself mortal and, therefore, is neither boundless nor invincible, yet that want is precisely the source of its transferential seduction, its ability to endlessly reproduce subjects in its own image. Only a poet who feels homeless in nature, one who has come to terms with the living death of a Father, with the loss of the moon who had once been his lover to "inwoven darkness," and with the paternal tyranny that persisted, unreasonably, within his orphaned imagination, could have written the closing lines of this most melancholic of all Romantic poems:

> Mont Blanc yet gleams on high:—the power is there,
> The still and solemn power of many sights,
> And many sounds, and much of life and death.
> In the calm darkness of the moonless nights,
> In the lone glare of day, the snows descend
> Upon that Mountain; none beholds them there,
> Nor when the flakes burn in the sinking sun,
> Or the star-beams dart through them:—Winds contend
> Silently there, and heap the snow with breath
> Rapid and strong, but silently! Its home
> The voiceless lightning in these solitudes
> Keeps innocently, and like vapour broods
> Over the snow. The secret strength of things
> Which governs thought, and to the infinite dome
> Of heaven is as a law, inhabits thee!
> And what were thou, and earth, and stars, and sea,
> If to the human mind's imaginings
> Silence and solitude were vacancy?

4

Depression and Vocation in the 1805 *Prelude:*

"The Homeless Voice of Waters"

> A deep and gloomy breathing-place, through which
> Mounted the roar of waters, torrents, streams
> Innumerable, roaring with one voice.
> The universal spectacle throughout
> Was shaped for admiration and delight,
> Grand in itself alone, but in that breach
> Through which the homeless voice of waters rose,
> That dark deep thoroughfare, had Nature lodged
> The soul, the imagination of the whole.
> WILLIAM WORDSWORTH, 1805 *Prelude,* book 13

> Writing was in its origin the voice of an absent person; and the dwelling-house was a substitute for the mother's womb, the first lodging, for which in all likelihood man still longs, and in which he was safe and felt at ease.
> SIGMUND FREUD, *Civilization and Its Discontents*

Nature's obdurate expressiveness in *The Prelude* depends upon lacunae that denote both loss and persistence. In her gloomy breaches, Wordsworth found a model for the vocation of the poet, one that exploits its melancholy by following rivers backward and downward to their silent sources as well as forward and upward to the mouth into which rivers and poems flow. Inviting the young poet to witness an imagination that nourishes and repairs itself by feeding on the infinity that lies hidden within her mute vacancies and vexed passageways, Nature in *The Prelude* is neither a maternal imaginary to be transcended nor a source only of material sustenance to be exploited. But neither is Wordsworth's Nature—like Shelley's Ravine of Arve or Mont Blanc—an emblem of the "want" that both fissures and facilitates the paternal tyranny of the Law. Rather, in *The Prelude* Nature possesses an intelligence, and a power, that, like the rivers, breezes, and tempests through which it speaks, refuses to respect the boundaries put in place by an eye that has forgotten its origins at the breast, in the father's house, and in the landscape. Now banished to a domain that lies beyond the eye and the reason it ratifies—tools for establishing both the transcendence and the prison house of the "human"—Nature in *The Prelude,* even in exile, calls out to its orphans through winds and waters, elements that vex the human words that would silence its speech. Co-opting and disrupting signification—that habitual, invisible, and inaudible medium of the Law of the Father and our daily depressiveness— Nature's reluctant metaphors, its blocked passages, when they refuse to bear meaning in fact may recover (even if to immediately re-cover) the dead. Nature in *The Prelude,* confounding the treacherous terrains that may be trespassed by human feet with those that thwart translation, teaches its foster son to find Nature where it, on Mount Snowdon, finds its own being: in visual spectacles of breath and fluency that are at once natural, supernatural, and, in a transformed sense, human.

Wordsworth, who lost by the age of thirteen both parents and (for a while) one sister, did not easily surrender any of the few objects of his anxious devotion. Yet he might not have sufficiently valued the hoardings of the hiding places revealed when Nature disrupts human systems of symbolic exchange had he not already come to appreciate, as a wanderer, the emotions encrypted when words cannot be exchanged, when they do not pass through the linguistic impediments of travel. Clearly this was the case in France and later, with Dorothy, in Germany. In a letter to Josiah Wedgwood in February 1799, just a few months after Wordsworth had begun composing the *Prelude,* the poet wrote from Goslar: "Our progress in the language has been very, very far short of what it would have been, had we been richer. . . . I mean by learning the language not merely the knowing that 'Liebe' is German for 'love,' and 'darum' for 'therefore' &c but the having your mind in such a state that the several German idioms and phrases without any act of thought or consideration shall immediately excite feelings analogous to those which are excited in the breasts of the natives. Unless our minds *are* in this state, what we call knowledge of language is a wretched self-delusion; words are a mere dead letter in the mind."[1] Wordsworth speaks from experience: during his long stay in France, he had indeed learned intimately what the words "love" and "therefore" mean (illegitimate fatherhood), and he had also learned the "therefore" (the consequences) of losing, yet again, a family. Yet equally foreign, and no less troubling, to Wordsworth were "dead letters," whether they were dissociative or rematerialized manifestations of a suddenly occluded signification. In urban settings, even where strangers spoke in his tongue, failures of legibility became for Wordsworth spectacles as full of wonder as a page of words before a child just learning letters but seeking the magic of a tale: a typesetter from a foreign land carries a "frame of images" upon his head, an actor wears a sign that declares he is "invisible," a blind man bears a message that he himself cannot read. Often in *The Prelude*, when Wordsworth explicitly states that he has been depressed, he experiences forestalled (or even prohibited) passages from one place, or one stage, to the next. Such encounters conclude in recovered delight or even "health," but they also end in the fecund reburial of the recently uncovered meaning, for it is associated with the repossession of an object, or a home, that had been lost.

In one such treasure-laden passage, the Cave of Yordas in book 8, "spectres" serve as retroactive emblems for the "spectacle" of slipping signifiers. The passage begins as a simile, just after the poet recalls experiencing "a weight" upon his "heart." In this simile the eye, adjusting itself to the skull-like enclosure and aperture of a cave, soon ignores the mysterious beauty and terror that line this visual passageway. The gaze is fixed on the scene that lies beyond: "The scene before him lies in perfect view / Exposed, and lifeless as a written book" (726–27). Such gazing concludes, however, not in lifelessness but rather in an encounter with infinity, "A spectacle to which there is no end" (741). As the poet passes from simile back to the urban memory that was its occasion, he finds himself facing a "burial-place" that is also a home: "That great emporium, chronicle at once / And burial-place of passions, and their home/Imperial" (749–51).[2]

In a different city, Wordsworth in Paris encountered "all the accidents of life" "pressed" into the daily work of terror (10.325–26). At night he dreamed of "despair / And tyranny, and implements of death" (374–75). Still far from fluent in French, he found the events themselves difficult to assimilate into consciousness, a "volume whose contents he knows / Are memorable but from him locked up, / Being written in a tongue he cannot read" (50–52). Wordsworth remembers this period as "lamentable . . . for man," but most "woeful" for those who, like the poet, still "had trust in man" (356, 358–60):

> Most melancholy at that time, O friend,
> Were my day-thoughts, my dreams were miserable;
>
> . . . .
>
> Such ghastly visions had I of despair,
> And tyranny, and implements of death,
> And long orations which in dreams I pleaded
> Before unjust tribunals, with a voice
> Labouring, a brain confounded, and a sense
> Of treachery and desertion in the place
> The holiest that I knew of—my own soul.
> (10.368–69, 374–80)

In such places of "desertion," encountered within or beyond the self, Wordsworth came to hear his vocation as a poet as a "voice" "labouring," often in futility, on behalf of whatever life might be imperiled. He discovered, in turn, that the dead themselves may speak from places that seem empty but that are in fact replete with repressed emotion. "O, blank confusion, and a type not false" (7.696), Wordsworth says in explanation of the imagination that productively imitates, even in populous places, a desertion of the human and of meaning, even as it co-opts the forms of communication: "type."

Yet no less troubling are his encounters with the soul's desertion in the wilderness. Meaning deserts the poet in London and Paris because he had sought, consciously and deludedly, to uncover truth by demystifying its origins. As a consequence, reason reduces all of experience to "one identity" (704). In the deserted landscapes of Snowdon and Simplon Pass, the poet may seem to experience a more exalted encounter with universal Truth, whether it is the unified and unifying Imagination of Nature that he discovers on Snowdon or, in Simplon Pass, the "workings of one mind, the features / Of the same face" (6.568–69). But what is in fact revealed to the poet through Nature's apocalyptic language (literally, the uncovering of what has been hidden) is neither truth nor transcendence but, rather, a vision of the origins of selfhood *in* "desertion, a separation that leads to a burial." Having first encountered on his journey across the Alps only "dejection" (a "melancholy slackening"), at last he makes a journey downward, along a road that is also the "stony channel of the stream," where he encounters Imagination as "an unfathered vapour," the very image of the poet who had been "lost" (because he had lost his father) but who now has "re-covered" in "infinitude" a "home" (527–39). In this "access of joy / Which hides" its sources "like the overflowing Nile" (6.547–48), Nature's mouth is a river that nourishes through alluvial flooding; such accidents (unlike those "pressed / Into one service" of death in Paris) hide even as they replenish their origins. Nature's sources not only originate and sustain life but, through their symbols, make sense of it. "Characters of the great apocalypse, / The types and symbols of eternity" (570–71), Nature's language gives to the "un-fathered" poet a mate for his own first pleasure in words, in his first foster home in language, at the traumatic opening where, psychoan-alytically and figuratively speaking, his father and mother first dis-appeared: the mouth. In that more intimate place of desertion, no less than in cities and on mountaintops, Nature persists as "an under-thirst," "never utterly asleep" (6.489–90) and never without resources to slake the poet's thirst for sources lost, and found, within the lacunae of the self.

One might say of the productive melancholia into which Words-worth converted the depressive features of his denials that he was creatively "cryptophoric." A term coined by Nicolas Abraham and Maria Torok to describe Freud's Wolf-Man, a brother who (like Wordsworth) refused to surrender his sister, the cryptophore "swal-lows" in order both to banish *and* to preserve the object he must surrender if he is to put words in its place, an act that leads to an "inexpressible mourning" through which the melancholic "erects a secret tomb inside the subject,"[3] that is to say, inside himself. "The words that cannot be uttered, the scenes that cannot be recalled, the tears that cannot be shed—everything will be swallowed along with the trauma that led to the loss." In so doing, the incorporative melancholic serves to "annul" figurative language in a process that Abraham and Torok call "antimetaphorical."[4] Wordsworth, who in crises of depression both lost and recovered his "calling" as a poet, heard, through Nature's voices, what he called a "ghostly language" through which he—unlike the cryptophoric Wolf-Man—could ar-ticulate publicly as well as hoard in a secret tongue, both recover and re-cover, an original home and a source of nurture that he, in so doing, "embodied" in "the mystery of words," providing "a mansion like their proper home" (5.621, 624). Radically revising the psycho-analytic processes not only of introjection but also of identifica-tion—the means by which the melancholic (and Oedipal) son works through mourning toward health by separating from the dead and identifying with the substitute "fathers" of language and of culture— Wordsworth feeds upon even as he identifies with Nature. In doing so his mind, like Nature's, remains an incorporative, permeable, and unbounded consciousness, one whose access to the unconscious enables it to preserve, where "darkness makes abode" (5.622) all of the objects that have themselves "preserved" him "still a poet."

It is to Dorothy, of course, that Wordsworth gives most credit for that preservation at a critical moment in his career, acknowledging that she gave back to him Nature's lost authority. While poetry alone could not reunite the poet with Nature, much less restore to life his mother and father, Wordsworth would have recognized in the daily, physical presence of Dorothy the persistence of his parents, discovering in her own face some semblance of theirs and hearing, through her voice, echoes from the past and from the grave.[5] Dorothy and William were brought together in 1787 for the first long period since their mother's death; significantly, their reunion (as it is recounted in bk. 6 of the *Prelude*) followed the poet's experience in college of a melancholy that was in many ways simply modish ("from humours of the blood / In part, and partly taken up, that loved / A pensive sky . . ." [192–94]). Yet Dorothy's restoration was still restorative, her brother recalls, a "grace" rendered "of heaven and inborn tenderness" (189). When in 1795 she and William were reunited, it was at the very moment when he, having abandoned in France a lover and an illegitimate child, having been thrown by England's war with revolutionary France "out of the pale of love" for his native country (10.760), and having "labour[ed] to cut off my heart / From all the sources of her former strength" (11.77–78), at last found reason itself failing before the philosophical tasks it had set for itself.

Entering what he later called "the crisis of that strong disease" (1850, 11.306), Wordsworth attributed his mental illness to a willful suspicion of received truths and his overly eager suspension of sonship in "the great family"—the family romance of sages, heroes, and poets—of "the past":

> Shall I avow that I had hope to see
> (I mean that future times would surely see)
> The man to come parted as by a gulph
> From him who had been?—that I could no more
> Trust the elevation which had made me one

With the great family that here and there
Is scattered through the abyss of ages past,
Sage, patriot, lover, hero; for it seemed
That their best virtues were not free from taint
Of something false and weak, which could not stand
The open eye of reason. Then I said,
"Go to the poets, they will speak to thee
More perfectly of purer creatures—yet
If reason be nobility in man,
Can ought be more ignoble than the man
Whom they describe, would fasten if they may
Upon our love by sympathies of truth?"
(1805, 11.57–73)

The melancholic despair that Wordsworth describes in books 10 and 11 of the 1805 Prelude took hold when he substituted for Nature, in which he was still "glorying," Reason's "glorious" "delight" in its own "self-knowledge and self-rule." Through "Reason," Wordsworth, following the rational principles of William Godwin, had hoped to "shake off" "The accidents of nature, time, and place, / That make up the weak being of the past, / Build social freedom on its only basis; / The freedom of the individual mind" (10.819–25).[6] While Nature continued to provide the poet with both "love as much as heretofore" and, indeed, a "secret happiness," it also possessed an equal power—through "accident" but also through time's passage—to deprive him of human love:

> . . . in Nature still
> Glorying, I found a counterpoise in her,
> Which, when the spirit of evil was at height,
> Maintained for me a secret happiness.
> Her I resorted to, and loved so much
> I seemed to love as much as heretofore—
> And yet this passion, fervent as it was,
> Had suffered change; how could there fail to be
> Some change, if merely hence, that years of life
> Were going on, and with them loss or gain
> Inevitable, sure alternative?
> (11.31–41)

When Wordsworth sought to articulate just how reason, in seeking to sever the self from its attachments (or, perhaps, to justify such

severance), had provoked despair,[7] he implicitly compared his reasonings to those of the laboratory scientist or, perhaps, to the melancholic and transgressive Democritus of Burton's *Anatomy of Melancholy*. He

> . . . took the knife in hand,
> And, stopping not at parts less sensitive,
> Endeavoured with my best of skill to probe
> The living body of society
> Even to the heart. I pushed without remorse
> My speculations forward, yea, set foot
> On Nature's holiest places.
> (5.872–77)

As Wordsworth acknowledges in retrospect, depressive reason,
when it most seeks to estrange itself from the "depravations" of
"passion" that it judges and scorns, in fact makes itself, perversely,
not only a tool for the acquisition of knowledge but also, in fact, a
narcissistic object of congratulation and desire, a fetishistic object
that supplants the shrines of Nature it has eagerly demoted or even
despoiled:

> This was the time when, all things tending fast
> To depravation, the philosophy
> That promised to abstract the hopes of man
> Out of his feelings, to be fixed thenceforth
> For ever in a purer element,
> Found ready welcome. Tempting region that
> For zeal to enter and refresh herself,
> Where passions had the privilege to work,
> And never hear the sound of their own names—
> . . . .
> Pleased with extremes, and not the least with that
> Which makes the human reason's naked self
> The object of its fervour. What delight!—
> How glorious!—in self-knowledge and self-rule
> To look through all the frailties of the world,
> And, with a resolute mastery shaking off
> The accidents of nature, time, and place,
> That make up the weak being of the past,
> Build social freedom on its only basis:
> The freedom of the individual mind,

Which, to the blind restraint of general laws
Superior, magisterially adopts
One guide—the light of circumstances, flashed
Upon an independent intellect.
(10.805–29)

In 1795, when melancholia followed such self-deluding demysti-
fication, Dorothy, in Wordsworth's words, "preserved me still / A
poet, made me seek beneath that name / My office upon earth," a
recovery that succeeded even as the "glory" of Napoleon became,
for the now-disenchanted revolutionary, "a gewgaw" (10.910–40).[8]
While these scenes from the past that she helps him recover painfully reenact the "accidental" incidents that he had hoped through
reason to control, they nevertheless return to him the dead. Dorothy led her brother back, in short, from his search for the universal
laws that allegedly govern human reason (and human communities) to what he terms Nature's alternative laws, those that "lie /
Beyond the reach of human will or power" (11.98). But in order to
recover for Wordsworth the spiritual authority of "Nature's secret
places," Dorothy had to help her brother turn from the "idolatry" of
reason's hardworking disavowals, its sham disenchantments:

Thus strangely did I war against myself;
A bigot to a new idolatry,
Did like a monk who hath forsworn the world
Zealously labour to cut off my heart
From all the sources of her former strength;
And, as by simple waving of a wand,
The wizard instantaneously dissolves
Palace or grove, even so did I unsoul
As readily by syllogistic words
(Some charm of logic, ever within reach)
Those mysteries of passion which have made,
And shall continue evermore to make—
In spite of all that reason hath performed,
And shall perform, to exalt and to refine—
One brotherhood of all the human race,
Through all the habitations of past years,
And those to come: and hence an emptiness
Fell on the historian's page, and even on that
Of poets, pregnant with more absolute truth.
The works of both withered in my esteem,

Their sentence was, I thought, pronounced—their rights
Seemed moral, and their empire passed away.
(11.74–95)

In order to overcome the self-divisiveness of his disillusion, Wordsworth had to reconceive what it might mean to be, in his words,
"creator and receiver *both*" (my emphasis). He realized, in 1795, that
he could not be a poet so long as he sought to make his mind
"work," hoping therefore to surmount the sorrows of the "merely"
natural self by subsuming, solipsistically, Nature into an aggran-
dized and superior self that tyrannically unifies the personality.
When Wordsworth announces in book 2 that memory leads him to
perceive "Two consciousnesses—conscious of myself, / And of some
other being" (2.32–33), that otherness is not only a now-alien past
self but also a Nature that *preceded* the self.

Nature several times in *The Prelude* "sustains" the poet just at the
moment when he might fall—weaned through his own willful-
ness—into orphanhood, providing him with a "nourishment that
came unsought" (2.7). The imagination of this most fortunate of
fostered sons works, at its best, "but in alliance with the works /
Which it beholds" (2.274–75), the agent rather than the master of a
Nature that is itself both matter and mind, *mater* and *pater*. Wordsworth's is a poetic mind, he claims, that "grows," that even "decays,"
and yet does not surrender this "first / Poetic spirit" that he earlier
calls "the filial bond / Of Nature" (276, 263–64):

> . . . Such, verily, is the first
> Poetic spirit of our human life—
> By uniform controul of after years
> In most abated and suppressed, in some
> Through every change of growth or of decay
> Preeminent till death.
> (2.275–80)

At this place of sustenance—in which the biological mother and
Nature are inseparable landscapes for a tiny human—anxiety and
aggression coexist with the dependence of reciprocal love. A forcible
"taking" ("that most apprehensive habitude") characterizes the infant's aggressive dependence even as it also receives a "discipline of
love" in this habitat where "feeling has . . . imparted strength." This
intimate "interfusion" with its surroundings forestalls the child's fall

into the "bewilderment" and "depression" of Oedipal anxiety, aggression, and exile:

> No outcast he, bewildered and depressed;
> Along his infant veins are interfused
> The gravitation and the filial bond
> Of Nature that connect him with the world.
> Emphatically such a being lives,
> An inmate of this *active* universe.
> From Nature largely he receives, nor so
> Is satisfied, but largely gives again;
> For Feeling has to him imparted strength . . .
> (2.261–69)

Through a "beholding" or "seeing" that "spreads" or "receives," the poet's mind gains "strength" in a manner closer to the infant receiving oral nurture than through a gaze that distinguishes the subject from its object by *creating* the subject. "Our puny boundaries," he writes in the passage that precedes the description of the "blessed babe" at the breast, "are things / Which . . . we have made" (2.223–24).

Itself circumscribed by such self-made boundaries, Romantic scholarship, even when it has challenged humanist models that exalt the imagination by demoting Nature, has ignored Wordsworth's insistent figuring of the mind as a place wherein the supernatural, the natural, and the human are not separable but rather, as in book 13 of *The Prelude*, create an "intellectual love" in which they "are each in each, and cannot stand / Dividually" (186–88). The humanist model that engages in such hierarchical separation of these entities may be best exemplified in Harold Bloom's "Nature and Consciousness," which argues that the "salient problem" for those considering the eponymous topic is "subjectivity or self-consciousness," the term that also defines (according to Bloom) Romanticism.[9] For Bloom "Nature poetry" in the Romantic age is finally "anti-nature poetry": "The strength of renovation in Wordsworth resides only in the spirit's splendor, in what he beautifully calls 'possible sublimity' or 'something ever more about to be,' the potential of an imagination too fierce to be contained by nature." In an essay also published in *Romanticism and Consciousness*, Geoffrey Hartman defines the link (or, rather, the severed link) between Nature and a "higher" consciousness as follows: "It is the destiny of consciousness, or as the English Romantics would have said, of Imagination, to separate from nature, so that it can finally transcend not only nature but also its own lesser forms."[10] And in a formidable reading that suggests that Nature (far from instructing the poet in its incorporative recoveries) must (like the mother) be not only consumed but also subsumed or sublated by her son's dialectically overachieving mind, M. H. Abrams in his 1974 *Natural Supernaturalism* describes this act of poetic domination: "In the final analysis the view that informs *The Prelude* is not naturalism, but humanism. . . . and if Wordsworth develops in *The Prelude* what Harold Bloom calls the 'myth of Nature,' this is incorporated within a higher and more comprehensive mind."[11]

I will discuss, at appropriate moments later in this chapter, contemporary theoretical approaches to specific passages in *The Prelude* in which Nature exists only as a historical or linguistic construct in (respectively) New Historicist and deconstructionist readings.[12] More urgent is my argument with those feminist scholars who have blamed Wordsworth for either his appropriation or his banishment of Nature, which they claim is only one of several underappreciated feminine personae in his poems. Presuming that the (male) Romantic poet may only "find" his vocation by asserting his adult independence (an aggressive act that is alleged to require him to surpass and to deny—and/or to appropriate—his mother, his sister, and Nature), Gayatri Spivak, Diane Hoeveler, Mary Jacobus, and Rachel Crawford find Wordsworth's praise of Dorothy in *The Prelude* to be insincere or inadequate (or both).[13] In their different accounts, these scholars conclude that Wordsworth uses Dorothy either to claim a (spurious) home in an androgynized and therefore colonized Nature or to reassure himself that he has passed well beyond dependent and incestuous ties to home. Spivak, in 1981, set the tone for a decade of feminist disparagement of *The Prelude* with these remarks in "Sex and History in *The Prelude*": "The itinerary of Wordsworth's securing of the Imagination is worth recapitulating. Suppression of Julia, unemphatic retention of Vaudracour as sustained and negative condition of possibility of disavowal, his sublation into Coleridge, rememorating through the mediation of the figure of Dorothy his own Oedipal accession to the Law, Imagination as the androgyny of Nature and Man—Woman shut out. . . . when a man (here Wordsworth) addresses another man (Coleridge) in a sustained conversation on a seemingly universal topic, we must *learn* to read the microstructural burden of the woman's part" (336).

In a sentence that picks up where Spivak ends, Mary Jacobus, in *Romanticism, Writing, and Sexual Difference* (1989), concludes that "in the Romantic family, the only good daughter is a dutiful one (Dora) or a dead one" (206). Like Nature, she contends, mothers, daughters, and sisters have no place in what she, like Spivak, identifies as the poetic son's "fetishism," a term that both critics apply not only to Wordsworth but also to the ideology of a "Romantic humanism": "Splitting becomes the means to defend an imaginary bodily integrity, warding off castration anxiety by means of the organic wholeness with which Romantic humanism is invested, whether its subject is man or simply his imagination" (Jacobus, 214). If there is a woman's voice to be heard in *The Prelude*, Jacobus implies, it is one that by definition the attentive critic, but not the poet, may learn to hear through Wordsworth's soundproof, poetic repression.[14]

Yet neither the sororal nor the natural need necessarily be viewed in *The Prelude* simply as substitutes for the mother Wordsworth wrote rarely of but whose nurture he never ceased to mourn. While it may be tempting to suggest that Dorothy and Nature, if viewed (incorrectly) as maternal substitutes, supply to the poet no more than the material (*mater*ial) satisfactions the poet remembers deriving, as a "blessed babe" at the breast, Wordsworth himself understood, as his representation of his 1795 depression demonstrates, the ways in which "rational" applications of "mind" that estrange it from "matter" merely substitute an invisible tyranny, the "self-rule" of ideology, for more obvious forms of paternal tyranny. Wordsworth in books 9 through 12 of the 1805 *Prelude* powerfully portrays the Oedipal and unhappy society of self-governing sons that succeeded (in England no less than in France) the crises of authority of the Age of Reason, Revolution, and Romanticism. A masculine and depressive culture that has exiled itself from home, from its sources of production, and from Nature, its bases of power are founded (as Wordsworth understood even in such early works as *The Borderers* and "The Ruined Cottage") on its capacity not only to subsume the authority of its traditional and ruling fathers but also to subdue and to exploit (1) women, who are visible only as wives, substitutes for the forbidden mother, and who themselves become an exploitable workforce of mothers and cottage laborers; (2) men, who share that labor with women in the rural home, until they find themselves at century's end either without work or tied to the production processes of a capitalism that depreciates the allegedly feminine attributes of *both* genders of the working class; and (3) Nature, which can only be construed, through those same processes, as either the nonexistent, or the merely material, "other" of a reason that misrecognizes its home in transcendence.

Jean-Joseph Goux, in a Marxist and Lacanian investigation of the culture of "general equivalence" that took hold in Europe at the end of the eighteenth century, makes clear the consequences of a culture of capital that consigns to one gender (the female) its undervalued material and biological labor, or reproduction, and to one class (the proletariat) its undervalued material and technological labor, which is also, of course, reproduction. A culture that thinks only in terms of "equivalence" can assimilate labor, woman, and Nature into its processes only through exploitative (and ecologically disastrous) technologies.[15] While the now-alienated, or self-orphaned, son in such a society may glimpse in imaginary productions (whether aesthetic, philosophical, or sexual) the satisfactions once derived in the mirror stage of a maternal dependence that was also the inception of his unitary and soon-orphaned self, he cannot, through such representations of that source of his own reproduction, so easily return to the negated Lacanian Real of Nature. The materialist absence that, like woman and labor, haunts what Goux calls a "paterialist" culture driven by symbolic exchange and mirror-stage nostalgia, Nature has become the Real insofar as it is an unsignifiable "thing" that can be neither fully exchanged nor fully assimilated into the symbolic on the imaginary. Criticizing as paterialist both Marx's "end" of history and Freud's trajectory for a satisfactorily concluded sexual development, Goux concludes that these masculine and heterosexual models both believe, erroneously, that cultural salvation lies in a denial (*through* work, one might add) of a *jouissance* they fear in Nature no less than in woman. If we are to negate the negations and denials of paterialist mourning, we might conclude from Goux, we may do so *not* by returning to the primordial and maternal imaginary where the separation of mind from *mater* originated but, rather, to Nature as itself a mind (one inseparable from its body) with an "organizing spirit":

What is rediscovered in the new materialism, or rather what is effected, is a *dialecticized reunion* of the two separated poles. There are not two separate principles of uninformed matter *versus* formative mind, of lifeless, passively receptive matter *versus* organizing spirit. Matter is organized, or rather, matter goes on *organizing itself.* Law, reason, order, form, controlling power are not preexisting transcendent principles, constituting a logic or logos to be conceived outside or apart from matter in movement; the existence of a dialectic of nature means, in other words, that matter and its organizational laws are one. Hence thought, consciousness, and mind again become functions of nature, products of matter when it is organized in a certain way. (235)

Indeed, should we seek beyond Goux's argument further grounds for recognizing in *The Prelude* the contemporaneity of Wordsworth's specific critique of a mind misguided by a reason divorced from Nature, it is available in the very different approaches to the natural world, and to cognition, that have succeeded the outmoded models Wordsworth himself repudiated.[16] In the words of the theoretical physicist David Bohm, mind and matter are no longer viewed by science as "separate substances. Rather, they are different aspects of one whole and unbroken movement. In this way, we are able to look on all aspects of existence as not divided from each other, and thus we can bring to an end the fragmentation implicit in . . . the atomic point of view, which leads us to divide everything from everything in a thoroughgoing way."[17]

"I Was a Chosen Son"

When we assume in advance that Wordsworth was a poet so driven by a need for imaginative independence that he needed Nature only as a silent muse and Dorothy only as an underappreciated amanuensis in, or as an admiring witness to, his poetic production, we exclude from our readings of the rich poems that emerged from their winter alone together in Germany the pleasure the siblings obviously shared in reviving not only Wordsworth's productivity (he did, after all, begin the major long poem that would be his most important work) but also their shared memories of the Nature that fostered both orphans. Spivak and Jacobus, like the humanists against whom their readings are directed, argue that the male Romantic poet could only be at home in the mind and its creations. Thus Wordsworth's "Paradise Regained" could not possibly be a home with Dorothy, much less a home that he has made *in* his mind *for* Nature. It could only be a poem, his "Home at Grasmere," which is, in Abrams's admiring and self-reflexive terms, "a home which is also a recovered paradise."[18] Like a good husband, the mature poet seeks only to marry an obedient Nature, and he is willing to work hard to support their union. Wordsworth, as this reading continues, entered into his birthright by returning, not to Grasmere, where he would continue to be a son, but rather to productive work on the poem named after his birthplace, his preliminary and spousal effort at the long (and never-to-be completed) *The Recluse*.[19]

If critics such as Abrams have eagerly exploited Wordsworth's own allusions to *Paradise Regained* in "Home at Grasmere," Milton's portrayal of God's chosen Son (who goes out into the world only to return to his mother's home) has not been the text favored by scholars who hear echoes of Wordsworth's admired literary father in *The Prelude*. The 1805 and 1850 versions both open where *Paradise Lost* ends, with the poet "homeward returning" even as "The earth remains all before me." And like Adam, according to most critics, Wordsworth had at last resigned himself to the labor and the rewards of fallen adults. Wordsworth, in this account, no less than Coleridge and anxious, older members of his family, had himself begun to understand that he must produce tangible, poetic evidence that what had seemed like idle years as a "gentleman vagrant" had been invested wisely in the vocation of poetry. The poet had now chosen a home, Stephen Gill reassures us, where he may undertake the "austere" and "high endeavour" of mental "reflection and study."[20] The promise of the philosophy to follow would then justify the less assuredly philosophical work of the aptly named *Prelude*. Result: the poet who had "spent" his youth writing poems about children, nature, and social misfits would redeem himself through the intellectual labor that lay like the world before the poet, who, like Adam (and as an orphan), cannot (and should not) go home again.

Yet the prospect that buoys the "home-bound labourer" that Wordsworth calls himself is hardly the physical toil that awaited the chastened couple Michael hurried from paradise:

> The heavy weight of many a weary day
> Not mine, and such as were not made for me.
> Long months of peace—if such bold word accord
> With any promises of human life—
> Long months of ease and undisturbed delight
> Are mine in prospect. . . .
> (1.24–29)

That critics typically, and expediently, banish this and other obvious discrepancies between book 12 of *Paradise Lost* and Wordsworth's poetic statements about his vocation is a failure closely tied to their virtually unanimous presumption that a poetic son can only follow the self-exile of the Oedipus complex. Accordingly, critics who accept the inevitability of the Oedipal model may either blame Wordsworth for denying a mother and a sister in his haste to abandon the pre-Oedipal paradise or, alternately, for shamelessly using them in his mistaken belief that he can return; others may accuse him of wistfully looking backward—"regressing"—like an unhealthy melancholic to infantile and effeminate delights; or they may praise him for driving forward with speed and strength, either in submission to the paternal Law or in creative rebellion against poetic predecessors.[21]

With no easy approach to the word "home," we must develop an approach to Wordsworth's use of that term in order to understand how he believed the poet's home also to be in a language that, while it heralds the dawn of subjectivity, evokes also the dusk of a larger and unbounded consciousness. To identify home as the site, both familial and natural, that calls the poet to a literary vocation is, of course, to challenge Bloom's appropriation of Freudian sexual development as the ephebe's necessary exile, a journey that follows, without halting, a single, undeviating path away from the home of his parents into the family romance of threatening predecessors. To shift our disciplinary focus to Wordsworth's "home-bound labour" is to appropriate a different Freud, the one who recognized (as in the quotation that opens this chapter) the abiding importance, sexually but also intellectually, of the voices that we hear in our first home, the Freud who in "Family Romances" recognized that the child, in fantasizing royal (or "glorious" origins) in fact restores to his or her own parents—or, we might extrapolate, *Nature*—their original glory. To read Wordsworth in relation to *that* Freud is to understand that Wordsworth's powerful identification with his "Great Original," Milton, could not help but be influenced by relationships that originated, even before he acquired words, in his first (and soon broken) home.[22]

The Prelude, as Hartman and Thomas Weiskel have especially illuminated, possesses many moments that are breathlessly suspended between the "it was" of a past that has been lost and the "this" of the present, where the poet's progress is halted or reversed. In these moments, as Hartman confirms, the poet feels not redeemed—"Was it for this . . ."—whether by works or grace, but "spent" by grief in the pensiveness of melancholy. In his trope of "the halted traveler,"[23] Hartman perceptively defines these as moments where the poet encounters an unassimilated sadness or an earlier, virtually "dead" version of himself. Yet Hartman, eschewing an opportunity to investigate just what constitutes the emotional power of the past in these liminal moments, defines them as moments when the Imagination, in the present, becomes aware that its own strength has surpassed the authority of what it has lost (Nature) and, even, of what it has gained (language and creativity). Weiskel, pursuing the Kantian echoes of Hartman's model, more specifically defines as *sublime* the mysterious feeling of strength that arises from melancholic loss (notably, the loss of God's presence at the center of one's being), a feeling of spent power that is succeeded by a surmise of a still-greater power from within.[24] A "labor of the mind," as Weiskel calls it, the sublime encounter puts the melancholic, idle mind to work through terror so that the mind may, as a consequence, experience relief. When a poet (Weiskel cites Collins, along with Wordsworth) uses the sublime to effect a "regressive" reunion with a maternal nature, rather than to challenge his poetic fathers and (Protestant) Father, he is succumbing to the idle pleasure of the positive sublime. In Wordsworth's most exemplary writing in *The Prelude,* however, Weiskel finds manifestations of a "negative sublime" in which the Imagination gains power by aggressively (that is, Oedipally) repudiating its origins, laboriously effacing the Word with the poet's own words.

According to both Hartman and Weiskel, the poet, by successfully passing through the halted or sublime moment of trial, ultimately asserts his imagination's freedom, a freedom underwritten by his absolute belief in the originality and authenticity of his own and solitary voice.[25] ("Solitary," it is important to recognize here, does not mean the hand-in-hand "solitary way" of *two* people, as it does in Milton. It is inevitably the condition of a single, male poet.) The vocation of poetry *demands* a break—a blockage or halt that can often be (Oedipally) blinding—from a (maternal) nature and (paternal) cultural past, from home and then from Milton, that allows the poet to find his true inner voice away from home: his independence is a prerequisite for his acquisition of "vocation," in both senses of the word.[26] Yet the poetic strengths of *The Prelude* may grow, rather than diminish, if we relinquish the burden placed on the poetic imagination's strength, independence, originality, and

maturation, recognizing that Wordsworth's rites of passage are au-
thored by Nature, not by a poet's self-authorship. For the poet who
still thinks of himself as a son, redemption lies not in a narrative or
in poetic feet that face only forward but, rather, in a poetry that
delays, a poetry whose feet idle, like the Leech-gatherer's, in the
eddies of memory where poems seem to come unbidden to a blood
that "interfuses" a landscape that is both home and *not* home.

Wordsworth, like Milton, understood the necessity of impeding
rather than hurrying into an unappealing vocation that had been
chosen for him by others. Milton, when he declined to enter the
church, asked his father nevertheless to support the extended travel
and reading that he would require as a writer, knowing full well that
he could finally justify choosing such a career only when he was able,
as an accomplished poet, to demonstrate that he, like Adam, regularly walked and talked in his imagination with the God whom
he—as a chosen son called to the vocation of poetry—could summon to his side.[27] As William Kerrigan has suggested,[28] Milton on
some level believed that he, no less than the Jesus he portrays in
Paradise Regained, heard "out of heaven the sovran voice" proclaim
"This is my son beloved, in him am pleased," an expression of paternal favor that is succeeded just a few lines later with the following:

> . . . my Father's voice,
> Audibly heard from heaven, pronounced me his,
> Me his beloved Son, in whom alone
> He was well pleased.
> (*Paradise Regained,* 1.84–85, 283 ff.)

Wordsworth, who in *The Prelude* also believed himself to be a son
"much-favored," recalls his difficulties with depression during his
time at Cambridge. Beset by "melancholy thoughts / From personal
and family regards," a melancholia associated not only with the past
but also with his vocational future, Wordsworth found relief from
such gloom not through academic work but, rather, through an
intuition of *grace* (which by definition, of course, cannot be earned):

> Why should I grieve?—I was a chosen son.
> For hither I had come with holy powers
> And faculties, whether to work or feel:
> To apprehend all passions and all moods
> Which time, and place, and season do impress
> Upon the visible universe, and work

> Like changes there by force of my own mind.
> I was a freeman, in the purest sense,
> Was free, and to majestic ends was strong—
> I do not speak of learning, moral truth,
> Or understanding—'twas enough for me
> To know that I was otherwise endowed.
> (3.83–93)

A son who believes himself to be chosen, even in the apparent absence of the father (or Father) whose voice he hears, and even in a college, or in a country, of foreign voices, is never far from home. He is "a free man" in book 3 in a sense that Wordsworth subsequently was not in 1795, for his mind has not yet been perverted by reason; it still "spreads," like the infant's, aware of "visitings" from the soul that lies "underneath":

> As if awakened, summoned, rouzed, constrained,
> I looked for universal things, perused
> The common countenance of earth and heaven,
> And, turning the mind in upon itself,
> Pored, watched, expected, listened, spread my thoughts,
> And spread them with a wider creeping, felt
> Incumbences more awful, visitings
> Of the upholder, of the tranquil soul,
> Which underneath all passion lives secure
> (3.109–17)

Having once received grace, he is able, when he begins the *Prelude* in 1799, to recover its "chear" and "perfect confidence" (1.160, 173), recognizing that he never ceases to be a poet, whether he is moved to speech or to silence:

> . . . To the open fields I told
> A prophesy; poetic numbers came
> Spontaneously, and clothed in priestly robe
> My spirit, thus singled out, as it might seem,
> For holy services. Great hopes were mine:
> My own voice cheared me, and, far more, the mind's
> Internal echo of the imperfect sound—
> To both I listened, drawing from them both
> A chearful confidence in things to come.
> . . . .
>   . . . but the harp

Was soon defrauded, and the banded host
Of harmony dispersed in straggling sounds,
And lastly utter silence. . . .
(1805, 1.59–68, 104–7)

In a subsequent passage, which was in fact written before the poet turned homeward, he hears his calling as an internal echo of the Derwent, a fluent, fatherly voice (a father who is not, significantly, singled out as exclusively a biological, heavenly, or literary father).[29] This murmuring voice is blended with the maternal song of a nurse (one that is not singled out as either human or Nature) in what were once the opening lines of the 1799 *Two-Part Prelude:*

> Was it for this
> That one, the fairest of all rivers, loved
> To blend his murmurs with my nurse's song,
> And from his alder shades and rocky falls,
> And from his fords and shallows, sent a voice
> That flowed along my dreams? For this didst thou,
> O Derwent, travelling over the green plains
> Near my "sweet birthplace," didst thou, beauteous stream,
> Make ceaseless music through the night and day,
> Which with its steady cadence tempering
> Our human waywardness, composed my thoughts
> To more than infant softness, giving me
> Among the fretful dwellings of mankind
> A knowledge, a dim earnest, of the calm
> Which Nature breathes among the fields and groves?
> (1.272–85)

While this music is made near the poet's "sweet birthplace," there are already signs that innocence is "shaded" by death and by imminent (or even recent?) "falls." That this riparian voice is heard retrospectively, at (or from beyond?) the gates of a timeless Eden, can be discerned through references to a "human waywardness" that now must be "tempered" to an infancy that is "more than infant softness." Yet it is important here that it is Nature, through the Derwent, that "composes" the poet who is himself beginning "composition." Her breath, delivered (like speech) from a home that is now distant, must reach the traveler from faraway fields, for this fallen son inhabits "the fretful dwellings of mankind."

One can think of a number of reasons why such a beginning to even the early and brief version of Wordsworth's autobiographical narrative may have proved fortuitous. If, at the beginning of such a retrospective poetic journey a young poet's feet may well have been (like Adam and Eve's as they left Paradise) wandering and slow, halting and poorly cadenced, then the fluent Derwent might serve as a model that would lend grace to the ephebe's metric gait. Indeed, "grace" would be the very term Milton himself might have used for a poetic motion that is moved entirely by his Father's voice, as in the "ceaseless music" of the "Nativity Ode" that the poet dare not interrupt, or the relief in learning that "career"—literally, movement forward as a poet—is propelled entirely by God, as in "Sonnet VII." But while Milton understood that the poetic voice that emerged as his own in his graceful, smoothly cadenced—"strictest measured"— lines were themselves the expression of not one but *two* fathers' favors, Wordsworth, deprived of his earthly father and possessing at this time far from orthodox beliefs, would have required other evidence of parental favor. His poetry would need to give graceful, "cadenced" voice to the language of his other home—his fosterage by Nature through both fear and beauty—that itself echoed the paternal voice and blended with the maternal song of his child- hood. In writing such poetry, he would reclaim not only *time,* "days / Disowned by memory" (TPP, 1.444–45), a past haunted by loss and an early manhood characterized by "idleness," but also the *place,* the home where his first parents remained buried and where Nature, his other parent, gave him poetic powers: the landscape of the Lake District, the foster home that taught him the lessons other children learn from a mother and father or through their surrogates in a classroom. Such lessons, of course, begin with words, the sym- bols that will make the child human but only at the cost of surren- dering innocence. How could the poet have learned from Nature such lessons in, first, hearing and speaking and, second, reading and writing, lessons that would give him the requisite skills to prove, through poetry, that he has indeed been "endowed" (from whatever parental source) with grace?[30]

Following Wordsworth's own lead, we might return to the pas- sages in *The Prelude* in which he suggests that he repeatedly re- covered his vocation (his calling as a poet *and* his poetic voice) by learning, through Nature, to overturn the eye, the organ that origi- nates a misleadingly unitary self at the very moment when the infant still feeds at the breast. The eye is both the origin and the agent of a subjectivity that judges and repudiates but believes it need not "need." In describing the origins of his 1795 depression, Wordsworth remembers that he turned from Nature's arts of representation to "rules of mimic art transferred / To things above all art" (11.154–55); in becoming her judge, the poet became "less sensible" to Nature's "moods," "the spirit of the place" (161–63):

> The state to which I now allude was one
> In which the eye was master of the heart,
> When that which is in every stage of life
> The most despotic of our senses gained
> Such strength in me as often held my mind
> In absolute dominion. Gladly here,
> Entering upon abstruser argument,
> Would I endeavour to unfold the means
> Which Nature studiously employs to thwart
> This tyranny, summons all the senses each
> To counteract the other and themselves,
> And makes them all, and the objects with which all
> Are conversant, subservient in their turn
> To the great ends of liberty and power.
> (11.171–83)

"But this," Wordsworth continues, "is matter for another song" (184), a comment glossed by his editors as a reference to *The Recluse.* Yet *The Prelude* itself, in its own fashion, clearly shows how Nature "thwarts" the "tyranny" of the eye, a visual sense whose temptations began when the poet as a boy was singled out in the wilderness. Like the young man in 1795 whom Wordsworth describes as "greedy in the chace" (11.189) for knowledge, as a boy he "roamed from hill to hill" (190) until Nature, in her most sublime and terrifying forms, chastised him. In the 1799 *Prelude,* as in book 11 of the 1805 version, the son knows he is chosen not merely when he stands in the presence of Nature's beauty—her "gentle visitation" (TPP, 1.73)—but also because of its sublime "Severer interventions, ministry / More palpable" (80–81; 1805, 1.355).

Such interventions, which rely on Nature's animation of senses beyond the visual sense strengthened by the mirror stage, are apparent in the very first lines of the 1805 *Prelude,* as Nature communicates through a wind that beats its message:

> Oh there is a blessing in this gentle breeze,
> That blows from the green fields and from the clouds

And from the sky; it beats against my cheek,
And seems half conscious of the joy it gives.
O welcome messenger! O welcome friend!
(1.1–5)

Subsequently Wordsworth will make Nature's—the river Derwent's—melodic powers his own by traveling with it to his "sweet birthplace," by bathing in its depths, and by participating in its metamorphosis into the powerful god of a thundershower. The same properties of speech that Nature possesses and bestows in images of water expressive of both voice and vocation enable Dorothy, *with* "Nature's self," in book 10 to "preserve" her brother as a poet through ministries that are both severe (hers is a voice of "admonition") and restorative, for to admonish is also, of course, to give back memory:

> . . . the belovèd woman in whose sight
> Those days were passed—now speaking in a voice
> Of sudden admonition like a brook
> That does but cross a lonely road; and now
> Seen, heard and felt, and caught at every turn,
> Companion never lost through many a league—
> Maintained for me a saving intercourse
> With my true self (for, though impaired, and changed
> Much, as it seemed, I was no further changed
> Than as a clouded, not a waning moon);
> She, in the midst of all, preserved me still
> A poet, made me seek beneath that name
> My office upon earth, and nowhere else.
> And lastly, Nature's self, by human love
> Assisted through the weary labyrinth
> Conducted me again to open day,
> Revived the feelings of my earlier life,
> Gave me that strength and knowledge full of peace. . . .
> (10.908–25)

In book 11, entitled "Imagination, How Impaired and Restored," the poet who imitates Nature's vocal joy, and praises it, begins to recover from the depression induced by misdirected consciousness (and to recover, through poetry, the breath—inspiration—of the breezes and flowing waters of the poem's opening praise and Dorothy's brooklike "saving intercourse"):

> Ye motions of delight, that through the fields
> Stir gently, breezes and soft airs that breathe
> The breath of paradise, and find your way
> To the recesses of the soul; ye brooks
> Muttering along the stones, a busy noise
> By day, a quiet one in silent night;
>
> . . . .
>
> Oh, that I had a music and a voice
> Harmonious as your own, that I might tell
> What ye have done for me. . . .
> (11.9–22)

When in Goslar the poet first began to imitate the music and the voice of the opening of the 1799 *Prelude* that Wordsworth subsequently placed in the first book of *The Prelude,* the Derwent's cadenced music—its halts and fresh starts—"tempered" the poet's "waywardness": "Which with its steady cadence tempering / Our human waywardness, composed my thoughts / To more than infant softness, giving me / Among the fretful dwellings of mankind . . ." (280–83). This is the first of many words associated with *tempus,* or time, that will appear in the text before the famous "spots of time" passage. From the first the association carries an additional, contradictory meaning: not the separate, up-down movements of "tempo" but the commingling of disparate elements under stress that produces a more resilient, *composite* texture, as in the *temper*ing of metal or the blending of "temporal" occurrences. In *tempests,* the poet will later suggest, originates *composition,* not just of poetic words but of thoughts themselves that continue to have value in the "fretful dwellings" of the present *because* they transport not only the memories but also the mental and emotional states of receptiveness of, and to, a no longer distant past. How does Nature convey to the poet those past states? Through breath: "Among the fretful dwellings of mankind / A knowledge, a dim earnest, of the calm / Which nature breathes among the fields and groves" (283–84). The element of air—the openings and blockings of air currents—associated with voice has now been integrated into that of the fluent (and yet cadenced) river.[31]

As Wordsworth suggests more than a decade later in his first essay on epitaphs, the child who ponders "a running stream" is pondering both origins and ends that are, in a word that suggests the familial as well as the parallel, "co-relative": "Origin and tendency are notions inseparably co-relative. Never did a child stand by the side of a running stream, pondering within himself what power was the feeder of the perpetual current, from what never-wearied sources the body of water was supplied, but he must have been inevitably propelled to follow this question by another: 'Toward what abyss is it in progress? what receptacle can contain the mighty influx?' "[32] Wordsworth's answer to the child's question in this passage, which would seem to lead ineluctably to "death," is first "infinity" and them "immortality." Yet we may well seek a more metaphorically interesting answer, for where do rivers and fathers, brooks and sisters, go if not to *mouths* that are fertile sources as well as terminal stops? What have their voices to do with the cadenced sounds and air that emerge from the mouth of a poet whose melancholy (as in the episodes of "feeding" that characterize the boy's encounters in, and growing understanding of, nature in book 2) typically manifests itself through tropes of incorporation that transform even—or *especially*—the visual sense that separates into one that reunites?

> How I have stood, to images like these
> A stranger, linking with the spectacle
> No body of associated forms,
> And bringing with me no peculiar sense
> Of quietness or peace—yet I have stood
> Even while my eye has moved o'er three long leagues
> Of shining water, gathering, as it seemed,
> Through the wide surface of that field of light
> New pleasure, like a bee among the flowers.
> (TPP, 1.404–12)

As Wordsworth writes, late in the 1805 *Prelude,* love cannot exist either where men and women "labour in excess and poverty" or where leisure distorts the judgments of a wealthy minority, for in such places "the eye feeds [love] not, and cannot feed" (12.197–203).

While rivers may seem to flow in one direction only—from source to mouth—transgressing, along the way, the borders of properties and states, the poet's dreams along which the Derwent flows may violate rapidly, and disconcertingly, the fixed temporal and spatial boundaries of everyday reality.[33] The voices of waters, which, Wordsworth tells us, flow along the boy's dreams, speak to Wordsworth in the poem, as often as not, through still spots of silence, openings that are themselves empty mouths. In his second reference to the river, Wordsworth refers not to its fluent passages but, instead, to what he called in the earlier, 1799 version, its "silent pools": ". . . a four years' child / A naked boy, among thy silent pools / Made one long bathing of a summer's day, / Basked in the sun, or plunged into thy streams" (TPP, 1.17–20). In such spots of water, and condensations of time, the poet anticipates what he will learn in the subsequent spots of time and on Mount Snowdon: the secrets of a poetry that plummets into unfamiliar linguistic lacunae where he encounters a death that involves language but that is not the death that Paul de Man has called "a linguistic predicament."[34] When Wordsworth surfaces from these condensed pools of illegibility, he has acquired through a re-Naturing of signification a heightened awareness of how words become most illegible *and* most useful to the poet precisely when he is divested of habitual fluency or hoped-for texts.

"Blank Desertion"

Nature in the first two books of *The Prelude* becomes most unfamiliar, and most frightening, when the poet as a boy seeks to establish his independence. When Nature, in turn, finds opportunities to remind the poet of past encounters on what had then seemed familiar terrain, that landscape becomes riddled by timeless loci of pleasure that are, disconcertingly, both intimate and illegible. The childhood memories that precede the spots of time in the 1799 *Prelude* all represent a boy who, in journeying out into the world in search of freedom and masculinity, instead discovers both his continued dependence on Nature and, through Nature, the mysteries of speech and writing. There may seem to be no necessary transition from the baptism of the thundershower to the recollection that follows, which begins with another form of precipitation, frost. Yet, in fact, in the stolen snares episode a subtle transformation has taken place in the boy's relationship to the nature in which he once basked on a riverbank. "Standing alone" may be the exemplary passivity that singles out Jesus as God's Son, himself a "naked god" devoted and immovable in his Father's presence. For the human child, however, "aloneness" will in turn produce speech and writing from riparian babble, skills that will orphan the child from parental love even as it weans the child from its authority. From such a posture the son may well believe that he is ready to wander, striding forth by himself into the wilderness. There he will enter the world of experience and of "difference," singling out the elements and creatures of Nature, naming them and (therefore) trapping them in an act that parodies Adam's verbal authority:

> 'Twas at an early age, ere I had seen
> Nine summers—when upon the mountain slope
> The frost and breath of frosty wind had snapped
> The last autumnal crocus, 'twas my joy
> To wander half the night among the cliffs
> And the smooth hollows where the woodcocks ran
> Along the open turf. In thought and wish
> That time, my shoulder all with springes hung,
> I was a fell destroyer. . . .
> (1805, 1.309–17)

Yet if this is, in some sense beyond the seasonal, "fall," it is not yet a fall into experience. Autumn transforms summer's fluency and humidity into the first frost of breath; "fell," the past tense of fall, is a Lake District term for a small mountain, an archaic synonym for "cruel," and it is also another word for "pelt." All of these meanings, as in the conjugation of the present tense of "fall" to "fell" and "befell," are evoked in Wordsworth's portrayal of the boy's precocious, "hurrying" movement into adult experience:

> I was a fell destroyer. On the heights
> Scudding away from snare to snare, I plied
> My anxious visitation, hurrying on,
> Still hurrying, hurrying onward. Moon and stars
> Were shining o'er my head; I was alone,
> And seemed to be a trouble to the peace
> That was among them. Sometimes it befel
> In these night-wanderings, that a strong desire
> O'erpowered my better reason, and the bird
> Which was the captive of another's toils
> Became my prey; and when the deed was done
> I heard among the solitary hills
> Low breathings coming after me, and sounds
> Of undistinguishable motion, steps
> Almost as silent as the turf they trod.
> (1.317–32)

Nature has entrapped the trapper. The child's theft from the "toils" of an adult could well be linguistic, a precocious pretense of work and of ownership of the carcasses of desired things—words—which no child can possess entirely through his own and solitary toil, no matter how he hurries. Nature's voice, however, has now become inarticulate; its "undistinguishable" sounds and winds that "breathe" follow the boy's footsteps homeward, changing, perhaps, his very relationship to the other foster home where he is now learning to write, to freeze on the page words captured in time and in space. Nature's speech in that lesson may be silent, but its breathings move (and move the poet) as surely as poetic feet may move the reader: "steps / Almost as silent as the turf they trod."

From the *spring*es of "fall" the poem shifts to the visual (but not aural) pun of *spring*time, and by now the boy who sought to steal a dead creature is a "plunderer" of the not-yet-living: a raven's eggs. Distancing himself from his first home by invading another's, the boy learns a lesson in Nature that seems to associate him with the steadfast Son who "stood alone" when Satan set him on the pinnacle that the tempter calls, significantly, the "Father's house":[35]

> Nor less in springtime, when on southern banks
> The shining sun had from her knot of leaves
> Decoyed the primrose flower, and when the vales
> And woods were warm, was I a plunderer then
> In the high places, on the lonesome peaks,
> Where'er among the mountains and the winds
> The mother-bird had built her lodge. Though mean
> My object and inglorious, yet the end
> Was not ignoble. Oh, when I have hung
> Above the raven's nest, by knots of grass
> And half-inch fissures in the slippery rock
> But ill sustained, and almost, as it seemed,
> Suspended by the blast which blew amain,
> Shouldering the naked crag, oh, at that time
> While on the perilous ridge I hung alone,
> With what strange utterance did the loud dry wind
> Blow through my ears; the sky seemed not a sky
> Of earth, and with what motion moved the clouds!
> (1.333–50)

Like Jesus in *Paradise Regained,* this boy-poet goes out to meet the temptations of the wilderness; unlike God's Son, his "views" are already "inglorious": he plans (still the springes-thief) to take as trophies the eggs of a bird of prey that is mythologically associated with the death-bearing mother. Even so, this favored son is arrested from falling by a "strange utterance" that "suspends" not only the son but also everyday reality itself.

From *pinnac*le and the current of breath or air, the poet returns to water and to thievery, stealing a *pinnac*e. This time the boy moves from speech to writing, for he is transported not by the mechanisms of voice and hearing but, rather, by the near-homonym that "pinnacle" and then "pinnace" evoke: the *pen*. The pinnace, like "metaphor," is a vehicle the boy is learning to master so that he can carry it (and himself) away from home (375). Through this fairy vehicle (the books Wordsworth first enjoyed, as we know from the later *Prelude*, were fairy tales) opens a landscape that from within such transport, and under the moonlight, looks altogether different at night. Without the guidance of the pastor whose boat he has claimed, dipping his penlike oars into the inky darkness of the still (and otherwise "silent") lake, the boy (who is once again alone) feels a power that he knows is greater than he can comprehend. He is acting like a man, whose "stately step" the child learns to reproduce first with his own limbs and, later, by reproducing the "cadences" and "echoes" of the written words he is no longer content only to hear or to read:

> I went alone into a shepherd's boat,
> A skiff, that to a willow-tree was tied
> Within a rocky cave, its usual home.
>
> . . . .
>
> The moon was up, the lake was shining clear
> Among the hoary mountains; from the shore
> I pushed, and struck the oars, and struck again
> In cadence, and my little boat moved on
> Even like a man who moves with stately step
> Though bent on speed. It was an act of stealth
> And troubled pleasure. Nor without the voice
> Of mountain-echoes did my boat move on . . .
> (1.373–90)

A critic focusing on the "stealth" and "troubled pleasure" of this episode is likely to perceive in the word the poet subsequently uses for this small boat—pinnace—a near-homonym (penis) that tidily conflates, in a single interpretation, power, guilt, and a poet's troubled, Oedipal passage. Yet to locate *only* in the locus of adult and male reproduction the physical sensations evoked generally by this discovery of a mysterious power and pleasure is to unduly limit the experience evoked in these lines. It is also to presume that Wordsworth believed that poetic language requires, like the Law of the Father, a substitution of one pleasure for another. The various sexual pleasures of childhood that Freud catalogs may be related to, but they are not identical with, the pleasure of putting a pen into liquid and then covering the surface of a page with words that summon objects that are greater—and sometimes more terrifying—than one anticipates. At such moments, the young writer does not wish to surrender for the compensations of the sunlit world the inky blackness of the words that call, almost supernaturally, mysterious objects into being. He may indeed feel that those words "echo" an unknown adult who is a hidden part of himself—a "consciousness" that *is* "some other being," supernatural or superegoistic. For writing, portrayed in the following lines both as dalliance and voice's echo, is also performative. It reconstructs the landscape:

> Leaving behind her still on either side
> Small circles glittering idly in the moon,
> Until they melted all into one track
> Of sparkling light. A rocky steep uprose
> Above the cavern of the willow-tree,
> And now, as suited one who proudly rowed
> With his best skill, I fixed a steady view
> Upon the top of that same craggy ridge,
> The bound of the horizon—for behind
> Was nothing but the stars and the grey sky.
> She was an elfin pinnace; lustily
> I dipped my oars into the silent lake,
> And as I rose upon the stroke my boat
> Went heaving through the water like a swan—
> When from behind that craggy steep, till then
> The bound of the horizon, a huge cliff,
> As if with voluntary power instinct,
> Upreared its head. I struck, and struck again,
> And, growing still in stature, the huge cliff
> Rose up between me and the stars, and still
> With measured motion, like a living thing
> Strode after me. . . .
> (1.391–412)

Even after the writer has returned home safely, he is haunted by that other self, and those unanticipated powers, that he has summoned, for they occlude—they literally "blank" and "desert"—the once-familiar landscape. Attracted and repelled by the act of creation that calls words to perform the poet's bidding—even as that act seems to alienate him from those very words and the strong magic that they work—the writer is afterward afflicted by a kind of melancholy, a "gloom" associated both with that "spectacle" and with the "blank desertion" of the familiar. The Derwent that flowed along the boy's dreams has been supplanted by a lake that, in its silence, is in fact representational:

> And through the meadows homeward went with grave
> And serious thoughts; and after I had seen
> That spectacle, for many days my brain
> Worked with a dim and undetermined sense
> Of unknown modes of being. In my thoughts
> There was a darkness—call it solitude
> Or blank desertion—no familiar shapes
> Of hourly objects, images of trees,
> Of sea or sky, no colours of green fields,
> But huge and mighty forms that do not live
> Like living men moved slowly through my mind
> By day, and were the trouble of my dreams.
> (1.416–26)

Such melancholy does not disappear even when the young poet's feet, in a subsequent episode, learn to fly across the frozen surface of the water, "all shod with steel." Like the writer who has learned, shakily, at last to maneuver the metal nibs of a pen, he moves with such exultation and confidence that he believes he "cares not" for the home he has deserted for the pleasure of this mastery. Yet "melancholy," an "alien sound," persists, even in the company of others where, in games imitative of his earlier and solitary hunts, "not a voice was idle":

> . . . With the din,
> Meanwhile, the precipices rang aloud;
> The leafless trees and every icy crag
> Tinkled like iron; while the distant hills
> Into the tumult sent an alien sound
> Of melancholy, not unnoticed; while the stars,
> Eastward, were sparkling clear, and in the west
> The orange sky of evening died away.
> (1.466–73)

Although Wordsworth associates the haunting, alien sound of the echoing feet with death in that final line, he nevertheless also associates it with Nature's language, "characters" that "work" in the following address to Nature:

> . . . can I think
> A vulgar hope was yours when ye employed
> Such ministry—when ye through many a year
> Haunting me thus among my boyish sports,
> On caves and trees, upon the woods and hills,
> Impressed upon all forms the characters
> Of danger or desire, and thus did make
> The surface of the universal earth
> With triumph, and delight, and hope, and fear,
> Work like a sea?
> (1.492–501)

In the 1799 *Prelude* the haunting that the boy next encounters in Nature is a drowned man's rising in the Vale of Esthwaite. In that episode the boy's oars become ears that are *pen*insulas and the "long poles" of grown men that reclaim the dead. The drowning in the 1799 text is immediately followed by the spots of time, in which water and wind forcibly instruct the boy in the inevitability of accident and of loss (notably, through flooding or drowning). By 1805, Wordsworth had separated these events from the Esthwaite drowning, which is itself separated from Nature's "ministry" in book 1.

In putting narrative distance between these episodes, Wordsworth clarified how Nature's instructive vocation may work productively with books, confounding the natural and the aesthetic. While Nature may express itself destructively, through accidents—"in flood or field, / Quarry or moor" (TPP, 1.280–81)—even the accidental becomes, when Wordsworth drops his "adversion" to it, Nature's lesson (which is communicated through a schoolmaster who is no longer alive) of what the boy had already learned through books, in the "shining streams / Of fairyland" (5.476–77). Itself the necessary means through which Nature, or its son, in the "face" of desertion (or "effacement") may yet create or compose anew, the flood that threatens the desert in book 5 transforms an orphan's "desertion" into both a natural landscape (a desert, or *moor*) and a father figure from literature: a Bedouin (*Moor*) who is also Don Quixote.

"Consecrated Works of Bard and Sage"

Adam weeps at the prospect, from the mountaintop, of God's destruction of creation by the Flood in book 11 of *Paradise Lost*, a text we know that Wordsworth and his sister had read (and wept over) early in 1802 when the poet resumed work on *The Prelude*. In the beginning months of that year he also wrote "The Rainbow" and began the Immortality Ode. Adam's tears, as critics have amply noted, manifest not only the first father's generous sympathy for the fate of his offspring but also, in their metaphorical appropriateness, the "naturalness" of metaphors (even in a fallen world) that establish correspondences between the human and nonhuman aspects of Creation.[36] Like the watery sympathy of the first and fallen father, the ghostly words of the ancient Father are in the Immortality Ode manifested in such natural covenants (and such natural expressions of supernatural aesthetics) as the rainbow that endures the Flood and the rose (both the flower associated with the Crucifixion and the past tense of "rise") that survives the Fall. Yet such emblems, however beautiful, cannot but remind us that glory has indeed passed from a Creation that God has left.[37] If there will never be another Flood, or another Fall, indisputably there are, regularly, in fallen Nature floods and falls, accidents that orphan children from their parents in fact as well as in metaphor. Yet Wordsworth's Nature in *The Prelude*, like the poet as chosen son, seems in many ways suspended between "fall" and "salvation": Nature enacts an economics of consecration, and even fetishism, that precedes and survives a covenantal fatherhood that sacrifices the son, surpasses the mother, and exiles the father.

Water, which contributed to Wordsworth's sense of his vocation in books 1 and 2, now, in Book 5 (which was begun in 1804, perhaps while Wordsworth was revising the Immortality Ode) directs his fear of destruction. The reflection into which Narcissus fell associates selfhood and death simultaneously with speculation, with connectedness (or separation from) a primary object of love and inspiration, and with unexpected encounters (fictional, contemporaneous, or memorial) that may lead to drowning. While water, in this sense, may elicit most obviously a discussion of the mirror stage of the "blessed babe"—indeed, Wordsworth frequently uses the words "breast" or "bosom" to describe still or silent waters that invite introspection—the rising of the drowned man from similar depths may also lead us to consider what Julia Kristeva has described as a paternal, rather than maternal, imaginary that "props" (to use Wordsworth's own term in book 2)[38] the child who is being weaned from the maternal breast with the offering of words and, as I will add, fairy tales and other narratives for children.[39] Kristeva calls this paternal figure the "loving father of individual prehistory," the object of the son's love who mediates both past and future, Nature, and Books. The son who loses a mother before he has entirely passed through the mirror stage may well see death in all kinds of reflections; if the father also dies, his absence will be reflected particularly in the verbal constructions of the literary imaginary, or books, no matter how fully the father's place may seem to have been usurped in the literary family romance. Wordsworth suggests in book 2 that Nature sustains the boy when the maternal "props of his affection" and of sustenance fall away; in book 5, that prop is literary, but Wordsworth nevertheless distinguishes "natural" from "unnatural" childhood reading.

As Peter Manning and Susan Wolfson have well documented,[40] Wordsworth's revisions of the Drowned Man episode are significant. Both an accidental drowning of a local schoolteacher and an accidental reencounter with (or memorialization of) the death of his mother,[41] in some sense the episode, by 1805, extends the poet's book 2 discussion of the child at the breast who "Doth gather passion from his mother's eye" in an act that is both oral and visual. The drowning seems also a variation of two episodes in book 4 in which water is associated with strange encounters. A boy who "hangs down-bending" from a boat to gaze, Narcissus-like, into the "breast / Of a still water" discovers, to his surprise and "delight" "shadows" as well as self-unity. At a later age, at the end of book 4, he comes upon a discharged soldier at a (significantly) "deserted" place where "restoration" may be imbibed with "stillness." Path, moon, stream, and hawthorn conjoin (as three of these elements do, later, in Wordsworth's description of Dorothy in book 10) before a figure of death and perhaps of military "desertion" emerges from the gloom. Like the Derwent, the stranger is "murmuring," but in such a way that his riparian speech associates him with disorder and even madness. At the end of book 4, "Back I cast a look," the poet recalls, "Then sought with quiet heart my distant home" (501, 503), a home that will seem different after this mirroring, döppelganger encounter with what might have been his own, alternative life.

But the lines that follow, as book 5 opens, carry the poet not homeward but to a melancholic reflection on desertion. Reflection is itself in this book more clearly linked to drowning (and, perhaps, to a womb that is also a precarious ark) than to mirroring and the breast, even before the reader reaches the Drowned Man episode. Waters rise in the dream of the Arab; the Boy of Winander dies into his own echoes, "received / Into the bosom of the steady lake" (5.413). The bodies of water of all of the preceding episodes now converge, as Manning suggests, in the fearful flood that threatens "all the adamantine holds"—or homes—of human truth.

Wordsworth must come to terms with Nature's accidents, its deadly and destructive responses to human voices (such as that of the Boy of Winander) that call "after" (in both senses) its own.[42] The skull upon which the melancholic Wordsworth implicitly muses as he begins this book that hints so often at death represents both the "adamantine" abode of a perishable (because Adam-like) mind—whose passion is "highest reason"—and the mind's "works," which are themselves "shrines" that are no less "frail":

> But all the meditations of mankind,
> Yea, all the adamantine holds of truth
> By reason built, or passion (which itself
> Is highest reason in a soul sublime),
> The consecrated works of bard and sage,
> Sensuous or intellectual, wrought by men,
> Twin labourers and heirs of the same hopes—
> Where would they be? Oh, why hath not the mind
> Some element to stamp her image on
> In nature somewhat nearer to her own?
> Why, gifted with such powers to send abroad
> Her spirit, must it lodge in shrines so frail?
> (37–48)

The human skull, an unreadable fossil upon which (and *in* which) the living mind of the poet dwells, would survive a second deluge; the physical organ that was once capable of reading, the books that it once read, and the books—works—that it once "wrought," would be swallowed by the rising waters. Our most exalted expressions of what it means to be human would become as "ghostly" and in-articulate as Nature's own and ancient language has become within the domain of the human. While Nature's "composure would en-sue," a scrubbed (adamantine) slate upon which surface crops would arise out of the decomposing matter exposed as the waters recede, no elegist would survive to weep for our species, a species lost in an accident not even reason would have been able to control. Like the stone and the shell that this poet next seeks to read (not in his own but in someone else's dream), the cultural relics of human hopes, thoughts, and fears will no doubt be illegible to the unimaginable beings born beyond the end of our history and our words. For like the poet dwelling upon the stone and shell, these future minds will neither have created nor have imagined the works that they will then consecrate *because* the meaning of our relics will have become inscrutable. They will indeed have become "the consecrated works of bard and sage" through which our humanity once "wrought, / For commerce of thy nature with itself," for commerce, like signification, will in such drowning die.

If they are words on paper, such shrines are as frail, as insubstantial, and as convertible as money; to imagine himself bereft of them makes Wordsworth "abject, depressed, forlorn, disconsolate." His melancholy, which even "the steadiest mood of reason" cannot relieve, derives not from his anticipation of the death of the human body on which is impressed (like coinage) "her prime teacher" (Nature) and a second teacher (culture). Rather, Wordsworth understands that between "Sovereign" Intellect and pound of flesh lies an indispensable, internalizable fetish that is simultaneously "sensuous or intellectual" and wrought by now-absent human labor. The book, a consecrated object beyond whose loss this mind shrinks, fearful, in its adamantine cave, is itself the mortal but adamantine object of someone else's (some future reader's) "meditation"; it is upon *that* object that Wordsworth, who writes for such readers, meditates. For the book signifies, like the totem of the murdered father that Freud made the founder of human cultures, both death and hidden power. Both book and skull elicit reflection because their origins, like the shell's, hide in their apparent openness; the skull, or the book, as *object* may facilitate another subject's meditation only after the object's original and perishable inhabitant has been dispossessed of its abode. Available, as such, to investments of fetishistic faith, the book and the skull are haunted with values and meanings ("commerce" and "signification") that are both foreign and inconvertible.[43]

Why is the book, like the shell and the skull, so near, Wordsworth asks, to the gray matter of the mind that creates poems out of the materials of death, and yet, inevitably, so distant from the future mind that will read it even after the author is dead?[44] Should books, the frail shrines that emerge (like human civilization, and like each human life) from the dark cave of creation, survive perilous journeys abroad (in the marketplace), even possible accidents during sea journeys (translation), they may yet end their lives as unreadable (but also as imprinted) as fossils. Even the book that is read may be endangered, for books are engendered ("stamped") like, but not quite like, living progeny; while each bears a different authorial stamp, and therefore a different "life," pedantic teaching methods are likely to produce unsympathetic, overwrought readers who read all texts the same way, readers whom Wordsworth calls mechanical "prodigies," "the monster birth / Engendered by these too industrious times" (296–97) and by "usurious" schoolmasters, "Sages who in their prescience would controul / All accidents" (380–81). Wordsworth's melancholic meditation on a skull might have led to the depressing conclusion that if all that will survive the uncontrollable flood will be either uninterpretable or misinterpreted, then perhaps it is better simply to accept (to dwell within rather than upon) the impermanent, adamantine prison house of ideology (of commerce and of signification) that, like bone, closes round the imagination, persuading "reason" that the "human" has already survived the inevitable, and perhaps even fortunate, death of Nature. For if Nature appears to have deserted the human, it is the human that ideology "consecrates." The poet turns from that possibility, however, and toward a different, no less skull-like, and still alien, dwelling: the "cave" of another's dream. Through it unfolds another morbid meditation on desertion and consecration.

Coleridge, who was on his way to Malta when Wordsworth addressed the 1805 *Prelude* to him, was the dreamer who described to Wordsworth the experience of falling asleep while reading *Don Quixote* within a cave by a sun-stricken, shimmering sea.[45] Dreaming that he had been left (or deserted) on an "Arab waste" (or desert),[46] he discovers a homeless, or "unmoored," Bedouin (a *Moor*) bearing a stone in one hand (Euclid's *Elements*), a lance in the other, and a shell beneath his arm (Poetry). Violating the laws of signification and of commerce, these objects are simultaneously illegible relics and legible books; indeed, the shell speaks to him in the poetic mode in which Wordsworth was working while composing book 5—the ode:

> . . . an unknown tongue,
> Which yet I understood, articulate sounds,

A loud prophetic blast of harmony,
An ode in passion uttered, which foretold
Destruction to the children of the earth
By deluge now at hand. . . .
(1805, 5.94–98)

The Arab describes the books he is about to bury: one "wedded man
to man by purest bond / Of nature"; the other bears "voices more
than all the winds" (105, 108). The dreamer, frightened, seeks to
"cleave unto this man" (116) who has, like the orphan, no family.
The dream ends, with the Moor / Quixote "looking backwards" at
"a glittering light" (128–29), "the fleet waters of the drowning
world / In chace of him" (136–37).

That Wordsworth, in usurping this dream of "waters," might
have sought the love and protection of a wanderer who is at home in
the "desart, crazed / By love, and feeling" (144–45), driven by "desertion" and by love to bear and to bury "Truth," is supported by the
fact that he found in book 5 two lost father figures: the drowned
schoolteacher's body surfaces later and the pedlar/schoolteacher of
the poems "The Ruined Cottage," "The Pedlar," and "Resolution
and Independence" ghosts the peripatetic Bedouin. Indeed, the
Moor appears to be a further metamorphosis of the "moorish flood"
and the "lonely moor" in and upon which the Leech-gatherer
worked. Wordsworth, who as an orphan turned with equal need to
Nature and to books, perceived in both of those "props" (to use his
own term in book 2) a feeding (like the Leech-gatherer's hosting
that is also a "conning," "As if he had been reading in a book")
that involves wandering, leaving home in a labor that is also
"homeward-bound."[47]

"Wandering" is how Wordsworth describes his (and Coleridge's)
youthful, virtually unpastured (un*pastored*) reading, an exuberant,
greedy incorporation of texts that he opposes to the cribbed and
guarded appetite of the Infant Prodigy, the disciplined but "melancholy" student, his diet restricted by the patriarchal schoolmaster.
That student will grow up to be neither a poet nor a true reader:

Oh, where had been the man, the poet where—
Where had we been we two, belovèd friend,
If we, in lieu of wandering as we did
Through heights and hollows and bye-spots of tales
Rich with indigenous produce, open ground
Of fancy, happy pastures ranged at will,

Has been attended, followed, watched, and noosed,
Each in his several melancholy walk,
Stringed like a poor man's heifer at its feed,
Led through the lanes in forlorn servitude;
Or rather like a stallèd ox shut out
From touch of growing grass, that may not taste
A flower till it have yielded up its sweets
A prelibation to the mower's scythe.
      Behold the parent hen amid her brood . . .
(5.232–46)

Unlike teachers who would pave a "broad highway" to prevent students from wandering into books or Nature, or teachers who believe that one may learn "the art / To manage books, and things, and make them *work*" (373–74; my emphasis), Wordsworth suggests in book 5 a different model for learning to read, implying that there is no unbridgeable difference between Nature's and teachers' texts:

    . . . he who in his youth
A wanderer among the woods and fields
With living Nature hath been intimate,
Not only in that raw unpractised time
Is stirred to ecstasy, as others are,
By glittering verse, but he doth furthermore,
In measure only dealt out to himself,
Receive enduring touches of deep joy
From the great Nature that exists in works
Of mighty poets. . . .
(610–19)

Implicitly, the reader who wanders like a pastoral Bedouin—whether through "heights and hollows and bye-spots of tales" or "among the woods and fields" of Nature—cannot "controul / All accidents," as would the false sages who, "skilful in the usury of time," are "stewards of our labour" (5.378–79).[48] Indeed, the reader who does not know in advance where reading may lead, but who follows nevertheless the odelike "turnings intricate of verse" into a place of desertion, may find in the darkness of a desert storm an "abode" that is a "proper home," and the words of the "shadowy things" that "work their changes there":

    . . . Visionary power
Attends upon the motions of the winds

Embodied in the mystery of words;
There darkness makes abode, and all the host
Of shadowy things do work their changes there
As in a mansion like their proper home.
Even forms and substances are circumfused
By that transparent veil with light divine,
And through the turnings intricate of verse
Present themselves as objects recognised
In flashes, and with a glory scarce their own.
(620–29)

In book 5, a book on the naturalness of a child who develops by roaming, apparently alone, within romances, the deaths of parental figures are forestalled: the mother ("parent hen"), an exemplary instructor in the arts of reading, feeds her children milk and homilies; the home of the father to which the son returns is not (yet) empty of his presence, and it is replete, also, with lost books. Even the schoolmaster returns (again), still dead but now "hallowed" because Nature's accidents have been conjoined to "purest poesy." The nightmare that opens book 5 is, in similar fashion, redeemed: the Arab wandering into the apocalypse, bearing the wind-voices of the poem-shell and following a "glittering light" as the "waters of the deep / Gather" is transformed, first, into the golden-backed *Arabian Nights* and, subsequently, into the Wordsworthian poet who has consumed that book, a poet who is not deluged, although he is vexed, or "stirred to ecstasy / By glittering verse."

Reading and writing poetry, one might conclude, is for Wordsworth wish fulfillment; for him poetry is, as Spivak herself implied in the earlier citation, that work of "consecration" Freud called a fetish: an object that allows one to deny, rather than to encounter, the death and absence that haunt its presence. To fulfill wishes is to avoid the consequences of accident. As if in evidence, Wordsworth elaborates a story of how a childhood book became a "precious treasure" for a band of schoolboys; the story begins at "that time" when the schoolmaster drowned, which establishes the event as a very early one in his days at his new fosterage, Hawkshead:

I had a precious treasure at that time,
A little yellow canvass-covered book,
A slender abstract of the *Arabian Tales;*
And when I learned, as now I first did learn
From my companions in this new abode,

That this dear prize of mine was but a block
Hewn from a mighty quarry—in a word,
That there were four large volumes, laden all
With kindred matter—'twas in truth to me
A promise scarcely earthly.
(482–91)

The book became for the boys, as did the Arab's stone and shell for the dreamer, an object that was both recognizable and impenetrable, possessing, like any other, otherwise ordinary object that is transformed into something "glittering," "a glory scarce [its] own," a value borrowed or even stolen. A part that stands in for an original, never-to-be-possessed whole, this block is "hewn from a mighty quarry" (perhaps, indeed, the "accidents" in "Quarry and in moor" that do *not* appear in the 1805 version of the Drowned Man episode). This one book in four entices the boys to pool their savings so that they may exchange money (gold) for the complete edition (will it, like the part or like gold, also be yellow?). Their hoarding scheme fails, and yet the very interruption of the act of exchange that they sought produces, as if by miracle, the "golden store of books" that surprises the poet when he returns to his father's house in the section of the poem that immediately follows.

The various fetishes of book 5 are not, in fact, produced by Wordsworth's denial of these consecrated objects' "natural" mortality, morbidity, or lack. Rather, these objects are present in *The Prelude* because Wordsworth understands that they express a child's earliest form of preservation, a burial that is, significantly, both an "interfusion" that makes the original object of love imperishable and an aggressive act of ingestion that is as destructive as any accident. Consecration depends upon burial; covenants do not. Words born not of accident but of a promise to pay the bearer, covenants, whether they are made between schoolboys or between an absent Father and an orphaned son, can never with certainty fulfill wishes in a world beset by accidents. Yet faith—mystification, consecration—may make the *words* exchanged, at least, imperishable. Scheherazade's words, as Manning and Wolfson remind us, can only forestall her death so long as mystery lingers from one uncertain ending to another until, at last, her paramour "preserves" her and puts her words into a book. In book 5, Wordsworth discovers belatedly in his father's abode the fulfillment of covenant but without paying (yet) the price: the golden store of books to whose loss he had prematurely resigned himself. In a book haunted by drownings, we may well wonder what the boy who carries that book with him on a fishing trip seeks to raise from the depths of the Derwent, again figured as a "murmuring stream," in what proves to be a productive confusion of appetites and of vocations. For, as the phrase "defrauding the day's glory" reminds us in book 5, in the opening lines of *The Prelude* few words were required of the poet whose harp "was soon defrauded." In book 5, the poet, still a boy, seeks words not for his own voice, but, rather, on which to feed:

> . . . I have lain
> Down by thy side, O Derwent, murmuring stream,
> On the hot stones and in the glaring sun,
> And there have read, devouring as I read,
> Defrauding the day's glory—desperate—
> Till with sudden bound of smart reproach
> Such as an idler deals with in his shame,
> I to my sport betook myself again.
> (5.508–15)

The word "reproach" is key in this passage: in book 1 the poet would "haply meet reproaches" in writing the poem that would "spur me on . . . / To honourable toil" (651–53). A word like "admonition" that suggests chastisement, "reproach," too, implies reunion—rapprochement—with something that has been lost, "days / Disowned by memory" (1.642–43). In book 5, the recovered (reproaching) books appease "Dumb yearnings, hidden appetites" (530) "And they must have their food" (531). If the child whom Wordsworth describes in book 5 as sitting "on the throne" (532) has more power than all of the "elements" (hinting, of course, at Euclid's adamantine book), his true friends—writers of romances—are disdained by reason's "ape" (Philosophy) as "Forgers," "Imposters, drivellers, dotards" (548–50), the frauds who would defraud the dreamer. The friends of the hungry and lonely child are the dreamers whose dreams the child (like the boy tutored by Nature earlier in *The Prelude*) appropriates precociously, dreamers who "make our wish our power, our thought a deed, / An empire, a possession" (552–53). The writer of romances is Creation's residual demiurge "to whom / Earth crouches, th' elements are potter's clay" (554–55).

"Even unto tears I sometimes could be sad," the poet continues, that he no longer can recover the pleasure he once derived from works that he, as a youth, "consecrated" (570). One might counter that, in "missing" imaginatively to the point of tears an *experience* of grief that once would have stricken him had he lost such works, the older poet in fact maintains possession of the child's correspondence with the various forms of water through which Nature once spoke to him, including the "trickling tear" through which the child, before he outgrew such tastes, once listened to the dreamers' stories with a "look / That drinks as if it never could be full" (189–92). Even so did Adam, and the Wordsworths, hear, tearfully, of the Flood. Compared with the "dimpling cistern" of the Infant Prodigy's heart (345), the tears of the boy and the poet are imitative of those shed by "Old Grandame Earth," who, "grieved to find / The playthings which her love designed for him / Unthought of—in their woodland beds the flowers / Weep, and the river-sides are all forlorn" (346–49). Yet, in a sense, tears have become for the disillusioned poet-reader simply tokens of a lost (or now unconscious) pleasure, its pleasure surrendered to a "conscious pleasure" in "words themselves":

> It might demand a more impassioned strain
> To tell of later pleasures linked to these,
> A tract of the same isthmus which we cross
> In progress from our native continent
> To earth and human life—I mean to speak
> Of that delightful time of growing youth
> When cravings for the marvellous relent,
> And we begin to love what we have seen;
> And sober truth, experience, sympathy,
> Take stronger hold of us; and words themselves
> Move us with conscious pleasure.
> (5.558–68)

Words may offer two, perhaps conflicting, rewards for the poet Wordsworth became. They may lead from immature "cravings for the marvellous" to a desire for "sober truth," yet words may also reproduce, when repeated and rhymed (as in poetry), a child's earliest pleasure in what Freud termed the "repetition compulsion." Wordsworth writes that he was thirteen when "My ears began to open to the charm / Of words in tuneful order" (577–78), spoken while wandering "abroad" (as once through tales or silently in Nature) "in the public roads" (585, 581–86). When put to the work of an adult mind, words indeed may unveil "truth," induct the speaker into "experience," divest consecrated objects of false glitter, in-

still habits of reasoning. They may seek a substitute garment—
"something loftier, more adorned, / Than is the common aspect,
daily garb" (599–600). Yet the process that Wordsworth clearly
values in the pleasure he came to derive from words divests words
themselves of their habitual (if invisible) work of *bearing* meanings
and values from lost objects to new truths. In so doing, the poet
reinvests (or, one might say, *buries*) in the very process of verbal
exchange the consecrating glory revealed in a brief and linguistic
apocalypse.

Wordsworth, recognizing in the word "vex" the same origins as
the words "divest," "invest," and "vestment," concludes in the
spots of time, as he did in his essays on epitaphs, that even when
words are "counter-spirits," wearing "poisoned vestments," they
may (through the wisdom of Nature) instruct poets. Another term
associated with the covering of human nakedness, the "habitual"
may be Nature's tool for re-naturalizing a thought that has estranged itself from its sources. Yet the *un*habitual is no less her tool.
"Habit" points to home, "habitat," and derives from an Old English word for "to hold" or "have." Habit, an unconscious and
repeated tendency, implies the death drive that Freud discovered in
a child's repetitive repudiation and reclamation of a play object, a
vexation that both denies and exposes loss. Like the fetish, habit
may be a covering of nakedness or, if the person clothed is female, of
a sexual absence. If we accept this restrictive interpretation of "absence," then the "shaking off" of habit may be viewed as the revelation of a "lack," in the feminine or in Nature, that accrues authority
to a mind gendered as masculine and figured as human reason.

Such has been the standard, and Oedipal, reading of the spots of
time, moments when the "deadly weight" of habit—"trivial occupations" and "ordinary intercourse"—are "relieved" because the poet
reencounters (from a safe distance) a woman whose "vestments" are
seductively "vexed" and a father whose absent place the boy may
now assume. Words arrive to stand in the place of both "lack" and
"absence," according to Oedipal readings of these vexatious moments in *The Prelude*, helping the poetic son to sublimate his desire
for the maternal body and to surrender his premature eagerness to
assume the father's place by identifying with the "habits" of masculinity. Yet words, for Wordsworth, are neither substitutes for lost
objects nor fetishes that deny loss even as they claim to expose truth.
Rather, they are, in his own terms "passages" of meaning and of "*life*
in which / We have had deepest feeling that the mind / Is lord and

master, and that outward sense, / Is but the obedient servant of her will" (11.269–72). If like Wordsworth we choose not to restrict mind and its will to the masculine ("her will"), then we may return to these moments of passage—spots of time—that are vexed by wind and attended by water to discover, in the alien and isolated objects that have been invested by memory with mysterious meaning and value, the experience Freud himself associated with vexatious repetition: not the Oedipal sublime but the uncanny, where the habitual becomes suddenly unhabitual, and where the aesthetic "order" of Nature, no less than of poetry, may "disorder."[49]

Wordsworth's first pleasure in "words in tuneful order," he writes in book 5, originated in walks with his friend John Fleming, "Repeating favorite verses with one voice" (588). While the verse was "overwrought" (594), "no vulgar power / Was working in us" as the boys exchanged "the common aspect, daily garb, / Of human life" for "a never-ending show" (600–601, 606). In such "adornment," Wordsworth writes in his discussion of melancholic crisis in book 11, Nature herself is restored to "glorious apparition, now all eye / And now all ear, but ever with the heart / Employed, and the majestic intellect!" (11.143–45). And so the cure for his depression comes with seeming simplicity: "I shook the habit off / Entirely and for ever, and again"—like the naked god standing in the thunder shower—"In Nature's presence stood, as I stand now, / A sensitive, and a *creative* soul" (253–56).

If the (bad) habit of judging with the unfeeling (and unfed) eye may be shaken off, perhaps it is because the habit itself originated in Wordsworth's "shaking off," through reason's effort to achieve "resolute mastery" over "The accidents of nature, time, and place" (10.821–22). Through a judging eye "blind" to "the restraint of general laws," that shaking off led to a denial of "the weak being of the past" (823). Yet a shaking off also occurs much earlier in *The Prelude,* at the very moment when the poet claims to have recovered his vocation. In book 1, unspecified "mountings of the mind" (mountings that seem, in every way, *not* equivalent to reason's mastery in later books) "came fast upon" the poet, who has declared that he "cannot miss [his] way" in his journey homeward, even if he wanders like the water-bearing cloud that is his guide:

> The earth is all before me—with a heart
> Joyous, nor scared at its own liberty,
> I look about, and should the guide I chuse

Be nothing better than a wandering cloud
I cannot miss my way. I breathe again—
Trances of thought and mountings of the mind
Come fast upon me. It is shaken off,
As by miraculous gift 'tis shaken off,
That burthen of my own unnatural self,
The heavy weight of many a weary day
Not mine, and such as were not made for me.

. . . .

Long months of ease and undisturbed delight
Are mine in prospect. . . .
(1.15–25, 28–29)

In book 1, Wordsworth shakes off the judging mind's admonishment to work, even in these passages that so strongly echo Adam
and Eve's "wand'ring steps and slow" in the final passages of *Paradise
Lost* as they leave Paradise for a life of labor. Yet the poet also may
well wish to avoid acknowledging that the ultimate "way" that he
cannot "miss," the ultimate "prospect" from which he may see the
future, is the final destination of life: death. In the hour in which he
is chosen to receive from nature a "gift" that, significantly, "*consecrates* my joy" (40; my emphasis) by blowing upon him "the sweet
breath of heaven," he feels "within / A corresponding mild creative
breeze" (41, 42–43). Yet that mild breeze soon becomes "A tempest,
a redundant energy, / Vexing its own creation" (46–47). If "shaking
off" imitates either the energy that creates and consecrates or the
redundant energy that vexes and may even destroy, it nevertheless,
as Wordsworth says of the spots of time, lifts "us up when fallen"
(11.267). Indeed, he attributes these gifts to an "efficacious spirit"
that hints at the distant "correspondent breeze" (11.268). Yet this
spirit, which the poet calls in the final line of the verse paragraph a
"beneficent influence" (278), "lurks" like a specter in what he calls
"passages of life" that are characterized as much by falling and by
submission as by "mountings" of the masterful "mind" (267; 1.20).

In each of the spots of time, as critics have amply noted, the
chosen son's hopes, confidence, and expectations mount, only to be,
literally, overthrown. In the first encounter, a five-year-old "through
fear / Dismounting" is "disjoined" from (deserted by) his older
companion on a "stony moor" (11.285–86). Descending, on foot,
the boy encounters a "monumental writing" inscribed upon the
(deserted) moor's face: where the "grass is cleared away" the "letters

are all fresh and visible," commemorating a public hanging that occurred there (294, 297–98). Susan Wolfson argues that Wordsworth's "confusion" of "a murderer at Penrith" (and his mother's death at Penrith) with "a hanging at Hawkshead a hundred years ago" "weaves a tangled web of death, guilt, and displaced punishment" in this spot.[50] In fact, however, there may be more interesting, and less Oedipal, connections to be made from this confusion. "Penrith" in a near-homonym connects this event with the hanging of the boy, suspended in book 1 from a "pinnacle," and the boy's experience of "blank desertion" after his writerly experience in the "pinnace" in that same book. This spot, where a hanging transpired, may also be linked to Gallow Hill, the happy home of the Wordsworths' close friends, the Hutchinsons, one of whom Wordsworth will have married by the time he returns to this "spot" in the 1805 *Prelude*. Wordsworth recalls visiting Penrith with Mary Hutchinson and his sister in 1787 (ll. 315–27), a recollection that is itself, even to the reiterative diction, a return to an earlier moment in *The Prelude*.[51] But the association of all of these events, somehow, with the mother's death at Penrith may well be confirmed by the events that follow the boy's encounter on the "stony" moor.

As he reascends a "bare" common, he glimpses, first, a "naked pool" (whose associations with the feminine, death, and silence we are now accustomed to recognize) and then an upright stone signal-beacon (source of a form of communication and also, of course, symbolically suggestive of the organ of paternal generation). Then a woman appears whose "vexed" clothing threatens to divest her (as they did the drowned man in the episode that once immediately preceded this one) of her garments. She is the vehicle of an object's passage from (perhaps) the "naked pool" to whatever destination (or home) the winds prevent her from reaching. She is the source also, one might argue, not only of nurture but also of life, even if we surmise this apparition (as is the poet's mother) to be dead. In the "pitcher" that this figure "bore" upon her head she may be, like the wandering cloud, carrying water or, in the waters borne within this uterine-shaped vessel, life—creation—itself. Her passage is imperiled, like that (one might say) of metaphor no less than of life (for metaphor has its origins in the word to "bear" and implies *death* as well as life): to "bear *away*"). Like the breeze of creation that began the *Prelude* ("A tempest, a redundant energy, / Vexing its own creation" [1.46–47]), she is vexed by a "strong wind":[52]

A girl who bore a pitcher on her head
And seemed with difficult steps to force her way
Against the blowing wind. It was, in truth,
An ordinary sight, but I should need
Colours and words that are unknown to man
To paint the visionary dreariness
Which, while I looked all round for my lost guide,
Did at that time invest the naked pool,
The beacon on the lonely eminence,
The woman, and her garments vexed and tossed
By the strong wind. . . .
(11.306–15)

In book 5 the poet compares the "isthmus which we cross / In progress . . . / To earth and human life" to "words" that "move" of (and by) "themselves," giving "pleasure" to the young reader without requiring him to abandon an object of need or desire (560–68). Language, this passage implies, is a narrow strip of land that connects the poet journeying (as in the Immortality Ode) from what he here calls a "native continent" (561) to his fosterage in the world, surrounded by waters that may sustain, inspire, or engulf. In this spot of time, the work (both pleasurable and fearful) of words—the perilous transference of meaning from object to word to auditor or reader that in book 5 depressed the meditative poet—is performed through all of the elements through which Nature previously inducted the young poet, sustaining him from falling altogether into alienation from Nature and its "voice," into the elements of his (and Nature's) vocation: water, wind, and feet. If this spot of time "repairs" the "depressed" imagination, if it even "re-pairs" that imagination with objects it has lost, the poet nevertheless continues to experience "dreariness" and "melancholy" as well as the regressive "pleasure" of an object that has been hoarded and withheld from exchange—the "gold" of "youth's golden gleam":

> . . . When, in blessèd season,
> With those two dear ones—to my heart so dear—
> When in blessèd time of early love,
> Long afterwards I roamed about
> In daily presence of this very scene,
> Upon the naked pool and dreary crags,
> And on the melancholy beacon, fell

The spirit of pleasure and youth's golden gleam—
And think ye not with radiance more divine
From these remembrances, and from the power
They left behind? So feeling comes in aid
Of feeling, and diversity of strength
Attends us, if but once we have been strong.
(315–27)

An element, like the "radiance" of the "divine," gold, no less than Nature and the original objects of love we lose even as we step from Nature's imminence, persists only *through* burial in a culture that founds value on the invisibility of money's original form and the banishment of the father who founds the Law. Its value is restored to Wordsworth in later years when he reencounters the vexing figure by journeying to this spot with Dorothy and Mary.[53] The word "strong" that concludes this passage, while it may be conventionally associated with masculinity, is qualified in an intriguingly feminine representation of creative power, and its nurture, as a "diversity of strength" that employs words to "enshrine" rather than *bare* the spirit it seeks both to reveal and to bury for "future restoration":

Oh mystery of man, from what a depth
Proceed thy honours! I am lost, but see
In simple childhood something of the base
On which thy greatness stands—but this I feel,
That from thyself it is that thou must give,
Else never canst receive. The days gone by
Come back upon me from the dawn almost
Of life; the hiding-places of my power
Seem open, I approach, and then they close;
I see by glimpses now, when age comes on
May scarcely see at all; and I would give
While yet we may, as far as words can give,
A substance and a life to what I feel:
I would enshrine the spirit of the past
For future restoration. . . .
(328–42)

In the second spot of time, a missing mount once again frustrates the boy. He is now thirteen and waiting to return to his father on horses that are to be brought to the brothers to "bear us home." Climbing, on foot, to an "eminence" to which he "repairs," a meeting point "Of two highways ascending," the boy is, in effect, protected by "nakedness": he "sate half sheltered by a naked wall" (352–57). On this day "Stormy, and rough, and wild," his imagination singles out a sheep, which is silent, and a hawthorn that "whistles" (unlike the thorn that accompanied his encounter with the discharged soldier in book 4). Mist allows only an "intermitting prospect" of the scene below. Ten days later, "I and my two brothers, orphans then, / Followed his body to the grave" (366–67). If this mist-enshrouded experience is, as has been so often read, a poet's submission to (or surpassing of) Oedipal identification with his father (like the mist that gathers at the laborer's heels at the end of *Paradise Lost*), it is also a recognition that where the father leads, the sons can only—all too soon—follow. If the poet's "anxiety of hopes," his "desires" have been corrected by God, not only has Wordsworth, in this scene, made God indistinguishable from Nature, but He has spoken, as Nature will itself in book 13, through a "*business*" of the "elements" that is also "music," "spectacles and sounds" that move, as though on foot, simultaneously (and in defiance of either signification or exchange) on "*two* roads" (my emphasis) even as they remain lodged in one place (and immovable) in his memory. Not only will the poet "repair" (and repair *to*) this memory ("whence depressed," as he said earlier, such spots "nourished and invisibly repaired" the mind), but also he will "*drink* / As at a fountain" (my emphasis). In so doing, the poet recovers "the bleak music of that old stone wall, / The noise of wood and water, and the mist" so that *he* may "recover" from depressive "dreariness." Yet this source of sustenance is so thoroughly "*re*-covered," becoming a spring buried deep within, that it seems undepletable. Both source and process, this spot returns the boy to the linguistic sustenance of a Nature that fostered him by both introducing him to, and forestalling, vocation. It reminds him that whether water heals or chastises, it involves "work" that is more like *grace:*

> All these were spectacles and sounds to which
> I often would repair, and thence would drink
> As at a fountain. And I do not doubt
> That in this later time, when storm and rain
> Beat on my roof at midnight, or by day
> When I am in the woods, unknown to me
> The workings of my spirit thence are brought.
> (382–88)

Wordsworth revised his original intention to make this sobering encounter a final revelation (much as Adam receives) from a mist-enclosed prospect. In choosing to conclude *The Prelude* with the ascent of Mount Snowdon—a vision in which the mist opens, followed by a revision of the meditation, caves, and engulfments of book 5—the poet represents Nature as an Imagination that discovers itself in a spot, a hiding place of power that seems only to be an emptiness, from which it receives nourishment, reparation, and even (as we shall see) an aesthetic pleasure that "feeds" and "repairs" rather than impairs "vision."

"The Homeless Voice of Waters"

In the mist-bound illusion that has closed in the poet's plodding consciousness at the beginning of book 13, the poet suddenly glimpses an opening through which he might, from great height, have "fallen." Having climbed Snowdon in anticipation of a sublime (and distant) prospect, the poet in fact experiences the disappointment of "a dripping mist / Low-hung and thick that covered all the sky" (11–12). Nature offers no invigorating breath or melodic murmuring in this ambiguous landscape "Half-threatening storm and rain" (13). Poet and Nature seem set against one another, much as the depressed poet had been in previous books at "war against myself." "With forehead bent / Earthward, as if in opposition set / Against an enemy, I panted up" (29–31).

Suddenly, however, the landscape is transformed by the moon's emergence. A metaphor earlier in *The Prelude* for mental errancy and correction, the moon then was a harbinger or even confirmation (for his was a "clouded," not a "waning" moon) of the recovery that Dorothy had wrought. Nature had then (as it will now) "Conducted me to open day" through "the weary labyrinth" (10.922–23) of confusion and depression; but the poet, on Snowdon, has usurped the role of his human guide (called, here, a conductor) by walking alone and in front. The moon reveals itself through an opening in the clouds, an opening that in turn reveals to the poet reflecting *in* its glory another opening beneath him. In the mist that opens he glimpses a spot that might have led to an accidental fall. There he also witnesses how Nature (in sublime but also in parodic imitation of the poet's earlier "gloomy" "usurpation" of its powers through an eye-governed reason that would control all accidents) puts the eye's "reality"—"the real sea" as he will call it—in its place even as Nature preserves this poet through the moonlight that "fell":

> For instantly a light upon the turf
> Fell like a flash. I looked about, and lo,
> The moon stood naked in the heavens at height
> Immense above my head, and on the shore
> I found myself of a huge sea of mist,
> Which meek and silent rested at my feet.
> A hundred hills their dusky backs upheaved
> All over this silent ocean, and beyond,
> Far, far beyond, the vapours shot themselves . . .
> (39–47)

Nature combines in this single setting all "the business of the elements" that threatened the boy in the spots of time, and the language through which it had instructed the poet in books 1 and 2. For in the passage that follows, the mist of "tongues" will dissolve into the open silence of Nature's "breathing-place," through which waters imitate the movement of the spots of time: they "*mount.*" Nature speaks in this scene both in the "roar of waters, torrents, streams" and in the "breach" of speech, "the homeless voice of waters." It has "lodged" an image of its "soul, the imagination of the whole" in the very places of loss, absence, or desolation—the "blue chasm, a fracture in the vapour," and "that breach":[54]

> Far, far beyond, the vapours shot themselves
> In headlands, tongues, and promontory shapes,
> Into the sea, the real sea, that seemed
> To dwindle and give up his majesty,
> Usurped upon as far as sight could reach.
> Meanwhile, the moon looked down upon this shew
> In single glory, and we stood, the mist
> Touching our very feet; and from the shore
> At distance not the third part of a mile
> Was a blue chasm, a fracture in the vapour,
> A deep and gloomy breathing-place, through which
> Mounted the roar of waters, torrents, streams
> Innumerable, roaring with one voice.
> The universal spectacle throughout
> Was shaped for admiration and delight,

Grand in itself alone, but in that breach
Through which the homeless voice of waters rose,
That dark deep thoroughfare, had Nature lodged
The soul, the imagination of the whole.

(47–65)

In this place where "heads" are also "lands," and where "headlands" are themselves Nature's playful, self-admiring, and self-delighting imitation of those that lie, earthbound, below (where the real sea encroaches), a mounting and even a surmounting occurs, but it is a mounting not of the poet's lonely mind or powers but, rather, of the "waters, torrents, streams / Innumerable" that now speak in unison. For in this sublime encounter awe mounts not (as it does in Kant's description of the sublime) in reason's aggrandizement of the "other" consciousness just revealed. Rather, in this "perfect image of "mighty mind" the unrepresentable—that absence or emptiness figured by the lacunae through which the vision appears—is, through Nature's genius, made palpable *as* the source on which Imagination "feeds." The poet recognizes in Nature's recovery of wholeness ("the imagination of the whole") a re-covering of a "hidden" source that must be figured as a "hole" (for, like the uncanny and maternal source of life in feminine "lack," it is both unrecognizable—unfamiliar—and simultaneously *too* familiar. "Some other being," which the poet describes as a consciousness that exists in addition to "self," Nature characterizes (and perhaps sexualizes) as an oracular authority that is, indeed, an orifice.[55] A Creator who, through metaphorical passages, exists inevitably in the troubled *vide* (the "blank desertion," the "homeless voice") that lies between two destinations, Nature at this climax joins the homeless Moor wandering on desert or moor, the books that travel mysteriously between "covenant" and the paternal dwelling, and the woman crossing from naked pool to the beacon of manhood. Nature, in turn, calls to the poet to bear both Nature's consecrated works (the shell and the stone) and the "consecrated works of bard and sage." In that still-mysterious uterine vessel, of the spot of time whose veiled meanings are transported across the self-vexing winds of speech, these missions are condensed. In Nature's apparent absence, the poet himself (as he did as a boy in the second spot of time) must make the difficult translation that is both thwarted and revealed in the "business of the elements." Nature's intervention *through* these elements is severe but also nurturing, impeding the orphaned son's inevitable arrival at a manhood—and a linguistic competence—that leads surely only to mutual death.

In response to this apocalyptic encounter with Nature's creative imagination, Wordsworth reconceives the act of meditation that earlier opened book 5. Dwelling no longer at reflective (and melancholic) distance on, and in, an empty, cave or shell of an "adamantine" skull, the poet on Snowden discovers meditation "rising" from within, for he (like Christ on his own pinnacle in *Paradise Regained*) does *not* fall into the open breach. When Nature's image "Had passed away" (68), we might have expected the poet, abandoned on a mountain that is itself, no less than the poet, lonely, to feel (as in book 5) "abject, forlorn, disconsolate" before what seems, in such passage, a kind of death. But in fact the poet has discovered that his mind is not only like Nature's, but that because he is *most* like Nature when he "represents," seeking and finding apt means of self-expression, he will also (as has Nature) discover within his own mind, wherever he makes his home, a presence that *is* Nature's very "under-presence." He bears, within himself, Nature's invisible "infinity" upon which his mind may "feed."

In Nature's haunted pasturage persists a "sense of God, or whatsoe'er is dim / Or vast in its own being" (72–73).[56] Nature, the poet continues, has "With circumstance most awful and sublime" thereby revealed "One function of such mind," a mind that Wordsworth, significantly, identifies at this point with both Nature *and* the God that Nature has disclosed. Nature, who can hide as well as reveal, in this moment used its "domination" "upon the outward face of things" *not* (demiurgically) to "mould," "endue," "subtract," "combine" but rather to make "unhabitual" this hidden object: Nature's soul, its imagination, which is to say, God, "whatsoe'er is dim." The power the poetic witness feels after this sublime encounter is in every sense "imitative" of Nature, which has created a "brother" in the poet's imagination that now belongs to the family of "higher minds" who "bear" Nature's "glorious faculty" "as their own":

> The sense of God, or whatsoe'er is dim
> Or vast in its own being—above all,
> One function of such mind had Nature there
> Exhibited by putting forth, and that
> With circumstance most awful and sublime:
> That domination which she oftentimes

Exerts upon the outward face of things,
So moulds them, and endues, abstracts, combines,
Or by abrupt and unhabitual influence
Doth make one object so impress itself
Upon all others, and pervades them so,
That even the grossest minds must see and hear,
And cannot chuse but feel. The power which these
Acknowledge when thus moved, which Nature thus
Thrusts forth upon the senses, is the express
Resemblance—in the fullness of its strength
Made visible—a genuine counterpart
And brother of the glorious faculty
Which higher minds bear with them as their own.
(72–90)

The "imitative" influence of Nature upon the "face," no less than Nature's power to "move" the soul whom it has created in its own image that it may, in turn, "create," might return us to that earlier moment in *The Prelude* ("blessed the infant babe") in which the mother's face appears to the poet at the very moment when he, in discussing "*habitual*" influence, found it difficult to recover "origins." In book II, Wordsworth describes how Nature "intervenient till this time" in its molding of the poet (often, in book 2, through acts of eating and drinking) becomes itself an object of his gaze and his desire, "sought / For her own sake" (2.207–8).[57] In making Nature an object, however, the poet encounters, even in retrospect, the frustration of separating what was once not only "intervenient" but, as he says in the "blessed babe" passage that follows, "interfused." As he reconstructs in book 2 the moment in which he believed (erroneously) that he had thrust Nature beyond his own boundaries, he discovers (as he does in books 10 and 11) that to seek to "point as with a wand" to the "portion of the river of my mind" that "came from yon fountain" is to engage—when we most think we are acquiring intellectual authority—in "weakness" (213–15).[58] We are making, the poet contends, of "Science" (whose "glory" is a "boast") "a prop / To our infirmity," a prop that is a phallic but impotent wand:

In weakness we create distinctions, then
Deem that our puny boundaries are things
Which we perceive, and not which we have made.
. . . .

Hard task to analyse a soul, in which
Not only general habits and desires,
But each most obvious and particular thought—
Not in a mystical and idle sense,
But in the words of reason deeply weighed—
Hath no beginning.
(2.222–24, 232–36)

Exemplifying an alternative use of reason that weighs deeply rather than seeks superficially, in the lines that follow (237–303) Wordsworth moves back to the imaginary moment of the blessed babe where the mind "spreads" and "receives"; that moment concludes with a prop that sustains (as "Science," analysis, and reason cannot) the orphan whose "mind lay open." For even after "the props of my affection were removed," even as the orphan is "left alone / Seeking the visible world, nor knowing why," because his mind has not yet opposed "self" to "world" through *eye*, "All that I beheld / Was dear to me." To "Nature's finer influxes / My mind lay open," maintaining "intimate communion" through the *heart* "with the minuter properties / Of objects which already are beloved, / And of those only."

Even as the poet in book 2 learns from the babe that to be created by a mother through Nature's interfused presence is to possess a wise and productive passiveness ("creator and receiver both"), the poet who has been inspired on Mount Snowdon comes to understand that the appropriate "spirit" in which to approach "all the objects of the universe" imitates the child's mind that (like Nature's) spreads: "They from their native selves can send abroad / Like transformation, for themselves create / A like existence" (13.93–95). "Willing to work and to be wrought upon," such minds "need not extraordinary calls" to a vocation "To rouze them" (100–101). In language that closely parallels the blessed babe passage, Wordsworth in lines 100–119 describes minds that are "powers" because they are—in a carefully ambiguous word—"*occupied.*" The "consciousness" that occupies the mind "infuses" (through "habit" in a more positive valence) "every image," "every thought," in a vocation that is an "endless *occupation* for the soul" (110–12; my emphasis). Such occupation is both linguistic ("discursive") and unconscious ("intuitive"). It leads to the overcoming of depression (to "chearfulness") and to a "delight / That fails not, in the external universe" because that universe is also, itself, an expression of a consciousness—*Nature* who is indivisible from the "*Deity*"—which occupies, and expresses itself, in and through both self and world.

"Genuine liberty" (122) in book 13 accrues, like the return of "imaginative power" in book 11 ("again / In Nature's presence stood, as I stand now, / A sensitive, and a *creative* soul" [255–56]), to a mind that preserves what Reason in books 10 and 11 sought to shake off. Recalling, in book 13 (128–43), that earlier period as a time when the "better mind" suffered "falls" through the very "accidents of life" it had tried to control, the poet recognizes that he at least avoided succumbing to Reason's most potent tyranny: an "enslavement" of the mind through the operations of the habitual that, in contemporary terms, we might call the interpellation (the "hailing" or "calling") of an ideology, the voice of authority that "substitutes a universe of death" by co-opting the same discursive and unconscious processes (using both "fear and love" and both "pain and joy") through which Nature has sought to instruct the poet to whom she has called in her own, life-giving, language.[59] To encounter in the landscape an echo of the unconscious processes, and loci, of these conflicting voices, may only be deemed "evil" (and, one might add, *Oedipal*) to the extent that one fails to hear Nature's voice, interpreting what seems at first its silence as its death:

> The tendency, too potent in itself,
> Of habit to enslave the mind—I mean
> Oppress it by the laws of vulgar sense,
> And substitute a universe of death,
> The falsest of all worlds, in place of that
> Which is divine and true. To fear and love
> (To love as first and chief, for there fear ends)
> Be this ascribed, to early intercourse
> In presence of sublime and lovely forms
> With the adverse principles of pain and joy—
> Evil as one is rashly named by those
> Who know not what they say. . . .
> (138–49)

Ideology, imitating the processes through which Nature had inducted the poet into its language, usurps the "under-presence" of power that had once been Nature's, turning Nature itself into an object of ideology's newly constructed subjectivity,[60] and creating subjects that speak the language of a slave without knowing what they say.

In that treacherous and echoing absence, the self may seem an Adam capable of so internalizing the Law that he misrecognizes as a higher love that which disjoins him from Eve, with "no other" to "divide with thee this work," no Nature to "intervene / To fashion" his "ability" (189–90). If we accept the "Imagination" (185) as a place where, as the poet may seem to imply, "Here must thou be, O man, / Strength to thyself," then we may conclude (as have so many readers of *The Prelude*) that the vision of Imagination to which Nature has led Wordsworth is indeed a state that transcends its own, a state that remains in some way not clearly specified associated with the freedom the poet sought earlier by way of reason's capacity to "cut off its sources." Yet there is a contrary reading that begins with the poet's description of Imagination and "intellectual love," in which they are described as "each in each, and cannot stand / Dividually" (185–93). Imagination, mind, and heart stand together only, finally, in one very important spot and time within the self, within "the recesses of thy nature, far / From any reach of outward fellowship" (195–96) and far, it would seem, also from the reach of ideology. For that place originated when the poet's infant heart imitated the tenderness of "a nursing mother's heart" (206) and, even if his soul has now "risen / Up to the height of feeling intellect," it will "want no humbler tenderness" (204–7). "This love more intellectual," Wordsworth writes earlier in refutation of the "habit to enslave the mind," "cannot be without imagination," which he calls "reason in her most exalted mood" (166–69). That mood he represents in a metaphor of a "cavern" that is as easily associable with feminine reproduction and nurture as with Plato's cave of blind men and false representations.[61] As in the blessed babe passage, this one begins with a question (and a problem) of origins that is associated with waters. As in book 5, these waters that originate with the image of a cave may threaten as well as create, leading to thoughts not only of "human life" but also of the "works of man":

> This faculty hath been the moving soul
> Of our long labour: we have traced the stream
> From darkness, and the very place of birth
> In its blind cavern, whence is faintly heard
> The sound of waters; followed it to light
> And open day, accompanied its course
> Among the ways of Nature, afterwards
> Lost sight of it bewildered and engulphed,

Then given it greeting as it rose once more
With strength, reflecting in its solemn breast
The works of man, and face of human life;
And lastly, from its progress we have drawn
The feeling of life endless, the one thought
By which we live, infinity and God.
(171–84)

Nature, from (and through) the chasm of its spectacle, earlier evoked in the poet a sense of infinity, or "God, or whatsoe'er is dim" through "That domination which she oftentimes / Exerts upon the outward face of things" (77–78). In this passage, however, Nature has been not only creation (soul) and creator (*moving* soul) but also the stream and its reflection. What "its solemn breast" returns, after an engulfment, is nothing less than "the works of man" and something so personal—the "face of human life"—that Wordsworth cannot leave its meaning unelaborated, even if it seems to have been subsumed, with those works, into the infinity on which we feed and "by which we live."

That face is Dorothy's, as we discover several lines later, the sister by the "thought of" whom Wordsworth indeed (and in every sense) "lived." Through her "countenance," he suggests, he "imbibed" and *imitated* an imagination that cannot be cut off from human "tenderness," even as it imitates the once-masculine sublime in its most terrifying aspects:

For all that friendship, all that love can do,
All that a darling countenance can look
Or dear voice utter, to complete the man,
Perfect him, made imperfect in himself,
All shall be his. And he whose soul hath risen
Up to the height of feeling intellect
Shall want no humbler tenderness, his heart
Be tender as a nursing mother's heart;
Of female softness shall his life be full,
Of little loves and delicate desires,
Mild interests and gentlest sympathies.

Child of my parents, sister of my soul,
Elsewhere have strains of gratitude been breathed
To thee for all the early tenderness
Which I from thee imbibed. And true it is

That later seasons owed to thee no less;
For, spite of thy sweet influence and the touch
Of other kindred hands that opened out
The springs of tender thought in infancy,
And spite of all which singly I had watched
Of elegance, and each minuter charm
In Nature or in life, still to the last—
Even to the very going-out of youth,
The period which our story now hath reached—
I too exclusively esteemed that love,
And sought that beauty, which as Milton sings
Hath terror in it. . . .
(201–26)

So, we might add in conclusion, have Wordsworth's recent readers. If it is no longer possible to read without embarrassment lines written by a male poet that celebrate "little loves," "delicate desires," and "gentlest sympathies," then we may well gauge the success of an Oedipalizing culture that depresses the modern reader (as it depressed Wordsworth) by its claims to demote emotion to sentiment, face to a prosopopoeia that elicits defacement, and Nature to flowers. Wordsworth, more fortunate than such readers, possessed a sister who knew that Nature, while she may bestow grace through the terror of faceless desertion (or of empty nests), also speaks through flowers that thrive in those chasms, flowers (however mean) that, in twinkling, bespeak their familiarity with the distant stars:

My soul, too reckless of mild grace, had been
Far longer what by Nature it was framed—
Longer retained its countenance severe—
A rock with torrents roaring, with the clouds
Familiar, and a favorite of the stars;
But thou didst plant its crevices with flowers,
Hang it with shrubs that twinkle in the breeze,
And teach the little birds to build their nests
And warble in its chambers. . . .
(228–36)

For in the passage from flower to star, or from the heavens to earth's crevices, we may yet witness metaphors that enable us to hear what Claudette Sartiliot, in her final book, calls a "language of flowers."[62] If death is "linguistic," Sartiliot muses in her implicit challenge to de Man's term, it is a predicament only if we strip from Nature her voices and her faces. To see and to hear, in the most contemporary ways that science now teaches us—and that poetry also may teach us—requires, in the words of Philip Kuberski, that we recognize in Nature's tropes a "passageway from the world of stars and seas, stones and water to the world of living creatures,"[63] which include, of course, ourselves.

Afterword:
"The Poet Is Dead in Me"

In my long illness I had compelled into hours of Delight many a sleepless, painful hour of Darkness by chasing down metaphysical Game—and since then I have continued the Hunt, till I found myself unaware at the Root of Pure Mathematics. . . . all sounds of similitude kept at such a distance from each other in my mind, that I have *forgotten* how to make a rhyme. . . . I look at the Mountains (that visible God Almighty that looks in at all my windows), I look at the Mountains only for the curves of their outlines; the Stars, as I behold them, form themselves into Triangles. . . . The Poet is dead in me.

SAMUEL TAYLOR COLERIDGE, letter to William Godwin,
March 25, 1801

The death of poetry will not be hastened by any reader's broodings, yet it seems just to assume that poetry in our tradition, when it dies, will be self-slain, murdered by its own past strength. An implied anguish throughout this book is that Romanticism, for all its glories, may have been a vast visionary tragedy, the self-baffled enterprise not of Prometheus but of blinded Oedipus, who did not know that the Spinx was his Muse.

HAROLD BLOOM, *The Anxiety of Influence*

"Romantic Love," Harold Bloom writes in *The Anxiety of Influence,* can only be "an oxymoron." "Romantic Love is the closest analogue of Poetic Influence, another splendid perversity of the spirit. . . . The poet confronting his Great Original must find the fault that is not there."[1] Even the "begetting" of a poem is an act for Bloom only of masculine aggression, and inevitably it is an act not of pleasure or of creation but of impotence, resentment, and "ursurpation" (37). To be "influenced," Bloom argues, is to be "anxious." To love, he writes in *Yeats,* borrowing a citation from Valéry, is in fact to hate: " 'One only reads well when one reads with some quite personal goal in mind. It may be to acquire some power. It can be out of hatred for the author.' "[2] In such aggressive avowals Bloom disavows the love that so clearly underwrites his devoted, overwrought readings of poems. Indeed, the example of Bloom might tell us that readers, no less than poets, suffer when they deny their devotion to the fetishized texts that father (or mother) them. For one only reads well when one's avowed hatred, one's usurpation of someone else's power, springs (whether one knows it or not) from the reservoir of a more archaic relation, one that we may define as need, desire, or love.[3] Bloom, master of the apt but unfathered citation, provocatively produced from his prodigious memories of readings, his own resentments and misreadings, and his sheer zeal for poetry, a sexually charged criticism that has itself, I would argue, been misread by a generation of Romantic readers.

That contemporary scholars of Romanticism now resist with such vehemence not only Bloom's rancorous humanism but also the seductions of the poetry to which he devoted his career may be testimony that Bloom's heirs have internalized unconsciously their Great Original's uneasy yet voluptuous relationship to literature. Certainly, they bear the birthmark of his more celebrated Oedipal aggression. In this polemical conclusion to my study of poets who do not (or cannot) disavow the dead, I will encourage those of us who teach and write about English literature, whether we teach Romantic poetry as part of a sophomore survey course or in the graduate seminar, to seek alternatives to a Romanticist scholarship that theorizes the reader's relationship to the dead who speak to us through texts as a process by which desire and pleasure (conventionally and too exclusively theorized as regressive and associated with the mother) are subsumed—and therefore made productive— by guilt and remorse (conventionally and too exclusively associated with the father). The scholar or the poet who reads "inappropriately," according to such terms, has failed to transform his or her relationship of pleasure in the consumable text into an anxiety induced by the threat of influence. Keats and Coleridge, orphans famously connected with an oral, nearly gustatory delight in words (and a corresponding literary delight in food), have been either "saved" by scholars from such contagion with demotic forms of pleasure by a *biographia* that seems to endorse, in Coleridge's case, a nearly heroic denial of his gift's importance and endurance or, as is more commonplace in contemporary readings of the poets, "condemned" to a thwarted development. Coleridge himself associated his failure of discipline with a premature death of the poet that he might have become. Yet it is Keats and not Coleridge (who will figure only occasionally in this brief afterword) who succeeds in theorizing pleasure as both absence and surplus, a poetry that is "capable" insofar as it is "negative," and a poetry that lives because it is—"ay, ages long ago"—already dead.

Because Romantic poetry so often calls attention to its oral origins, it has provoked in certain critics a powerful urge to "resist" (to use Jerome McGann's term) "incorporation":

> Works of the past are relevant in the present, it seems to me, precisely because of this difference. We do not contribute to the improvement of social conditions or even to the advancement of learning—insofar as scholars improve or advance anything outside the field of scholarship—by seeking to erase this difference, but rather by seeking to clarify and promote it. . . . the cooptive powers of a vigorous culture like our own are very great. If such powers and their results are not always to be deplored, cooptation must always be a process intolerable to a critical consciousness, whose first obligation is to resist incorporation, and whose weapon is analysis.[4]

While McGann has more recently encouraged Romanticists to share in his reconception of the "material" text as the product of a poet's lonely and private labor with pen, paper, and ink, nevertheless young scholars who sharpened their pencils in the margins of his still widely read *The Romantic Ideology* continue to make of its legacy similarly debilitating and yet self-aggrandizing professional pronouncements. Alan Liu, in a study of Wordsworth that has become nearly as influential (and certainly as anxiously Oedipal) as the work by McGann that he cites admiringly, urges his readers to "correct" the poet by "resisting" "complicity":

> How to resist complicity and correct the poet even in those passages where he declares himself most correct, most fit to be ordained a Poet. . . . It would be possible at this point to proceed as others have done and—starting upon the observation that Wordsworth's mature Imagination is avowedly logocentric—go on to read the endless decentrings that signal the necessary reversion of logos to those things that begot it: "absence, darknesse, death; things which are not." . . . Such would be one way to correct the poet. . . . But while the particular bent and texture of this book would not have been possible without some devotion to the turnings intricate by which deconstruction itself illuminates its texts, it is also true that my purpose all along has been to put the content back in the method of absence—and so to validate the power of such method upon the most basic absence there "is": history.[5]

Liu explicitly distinguishes his New Historicist work on the English Romantics from that of a "logocentric" deconstructionism that he attacks as cheerfully as he corrects the poet. Yet New Historicism and de Manian deconstruction are in fact linked by a mutual resignation to what they perceive as the futility of their vocation—the teaching of poetry—and by a jocund representation of history itself as the inevitability of thwarted desire, frustrated Prometheanism, and endless repetition. Cynthia Chase writes of *The Prelude*, "Wordsworth's misreading is a powerful example, a literally compelling model. We may see his mistake, but we are bound to repeat it."[6] Whether history or language is made the all-too-human horizon of poetic flight, it has become customary in Romantic scholarship to accuse canonical poets of vainly grasping for immortality, for seeking but failing to escape from an originary, parricidal guilt that necessarily confines the poet to a no less parricidal Law of the (banished) Father.

Perhaps it should not be surprising that the second annual graduate student conference on Romanticism, held at Yale in the fall of 1994, concerned the difficulties of following in the "Wake of Romanticism." On the one hand, the beginning scholar may follow the sleuth work of the New Historicists whose memories are resolutely public, whose memorials are the balance sheet and the courthouse archive. Yet however allegedly empirical their approach, theirs is a critical agenda that, in the words of one of its most influential purveyors, Marjorie Levinson, feels "distinctly guilty" when it has most successfully, and gleefully, ended Coleridge's metaphysical "hunt" by tracking the poet to his lair in the allegedly antisocial "imagination."[7] Trapped in his so-called solipsism, the ideologically culpable bard is quickly dispatched. On the other hand, the new scholar in the field of Romanticism may be attracted to the ritual and cultural deaths of a Romanticist deconstructionism for which such predicaments are always already linguistic, recurring as regularly and as predictably as the repetition compulsion of Freud's death drive.

Yet the archaic muse of melancholy somehow continues to inspire the contemporary Romantics scholar to memorize even as she murders the poems she cannot help but thereby memorialize. While such scholarship may believe itself to perform an act of "healthy" mourning (one that imitates and therefore assumes the authority of the poet/father who has been effectually murdered), it is, arguably, more likely to originate in melancholia (a refusal to acknowledge the death of the object that it desires as much as it despises). Melancholia, a refusal to surrender the "regressive" pleasure yielded by an object of desire that has been incorporated (and thereby preserved) commemorates the dead who are buried in the unconscious through daily acts of imitation (or identification). Because the child learns to speak only after relinquishing his or her earliest sources of nourishment, the first objects of need, desire, and love exist *as* a negative space in the psyche, a void that will not cease to be inseparable from insatiation, whether that hunger is for love, for books, or for food and drink.[8] If poetry is "cryptic," it is because (as Nicolas Abraham and Maria Torok have suggested) it returns language to the "crypts" that are the birthplaces of the words that henceforth must stand in for now-forbidden (or taboo) objects.[9] To read a poem, whether as a child hungry for knowledge, a poet eager for models, or a critic anxious for fodder, may in every case, consciously or unconsciously, be simultaneously an act of love (identification), of desire and/or need (incorporation), even as it may also, and at the same time, be an act of anxiety, fear, and loathing.

Romantic scholarship in America is haunted by the absence of its own earliest ties to a melancholic object that it has banished, a fetishistic relationship to literary texts that it has denied out of a fear, and a failure, of love. We become what we repudiate, no less than what we eat or what we love, because the object that we disavow is likely to be one we have already cannibalized. The bodily temple of academic, literary discipline, like Keats's temple of "veiled Melancholy" and of amorous delight, is—to borrow Judith Butler's term—a masculine *morphe* formed (and deformed) by censorship. That includes censorship of the homosexual desire for the father, the melancholic object that the son first incorporates and then subsequently fails to master and refuses to love:

And if one must either love or fall ill, then perhaps the sexuality that appears as illness is the insidious effect of such a censoring of love. Can the very production of the *morphe* be read as an allegory of prohibited love, the *incorporation* of loss?

The relation between incorporation and melancholy is a complicated one. . . . What is excluded from the body for the body's boundary to form? And how does that exclusion haunt that boundary as an internal ghost of sorts, the incorporation of loss as melancholia?[10]

As Butler reminds us, "constitutive identifications are precisely those which are always disavowed."[11] A scholarly and poetic imagination that exploits rather than impedes its unconscious resources acknowledges, as Eve Kosofsky Sedgwick has suggested throughout her career as a writer, its earliest debts to the fetishized, totemized, and taboo literary *corpus*/corpse. In such acknowledgments we are in fact imitating rather than disavowing the very sources of power (which are inevitably, in our culture, *hidden*—or fetishized—sources of power) that yield Romantic poetry.

In the century that has seen the genealogical descent of Matthew Arnold's already secular aestheticism into the disillusioned practices I have identified in contemporary Romanticism, it is hardly surprising that we have made the aesthetic fetish as suspect as the commodities that we (fetishistically) both condemn and consume. We shape ourselves in the cracked mirror of begrudging servitude, that is, in our misrecognition of Coleridge, who himself misrecognized his disappointed ambition on behalf of—and, arguably, his unexpressed love for—Wordsworth as the murder of the poet within himself. While we may claim to eschew Arnold's belief that English poetry, like Christianity in a former age, could civilize philistines, or Leavis's faith that a poetry of "normality" might regularize the private as well as the public standards of the English middle classes, we maintain a clear, if unspoken, distinction between the "truth" (if not the beauty) possessed and disseminated by our own implicitly "civilized" metaphysics (material history and poststructural linguistics, for example) and the superstitions and ideologies that allegedly delude our implicitly "barbaric" and "regressive" subjects of study: the poets whose once-canonical status has made them suspect. Indeed, a critic like Liu more or less proclaims that what *we* do is "work"; what Wordsworth does is profit unjustly from the work of the laboring poor, thereby refusing to "work through" loss.

Yet the melancholic poet remembers, as the melancholic scholar may have forgotten, that all words retain their oral origins in a totemistic consumption and internalization of now-dead objects, objects that haunt the psyche's unworshiped shrines. If in the "Ode to Psyche" Keats praises the mortal ruins of an imagination that longs for immortality, in his Nightingale Ode he reminds us that poetic flights toward immortality, inspired by imagined song and drink from the "deep-delved earth," may nevertheless end in the sensation of earthbound burial: "to thy high requiem, become a sod." Death, in fact, haunts Romantic poetic labor at precisely the moments when it is most productive, when words are most effortlessly harvested so that they may sustain both daily life and future harvests. If, as Freud suggests, the newborn's first and terrifying passage from the womb into the world is evoked as "uncanniness" in the adult's dreams of live burial, then perhaps it is not surprising that a similar bodily orifice—the mouth—may, in poetry, be linked simultaneously with ingestion (a "*beaker* ful of the warm South"), with poetic song (the *beak* of the nightingale), and with death (the *beak* of the dead and death-bearing mother that Freud identified in da Vinci's dreams of flight). The melancholic productivity that we call poetry emerges from the same mouth that, according to popular stereotype, too often makes the Coleridgean and Keatsian poetic laborer himself a victim of excessive consumption; indeed, in tubercular consumption (where no amount of dietary or other discipline can thwart the progress of the disease) the wine that bursts upon the palate fine literally (if nearly unthinkably) becomes blood. Whether a consumer or a consumptive, the dejected Romantic poet allegedly wastes his substance in the ideal, sometimes ecstatic, but inevitably death-infused states of longing that occur between wake and sleep, between hearing a nightingale or a solitary reaper and appropriating that voice as one's own, between the untranslatable language of dreams and the translation of the self into the non-self of a poem.

Yet it is, after all, that imagined "beaker" that metonymically empowers Keats, for a brief but ecstatic moment, to assume both the wings and, poetically, the song-bearing "beak" of the bird whose voice calls, invisibly, to the homesick poet who himself called out for Death. Such imagined (or real) internalized supplements to the muse may produce, in a state where one feels unexpectedly close to the *sod* from which we are supposed to be alienated (and to Ruth, the rural laborer who harvests the alien corn), a feeling of *sod*denness, the euphoric and terrifying feeling of being saturated with what Keats described as the "embalmed darkness" of an alien presence. In Keats's ode, the thought of a foreign substance that enters the orifices of the self evokes an immortal, mythical bird; the violence of Philomela's usurped voice; an exploited, female harvester in exile; the sadness of "ruth"; the wet *sod* of the dead. But it also evokes the voice, or vocation, of Keats's literary father, Wordsworth, the author of "The Solitary Reaper."

While vacationing in Scotland, Wordsworth had himself discovered that not even the visiting cosmopolite may easily distinguish hearing a "melancholy *strain*," working (in identity with the Scots singer) the *grain*, consuming that strain/grain (visually, aurally, and orally), and then *becoming* it, growing from the seed that was harvested in exile, mulched in memory, and recollected in tranquility a poem. To seek to identify with poetic immortality is to summon, as Wordsworth discovers, a painful, pensive surmise of one's own and imminent "passing," as in the epitaphic warning that Geoffrey Hartman has so helpfully called to our attention: "Stop here, or gently pass!" While the melancholic poet may seem to be either languishing or idling, in fact he labors (in the reproductive as well as the productive sense) intensively on behalf of the unintelligible speech of the once, now, and future dead: "The music in my heart I *bore*, / Long after it was heard no more" (my emphasis).[12] Conflating the categories of writing and speech, pleasure and procreation, Wordsworth both acknowledges the difference, and refuses to distinguish between, his seed and the reaper's.[13] The poet, paradoxically, both hoards and feeds on, plagiarizes and "bears," a voice that he acknowledges as "alien." For the melancholic poet intuits that all speech is founded not only on *aural* or *visual* acts of culturally improving "identity" (that is, metaphor) but also on now-forbidden, almost forgotten forms of metonymic, *oral* ingestion. The poet-reader who needs, desires, and loves the internalized, fetishized *corpus* of his father literally feeds on, and grows from, the poetry of his predecessors.

No less than the orphans Wordsworth and Coleridge, Keats learned early the solace brought by the phantom voices of poets, the rhythms of their verse echoing with coronary force within the covers of books. Yet while readers of poetry are likely to hear Wordsworth's genuine calling to poetry, or to share Coleridge's dejection when vocation falls silent, our response to the demonstrative, corporeal, synaesthetic appeal of such poems as "This Living Hand Now Warm and Capable" may well be troubled. Alive and yet capable of negative self-surpassal, Keats called out to, and for, death in the Nightingale Ode. Death answers when the poet imitates his interlocutor, transforming a poet's call into a performative speech act that seems to make manifest the uncanny presence, and power, of his deadly auditor:

> Darkling I listen; and, for many a time
> I have been half in love with easeful death,
> Call'd him soft names in many a mused rhyme,
> To take into the air my quiet breath;
> Now more than ever seems it rich to die,

To cease upon the midnight with no pain,
While thou art pouring forth thy soul abroad
In such an ecstasy!
Still wouldst thou sing, and I have ears in vain—
To thy high requiem become a sod.[14]

If the poetic performative restored the melancholic Wordsworth and even the dejected Coleridge to literary life in 1802, Keats's final, extraordinary work in 1819 made Coleridge's metaphor for melancholy—"The Poet is dead in me"—unthinkably real. Keats remains to us still more boy than man and yet, simultaneously, a poet who is not living but dying.

This poet whose letters betray personal sanity, industry, cheerfulness, and even courage has, paradoxically, provoked in critics anxieties more typically found in friends and supervisors of grieving orphans. Will he, they worry, finally grow up to enjoy a normal life? Invariably, the focus narrows to the poet's physical traits, the melancholic *morphe* that (as Butler suggests) is shaped by love's absence and its supplements: Keats's unusually small stature, his tubercular delicacy, his self-taught and self-conscious "palate fine." Walter Jackson Bate's life of Keats, in many ways itself the bildungsroman M. H. Abrams has suggested is the paradigmatic Romantic art form, confirms what one may surmise through the letters: that the young poet was astonishingly, even precociously, a warm-blooded, worldly man committed to friends and to family. Yet certain poems by Keats—most notably the romances—have encouraged Bate and others who are usually sympathetic readers of the poet to qualify that portrait. The romances, more than other poems, remind Keats's critics that the poet-prodigy derives his precocious sagacity as much from books as from life, a precocity that implies character traits developed through a sentimental education that scholars especially may intuit (because they share them) but nevertheless disavow. "Precocity" evokes the adolescent whose sexuality is acquired (only?) from books; the lovesick idealist who knows how but is unable or unwilling to consummate desire, whether erotic or ambitious; the ill-equipped social climber who stumbles, like Keats's dreamer, before Moneta, on the steps of imagined celebrity; even the pervert who haunts, without commitment, the forbidden territory between Eros and Thanatos. While Marjorie Levinson's pathbreaking *Keats's Life of Allegory* is the first study to state boldly these misgivings, scholarly readings of Keats have been haunted for decades by the textualized body (and sexualized texts) of the poet who made his life and his art from his early romance with books.[15]

Efforts to delineate clearly the "mature" or "adolescent" contours of that body have particularly characterized discussions of *The Eve of St. Agnes,* discussions that invariably move from desire (the poet's, or the poem's characters', or the reader's) to discipline (his, theirs, or ours).[16] John Bayley in 1962 raised the question forthrightly, using, as has become standard in discussions of these matters, the terminology of masculine sexual development as a benchmark for Keats's development as a poet:

> The most emphatic aspect of the *gemein* in Keats is, of course, the way he writes about sex. I do not think that any critic, not even Leigh Hunt, has found himself able to praise Keats's treatment of the subject, and I feel some qualms in attempting to do so now. But considering the general agreement that he is a fine poet, this negative attitude is odd, to say the least. How does this side of Keats come to be so customarily dismissed—as indeed Keats himself was only too ready to dismiss it—with epithets like "mawkish" and "adolescent"? The critic's route of escape from the topic seems to be that Keats outgrew all that nonsense when he became full of flint and iron, or that it is in any case of little importance, something sloughed off in his finest poetry. Distrust of it unites the most dissimilar critics.[17]

Bayley is correct in noting that embarrassment about *St. Agnes* has created strange bedfellows. He alleges that *he* feels no embarrassment about these matters because he shares with Keats a "mature" understanding of what constitutes a "real woman" and real (masculine) desire. Assured of his own masculinity, Bayley may proclaim what so many readers in our discipline have either denied or qualified: a liking for Madeline, the heroine of his favorite Keats poem. "It is this kind of existence, the existence that Keats can give to sexual fantasy, that is the kernal of his poetic achievement," Bayley boldly affirms; Keats is, he continues, "unique among English poets in his power of generalizing the most personal and the most intimate sexuality back into a great and indeed an august idea of nature and life. It is a peculiarly romantic power." In other words, neither critics nor analysts should notice a sexuality that is so commonplace—so normal—so universal—that it is no longer sexual at all. Keats's sexuality disappears into "august" "nature," or life itself.

The embarrassed critic who finds *St. Agnes* a deviant poem in an otherwise healthy oeuvre may yet attribute to its composition motives that redeem it. Bate, for example, at first cannot understand why Keats, facing forward on the road to greatness, momentarily digressed—indeed, regressed—by writing the erotically charged *St. Agnes,* a poem in the "mawkish" genre he had claimed to abandon. Bate makes excuses for Keats: it is a poem "begun with mixed and even negative feelings (including fatigue and grief, the need to keep his mind occupied in this trying time . . .)." And then illumination arrives: *St. Agnes* is a "poem that at the same time turns into a feat of craftsmanship—a triumph of idiom and versification over the limitations of the subject—because the new artistry he had gained through *Hyperion* was freshly yet very simply challenged."[18] Nevertheless, Bate concludes, a reader who expresses a preference for *St. Agnes* should question his or her own "poetic interests": "It is still frequently said that, in turning from *Hyperion* to the *Eve of St. Agnes,* Keats was changing to a theme and mode of poetry more 'congenial' to his talent. In this case we are either assuming that the more 'congenial' is that which demands less, and are therefore stooping with a condescension grotesquely out of place, or else (if the remark is meant as a compliment to the *Eve of St. Agnes*) we reveal the gentle bias of our own poetic interests."[19]

If Bate feels he must defend the poet from readers who might "embarrass" Keats by seeking out certain poems for the wrong reasons, Christopher Ricks in *Keats and Embarrassment* establishes a breezy urbanity in his matter-of-fact assertion that civilized poet and reader alike are (and should be) instructively discomfited by witnessing certain private acts that nevertheless make us human. Ricks's cold, disciplinary eye is bent not on Keats but rather on Keats's embarrassed reader. Reading, like writing, is for Ricks a form of good behavior; decorum can allow one to travel anywhere and witness anything without damage to one's character. Just as "rules, constraints, and self-discipline are explicitly invoked as guiding Madeline herself," Ricks argues, they are also "implicitly manifested in the art with which Keats creates Madeline."[20] Echoing Yeats, Ricks notes that even dreams or fantasies are not free of "responsibilities"; the writer's first responsibility is "generosity" toward his subject: "I have said that it is hard, when contemplating the loving physicality of others, to let the inevitable sense of a possibility of the distasteful be accommodated within a full magnanimity. The ambivalence of such physicality (ambivalent within oneself, and ambivalent because others are not oneself) involves a recognition of the need for such generosity" (95). Interestingly, while Ricks often notes the reader's embarrassment, rarely do we sense that he retains as a reader himself a joyful vicariousness in the erotic moment he can so skillfully "dis"compose. (If even the image of Madeline's seaweed is repugnant to this sensitive reader, then he is himself generous in enduring rereading such passages at all.) Keats's generosity, Ricks argues, disciplines the reader's erroneous imagination through the pedagogical tool of embarrassment: "Certainly art has its freedom which life does not, but such freedoms are the purposeful suspension of responsibility, not the ignoring or abolishing of it. . . . When Keats not only lets us see so vividly the undressing of Madeline and Porphyro's watching it, but lets us share his richly intimate equanimity, he gives us an example of how we should—in the largest sense—behave. His art, though not didactic, is concerned to educate our thoughts, feelings, and sympathies, and it does so by being exemplary" (95). Understanding clinically how blushing divulges what should be kept private, Ricks can coolly discuss such matters as masturbation, scopophilia, and even "ereutophobia" in Keats's poetry with the ease of the clinical experts he so often summons for evidence that we may indeed learn to "read" bodies for expressions of "decorum":

Art, with its discipline and respect, can convert such impulses to true ends; the writer and the reader, like the ereutophobe but unsuccumbing, makes use of imagined others as a mirror in order to look at themselves with a clear conscience—genuinely clear, not self-flattering. Again, the vistas of voyeuristic embarrassment resemble those of art, especially of Keats's art: "Another adult male patient once noticed that an old man was looking at a scene in which a young man was heavily courting a girl in public. The patient blushed." Yet all such blushing asserts decorum, and like all decorum it is an equivocal blend of innocence and experience. (88)

It may be *because* innocence and experience *do* equivocate with such disturbing consequences in Keats's *St. Agnes* that critics with fewer devices for disengagement (or for disciplining their reading) have taken refuge in ever more ingenious definitions of imagination either to justify the decorousness of Keats's desire or to discipline (someone's) indecorous body. The silent, dreaming, female body at the center of this poetic fantasy has served as the cathectic center of a critical tradition that sees in "Adam's dream" experience, perceptiveness, and truth, but in Madeline's dream perceives deluded and prolonged innocence. The major scholars who have written about this poem urgently seek to define the kind of sexual encounter—

innocent, experienced, or in between—that Madeline did or did not enjoy that night, perhaps believing that their task, as professional readers, is to distinguish reality from dreams, truth from illusion, the culpable from the naive (which makes their task as critics of *St. Agnes* litigious as well as schoolmasterly). Ricks suggests in his reading of *St. Agnes* that we must value literature for "giving us a sense of what is true and false, what can be both realistic and healthy, about our attitude to our own 'expressive delight,' our attitude to that of others which we imagine, and to that of others whom we imagine" (132–33). The "serious" reader may recuperate not only an embarrassing romance but even its heroine, so long as her dream is reconceived as part of Keats's "lesson" to us. Witness, for example, Earl Wasserman's reading: "Madeline would no longer be torn between truth and beauty, for the two would coincide; and the ideal Madeline and the human Porphyro could unite to experience the conditions of heaven."[21] Far more typically, critics view Madeline's dream not as an ideal but rather as an error, a delusion that, if not yet a sin, nevertheless, like Eve's dream of temptation, must be corrected. Jack Stillinger, the critic most famous for defining Madeline's scene of sexual instruction as the correction of illusion, writes with undisguised prurience: "When she awakens to find herself with Porphyro, she is anything but warm: rather, she wakes up to 'flaw-blown sleet' and 'iced gusts' . . . it's no virgin morn for her."[22] It would seem that the gulled can nevertheless be guilty, if the sin is seduction.

If Madeline is taught by scholarly disciplinarians to reject fantasy and to accept "reality," Porphyro is praised for having already learned the value—and, indeed, the resourcefulness—of what critics prefer to call his "imagination." In fact, we may surmise that it is when critics uncomplicate, empty, or even neuter Madeline's dream of even "regressive" content, as in Leon Waldoff's reading, that the allegedly innocent victim is most assuredly denied access to the creative, poetic imagination attributed to the experienced seducer/rapist:

There are, after all, two significant imaginations to consider—Porphyro's and Madeline's (not to mention the narrator's)—and the idea of imagination in the poem is more complicated than Madeline's dream alone suggests. Although Porphyro and Madeline face the same problem—their separation from each other—they use their imaginations to solve the problem in quite different ways.

Madeline turns to dreaming. She places her trust in a world of legend and romance where dreams are supposed to come true. To a large extent she is a creation of the Keats who . . . said that he would "from detested moods in new romance / Take refuge." . . . the idea of taking refuge in dream and romance is certainly present in Madeline's fascination with "faery fancy," and it recurs throughout Keats's poetry. This dreaming or visionary imagination is in some degree regressive and escapist, and it can be dangerously deceiving, even to the point of incurable melancholy or death. . . . Madeline "sweet dreamer" though she is, does not suffer either fate and hers is not the crucial imagination in "The Eve of St. Agnes."

Porphyro, on the other hand, is not a dreamer. He employs his imagination to solve the problem of his separation from Madeline in a bold and resourceful way.[23]

In similar fashion Ricks praises Porphyro's ingenuity but disciplines, with relish, the daydreaming Madeline. Noting, with approval, that Madeline goes "supperless to bed" like a chastened schoolgirl (he does not speculate on her adventures in solitude), Ricks gives Porphyro high marks for "erecting" a scheme for violating her, using a well-developed imagination that "is itself akin to the final enjoyment of its success in the plan, and so includes within itself again Keats's sense of the imagination as a nobly self-fulfilling prophecy. 'That which is creative must create itself'" (165). While we might wonder just how Porphyro's "self-creation" and Madeline's "dream" could receive such different evaluations, Ricks hints that it has to do with the connections between "a type both of erection and of orgasm . . . Keats, whose sense of imaginative and of erotic creation is so strongly proleptic, so akin to the self-fulfilling erotic prophecy of Adam: 'The Imagination may be compared to Adam's dream—he awoke and found it truth.' Finding the imagination truth meant for Adam (and for Milton and Keats) immediately consummating the truth and proving it upon love's pulses; this is what Adam and Eve immediately do."[24]

Yet Tilottama Rajan in *Dark Interpreter* reminds us that illusion and truth (like seduction and rape) raise questions about the very status of innocence, both in the "unrealistic" genre of romance and in the "real" world of men and women. Rajan equates dreams with ignorant and regressive innocence—notably "Madeline's desire to preserve the unravished purity of illusion"—and reality with experience, Porphyro's "desire to awake into reality, his fear of lapsing into the undifferentiated unity of sleep."[25] Keats, she argues, is unwilling to occupy a space that excludes either, an unwillingness that she implicitly equates with immaturity. Were Keats "sufficiently" committed to reality, he might develop "a new awareness of the work of art as constituted by its tragic emergence from the ideal. . . . But the poem seems sentimentally unwilling to commit itself to so radical a revision in its sense of what poetry is" (112). Hence, the poet and his poem are caught uneasily between two unacceptable alternatives and, when the poem at its erotic climax attempts to propose a union, she argues that the poetry falters because it attempts to "elide" the states of "virginity" and "consummation." Clearly, Rajan herself experiences as a reader the uneasiness she attributes to Keats concerning undifferentiated states, with being "between" sexual identities, "between" illusion and truth, "between" desire and its heterosexual satisfaction. Yet she feels less discomfort (or "guilt") than Levinson in reminding critics that their task, like that of the responsible poet, is to confront the dream with reality, where it must be "made to disclose its potentialities":

The peculiar, inconclusive ecstasy toward which the lovers proceed must be seen as a kind of optical illusion designed to realize the dream while preserving its fictionality and immunity from time. In this manner Keats, by a kind of automatonism characteristic of the sentimental poem, avoids confronting a crucial lacuna in his sense of what happens to the dream when it is incarnated in reality and made to disclose its potentialities. Keats might perhaps have wished that he could create a naive poem: a poem in which romance could become real without also awakening into tragedy. But the lacuna whose menace is covered up in the relationship of the lovers to their dream appears outside their world in the analogous relationship of the narrator to his fiction. Even if we can go against all the canons of logic and believe that the lovers can realize their dream without awaking into reality, we cannot believe that the narrator can keep his dream fictive, pure, and untainted by mortality, while at the same time bringing it to life in the real world. In his world, at least, Adam's dream cannot be simultaneously true and a dream. . . . The mutually irreconcilable alternatives which confront the narrator raise again the impossible choice between fiction and mimesis that divides Keats's poems considered as works that are concerned with their own epistemological status. Insofar as the dream remains a fiction it also remains something phantasmal, unconsummated, a mere intent of consciousness from which the sense of concreteness has evaporated. (114–15)

The word that Rajan uses repeatedly—lacuna—describes, in fact, what is at stake in readings of St. Agnes that claim to recuperate for

Keats's romance the terms "experience," "realism," and "truth." If the "tragic" truth of human existence lies in the distance between our dreams and our reality, if, in the fallen world of experience, fiction and mimesis are "irreconcilable alternatives," then neither the dreamer nor the poet can bring to life, performatively, the nonliving "thing" called art. Yet there is a genre in which the regressive fantasies of melancholics can find confirmation—the gothic romance—for it violates, implicitly, our expectation that the hero or heroine, and the reader and poet, will grow up "normally" through a process that will lead to a clear difference between self from other. For within the gothic, it becomes notoriously difficult for the reader to distinguish entering into another's nightmare and having one's own dreams invaded by another's; to conclude whether the experience the reader acquires by engaging in the desires of characters makes the reader less innocent, or more "consummated," than before; or to know where the absent writer exists in relation to the fictional corpus, and in relation to the reader's own responsive flesh.

Yet in *St. Agnes* Keats created a poem that is both cold pastoral and overheated gothic, a text that confronts the responsive reader with the multiple subjects (identifying, simultaneously, with Madeline, Porphyro, the Beadsman, Angela) who read, in privacy, from within the reader's single, many-chambered mind. The reader of *St. Agnes,* like Madeline, may look up from the dream-text and express unwillingness to have it end. Like Porphyro, the reader may discover that to dissolve into another's textual dream is to confuse (pleasurably and productively) boundaries between innocence and experience, or between "peculiar, inconclusive ecstasy" and mature, sexual experience. Like both lovers, the reader may reach the end of the text and discover that, with its conclusion, the part of the self that dies at the end of the reading would, uncannily, have "died, ay ages long ago," and believe, nevertheless, that the poem may be reentered and relived immediately. No matter how often we have learned that the lovers are already dead before the story has begun, that knowledge resides in a different chamber from our belief that the lovers continue to inhabit the vital and sensuous enclosure that Keats has created, indeed with each rereading, continues to create, with a warm and still-living hand.

The lovers, the poem, and the poet, all remain both alive and dead within the imagination of even the professional reader, or perhaps *especially* in the imagination of the professional reader. For that reader's exceptional verbal facility betrays knowledge (sexual and otherwise) gained through youthful intellectual curiosity, a precocity that, through books, at some point introduced into the once-innocent mind knowledge it could not consciously have been permitted to know. Such knowledge, like the child's first objects of love and desire, is melancholically incorporated and then encrypted in the gothic graveyard of the unconscious, where it remains both banished and preserved. *The Eve of St. Agnes,* Keats's self-consciously gothic shrine, miraculously and repeatedly revives from death the lovers, the poem, the poet, and—in a certain sense—ourselves. Yet Keats in *St. Agnes* deliberately and artfully foregrounds the ongoing threat of violent death, suggesting that the voluptuous palace of art—even, or especially, if it was once hallowed by the church before becoming a trophy of war—can never escape the history of its rapacious spoils.[26]

It is with those spoils, peering coldly yet "ever eager-eyed" from the walls, that, with the negatively capable Beadsman, the reader first identifies, their "frieze" invading (like the "freezing" cold) the invisible border between artifice and reality. Soon we will meet characters who, like ourselves, have become the art that surrounds them: an impenetrable girl like a "carved angel," or like a saint, who is more dead to the world than alive, and her "cold" lover, "pale as smooth-sculptured stone" (st. 33). Unlike the castle's inhabitants, who make and remake themselves in the image of its lore, its music, and its museum pieces, we may distract our gaze, and our desire, from the aesthetic agony on the walls or the music snarling in pain by turning (as the poem leads us) to the distracted, dreaming somnambulist at the poem's center. In doing so, we will, in a certain sense, "become" Madeline, even to the point of investing her dream with substance. Yet because our critical gaze is also, like Porphyro's, possessive, we will also "desire" Madeline. The "solution sweet" to the reader's conflict between being and having is, of course, the poem's: we dissolve, with Porphyro, into the dream *as* into the body *as* into the poem.[27] The boundaries between these entities dissolve in a solution where the stained glass's violently "blushing scutcheons" become Madeline, the tinctured object of desire, and where staging, consuming, and becoming Porphyro's laid table are all simultaneous. We become what we read, no less than (because it is also) what we eat. If the reader is in Ricks's terms "disciplined" by the poet's "instruction" to blush, nevertheless the reader is also becoming, at the moment of blushing, in identification with Madeline, a living memorial of the text consumed.

The melancholic futility of scholarly endeavors to escape *from* the literature they have already—paradoxically—both incorporated and escaped *into* is nowhere more evident than in Marjorie Levinson's zealous indictment of a class, its alleged perversions, and its poetry.[28] *St. Agnes,* she suggests, has found its most engaged readers among those who fear, and yet who cannot recognize, "real" desire and "real" death: the middle-class professionals of Keats's day and (by extension) our own. "Busy for luxury" (in fact, no better phrase could summarize Levinson's own work), even as their lives and work amount to nothing, these readers, Levinson argues, deny—melancholically—their missing origins and their missing (in many senses) ends. What better poet for such readers than the one Levinson portrays as an orphaned nobody? "Keats had to make for himself a life . . . while writing a poetry that was, structurally, a denial of that life. . . . Is it any wonder that the poetry produced by this man should be so autotelic, autoerotic, so fetishistic and so stuck?"[29] Byron, the poetically prolific and profligately procreative member of a different class, got it right, she claims; Keats's poetry is just "frigging the imagination," both his and ours, in a desire that amounts to nothing:

> What Byron is driving at is the contradiction which organizes both masturbation and the reproductive habits of the middle class. Below, I propose that the dream or the concept of masturbation is one of conscious unconsciousness: "the feel of not to feel it," or, as in the Nightingale Ode, sensible numbness. (Here again, we detect a debased because reified version of that Wordsworthian paradigm, "wise passiveness.") Inasmuch as one is both worker and pleasurer, giver and receiver, subject and object in masturbation, the act should produce a rare psychic consolidation. However, both the technical groundplot (a part of the body is fetishized and overworked), and the absence of a distracting other to absorb the purposiveness of the activity and naturalize the techne, install with unusual force the divided psyche, which must know itself busy for luxury. (23)

Levinson's implicit cure for the regressive behavior of the middle-class—presumably, whether it is manifested in the poet or the reader—is to overcome narcissistic "psychic dissonance," to give up merely dreaming a "solution sweet," by getting a life rather than reading a fetish. This may be done, she prescribes, through healthy, object-oriented sex that reaches an authentic climax and produces offspring; by performing "real" work that cannot be confused with leisure; and by avoiding "incorporative" psychic and consumer behavior. *St. Agnes,* she concludes, is a symptom of a perverted class that thinks (like Keats) it may do nothing and yet *make* something—"beauty" and "truth"—*out* of nothing, that is, out of its bodily and social impotence:

An ego *in the place of* an authentic, natural body; and, in addition to an unself-conscious, natural body: a body that cannot mean, cannot "project" itself, can only *be.*

The middle class of Keats's day could neither experience nor imagine its authenticity. To be genuine is to be naturally derived and to anticipate a natural immortality in one's natural offspring. A class that refuses its sociogenetic past—whose identity *as* a class requires this genealogical erasure— cannot imagine a relation with the future that is other than its parodic relation to the present. It has no means for the identification which alone makes the future ours: our children's, that is. Moreover, it recognizes by the very logic that brought it into being the "hunger" of the coming generations who are its own class offspring and whose identity must therefore be *their* bad derivation. (175–76)

The "virtue" of Keats's autoerotic, unregenerative art, Levinson concludes, is that its reality is so "virtual." An empty, artificial space created by an orphaned nonentity, *St. Agnes* presents as self-parody a class that can be "called" anything (and, by extension, hailed by any ideology) precisely because it has lost its origins and its ends:

One fact emerges over and over in all the biographies, the letters, the reviews, and also in the poetry itself. Keats was *named:* apothecary, Johnny Keates, Jack Ketch, Mankin, Self-polluter, Master John, copyist, Cockney. He was named, moreover, not so much as Other and adversarial but as "nothing," the dissociated figure of an allegory. The child of unnatural parents, orphaned at an early age, separated from his siblings and his inheritance, ambitious for an identity that was socially prohibited, and isolated by his disease, Keats was detached in an unusually thoroughgoing way from the origins and ends that naturalize most people's lives by fusing their figural aspect (image, attribute, name) to their inwardness.

A man who is allegorized will, to liberate himself from that suffered objectivity, *invent* a life of allegory. . . . We grasp the necessity of this bitter solution by remembering that a man who experiences his identity as his nothingness and desire cannot afford the luxury of full gratification and its natural closures. This is to say that Keats's creativity was powerfully mediated by a set of psychic circumstances that would seem to require rather than resist his particular social reality. (126)

To refute an entire class's "confusion" of truth with beauty by adverting to the "naturalness" of the body and its productions is also to call into question, as Levinson does, not only the *naturalness* of poetic labor but, finally, of course, its *value*. In a world that cannot be changed without "work" and without the sacrifice of "consumption" (and, perhaps, of lives), poetry, she concludes, becomes a luxury and a fetish. More precisely, it is a talisman that wards off an "incorporative" class's fear of being "incorporated":

As poetry recognizes its loss of practical power in the world, it assumes the magic, oxymoronic virtue of the ceaselessly self-deconstructive structure. *It offers us a meaning which we cannot consume and which promises not, therefore, to consume us.* It's not hard to conjecture the value of such a meaning to a culture afraid of satisfaction, which it feels as death, and afraid of death, which it imagines as absolute and unrecompensed. As I said, a group that knows no natural inheritance cannot guess at immortality. Such a group must want to own everything because it knows that it never owns anything—can never *let* itself own anything—properly or forever. (177–78; my emphases)

Citing Sartre, Levinson admonishes those critics who persist in enjoying poetry ("the ideal commodity") rather than seeking something more real ("instinctual gratification"):

Consider the value of these unconsumable meanings to a culture that tries to remake everything in its own image but which must then reject those renovated objects as being unworthy, since they are only images of a profoundly "bad" self. For this culture, academically processed, Keats's poetry is the ideal commodity. It provides "real pleasure," not for its own sake but in the service of an impossible attempt to coincide, in the realm of the imaginary, with the essence of an owner of things. As a result, the whole system is derealized, the very enjoyment becomes imaginary. This is to say, the enjoyment is incomplete, self-conscious and self-perpetuating: a pleasant pain. A poetry that teases out of thought saves us from the instinctual gratification that would, we fear, annihilate identity. (178)

A reader who shares Levinson's claim to read literature through Marx, history, and psychoanalysis could challenge her reading of Keats's life and art by citing Slavoj Žižek's observation that there exists no "natural" life (sexual or otherwise) in modern states (capitalist or socialist) because the reproduction of ideology (the "naming" of the orphaned "nobody" by the Father) relies as much on the "regressive" autoeroticism of the pleasure principle (which generates a surplus of commodified desire) as on the so-called reality principle that Levinson advocates. One could also turn to Julia Kristeva, who has observed that all cultural ideals are founded on the priority and the persistence of melancholic incorporation of the maternal object and of narcissistic, neo-Platonic identification with first a parental object and then the Father. As an advocate for psychoanalytic alternatives to Freudian models of sexual development, one could enlist the support of Eve Kosofsky Sedgwick's and Judith Butler's work on fetishism, performativity, homoerotic identification, and the construction (and cultural denial) of same-sex desire. From any of these theorists we would learn that the melancholic object from which Levinson, as a reader, seeks disciplinary distance is also the object of ambivalence that she desires: the image of an autoerotic dreamer who seems, like the body of a dead poet, suspiciously suspended between life and death.

The persistence of Levinson's affection for Keats, manifested in her fascination with that image but also in her own, powerful reading of *St. Agnes,* demonstrates in itself the enduring power and value of Keats's bookish art *as* bookish life, a life where, as in melancholia, ambivalence leads to recurring failures of "detachment" and of "attachment." Levinson, in her dense, difficult, and sometimes repetitive ninety-odd pages on *St. Agnes* reads that poem with the over-engaged curiosity, openly stimulated libido, and eagerness both to see and to question that, as we have learned from the New Critics, can so often serve to reward close readers. Transforming the world of *St. Agnes* into a claustrophobic panopticon, Levinson continually rediscovers her own responses as a reader (discoveries that help her readers in turn to discover their own) by foregrounding the artificial beauty (what she calls the "virtual reality") of the poet's words no less than that of the objets d'art in the Baron's castle. Levinson asks us from the beginning to seek, with her, the "absence" circumscribed by the current field of our discipline's discourse, which is itself inscribed by the invisible hand of ideology. With her own overworked contribution to that field, the absence which she has exacerbated becomes visible: it is the negatively capable poet whose contours Levinson has sought and so fabulously failed to delineate, however rich and strange her evocations of Keats's densely textured, polyvalent corpus. In the few pages that remain, I will argue that what Levinson calls absence—and what Rajan calls a lacuna—is a negative capability that makes manifest an ideology that is usually invisible, twisting it into the chambers of his poem's (and his heroine's) heart. Levinson's erotically charged, overheated rhetoric undermines her stated presumption that the subject (or "substance") matters so much more than its highly wrought form.[30]

The poet who would turn as deliberately as Keats did to art in compensation for the early loss of love might inevitably have developed the highly stylized, or textualized, life and self that Levinson calls at best autotelic and, at worst, a nonentity. To blame Keats for living his life in books hardly corrects the conventional praise of Keats for living his life on the pulses. Between Levinson and Bate lies the corpus of a poet that is neither entirely word nor entirely flesh, a self that is (rather like our own) a monument to the books that were consumed, a cemetery for the writers no less than for the parents who were encrypted in a psychic space inhabited (inevitably) by others (including the Other of ideology). Levinson, while extenuating such circumstances in the impoverished life of an orphan, nevertheless accuses Keats of weakness in his melancholic incorporation of his literary forebears, charging that he sought to possess them only after he could not become them:

What if a person cannot, for profound social reasons and the psychic distortions they impose, realize his ego ideal, and what if, for the same reasons, the ego is extravagantly diminished by its object cathexes? What happens, moreover, when the psychic economy will not permit a merger with the ego ideal, even if material conditions *were* favorable? Finally, what about people who, because of primary as well as sustained and severe object loss, cannot tolerate any effacement of identity in loved objects, even if that effacement comes about through internalization? I'm describing Keats, of course. Or rather, I'm describing a textual solution to a psychic dilemma. That solution is, as I've suggested, the "sweet," regressive solution of a return to narcissism. One chooses a sexual ideal that is also an ego-ideal. One loves that which one lacks and couldn't otherwise attain; that is, one tries to *obtain* it. Keats doesn't want to *have* Milton, originally. He wants to *be* Milton, but the only way to do that, given Keats's circumstances, is to make of Milton the introjected erotic object: the possessed otherness that is inalienable because always already alien. (172)

In fact, Levinson reverses Keats's probable process of identification with Milton, Wordsworth, and Shakespeare.

Judith Butler argues persuasively that melancholic incorporation is in fact not a subsequent but rather the founding act not only of subjectivity (the "inner" self) but also of the sexually differentiated body. Incorporation begins in the child's desire for the parent of the same sex and ends with the child's internalization of the homosexual incest prohibition *as* heterosexual identification with the parent of the same sex. It is, as she says in the earlier citation, a "censoring of love." The once-desired (homosexual) object that became an object of (heterosexual) identification persists, encrypted, *as* the poet's *morphe* and as the poetic *corpus*. Following this, style may be defined as the deepest structure and the most "real" substance of selfhood. To be influenced by another poet's style is, as in the case of Keats, as much an avowal of love (and perhaps much more an *open* avowal of love) as it is an (ambivalent) expression of anxiety. To use a related example, Levinson's own ambivalence toward *her* (incorporated) melancholic object—the morphe and corpus of Keats/Madeline—may well persist not only in her repeated disavowals of some other class's (and some other reader's) regressive, fetishistic reading of Keats's sexuality/textuality but also, and just as important, in her lush and self-delighting prose.

If aesthetic engagement depends on acts of identity and incorporation that produce the reader no less than the poet, the aesthetic relationship itself inevitably, in some fashion reproduces ideology, even if the aesthetic work itself calls attention to ideology's designs on both poet and reader. As readers of *St. Agnes,* we might learn this from encounters with the invasive Otherness of the castle's artifacts, where the Baron's power shapes Madeline's dream (and ours) no less than Porphyro's desire (and ours). The linguistic and aesthetic "performative," as Butler and as Žižek have argued, is not the exclusive property of poets and transvestites, and it is not necessarily empowering, for it also characterizes the mundane reiteration of the Name of the Father where subjectivity, like sexual identification, begins in an aesthetic act of mirroring that also, paradoxically, brings into being that all-powerful Other. Symbolic identification returns to us a lacuna (a "want") that we cannot perceive, but one that we will henceforth experience as desire (want). Entering into language and its productions (books, for example), we cease to see ourselves in imaginary relation to a loved and desired other (originally, one or both parents) and begin to identify with a loved, desired, and feared Other (the Law of the Father). Yet the image that we recognize in that Other (or the voice that we hear calling from its space) is, in fact, its "nothingness." It is with the Other's lack that we identify, a lack that is, in fact, the drive that Freud called "death." That lacuna in the Other, a lacuna incorporated into the very center of the self, is the same space that Keats in *St. Agnes* represents as a dreaming girl, an *objet petit a,* the cathectic yet vulnerable center of the Other's violent, seemingly inviolable palace of art and power. Her lack is its (and the Baron's) lack, and so while Madeline's dream can never, sadly, be a place of innocence, neither—and more hopefully—can it reproduce the Other as an all-powerful place of plenitude and of potency.

Eve Sedgwick has observed, in tracking the presence of innocence and experience in another text that centers upon an illegible figure of feminine desire, that we learn to desire at the same moment in which we learn to discipline desire. Both moments occur within the Father's Law (and under his Name) and are likely to have occurred through books. It may be difficult to determine whether "innocence" is "the time before we became literate or the time before we became expert at interpreting the signs associated with sexuality."[31] Eager readers, especially, acquire early some version of the trait that Freud would call "epistemophilia." Keats called it "negative capability," the imagination of an avid reader whose writing may be defined by its identification with absence, by its ready assumption of another's form.

Keats's conception of negative capability altered between 1817— when that term arose as Keats critiqued a reproduction of reality (a painting by West called *Death on the Pale Horse*)—and the late winter and spring of 1819, when Keats wrote *The Eve of St. Agnes* and all of the odes but "To Autumn." In Keats's now-famous letter to George and Tom Keats of December 1817, he uses the adjective "negative" to praise a relationship to art that Freud might have criticized by calling it either negation or, perhaps, rather, denial: the substitution of a fetish ("Beauty," say, an *objet petit a*) for a now-absent (or now forbidden) object. Certainly, Keats defines West's failure as an evocation of something that is nevertheless missing, an absence that makes the painting "repulsive":

> But there is nothing to be intense upon; no women one feels mad to kiss; no face swelling into reality. the excellence of every Art is its intensity, capable of making all disagreeables evaporate, from their being in close relationship with Beauty & Truth . . . but in this picture we have unpleasantness without any momentous depth of speculation excited, in which to bury its repulsiveness. . . . I had not a dispute but a disquisition with Dilke, on various subjects; several things dovetailed in my mind, & at once it struck me, what quality went to form a Man of Achievement especially in Literature & which Shakespeare possessed so enormously—I mean *Negative*

Capability, that is when man is capable of being in uncertainties, Mysteries, doubts, without any irritable reaching after fact & reason—Coleridge, for instance, would let go by a fine isolated verisimilitude caught from the Penetralium of mystery, from being incapable of remaining content with half knowledge. This pursued through Volumes would perhaps take us no further than this, that with a great poet the sense of Beauty overcomes every other consideration, or rather obliterates all consideration.

Within a month, Keats's focus in his poetry would imply that Beauty's truth *is* the negativity and the mystery of death's nothingness (the very absence that Beauty is supposed to efface in the above passage), a truth that takes form in the negative capability of a literary act that prefers to Beauty the "unreflecting" Real (to use Lacan's term) that is Death, a truth that imitates death's ultimate, and solitary, reaping:

> When I have fears that I may cease to be
>   Before my pen has glean'd my teeming brain,
> Before high piled books, in charactry,
>   Hold like rich garners the full ripen'd grain;
> When I behold, upon the night's starr'd face,
>   Huge cloudy symbols of a high romance
> And think that I may never live to trace
>   Their shadows, with the magic hand of chance;
> And when I feel, fair creature of an hour,
>   That I shall never look upon thee more,
> Never have relish in the fairy power
>   Of unreflecting love;—then on the shore
> Of the wide world I stand alone, and think
> Till love and fame to nothingness do sink.

The poet fully capable of imagining nothingness constructs death in *St. Agnes* as a romance, or a dream, that was already over (and hence is an absence, a lacuna, "nothingness") before our entry into its space. Death in the later poem "To Autumn" is a blank horizon, a vacant psyche through which swallows pass on the way to somewhere else, echoing momentarily their songs, until all that remains is silence. The terms that come to mind for Keats's "negativity" in such poetry—stoicism, skepticism, existentialism, or even the health of an anticipatory mourning—fail to represent his complex understanding of death and its ambivalent Beauty, his intimacy with oblivion (or is it eternity?) that allowed Keats to reap such poetry in the short autumn of his career. It is we who need, and who therefore cannot help but see, even in such negative delineation, the body of a poet who was too young to write so knowingly of death, or to have known so much about the love that was so rarely returned. It is we who must learn—if one "must" learn anything from these poems—neither to deny the body nor the need, a need that has shaped, and will continue to shape, our criticism, our teaching, and our lives. Keats might teach us that love and death, desire and discipline, and poets and critics mutually construct and feed upon (if they do not, also, poison) each other whenever the critic stares into that most intimate of spaces and obscure of all objects of desire—a poem:

> She dwells with Beauty—Beauty that must die;
>   And Joy, whose hand is ever at his lips
> Bidding adieu; and aching Pleasure nigh,
>   Turning to poison while the bee-mouth sips:
> Ay, in the very temple of Delight
>   Veil'd Melancholy has her sovran shrine,
>   Though seen of none save him whose strenuous tongue
>   Can burst Joy's grape against his palate fine;
> His soul shall taste the sadness of her might,
>   And be among her cloudy trophies hung.

Notes

Introduction

1 Slavoj Žižek, as may be clear to his readers, is the theorist who informs much of my own thinking in these matters. See especially *The Sublime Object of Ideology* (New York: Verso, 1989), where, in "How Did Marx Invent the Symptom?" Žižek discusses "enjoyment," the very surplus of desire, as the symptom of our conscious cynicism:

> It is this paradox which defines surplus-enjoyment: it is not a surplus which simply attaches itself to some "normal," fundamental enjoyment, because *enjoyment as such emerges only in this surplus.* . . . If we subtract the surplus we lose enjoyment itself, just as capitalism, which can survive only by incessantly revolutionizing its own material conditions, ceases to exist if it "stays the same," if it achieves an internal balance. . . . Is not the paradoxical topology of the movement of capital, the fundamental blockage which resolves and reproduces itself through frenetic activity, *excessive* power as the very form of appearance of a fundamental *impotence*—this immediate passage, this coincidence of limit and excess, of lack and surplus—precisely that of the Lacanian *objet petit a,* of the leftover which embodies the fundamental, constitutive lack? (52–53)

2 See, for example, Colin Martindale's "Father's Absence, Psychopathology, and Poetic Eminence," *Psychological Reports* 31 (December 1972): 843–47. Constructing a horizontal scale of "psychopathology" that intersects with a vertical scale of "cross-sexual identification," Martindale concludes that Blake was clearly a psychopath, that there is no evidence that Byron ranked on either scale, that Wordsworth was "normal," and that Keats and Shelley reside somewhere in the middle on both scales. While Coleridge is cleared of the charge of cross-sexual identification, he nevertheless veers toward psychopathology.

3 On the other hand, one should not infer that the critics and psychoanalysts are either consistent with each other or uniformly unhelpful. For example, Bloom's assertion that poets have highly charged relationships with other poets is an indispensable insight. In the afterword, I will make clear my own indebtedness to Bloom, yet because not all poets have the same families, the same psyches, or the same relationships to political and social authority, one "family romance" is unlikely to serve for all poets (even for all the "strong" poets in Bloom's restricted

canon). John Bowlby (*Loss: Sadness and Depression*, vol. 3 in the three-part series *Attachment and Loss* [New York: Basic Books, 1980]) makes it clear that the one identifiable difference between orphans and children who do not experience loss at an early age is that the orphan finds it difficult not only to surrender the original loved object but also subsequent ones as well, throughout an otherwise normal lifetime. The psychologist Edith Jacobson ("The Return of the Lost Parent," *Canadian Psychiatric Association Journal* 11 [1966]: S259–S266) has found that orphans construct family romances that are often very different from the fantasies of different, aristocratic parents dreamed up by Freud's "highly creative" children in "normal" families. In these day-dreams, the original parents return, even if disguised (of course, Freud himself reminds us that the lineaments of the "real" parents also shine through the substitute parents in the fantasies of children who are not orphans). Jacobson concludes that the orphaned child persists in refusing to accept the loss of the parent and continues to expect that the parent will one day return.

4 See Lawrence Stone's portrayal of the "privatization" of the middle-class, child-centered home in *The Family, Sex, and Marriage in England, 1500–1800* (New York: Harper & Row, 1977).

5 See especially Abraham and Torok's *The Wolf Man's Magic Word: A Cryptonymy*, trans. Nicholas Rand with a foreword by Jacques Derrida (Minneapolis: University of Minnesota Press, 1986), and the recent publication of volume 1 of their essays, *The Shell and the Kernel*, also translated by Rand (Chicago: University of Chicago Press, 1994).

6 Jean Baudrillard's *Symbolic Exchange and Death*, trans. Ian Hamilton Grant (Thousand Oaks, Calif.: Sage Publications, 1993), might have figured more largely in the chapters that follow had I encountered this fascinating and important work earlier. Baudrillard defines late capital as the supersedure of symbolic exchange (in which production still drives capital) and introduction of the "hyperreality of the code and simulation" (2). Our age, he argues, is governed by the aleatory processes of the death drive. Death itself haunts us (as, in this sense, I would claim it haunted the Romantics) because it disrupts the identificatory processes of culture that "fails to inscribe its own death" within its code. In this sense, Baudrillard anticipates what Žižek will describe as the deathly Real that haunts the Symbolic Order by reminding it of its own inevitable death. I follow Žižek rather than Baudrillard in finding the term "symbolic exchange" not yet outmoded for discussing the economic and linguistic structures of contemporary culture that I suggest are extensions of Romanticism and late-eighteenth-century capitalist expansion.

7 Robert Burton, *The Anatomy of Melancholy* (Philadelphia: J. W. Moore, 1855). "I have lived a silent, sedentary, solitary, private life, *mihi et musis* in the University, as long almost as Xenocrates in Athens, *ad senectam ferè* to learn wisdom as he did, penned up most part in my study. For I have been brought up a student in the most flourishing college of Europe . . . ; for thirty years I have continued (having the use of as good libraries as ever he had) a scholar, and would be therefore loth, either by living as a drone, to be an unprofitable or unworthy member of so learned and noble a society, or to write that which should be any way dishonorable to such a royal and ample foundation. Something I have done, though by my profession a divine, yet *turbine raptus ingenii,* as he said, out of a running wit, an unconstant, unsettled mind, I had a great desire (not able to attain to a superficial skill in any) to have some smattering in all. . . . This roving humour (though not with like success) I have ever had . . . I have read many books, but to little purpose, for want of good method; I have confusedly tumbled over divers authors in our libraries, with small profit, for want of art, order, memory, judgment. I never travelled but in map or card, in which my unconfined thoughts have freely expatiated, as having ever been especially delighted with the study of Cosmography. Saturn was lord of my geniture, culminating, &c., and Mars principal significator of manners. . . . I am not poor, I am not rich; *nihil est, nihil deest,* I have little, I want nothing: all my treasure is in Minerva's tower" (16).

8 Slavoj Žižek reminds us, as in the following passage from *Enjoy Your Symptom! Jacques Lacan in Hollywood and Out* (London: Routledge, 1992) that Burton is right: the "natural" condition of the capitalist "free" economy is disorder, upheaval, and the routine dispossession of those who previously had wealth. Historically, cultures have been no more willing than Burton to blame the marketplace for their "disease," preferring to find scapegoats (as Burton does in indicting "malingerers") among those who appear to benefit to the detriment of others from the "vast chaos" of unregulated markets. Žižek cites the example of anti-Semitism, where the Jew becomes the bad *objet a* that sustains the illusions of an economy based on sacrificial, symbolic exchange (of objects for words, of things for cash):

What we encounter here is the paradox of the *sacrifice* in its purest: the illusion of the sacrifice is that renunciation of the object will render accessible the intact whole. In the ideological field, this paradox finds its clearest articulation in the anti-Semitic concept of the Jew: the Nazi has to sacrifice the Jew in order to be able to maintain the illusion that it is only the "Jewish plot" which prevents the establishment of the "class relationship," of society as a harmonious, organic whole. . . . One is tempted, here, to paraphrase the above-quoted Jacques-Alain Miller's proposition: "The Jew is not what hinders the advent of the class relationship, as the anti-Semitic perspective error makes us believe. The Jew is on the contrary a filler, that which fills in the relationship which does not exist and bestows on it its fantasmatic consistency." (89–90)

9 "What's the market? A place, according to Anacharsis, wherein they cozen one another, a trap; nay, what's the world itself? A vast chaos, a confusion of manners, as fickle as the air, *domicilium insanorum*, a turbulent troop full of impurities, a mart of walking spirits, goblins . . . the academy of vice, a warfare . . . in which kill or be killed; wherein every man is for himself, his private ends, and stands upon his own guard. No charity, love, friendship, fear of God, alliance, affinity, consanguinity, Christianity, can contain them, but if they be any ways offended, or that string of commodity be touched, they fall foul. Old friends become bitter enemies on a sudden for toys and small offences, and they that erst were willing to do all mutual offices of love and kindness, now revile and persecute one another to death, with more than Vaninia hatred, and will not be reconciled. So long as they are behoveful, they love, or may bestead each other, but when there is no more good to be expected, as they do by an old dog, hang him up or cashier him. . . . In a word, every man for his own ends. Our *sumum bonum* is commodity, and the goddess we adore *Dea moteta*, Queen money, to whom we daily offer sacrifice, which steers our hearts, hands, affections, all: that more powerful goddess, by whom we are reared, depressed, elevated, esteemed the sole commandress of our actions, for which we pray, run, ride, go, come, labour, and contend as fishes do for a crumb that falleth into the water" (43).
10 My indebtedness to Max Weber and Michel Foucault in this summary will be clear as my argument unfolds. See Weber, *The Protestant Ethic and the Spirit of Capitalism*, trans. Talcott Parsons (New York: Routledge, 1985). Foucault will be cited more specifically in subsequent notes.
11 Michel Foucault, *Madness and Civilization: A History of Insanity in the Age of Reason*, trans. Richard Howard (New York: Vintage Books, 1973). Paul Youngquist, in *Madness and Blake's Art* (University Park: Pennsylvania State University Press, 1989), considers the implications of Foucault's discussion of work and madness in relation to Blake's art, although he does not link his fascinating conclusions to Foucault's larger contribution to our understanding of reason and ideology. See especially pages 25 to 30.
12 See especially Foucault's discussion of "workhouses," the first in-

stitutions for the "disorderly," a term that covered not only the insane but also paupers, orphans, widows, and the unemployed. Not only did such houses absorb disorderly behavior, but they also artificially regulated capitalist production. Such enforced labor, of course, is itself an irrational violation of the new faith in free-market capitalism.

13 Wolf Lepenies, *Melancholy and Society*, trans. Jeremy Gaines and Doris Jones (Cambridge: Harvard University Press, 1992).

14 Geoffrey Hartman, *Wordsworth's Poetry 1787–1814* (New Haven: Yale University Press, 1964), p. 12.

15 Eleanor Sickels, *The Gloomy Egoist: Moods and Themes of Melancholy from Gray to Keats* (New York: Octagon Books, 1969). Sickels's well-conceived and admirably wide-ranging accumulation of the evidence of "white," "black," and "love" melancholy in English literature since Milton relieves succeeding studies of the burden of such fact gathering and categorization. What makes her work particularly persuasive, and even contemporary in its methodology, is its summation and correlation of noncanonical as well as (now) canonical works that were read in any given year of the century. In the following she states the premise of her singular work: "What happened between 1740 and 1810 to turn poetic optimism from 'The Essay on Man' to 'Prometheus Unbound,' poetic pessimism from 'The Vanity of Human Wishes' to 'Childe Harold's Pilgrimage'? Whence came the mystery, the imaginative sympathy, the introspection, which are implicit even in Shelley's ecstasies and are the very warp and woof of Byron's lamentations? It is a question often answered by those wiser and more erudite than I; yet it must be here answered once again from the particular angle of our inquiry" (296).

16 Kay Redfield Jamison, *Touched with Fire: Manic-Depressive Illness and the Artistic Temperament* (New York: Free Press, 1993), p. 9.

17 Kurt Heinzelman, *The Economics of the Imagination* (Amherst: University of Massachusetts Press, 1980), p. 141. Heinzelman's reading of texts, literary and economic, is both broad and well informed. While I do not share his premises or reach his conclusions concerning the "work" of poetry, his survey of the field could serve as a beginning point for the reader of literature who seeks an introduction to the workings (in every sense) of capital.

18 M. H. Abrams, *Natural Supernaturalism: Tradition and Revolution in Romantic Literature* (New York: W. W. Norton, 1971), pp. 260–61.

19 Acknowledging the influence of Abrams, James Engell in *The Creative Imagination: Enlightenment to Romanticism* (Cambridge: Harvard University Press, 1981) enthusiastically traces the development of a "philosophy of the imagination" in modern Europe that so "elevated"

the creative mind that, without fear of contamination, it could metaphorically reunite mind and body, man and nature.

20 Jerome McGann, *The Romantic Ideology* (Chicago: University of Chicago Press, 1983), p. 1.

21 Terry Eagleton, *The Ideology of the Aesthetic* (London: Basil Blackwell, 1990).

22 Thomas Love Peacock, "The Four Ages of Poetry," *Critical Theory since Plato,* ed. Hazard Adams (New York: Harcourt Brace Jovanovich, 1971), pp. 509–14.

23 Jacques Derrida, *Dissemination,* trans. Barbara Johnson (Chicago: University of Chicago Press, 1981), p. 152.

24 Tilottama Rajan, "Mary Shelley's *Matilda:* Melancholy and the Political Economy of Romanticism," *Studies in the Novel* 26, no. 2 (summer 1994): 43–68; "Coleridge, Wordsworth, and the Textual Abject," *The Wordsworth Circle* 24, no. 2 (spring 1993): 61–68. I discovered, late in the production of *The Orphaned Imagination,* Rajan's "Language, Music, and the Body: Nietzsche and Deconstruction," in *Intersections: Nineteenth-Century Philosophy and Contemporary Theory,* ed. Rajan and David L. Clark (Albany: State University of New York Press, 1995), pp. 149–69. It is a persuasive and eloquent argument on behalf of Kristeva's material poetics and politics. See also in that fine collection Clark's sophisticated reading of Romantic darkness in his essay, "The Necessary Heritage of Darkness: Tropics of Negativity in Schelling, Derrida, and de Man," pp. 79–146.

25 Esther Schor, *Bearing the Dead: The British Culture of Mourning from the Enlightenment to Victoria* (Princeton: Princeton University Press, 1994).

26 Jacques Derrida argues in "Economimesis" (*Diacritics* 11 [1981]: 3–25) that idealist philosophies that have (like Urizen) orphaned the imagination cannot, by definition, understand a poetry (or a *poet*) whose origins precede and pervade the free self and its fallen, symbolic relationship to the world. Derrida's project is not to specify or investigate what those origins are, or, indeed, to urge that poetry readers return to such origins for the real "truth." Such a project, he implies, would only perpetuate the philosopher's search for an *acceptable—* because *ideal—*original truth that cannot be disputed. For example, the "original genius" established by late-eighteenth-century philosophy as the origin of the poetic imagination is in fact, according to Derrida, revered as an (imaginary) site of production because such an origin would imitate that Being who, paradoxically, is original precisely because He can be neither imitated nor represented by another imagination: God, the Creator who precedes (and will outlive) Creation.

Through the poet-son's identification with the Creator-Father, in a process that bears close resemblance to the death-denying, healthy mourning that Peter Sacks in *The English Elegy: Studies in the Genre from Spenser to Yeats* (Baltimore: Johns Hopkins University Press, 1985) attributes to the elegiac poet, the poet as conceived (in his own ideal image?) by the idealist philosopher "hears" a "vocation of autonomy," which may be subsequently defined as the pleasure of "hearing one's self speak" in a voice that is very close to the origin of thought itself (14). Poetry is the highest expression of an aesthetic faculty (a faculty that is, nevertheless, inferior to the moral faculty or reason) because poetry's "voice" most imitates the way reason "hears" itself in operation. If such poetry is a positive pleasure, literally a pleasure that (like the Urizen who "thinks" him-self into being) *posits* itself and therefore exists, then what is the negative that, like the Chaos of nonbeing that surrounds Urizen, defines what is meant by "poetic"?

Derrida, after disqualifying Kant's own example of negative pleasure as the sublime, concludes that Kant's conception of a pleasure that is entirely internal ("inner hearing") is related to his definition of aesthetic consumption (a disembodied "taste" that "digests" the art work "ideally") as an altogether subjective, internal, "disinterested pleasure" that has nothing whatsoever to do with the physical, quasi-external sense of taste that occurs within the physical organ of speech (the mouth). That empty, unoccupied mouth leads Derrida to propose that Kant's conception of a poetic speech that is analogous to the divine word is based on an absence, or void, and to ask what lies between the two self-refracting objects of identity—Creator and creative imagination—both of whom have no origins. Is it related to the empty mouth of a poet whose speech is entirely mental? Derrida does not name this absence in Kant's thought (although he proposes its association with a response to the repulsive: "vomit"), because a haunting, absent presence is, by definition, an "unrepresentable, unnameable, unintelligible, insensible, unassimilable, obscene other which forces enjoyment and whose irrepressible violence would undo the hierarchizing authority of logocentric analogy—its power of *identification*" (25).

1. Byron's In-Between Art of Ennui

1 All quotations of *Don Juan* are from the edition edited by T. G. Steffan, E. Steffan, and W. W. Pratt (New York: Penguin, 1986). See n. 6 regarding form of citations.

2 W. H. Auden, "Don Juan," *The Dyer's Hand and Other Essays*, se-

lected by Edward Mendelson (New York: Vintage International edition, 1989), p. 399. "What had been Byron's defect as a serious poet, his lack of reverence for words, was a virtue for the comic poet. Serious poetry requires that the poet treat words as if they were persons, but comic poetry demands that he treat them as things and few, if any, English poets have rivaled Byron's ability to put words through the hoops."

3 Canto 10, stanza 76.

4 Canto 14, stanza 17.

5 Canto 14, stanza 8.

6 All quotations of Byron's poems (with the exception of *Don Juan*) are from Robert Gleckner's edition of *The Poetical Works of Byron* (Boston: Houghton Mifflin, 1975). Most of the citations, such as 13.101.15, refer to canto, stanza, and line number. Verse drama citations, such as 1.1.9, refer to act, scene, and line number.

7 In this sense, Byron would have agreed with one of his fans, the contemporary poet Paul Muldoon, who in "7, Middagh Street" has Gypsy Rose Lee revise Yeats's lines on poetic enterprise: "there's more enterprise in walking not quite / naked" (*Meeting the British* [Winston-Salem: Wake Forest University Press, 1987]). Muldoon has edited a selection of Byron's verse.

8 Robert Gleckner in *Byron and the Ruins of Paradise* (Baltimore: Johns Hopkins University Press, 1967) has described *Don Juan* as a poem of "endless repetitions of the Fall." I am indebted to this text for much of my thinking concerning the "sepulchral" and melancholic Byron who is also a lifelong defender of the innocent.

9 Not all who exfoliate experience benefit equally from such renewals, as Juan learns from his fellow captive in canto 5:

> "You take things cooly, sir," said Juan. "Why,"
>   Replied the other, "what can a man do?
> There still are many rainbows in your sky,
>   But mine have vanished. All, when life is new,
> Commence with feelings warm and prospects high;
>   But time strips our illusions of their hue,
> And one by one in turn, some grand mistake
> Casts off its bright skin yearly like the snake.
>
> " 'Tis true, it gets another bright and fresh,
>   Or fresher, brighter; but the year gone through,
> This skin must go the way too of all flesh" . . .
> (5.21, 22)

Paul West in *Byron and the Spoiler's Art* (New York: St. Martin's Press, 1960) would argue that Byron's art of "elimination" or repudiation is closer to the hopelessness of the English soldier of fortune than to what I am describing (following, in part, Peter Manning's model) as an art through which Byron repeatedly revives himself *and* his ability to love. West believes that "reduce everything [Byron] ever wrote, and you will find an essential act of repulsion . . . chameleonic and irresponsible" (13). To the contrary, I am arguing that Byron sets a better example of paternal—that is, of *creative*—responsibility than his own father (or Father). While Byron is honest about his failings as a husband and a parent, I take Byron seriously when he stated in his letters to Lady Melbourne, "I cannot exist without some object of love," even if his "heart always alights upon the nearest *perch*," if not always the wisest (Nov. 9, 1812; Apr. 30, 1814).

10 Leslie Marchand, in *Byron: A Portrait* (New York: Alfred A. Knopf, 1970), offers the following observation: "Like many of his contemporaries, he had escaped rationally but not emotionally from the Calvinistic sense of sin that haunted his subconscious mind. But that fatalistic conception of human depravity blended with his own weakness to drive him on to further violation of his inhibitions" (148).

11 Reinhard Kuhn, *The Demon at Noontide: Ennui in Western Literature* (Princeton: Princeton University Press, 1976), p. 10.

12 In *Don Juan*, Byron implies that election is little better than the collusion of a tyrant with his hypocritical, sycophantic followers to dispossess more honest—but less obedient—subjects of their ancestral estates. Donna Inez, that noted hypocrite,

> . . . went to heaven in as sincere a way
> As anybody on the elected roll,
>   Which portions out upon the judgement day
> Heavens' freeholds in a sort of doomsday scroll,
>   Such as the conqueror William did repay
> His knights with, looting others' properties
> Into some sixty thousand new knights' fees.
> (10.35)

13 Peter Sacks in *The English Elegy: Studies in the Genre from Spenser to Yeats* (Baltimore: Johns Hopkins University Press, 1985) describes this source of literary productivity as one that "emerges from, and reacts upon, an originating sense of loss. . . . the work of mourning" (1).

14 *Byron's Letters and Journals*, ed. Leslie A. Marchand (London: John Murray, 1973), letter of January 2, 1821.

15 I do not pursue in this chapter what may be now, to most readers of psychoanalysis, the obvious similarities of Byron's creative process to the death-driven miserliness and sadism of Freud's anal stage. My neglect of this topic will become increasingly apparent, particularly when I interpret certain aspects of Byron's early childhood through the work of Julia Kristeva on "abjection," a condition that she characterizes, in part, by its anality. While I do not find the Byron studies on this subject (including West's) altogether misguided, neither do I find that such investigations have illuminated the most interesting poetic themes and textures produced by Byron through (or in resistance to?) these needs. Notably, it becomes too easy to conclude that Byron was a psychotic victim of arrested development (based on an assumption that healthy maturity requires the achievement of genital sexuality), and that his disease led Byron into bisexuality, even as it diverted his interests as a poet in philanderers, tyrants, and misers.

16 Much as Robert Burton finds his discussion of melancholic societies drifting into a critique of their capital economies, Byron in describing ennui evokes the phenomenon that Karl Marx will call commodification, and that Georg Lukács in turn will elaborate as the reification and alienation of everyday, modern life in capitalist societies. Each of these phenomena deserves more attention than I am able to provide within the space of this chapter, particularly as these phenomena relate to the operations of symbolic exchange.

17 Byron offers a clue to Harold's mysterious ennui in canto 2 of *Childe Harold* that is related to the reflections in this journal:

> If, kindly cruel, early Hope is crost,
> Still to the last it rankles, a disease,
> Not to be cured when Love itself forgets to please.
> (2.35)

18 Wolf Lepenies, *Melancholy and Society,* trans. Jeremy Gaines and Doris Jones (Cambridge: Harvard University Press, 1992), p. 36.

19 Fredric Jameson, "The Vanishing Mediator, or, Max Weber as Storyteller," *The Ideologies of Theory: Essays 1971–1986,* vol. 2 (Minneapolis: University of Minnesota Press, 1988).

20 Percy Shelley, after reading *Cain,* described Byron in the following terms: "Space wondered less at the swift and fair creations of God, when he grew weary of vacancy, than I at the late works of this spirit of an angel in the mortal paradise of a decaying body" (Marchand, *Byron: A Portrait,* p. 361).

21 Jerome Christensen, *Lord Byron's Strength: Romantic Writing and*

Commercial Society (Baltimore: Johns Hopkins University Press, 1993), p. 19.

22 Christensen seems to imply three things in the passages that address the question of Byron's biography at the end of *Lord Byron's Strength*. First, any effort to establish such a referent fails to escape tautology. Second, Byron's psychic "plasticity" approaches (or may be synonymous with—Christensen is coy on this matter) psychosis. Finally, his *physical* plasticity, his well-known bouts with bingeing and purging, defy the "integrity" implied by the "biographical subject-form of the writer": "Because the body of the writer of the English Cantos has been fully textualized, it can give no metaphysical coherence to the metaphysical concept of a biographical subject-form" (356).

23 W. H. Auden in his essay "Don Juan" notes that while Byron in his life never perfected the role of lordship, through Juan he played that role to perfection: "When one compares Don Juan with what we know of his creator, he seems to be a daydream of what Byron would have liked to be himself. Physically he is unblemished and one cannot imagine him having to diet to keep his figure; socially, he is always at his ease and his behavior in perfect taste. Had Juan set out for Greece, he would not have had made for himself two Homeric helmets with overtowering plumes or had engraved on his coat of arms the motto *Crede Don Juan*" (393).

24 In his letter to John Cam Hobhouse of August 10, 1811, written before Byron would learn of Edleston's death, Byron described his reaction to the deaths of his mother, Matthews, and the earlier loss of his friend John Wingfield:

My dwelling, you already know, is the House of Mourning, I am really so much bewildered with the different shocks I have sustained, that I can hardly reduce myself to reason by the most frivolous occupations. . . . There is to me something so incomprehensible in death, that I can neither speak or think on the subject.—Indeed when I looked on the Mass of Corruption, which was the being from whence I sprang, I doubted within myself whether I *was* or She *was not.*—I have lost her who gave me being, & some of those who made that Being a blessing.—I have neither hopes nor fears beyond the Grave. . . .

25 Robert Gleckner in *Byron and the Ruins of Paradise* describes in the passage that follows Byron's association of the Father, his love, and language (the Law of the Father) in his early lessons in reading:

At the same time that he was fascinated by a vengeful, punishing God, he also, in the first school to which Mrs. Byron sent him, was drilled to repeat by rote,

"God made man, let us love him," his "first lesson of Monosyllables." Yet, if he listened to its meaning, his automaton-like repetition of the sentence did not teach him to read: "Whenever proof was made of my progress at home, I repeated these words with the most rapid fluency; but on turning over the new leaf, I continued to repeat them, so that the narrow boundaries of my first year's accomplishments were detected, [and] my ears boxed." This disturbing juxtaposition of God's love and the divinity of man with the insensitive brutality of one of his created beings is similar to the incident of May Gray, the young Scottish girl who succeeded her sister Agnes as Byron's nurse and continued teaching him the Bible. As Hobhouse wrote of it: "When [Byron was] nine years old at his mother's house a free Scotch girl used to come to bed to him & play tricks with his person." . . . Clearly such an experience affected his mature sexual life—or at least his attitude toward sex. (xix–xx)

26 Marchand, *Byron: A Portrait,* p. 14.

27 The relationship between Byron's sense of damnation, his strong self-criticism, and his hatred of his own infirmity is fascinating in itself. For example, young Byron once sought to have that foot amputated; the doctor whom he consulted refused. In a lighter mood, Byron once wrote to Francis Hodgson the following: "And our carcases, which are to rise again, are they worth raising? I hope, if mine is, that I shall have a better *pair of legs* than I have moved on these two-and-twenty years, or I shall be sadly behind in the squeeze into Paradise" (Sept. 13, 1811).

28 I, 155–56. To create, and to fail, and to begin again is to engage (according to Lucifer) in the death-driven activity that Freud would call the "repetition compulsion."

29 Byron's use of the new science of archeology to express the melancholy of belatedness anticipates the poetry of the Victorians. In a letter to William Gifford (June 18, 1813) Byron places his skepticism about immortality—"our pretensions to eternity might be overrated"—in the context of his belief that Earth and mankind are insignificant "when placed in competition with the mighty whole of which it is an atom."

30 A decade before he began *Cain,* Byron used similar language to express his aversion to a religion based on the "injustice" of sacrifice in a letter he wrote to Francis Hodgson (Sept. 13, 1811):

[T]he basis of your religion is *injustice;* the *Son of God,* the *pure,* the *immaculate,* the *innocent,* is sacrificed for the *guilty.* This proves *His* heroism; but no more does away with *man's* guilt than a schoolboy's volunteering to be flogged for another would exculpate the dunce from negligence, or preserve him from the rod. You degrade the Creator, in the first place, by making Him a begetter of children; and in the next you convert Him into a tyrant over an immaculate and injured Being, who is sent into existence to suffer death for the benefit of some millions of scoundrels, who, after all, seem as likely to be damned as ever.

Byron may call it a "degradation" to make God a "father" in these lines written as a son who still resents his own father's absence, but by 1821 he has found paternity—as a poet, and as a man—a more meaningful and creative role.

31 Jacques Derrida, *Dissemination,* trans. Barbara Johnson (Chicago: University of Chicago Press, 1981), p. 145.

32 Socrates in the *Phaedrus* may stand in for the Father and his commandments (much as Plato the writer may stand in for Socrates without incurring the "sin" of writing) because he "hears" his voice: "I am subject to a divine or supernatural experience [*phone*]. . . . It began in my early childhood—a sort of voice . . . which comes to me, and when it comes it always dissuades me from what I am proposing to do, and never urges me on" (ibid., p. 147).

33 Byron himself makes several observations in relation to the Word— spoken or written—founded on his absence, in the letter, quoted earlier, to Hodgson (Sept. 11, 1811):

> I do not believe in any revealed religion, because no religion is revealed; and if it pleases the church to damn me for not allowing a *nonentity,* I throw myself on the mercy of the "*Great First Cause, least understood,*" who must do what is most proper; though I conceive He never made anything to be tortured in another life, whatever it may be in this. I will neither read *pro* nor *con.* God would have made His will known without books, considering how very few could read them when Jesus of Nazareth lived, had it been His pleasure to ratify any peculiar mode of worship. As to your immortality, if people are to live, why die? . . .
>
> . . . Let us make the most of life, and leave dreams to Emanuel Swedenborg. Now to dreams of another genius—poesies . . .

34 "Writing and speech have thus become two different species, or values, of the trace. One, writing, is a lost trace, a nonviable seed, everything in sperm that overflows wastefully, a force wandering outside the domain of life, incapable of engendering anything, of picking itself up, of regenerating itself. On the opposite side, living speech makes its capital bear fruit and does not divert its seminal potency toward indulgence in pleasures about paternity" (Derrida, *Dissemination,* p. 152).

35 Again, Derrida offers a description of writing as a banished, straying son: "This signifier of little, this discourse that doesn't amount to much, is like all ghosts: errant. It rolls . . . this way and that like

someone who has lost his way, who doesn't know where he is going, having strayed from the corrupt path, the right direction, the rule of rectitude, the norm; but also like someone who has lost his rights, an outlaw, a pervert, a bad seed, a vagrant, an adventurer, a bum. Wandering in the streets, he doesn't even know who he is, what his identity—if he has one—might be, what his name is, what his father's name is. He repeats the same thing every time he is questioned on the street corner, but he can no longer repeat his origin. Not to know where one comes from or where one is going, for a discourse with no guarantor, is not to know how to speak at all, to be in a state of infancy. Uprooted, anonymous, unattached to any house or country, this almost insignificant signifier is at everyone's disposal, can be picked up by both the competent and the incompetent, by those who understand and know what to do with it, and by those who are completely unconcerned with it, and who, knowing nothing about it, can inflict all manner of impertinence, upon it" (*Dissemination*, pp. 143–44).

36 Peter Manning in *Byron and His Fictions* (Detroit: Wayne State University Press, 1978) is correct in stressing Catherine Byron's "smothering" influence on the fatherless son who so early began finding consolation in fictions of the self and who would, throughout his life, find himself drawn to difficult boundaries: ". . . the characteristic fragmentation and multiplication of the self in Byron's work and its skeptical challenge to the knowability and reliability of phenomenon are specific to . . . that first stage in which the infant is wholly dependent on the mother whose 'good-enough' mothering is the indispensable requisite to his trust in the stability of the self and world" (13). To supplement Manning's illuminating investigation of a "passive boy and a domineering mother," we might add two key psychoanalytic insights: *ambivalence* and *incorporation*. While Manning himself dismisses the usefulness of these terms, claiming that they are not required for studying an author for whom "the world in *Don Juan* remains healthily external, not assimilated by the encompassing self but a means of self-definition" (286), in fact Manning leads us, nevertheless, toward an enlarged understanding of the incorporative, abject nature of Byron's "in-between" art:

His ever-shifting, all-encompassing voice, allowing nothing to remain outside itself, enables Byron to be at once everywhere revealed and everywhere concealed, nowhere to be pinned down. Turning back upon himself and revising his themes as he advances, proceeding from confessions of personal confusion to moral argument and inclusive philosophic speculation, calling into doubt even the language through which he appears, Byron is overwhelmingly present yet forever elusive. The capriciousness of fame, the little likelihood of preservation, the universality of transience, and the treachery of memory are topics which haunt him throughout the poem, and they are all instances of the sense of futility which threatens him from within and without. (242–43)

37 Byron comments at length on his father, John Byron, only once in his collected letters and journals. He does so to reassure his correspondent that his father was *not* the "harsh" and "brutal" figure he had been portrayed as being. Such an observation only confirms that John Byron's major injury to his son was neglect, and that Byron's strong feelings toward tyrannical fathers and Fathers are a result of the process of abjection (based on the phantom superego) that Kristeva describes.

38 The implications for Byron's readers of Kristeva's multiple lines of thought in *Powers of Horror: An Essay on Abjection* (trans. Leon S. Roudiez [New York: Columbia University Press, 1982]), notably her investigation of abjection, taboo, and religious sacrifice, extend far beyond those pursued in this chapter.

39 *Byron's Don Juan: A Variorum Edition*. Edited by Truman Guy Steffan and Willis W. Pratt (Austin: University of Texas Press, 1957).

40 As an ephebe, Byron takes kisses very seriously, refusing to find consolation in "cold compositions of art" for the loss of the warm flesh that met in the "first kiss of love," for the memory of pressed flesh is the only "memorial" that literally "matters":

The First Kiss of Love

. . . .

I hate you, ye cold compositions of art!
   Though prudes may condemn me, and bigots reprove,
I court the effusions that spring from the heart,
   Which throbs with delight to the first kiss of love.

. . . .

Oh! cease to affirm that man, since his birth,
   From Adam till now, has with wretchedness strove;
Some portion of paradise still is on earth,
   And Eden revives in the first kiss of love.

When age chills the blood, when our pleasures are past—
   For years fleet away with the wings of the dove—
The dearest remembrance will still be the last,
   Our sweetest memorial the first kiss of love.

41 As Byron admitted to John Hanson, he had become the very agent of exchange whose obligations he would, throughout his life, disdain—

the merchant of money: "I have one word to add about Rochdale[;] when it is sold, I wish the purchase money to be applied to the liquidation of my debts of all descriptions, and what overplus there may be (if any) to be laid out in securing annuities for my own life at as many years of purchase as it may be lawful & right to obtain; you see I must turn Jew myself at last—" (June 25, 1809).

42 Stuart Curran, *Poetic Form and British Romanticism* (New York: Oxford University Press, 1986).

43 In the previous chapter on Wordsworth, I discuss this matter at greater length.

44 Jean-Joseph Goux, *Symbolic Economics: After Marx and Freud*, trans. Jennifer Curtiss Gage (Ithaca: Cornell University Press, 1990). Byron hints as much in rhyming "matter all" and "supernatural" in a stanza that begins with politics (15.93).

45 Judith Butler in *Gender Trouble: Feminism and the Subversion of Identity* (New York: Routledge, 1990) and *Bodies That Matter: On the Discursive Limits of "Sex"* (New York: Routledge, 1993) illuminates "melancholic" heterosexual identification by locating its origins in an earlier, repressed desire for the same-sex parent.

46 In the passages cited below, Goux follows Marx as he elaborates his understanding of how these two kinds of value are different:

[U]se-value is determined solely by the "physical properties of the commodity"—that is, by the empirical object, as a prop, with the diverse and accidental qualities inherent in corporeality—exchange-value, on the other hand, expresses the commodity's substantial, permanent base, its essential, universal identity; it rests on the elimination of all empirical determination. What equivalence affirms, Marx shows, is an *identical essence.* The expression of value, transforming diverse products of labor into identical *sublimates,* is a language of alchemy, of essence and quintessence, of distillation and sublimation. This difference between use-value and exchange-value, then, exposes all the oppositions between body and soul, as Marx's frequent metaphors in this register demonstrate. Use-value is the physical, incarnated, perceptible aspect of the commodity, while exchange-value is a supernatural abstraction, invisible and supersensible. (19)

The materiality of value is abandoned for the abstraction of value in a hypostatized sublimation, a movement toward pure consciousness, convention—a trend that is perhaps consciousness itself. . . . [V]alue is gradually taken over by transcendence. The energetic investment of value (labor, libido) is withdrawn from the material support to be referred (displaced) onto an abstract transcendence that, in the fallen world, is merely represented by a simple diacritical sign. (49–50)

47 Kurt Heinzelman, "Byron's Poetry of Politics," *Texas Studies in Literature and Language* 23, no. 3 (fall 1981): 360–88. Citation is on page 373.
48 Karl Marx, *Marx's Capital: A Student Edition*, ed. C. J. Arthur (London: Lawrence & Wishart, 1992), p. 7.
49 Champagne, reproduction, and economies are also associated in the following stanzas from Canto 2, a digression during which Juan and Haidée are wandering, like Adam and Eve "hand in hand" (st. 184). While they have not yet (technically) fallen, something has been "spilt":

> And the small ripple spilt upon the beach
>> Scarcely o'erpassed the cream of your champagne,
> When o'er the brim the sparkling bumpers reach,
>> That spring-dew of the spirit, the heart's rain!
>
> . . . .
>
> Man, being reasonable, must get drunk;
>> The best of life is but intoxication.
> Glory, the grape, love, gold, in these are sunk
>> The hopes of men, and of every nation;
> Without their sap, how branchless were the trunk
>> Of life's strange tree, so fruitful on occasion.
>
> (2.178, 179)

50 "Dawn," like Byron's other terms for new beginnings, is associated with Aurora through whom the jaded Juan could, perhaps, reclaim something of his innocence (and even, perhaps, immortality), while Haidée, that more innocent love, was associated *not* with dawn but with dusk and mortality. Nevertheless, both heroines are characterized, consistently, as "golden."
51 "These objects, gold and silver, just as they came out of the bowels of the earth, are forthwith the direct incarnation of all human labour. Hence the magic of money. In the form of society now under consideration, the behaviour of men in the social process of production is purely atomic. Hence their relations to each other in production assume a material character independent of their control and conscious individual action" (Marx, *Capital*, p. 47).
52 Peter de Bolla's work on the sublime and England's national debt illuminates the poetic art of Byron, an art that is so often described as one of surfaces rather than depths. See *The Discourse of the Sublime: Readings in History, Aesthetics, and the Subject* (Oxford: Basil Blackwell, 1989).
53 Biographically, of course, Byron would have reason to feel haunted

by ghosts in this imaginary return to English soil, English ruins, and English ennui.

54 *Byron's Letters and Journals,* vol. 9 (1821–1822), p. 47.

2. Spectral Generation in *The Four Zoas*

1 David V. Erdman, ed., *The Complete Poetry and Prose of William Blake* (New York: Doubleday, 1988), 716. All quotations of Blake's letters are from this text.

2 Thomas Pynchon, "Nearer, My Couch, to Thee," *New York Times Book Review,* 6 June 1993, 3.

3 Jacques Derrida offers a model for such a departure in his own examination of mourning, specters, and Marx in *Specters of Marx: The State of the Debt, the Work of Mourning, and the New International,* trans. Peggy Kamuf (New York: Routledge, 1994).

4 Mark Bracher, "Rouzing the Faculties: Lacanian Psychoanalysis and the Marriage of Heaven and Hell in the Reader" in *Critical Paths: Blake and the Argument of Method,* ed. Dan Miller, Mark Bracher, and Donald Ault (Durham: Duke University Press, 1987), pp. 168–203; Slavoj Žižek, *The Sublime Object of Ideology* (New York: Verso, 1989); and Julia Kristeva, *Black Sun: Depression and Melancholia,* trans. Leon S. Roudiez (New York: Columbia University Press, 1989).

5 David Aers, "Representations of Revolution: From *The French Revolution* to *The Four Zoas,*" in *Critical Paths.*

6 These may also be configured, as in Freud's paranoid Schreber, as the sexualized places a solar god enters, including the anus. While the scope of this chapter is too limited to pursue the many ways in which the paranoid's hiding and seeking from a paternal object (and agent) of desire is relevant to this discussion of a sexual procreation in the *Zoas* that elides sexual difference, I will later return to the homoerotic implications of Blake's resurrection of the father, and of the Father as Son.

7 All quotations of *The Four Zoas* are from *The Complete Poetry and Prose of William Blake,* ed. David V. Erdman with a commentary by Harold Bloom (New York: Doubleday, 1988). I will refer to that volume as E, with numbers indicating the Night, Blake's pagination, and lines, as well as the page number of the Erdman text.

8 In many ways David Erdman's reading of Blake's political and social contexts and beliefs in *Blake: Prophet against Empire* (Garden City, N.J.: Anchor Books, 1969) remains unsurpassed in establishing that *The Four Zoas* is in an important sense an outcry against the reactionary politics of war abroad and, at home, surveillance, pestilence, and economically engineered famine. Erdman's indispensable reading of the *Zoas* precedes, of course, Marxist approaches that presume that language (including poetic language) can only be complicit with hegemonic practices that are underwritten by the linguistic Law of the Father. Two essays published in Nelson Hilton and Thomas A. Vogler, eds., *Unnam'd Forms: Blake and Textuality* (Berkeley: University of California Press, 1986), suggest the ways in which New Historicist and poststructuralist readings may converge in this shared presumption. David Simpson in "Reading Blake and Derrida" concludes that Blake deludes himself that a revolution in the labor that produces books—or, for that matter, any revolution in language—may revolutionize a society that oppresses the laboring class. Stephen Leo Carr, who argues in "Illuminated Printing: Toward a Logic of Difference" that Blake, in making each of his "products" different, deliberately exploits (or *reveals*) a language that alienates labor and product, also presumes that Blake as a laborer engages in a "play of differences" that is also the alienation of product from laborer whereby "the ability of a sign to function in the absence of its author, to effect new meanings when reproduced in different contexts, always distances a signifier from its origins: it reveals the systematic working of some irreducible quality that is not solely determined by the initial inscription" (187). Simpson calls Blake's "play" a strategy of avoiding political engagement. Note Simpson's own repeated use of the words "work" and "labor":

Not only might Blake's books have terrified many readers, if he [sic] had had them, it is part of his very *purpose* that he did not. As with Blake, so for Derrida?

We know that times were hard in England after 1794, and that it was dangerous to say anything in public that could even be interpreted as democratic. Working as we now can with a "Blake" who is free from the chains of unitary or monolithic subjectivity and its existential dichotomies (this being as I have said the most valuable contribution of the Derridean movement, though not unique to it), we can understand the obscurity of Blake's writings without any accusation of bad faith. Because his *text* is radical, sublime in the aesthetic sense, we move, in a gesture that surreptitiously inscribes the importance of our own discipline of exegesis, to a radical Blake. The radical text was very possibly written on the assumption that it would not be read, and indeed it was produced in such a form that it could *never* have had mass circulation or radical effect (unless we make an argument for the policy of changing the minds of the rich and powerful). . . .

Perhaps I am laboring the point, but the radical Blake, as we know him, may be a consequence of our allowing the space vacated by the old-fashioned subject "William Blake" to be reoccupied by text or language *alone,* imaged as an autonomous organism generating a self-engaging play, rather than language as the play of *powers* in the *structuring* of the *historical* psyche. . . . (22–23; Simpson's emphases)

9 "The opacity of things, like that of the body untenanted by meaning—a depressed body, bent on suicide—is conveyed to the work's meaning, which asserts itself as at the same time absolute and corrupt, untenable, impossible, to be done all over again. A subtle alchemy of signs then compels recognition—musicalization of signifiers, polyphony of lexemes, dislocation of lexical, syntactic, and narrative units—and this is *immediately* experienced as a psychic transformation of the speaking being between the two limits of nonmeaning and meaning, Satan and God, Fall and Resurrection." Kristeva, *Black Sun,* p. 101. See also Kristeva's *Revolution in Poetic Language,* trans. Margaret Waller (New York: Columbia University Press, 1984).

Nelson Hilton has argued in *Literal Imagination: Blake's Vision of Words* (Berkeley: University of California Press, 1983) that "Blake sets himself against the splenetic, fashionable, melancholic inwardness that is, at heart, an expression of the self's despair at its 'dumbness'—its inability to connect to another or to a medium of connection. Blake must supply a language with which to break down the rising prison walls of bourgeois individualism and self-sentimental narcissism" (53). One need not reach Hilton's conclusion—that Blake, in surpassing Gray, Collins, and Young, turned narcissistic and sunless grief and fear into the healthy mourning (the sunlit "morning") of poetic self-empowerment—in order to extrapolate from Hilton's indispensable textual interpretations a more radical perception in Blake's poetry of a melancholia that resists its own removal.

10 Robert F. Gleckner, *The Piper and the Bard: A Study of William Blake* (Detroit: Wayne State University Press, 1959), p. 45.

11 Gleckner attributes that last citation to Max Plowman. In subsequent sections my indebtedness to Gleckner's powerful reading of Blake's revolutionary art will become apparent.

12 See especially *Blake and Spenser* (Baltimore: Johns Hopkins University Press, 1985), where Gleckner shows how Blake reconceives the *eros* (and the error) of courtly love, and of "allegoresis," as a redemptive and embodied love of his own poetry, "Generation," Gleckner argues, "is thus not merely the '*Image* of Regeneration'; it is also its enabling means" (69).

13 See Gleckner, "Most Holy Forms of Thought: Some Observations on Blake and Language," in *Essential Articles for the Study of William*

Blake, 1970–1984, ed. Nelson Hilton (Hamden, Conn.: Archon Books, 1986), pp. 101–2. Gleckner further observes that "[t]he Word then is not so much a linguistic unit as an event, a sharing, an act of love, a coming together. Blake used the splendid word 'comminglings' to describe it. . . . Thus Eternity is in the form of a man, and the Word is a man, and all things are human-formed, each in each without separation, mergeable identities interpenetrating without end." Gleckner's vision of Blake's humanity challenges humanist assumptions about freedom, selfhood, and the fortune of our fallenness *as* the "work" of "healthy mourning," restoring to Blake's "interpenetrating" art the full potential of its embodied (and procreative) poetics, its radical challenge to the healthy work of mourning accomplished through identificatory ego development. In *The Piper and the Bard* Gleckner suggests that "Blake posits sexual union as the one valid method of achieving the eternal oneness" (37), a dialectical act of generation in which war— sexual *and* intellectual—ultimately leads to recovered innocence. Returning words to their origins in the corporeal self, Gleckner concludes, in "Most Holy Forms of Thought" that words must be seen as "human forms acting out the drama of fall, redemption, and acocalypse that takes place within one's own mental universe," a universe that cannot (and should not) transcend its bodiliness: "This intellectual intercourse (clearly the external analogue of sexual intercourse) makes clear Blake's otherwise seemingly peculiar notion that the sense of touch (the Tongue) is the 'Parent Sense' (*Jerusalem* 98:17). Without such engagement and commingling Blake's poetry seems much wind and splutter" (114). Blake, Gleckner concludes, asks us to enter the "graves" as well as the bodies that ordinary language asks us to abandon:

"If," [Blake] writes in *A Vision of the Last Judgment,* "the Spectator could Enter into these Images in his Imagination approaching them on the Fiery Chariot of his Contemplative Thought if he could Enter into Noahs Rainbow or into his bosom or could make a Friend & Companion of one of these Images of wonder which always intreats him to leave mortal things as he must know then would he arise from his Grave then would he meet the Lord in the Air & then he would be happy." And then he will recognize the dross of language to be the Baconian-Newtonian Lockean-Urizenic illusion that obscures, debases, and falsifies, but never hides the "Visionary Forms Dramatic" redounding *from* the plate or page as they do from all unfallen tongues and minds. Thel was told about the grave: "Tis given thee to enter / And to return; fear nothing." In the sense that I have been attempting to develop, Blake's linguistic text, indeed the whole of each grand plate, is our "grave." It is not much to ask us to enter, but it is everything. (114–15)

14 Thomas A. Vogler, "Re: Naming MIL/TON," in Hilton and Vogler, eds., *Unnam'd Forms*, p. 174.

15 While they are not primarily concerned with Blake's representations of leisure and labor, two other studies to which I am indebted also acknowledge the importance of Blake's "material" "labor." Donald Ault has demonstrated in *Narrative Unbound: Re-Visioning William Blake's "The Four Zoas"* (Barrytown, N.Y.: Station Hill Press, 1987), the most comprehensive reading of *Zoas* yet to appear, that Blake makes a virtue of revision, of re-production *as* labor: "[T]he textuality of *The Four Zoas* challenges cherished assumptions concerning what in fact a text is. In its naked preservation of the traces of its struggle to be (re)composed, *The Four Zoas* pushes to the foreground the productive labor of writing: it is a text that insists on its own radical heterogeneity, on its own struggle to be different from itself, indeed, ultimately on its process of eradicating a potentially unitary textual 'self' on which 'it' could 'differ'" (xiii). In a less optimistic reading of Blake's foregrounding of that labor, Paul Mann, recognizing in "*The Book of Urizen* and the Horizon of the Book" (in Hilton and Vogler, eds., *Unnam'd Forms*, pp. 49–68) that what Blake calls "Urizenic reproduction" is a material and sexual relationship in which "book and body continually intersect," concludes that the material production of books is not only also sexual but a usurpation as well of all other forms of "genesis," a "binding" of "genesis" (origins, eternal or sexual) to the book. As will become clear, my own reading of Urizen's—and Blake's—production of words departs both from Ault's structuralist account and Mann's poststructuralist reading.

16 See my discussion later in this chapter of Judith Butler's important work on melancholia and same-sex identification and my other applications of her findings in the introduction and chapter 3. While Vogler's essay does not deal explicitly either with melancholy or with sexual formation, Vogler, in his readings of Kristeva, Lacan, and Derrida, recognizes the liberatory potential of a poststructuralist literary practice that need not and inevitably seek recourse to the "always already" of the Law of the Father or of heterosexual hegemony. In this sense his work is distinguished from the theoretically sophisticated and otherwise insightful readings of Blake offered by Stephen Leo Carr and Paul Mann in the same collection of essays.

17 Fredric Jameson in *The Seeds of Time* (New York: Columbia University Press, 1994) reminds us of the importance of this metaphor to utopian thinking not only for Marxisms of the past but also in our own age.

18 E. P. Thompson in *Witness against the Beast: William Blake and the*

Mortal Law (New York: New Press, 1993) offers historical and bio-graphical as well as textual evidence for interpreting the erotic and serpentine elements in Blake's illustrations in relation to antinomian traditions that offered tools for resisting hegemony. I will return to this important work later in this chapter.

19 This pattern has the compulsive repetitiveness of the *fort-da* game through which Freud discovered the death drive.

20 In Night the Seventh the question of "feeding" becomes closely associated with an innocence in which humans and Eternals, "They in us & we in them alternate Livd / Drinking the joys of Universal Man-hood" (84.10–11). Further, after Los learns the secrets of creation—and of creativity—from Urthona's Spectre ("For thou art but a form & organ of life & of thyself / Art nothing being Created Continually by Mercy & Love divine" (86.1–2), even Enitharmon's Evelike eating of the fruit ("Life lives upon Death & by devouring appetite" [87.18]), thanks to the Spectre's mediation, transforms their fallenness into an opportunity to "fabricate forms sublime" for the spectres' "war." Only at that moment do Los and Enitharmon become, truly, partners.

21 By the end of Night the First, it has become clear that: (1) Tharmas experiences the loss of a daughter/granddaughter who is also (in-cestuously) a female partner, (2) that the daughter/granddaughter has in fact not yet come into being, and (3) that the fear itself will, paradox-ically, engender the daughter/paramour only after it, first, engenders (in both parents) suspicion, secrecy, and a pretense of "death." The daughter that Tharmas claims already to have lost is one that he had himself hoped to banish by sequestering her within himself: "Let her Lay secret in the Soft recess of darkness & silence." (4) Throughout the *Zoas,* Jerusalem, Enitharmon, and Vala are associated with hidden se-crets whether divine (Jerusalem, the Saviour) or monstrous (the Satan "embosomed" by the tabernacle of Mystery).

22 While it is beyond the scope of a single chapter on Blake, the importance of the visual aspects of specters, spectator-ship, and spec-ulation to the phenomenon of the Lacanian "gaze" deserves more at-tention than it can receive here. See especially Hilton's very fine analysis of the word "specter" and its history in a century of scientific discovery (or "speculation") and revolutionary specters in *Literal Imagination.*

23 In this sense we might also view Schreber's paranoia as (1) produced by the surveillance of a society suspicious of homosexuality *because* (following Butler's argument) it must forget the heterosexual body's origins in homosexual desire for the same-sex parent and as (2) produc-tive (or reproductive) of paranoid desire for, as well as fear of, the Father, a solar parent who seeks (through the paranoid's fears and hopes) to beget offspring through the sexualized spaces of "His" absence in the male body. Blake, in making fear and desire reflexive between a male who reproduces and a female who generates art productively confounds the certainties of heterosexual melancholy.

24 See commentary by Harold Bloom in *The Complete Poetry and Prose of William Blake*, pp. 948–67.

25 The Daughters of Beulah have created, in other words, what Freud called the "splitting of the self" that, in restricting the experience of loss to the melancholic unconscious (the unconscious is itself generated in this very act of splitting), allows the conscious self to go about its business while experiencing, occasionally, a "haunting" from the unconscious crypt where the repressed materials are uneasily buried.

26 Victor Frankenstein discovers the same ambivalence in his relationship to the work of art/monster he brings to life from the dead.

27 In this sense Enion, and the Daughters of Beulah, may be usefully compared to the Eternals in *The Book of Urizen* who, in withdrawing from the demiurge who imitates the Creator, re-create the artist as a reflection of their abjection.

28 And, as we learn later, Urthona's specter, who offers quite a different account of that birth, one that begins in a different labor: Urthona's work at the forge.

29 Julia Kristeva has argued in *Black Sun* that the banishment of the mother from the psyche of the child who is acquiring language and other means of acculturation is equivalent to "matricide," a murder that is the earliest loss (and the earliest basis for melancholy) that we experience. Those who resist engaging in "healthy mourning," that is, the denial of the mother that will ensure successful entry into culture, are the melancholics who, Kristeva writes, are "foreigners in their maternal tongue. They have lost the meaning—the value—of their mother tongue for want of losing their mother. The dead language they speak, which foreshadows their suicide, conceals a Thing buried alive" (53). The alternative to such signifiable sadness is a denial and negation in which the "healthy" subject, having engaged in matricide, unconsciously converts the guilt into a fear of an archaic and all-powerful mother figure:

For man and for woman the loss of the mother is a biological and psychic necessity, the first step on the way to becoming autonomous. Matricide is our vital necessity, the sine-qua-non condition of our individuation, provided that it takes place under optimal circumstances and can be eroticized—whether the lost object is recovered as erotic object (as is the case for male heterosexuality or female homosexuality), or it is transposed by means of an unbelievable symbolic effort, the advent of which one can only admire, which eroticizes the *other* (the other sex, in the case of the heterosexual woman) or transforms cultural constructs into a "sublime" erotic object (one thinks of the cathexes, by men and women, in social bonds, intellectual and aesthetic productions, etc.). The greater or lesser violence of matricidal drive, depending on individuals and the milieu's tolerance, entails, when it is hindered, its inversion on the self; the maternal object having been introjected, the depressive or melancholic putting to death of the self is what follows, instead of matricide. In order to protect mother I kill myself while knowing—phantasmatic and protective knowledge—that it comes from her, the death-bearing she-Gehenna . . . Thus my hatred is safe and my matricidal guilt is erased. I make of Her an image of Death so as not to be shattered through the hatred I bear against myself when I identify with Her, for that aversion is in principle meant for her as it is an individuating dam against confusional love. Thus the feminine as image of death is not only a screen for my fear of castration, but also an imaginary safety catch for the matricidal drive that, without such a representation, would pulverize me into melancholia if it did not drive me to crime. No, it is She who is death-bearing, therefore I do not kill myself in order to kill her but I attack her, harass her, represent her . . . (27–28; Kristeva's ellipses)

While I will focus, in the limited space available, on Blake's melancholic relationship to his father, the implications of Enion's importance in the *Zoas* as the exiled "Ancient Mother" who so often speaks *for* Blake, and as her manifestation in the deadly Vala/Tirzah who will be transformed into a more generative and nurturing figure in Night the Ninth, warrants further study.

30 See the fuller quotation of that letter in the first paragraph of this chapter.

31 John E. Grant in "Jesus and the Powers That Be in Blake's Designs for Young's *Night Thoughts*" proposes that the conversion occurs after the illustrations of *Night Thoughts* are completed (between 1795 and 1797): "The plain senses of Blake's letters during these troubled years (e.g., E720) do seem to indicate that Blake had recently experienced a major religious crisis, as the result of which he had emerged either as a Christian or as a better Christian than he had been before" (71). Grant, noting the frequent and disturbing portrayals of Jesus in *Night Thoughts* rightly suggests that Blake's conversion "ought to be called 'Jesus-ism' rather than Christianity" (72). Grant's essay appears in David V. Erdman, ed., *Blake and His Bibles* (West Cornwall, Conn.: Locust Hill Press, 1990), pp. 71–116. While there is insufficient space in this chapter to fully consider the implications of Blake's incorporation of the *Night Thoughts* plates (and his revision of Young's representation of mourning) in his production of the *Zoas* manuscript, see also the exchange of proposals on this topic that took place in issue no. 18 of the

Blake Illustrated Quarterly: "*The Four Zoas:* Intention and Production" (Robert N. Essick) and "The Final State of *The Four Zoas*" (Paul Mann).

32 In *Of Two Minds: Poets Who Hear Voices* (Hanover, N.H.: Wesleyan University Press, 1993), Judith Weissman also notes that the tradition of oral poetry, even in the contemporary bardic verse that Albert Lord studied in Yugoslavia, is predominantly male. She concludes that visionary and oral poetry has transmitted poetry as a vocation of patriarchy. Yet she cites "one of the oldest codes of ethics we possess, the one in the Book of Proverbs," to suggest it needn't have happened that way (xx–xxi). I am indebted to Weissman's readings of Blake, which are close and perceptive, but I depart from her in suggesting that the voice of a loving Father who is also a Son—and the voice of a mother who has been banished, as Julia Kristeva argues, by patriarchy *to* the crypts of the self's unconscious—competes with the voices of the Law within the imaginations of the Romantic poets who are the subjects of my study.

33 See Hilton's *Literal Imagination* and Youngquist's *Madness and Blake's Myth* (University Park: Pennsylvania State University Press, 1989).

34 Hilton's argument is psychoanalytically sound and historically perspicacious, drawing on Adam Smith's discussion of the "spectator" as well as the etymological history of the "specter" in suggesting how the melancholic specter enacts an "internalized split in the self, represented by conscience" (*Literal Imagination,* p. 154). My argument with Hilton's interpretation of Blake's specters derives from my different sense of the nature of Blake's two decades of remorse, that is, my sense that he found a way *not* to work through his loss of the father but rather to keep alive, through his art, the almost-physical presence of a father (and a Father).

35 Judith Butler, *Gender Trouble: Feminism and the Subversion of Identity* (New York: Routledge, 1990).

36 By this time it is no doubt clear to readers of Leslie Brisman's *Romantic Origins* (Ithaca: Cornell University Press, 1978) that I do not share his belief that Blake opposes to "natural" origins poetic originality, "the author of his own sense of transcendence" (225). In a chapter titled "Re: Generation in Blake," Brisman makes the following claims:

> For Blake, prophet of psychic regeneration, the attempt to discover natural causes of mental states is likewise a misdirection. The traveler on the path from generative nature to regenerated human nature must leave behind him the figures and events of his biographical past, or at least come to distinguish their historicity from their reconstituted presence as phantoms of the psyche. In a letter to Thomas Butts, Blake depicted himself as such a traveler, met by an

admonitory Thistle: " 'If thou goest back,' the thistle said, / 'Thou art to endless woe betrayed.' " Instead of going back or continuing on his way burdened by the actual past "With my father hovering upon the wind / And my brother Robert just behind," Blake strikes the thistle, separating it from its "delving root." This defiance results in apocalyptic sight: "My brothers and father march before; / The heavens drop with human gore." Whatever the precise meaning of that apocalyptic gore, some visionary resistances have been overcome, and this personal poem draws to a close with renewed power: "Now I a fourfold vision see, / And a fourfold vision is given to me." (224–25)

Brisman continues: "Insofar as biography offers natural rather than spiritual history, it misleads as well as impedes. Attempts to locate the origins of psychic phenomena outside the psyche are attempts to naturalize—to reduce man to nature, and the productions of inspiration to natural causes" (225). He further states that "the *father* of falsehood is the devil, the 'Mind of the Natural Frame.' To such a mind no man can be understood to be a source or image of God as First Cause; every man in mind and body is the son of his natural mother, with a body moved by natural needs and a sciential mind busied in searching after second or natural causes" (225–26).

37 Robert Essick, *William Blake and the Language of Adam* (Oxford: Oxford University Press, 1989).

38 See Ault's *Narrative Unbound: Re-Visioning Blake's "The Four Zoas"* (Barrytown, N.Y.: Station Hill Press, 1987).

39 Gleckner argues in "Most Holy Forms of Thought" that "the wars of Blake's mythology directly pit the poet (the human imagination) against the non-poet (the sense-dominated reason-controlled man). More to the point, that war takes places within each man. As his imagination strives to produce 'most holy forms of thought' for the redemption of his total being, his reason produces space-bound, time-bound monsters which struggle for personal dominion. . . . The major products of their infernal creations are two: the law and bad art (which are the same thing)" (107–8).

40 The Muggletonians proposed that God was himself confined to the sepulchre, cohabiting there with (in) the Son until the Son raised the Father on the third day.

41 It is beyond the scope of this chapter to represent fully Thompson's fascinating evidence, particularly his citations of Muggletonian creed. See, for example, his quotation on page 73 of the "Articles of Muggletonian faith." Thompson particularly takes pains to compare and to contrast the beliefs of this sect with the gnostic and Neoplatonic ideas typically attributed to Blake because of his interest in Swedenborg and Böhme.

42 This is, of course, a recapitulation of Enion's encounter with the specter her suspicion and sorrow evoke.

43 *The Four Zoas* (1:3 E300) refers, in marginalia, by chapter and verse number in these two quotations, John 17.21–23. My citation is from the King James version.

44 David Simpson, "Reading Blake and Derrida," in Hilton and Vogler, eds., *Unnam'd Forms.*

45 In response to Urizen's "lab'ring," his probing into Eternal secrets— "Why will you die, O Eternals?"—the Eternals become what they have heard:

> Eternity roll'd wide apart,
> Wide asunder rolling
> Mountainous all around
> Departing; departing; departing:
> Leaving ruinous fragments of life
> Hanging frowning cliffs & all between
> An ocean of voidness unfathomable.
> (ch. 3, plate 5, lines 5–11 E73)

It is the creator's task, Blake suggests in *The Four Zoas,* to restore the presence of Eternity to an art that may begin, as Derrida argues, in "absence," but that nevertheless requires the creator—the poet and artist—to give birth to his or her own best models. When the Eternals "Dictate swift winged words," Blake returns them to his Eternal source, transforming his inner ear, the "Auricular Nerves of Human Life," from a tomb into a womb, and a loom.

Blake tells us in the opening lines of *The Four Zoas* that the Creator himself keeps secrets, and that the knowledge He keeps to himself will never be available to those who (like Urizen) seek it: "[*What*] are the Natures of those Living Creatures the Heavenly Father only / [*Knoweth*] no Individual [*Knoweth nor*] Can know in all Eternity" (1.3.7–8). Indeed, one might argue that the "hidden" becomes dangerous, or perhaps simply threatening, only when it becomes the object of a "seeker" estranged from whatever is now "lost," a loss that occurs whenever a word intervenes (is substituted for) that original object. In "*The Book of Urizen* and the Horizon of the Book" (in Hilton and Vogler, eds., *Unnam'd Forms*), Paul Mann has argued that "what the engraved book and body obstruct is Eternity, and they obstruct it as writing over speech" (53). The Eternals themselves "lose" Urizen once They have been exiled to a transcendental Heaven.

46   And many said We see no Visions in the darksom air
      Measure the course of that sulphur orb that lights the darksom day

Set stations on this breeding Earth & let us buy & sell
Others arose & schools Erected forming Instruments
To measure out the course of heaven. Stern Urizen beheld
In woe his brethren & his Sons in darkning woe lamenting
(2.28.17–22 E318)

47 Los first forges the chains of the former master, Urizen, and then (in Night the Fifth) those of Orc, Los's rebellious son: "Concenterd into Love of Parent Storgous Appetite Craving / His limbs bound down mock at his chains for over them a flame / Of circling fire unceasing plays to feed them with life" (5.61.10–12 E341).

48 Derrida reminds us that "host" and "ghost" are etymologically related. See *Aporias*, trans. Thomas Dutoit (Stanford: Stanford University Press, 1993).

3. Shelley's Absent Fathers

1 I will later discuss more precisely these processes as what Slavoj Žižek calls "imaginary" and "symbolic" identification in *The Sublime Object of Ideology* (New York: Verso, 1989).

2 Freud, of course, explains narcissistic identity as a consequence of a "transferential" misrecognition that derives from (literally) blind faith; Lacan explores these processes as events that begin in the child's mirror stage and continue in that stage's corresponding domain, the imaginary. Identification and transference will be immediately recognizable to readers of Shelley's *Epipsychidion*, his fullest exploration of ocular mirroring and transference, where an "orphaned" poet ("Sweet Spirit! Sister of that orphan one") identifies with a waning moon, a comet, and the sun.

3 Shelley, like Blake, came to possess a healthy skepticism toward the Enlightenment, understanding that reason (Urizen) is founded on repression, including the denial that passion is ambivalent and forceful.

4 Unless otherwise indicated, all quotations of Shelley's poetry are from *Shelley's Poetry and Prose*, ed. Donald H. Reiman and Sharon B. Powers (New York: W. W. Norton, 1977). The citations, such as 3.76–83, refer to stanza and line numbers.

5 I am indebted to Julia Kristeva's *Tales of Love* (trans. Leon S. Roudiez [New York: Columbia University Press, 1987]) for much of my conceptual framing of these terms within philosophical and literary traditions. Kristeva discusses how Freudian transference and Freud's understanding of the presymbolic construction of the ego through identification

with a "loving father of individual prehistory" are related to Plotinus's neo-Platonic transformation of narcissism into philosophical self-reflection. See especially her reading of Plotinus's *Enneads* (pp. 110–11), where she considers that philosopher's debt to (and departure from) Narcissus. For Plotinus, the mirror-stage unification of the self (through unification—"loving reverberation"—with the remote One) "proceeds through *love* and the exclusion of the impure," a process of transference and identification that transpires between "souls" and that excludes the physical body and its association with "regressive" and even "ugly" material (and, by implication, maternal) processes. "In the final analysis it is love that constitutes the inner unity of the soul: as in the *Symposium,* but in explicitly autoerotic fashion, the soul is established through loving itself in the ideal" (110–11).

6   This observation derives in part from Sandor Ferenczi's "Confusion of Tongues between Adults and the Child," in *The Assault on Truth,* ed. Jeffrey Moussaief Masson (New York: Farrar, Straus & Giroux, 1984). Ferenczi in his 1932 essay investigates the trauma experienced by the young child who turns openly to a trusted adult in expectation of physical tenderness and discovers, instead, the force of an adult's unfamiliar desires. In the second stage of that experience the child, far from resisting such an adult, internalizes that adult's aggression through identification. The infliction of pain (and the child's identification with adult guilt) may also lead to precocious intellectual development, as the child learns all too rapidly the "language" of adult passion.

7   Žižek in *The Sublime Object of Ideology* summarizes this process as follows: "What is 'repressed' then, is not some obscure origin of the Law but the very fact that the Law is not to be accepted as true, only as necessary—the fact that *its authority is without truth.* The necessary structural illusion which drives people to believe that truth can be found in laws describes precisely the mechanism of *transference:* transference is this supposition of a Truth, of a Meaning behind the stupid, traumatic, inconsistent fact of the Law. In other words, 'transference' names the vicious circle of belief: the reasons why we should believe are persuasive only to those who already believe" (38). Žižek understands, as did the philosophical skeptic Percy Shelley, that reason cannot finally banish belief: "act *as if* you already believe, and the belief will come by itself" (39).

8   Thomas Weiskel in *The Romantic Sublime: Studies in the Structure and Psychology of Transcendence* (Baltimore: Johns Hopkins University Press, 1986) in fact explains, in part, the pervasiveness of the sublime in eighteenth-century experience as an Enlightenment (and, notably, a

skeptical) evacuation of the Father who became, in absentia, a palpable
and terrifying vacancy (the Real) that threatens Law:

> If the only route to the intellect lies through the senses, belief in a supernatural
> Being finds itself insecure. God had to be saved, even if He had to marry the
> world of appearances. And so, in the natural sublime, He did. The first de-
> velopment, in the seventeenth century, was the identification of the Deity's
> traditional attributes—infinity, immensity, coexistence—with the vastness of
> space newly discovered by an emergent astronomy. The emotions traditionally
> religious were displaced from the Deity and became associated first with the
> immensity of space and secondarily with the natural phenomena (oceans,
> mountains) which seemed to approach that immensity. . . .
>
> There were, however, currents more turbulent and less visible running
> through the Lockean psychology. Locke had removed the soul from the circuit
> of analogical relations in which it had been installed, thereby decisively dis-
> placing the locus of order. . . . The "essence" of the soul is now unknowable or
> even hypothetical; Locke had emptied it out. The soul is a vacancy, whose
> extent is discovered as it is filled. Inner space, the infinitude of the Romantic
> mind, is born as a massive and more or less unconscious emptiness, an
> absence. . . . (14–15)

9 Neil Hertz explores that fissure as the *vide* of difference in the phenomenon of narcissistic identification that he calls "the end of the line"
in *The End of the Line: Essays on Psychoanalysis and the Sublime* (New
York: Columbia University Press, 1985). See the Wordsworth chapter
for a fuller discussion.

10 Ferenczi, in an appendix to "Confusion of Tongues between Adults
and the Child," explores the passage from "tenderness" into "suffering"
as the introduction of *ambivalence,* that combination of love and hatred
that characterizes, especially, the melancholic's relationship to his own
ego. Ambivalence transforms the ego, an entity that comes into existence by identifying with love for and from an other, into an object of
punishing self-hatred.

11 See the quotation that opens this chapter. Harold Bloom, *The Anxiety of Influence: A Theory of Poetry* (Oxford: Oxford University Press,
1973), p. 96.

12 Kristeva in *Tales of Love* suggests that the "hysteric speaks of Agape
and dreams of Eros Thanatos" (52). Shelley's most apparently dispassionate and abstract appeals to a universal love that will palliate human
suffering frequently (and disturbingly) betray an ambivalence that
seems, like a hysterical symptom, to have an unconscious existence of
its own.

13 In the following (and in subsequent) citations from Frederick L. Jones's two-volume edition of Shelley's *Letters* (Oxford: Clarendon Press, 1964), I follow the editor's faithfulness to Shelley's orthography, punctuation, and capitalization.

14 In this sense also, Shelley shares Blake's outrage against an institution that professes love and redemption when in fact it favors death over life, war over peace, and tyranny over freedom.

15 As early as 1811, Shelley praised *Caleb Williams* as a work of importance to him. See Richard Holmes, *Shelley: The Pursuit* (London: Penguin Books, 1987), pp. 97–98. All citations of the novel are from Godwin, *Things as They Are, or the Adventures of Caleb Williams*, ed. Maurice Hindle (London: Penguin, 1988).

16 For a fuller account of panic and pursuit in *Caleb Williams*, see Eve Kosofsky Sedgwick's reading of that novel in *Between Men: English Literature and Male Homosocial Desire* (New York: Columbia University Press, 1985).

17 The morbidity of Mary Shelley's literary themes is, arguably, matched by the formal, inert prose that she developed through melancholic, self-annihilating identification with such figures. Mary first learned the alphabet by tracing her own name on her mother's gravestone, a site to which she returned frequently throughout her childhood and where, significantly, she and Shelley conducted their courtship.

18 *The Poetical Works of Shelley*, ed. Newell F. Ford (Boston: Houghton-Mifflin, 1974), pp. 551–52.

19 Eustace Chesser, *Shelley and Zastrozzi: Self-Revelation of a Neurotic* (London: Gregg Press, 1965), p. 77.

20 "Lines Written for Prometheus Unbound," in *Poetical Works of Shelley*, ed. Ford, p. 445.

21 We do not know until the final pages of *Zastrozzi* just why the eponymous villain seeks to torture and then kill the novel's masochistic hero.

22 Eve Kosofsky Sedgwick, *The Coherence of Gothic Traditions* (New York: Methuen, 1986), pp. ix–x, xi.

23 This statement appears in Jerome Christensen's *Lord Byron's Strength: Romantic Writing and Commercial Society* (Baltimore: Johns Hopkins University Press, 1993). Christensen also cites a passage from Bloom that could serve aphoristically in this chapter: " 'The poem is *within* him, yet he experiences the shame and splendor of *being found* by poems—great poems—*outside* him. To lose freedom in this center is never to forgive, and to learn the dread of threatened autonomy forever' " (xxii).

24 Earl R. Wasserman, *Shelley: A Critical Reading* (Baltimore: Johns Hopkins University Press, 1971).

25 Harold Bloom, "The Unpastured Sea: An Introduction to Shelley," in *Romanticism and Consciousness: Essays in Criticism*, ed. Harold Bloom (New York: W. W. Norton, 1970).

26 Jerrold E. Hogle, *Shelley's Process: Radical Transference and the Development of His Major Works* (New York: Oxford University Press, 1988). In the teleology of Shelley's psychic development that Hogle describes, Shelley moves from a "gothic" preoccupation with loss, death, and paternal persecution, to Deism (where "Soul is there primally, instead of the Gothic vacancy" [32]), to a philosophical skepticism (combined with Lucreation materialism) that is aware that origins always recede from our pursuit. Result: Shelley's "higher" understanding of "reality" that Hogle calls "transferential." For Shelley, he concludes, there is "an invisible causality . . . in the intervals between thoughts to serve as the drive from one idea to the next" (36). Man cannot know the origins of thought, because all that is knowable is the relation or exchange called "transference" (or, to use Derrida's terms, the "difference" and "deferral" of desire). Consequently, Hogle reads "Alastor" as a bildungsroman in which the Poet at last understands the futility of his youthful pursuit: "All these constructs suppress what the Poet's demon really is and so what the Poet most fears to confess: the incapacity of any signifying structure, object, person, or dream to pass on its own from being a formation of desire to reaching the presence of desire's ultimate object" (54). In other words, the Poet of "Alastor," like Shelley himself, comes to understand that there is no God but, rather, only thought itself, "a vast relational exchange, a play of turns, flowing into curves (or paradises) of apparent unity while also dashing from one element to another in a way that threatens every unity" (57). Hogle's "deconstructive" Shelley fails to appreciate the poet's ongoing preoccupation with an absent God who is more "Gothic" (and therefore "Real") than imaginary and symbolic.

27 Barbara Charlesworth Gelpi, *Shelley's Goddess: Maternity, Language, Subjectivity* (New York: Oxford University Press, 1992).

28 Laura Claridge, *Romantic Potency: The Paradox of Desire* (Ithaca: Cornell University Press, 1992), p. 128.

29 As he was writing "Alastor," Shelley was also exploring "nothingness" within what he called the "river" of thought processes in the essay "Speculations on Metaphysics" (see *Shelley's Literary and Philosophical Criticism*, ed. John Shawcross [London: Humphrey Milford, 1923]). In the opening paragraph, the word "nothing" is repeatedly linked to "thinking," "reason," and an originary act of perception: "It is an axiom in mental philosophy, that we can think of nothing which we have not perceived. When I say that we can think of nothing, I mean, we can

imagine nothing, we can reason nothing, we can remember nothing, we can foresee nothing" (64). The originary "perception" that inspires "thought" eludes pursuit in the narcissistic—even paranoid—and gothic description that follows:

> A mirror would be held up to all men in which they might behold their own recollections, and, in dim perspective, their shadowy hopes and fears,—all that they dare not, or that, daring and desiring, they could not expose to the open eyes of day. But thought can with difficulty visit the intricate and winding chambers which it inhabits. It is like a river whose rapid and perpetual stream flows outwards;—like one in dread who speeds through the recesses of some haunted pile, and dares not look behind. The caverns of the mind are obscure, and shadowy; or pervaded with a lustre, beautifully bright indeed, but shining not beyond their portals. If it were possible to be where we have been, vitally and indeed—if, at the moment of our presence there, we could define the results of our experience,—if the passage from sensation to reflection—from a state of passive perception to voluntary contemplation, were not so dizzying and so tumultuous, this attempt would be less difficult. (68–69)

If we return to the opening passage of the essay and reverse the obvious, negative reading of these sentences (that is, that thought is impossible without something at its beginning or its end: an *object*), then we might read Shelley as instructing us that we *can* think of a *something* that is called *nothing*. In making "nothing" an object, we may begin to see how Shelley had already exceeded the insights he had found in Godwinian reason.

30 Chesser in *Shelley and Zastrozzi* cites Shelley's inability to live happily with one woman at a time, combined with his preference for opening his home to an extended family of friends, as evidence of his "repressed homosexuality." I am less interested in putting Shelley's motives under surveillance than in looking at the larger forces at work in a culture that is both homosocial and homophobic.

31 Richard Holmes, *Shelley: The Pursuit* (London: Penguin Books, 1987), p. 83.

32 Holmes suggests that Shelley developed early a taste for power in his family home when, as an older brother, he delighted in, first, persuading his frightened younger sisters that he could conjure ghosts and then "comforting" them.

33 Žižek distinguishes "imaginary" and "symbolic" identification as the difference between *believing in* the ideal others and the images that such others project for us to imitate in a given society and *identifying with* an Other, the Law of the Father, that pretends to be the ideal site

from where judgment (and punishment) derive: "The relation between imaginary and symbolic identification—between the ideal ego [*Idea-lich*] and the ego-ideal [*Ich-Ideal*]—is—to use the distinction made by Jacques-Alain Miller (in his unpublished Seminar)—that between 'constituted' and 'constitutive' identification: to put it simply, imaginary identification is identification with the image in which we appear likeable to ourselves, with the image representing 'what we would like to be,' and symbolic identification, identification with the very place *from where* we are being observed, *from where* we look at ourselves so that we appear to ourselves likeable, worthy of love" (*The Sublime Object of Ideology*, p. 105).

34 First published with *Alastor* in 1816. Cited from *The Complete Works of Percy Bysshe Shelley*, ed. Thomas Hutchinson (Oxford: Oxford University Press, 1940), pp. 521–22.

35 While the most-often cited studies of Shelley's reading of Words-worth's Immortality Ode and *Excursion* remain Wasserman's chapter on "Alastor" in his *Shelley: A Critical Reading* and Bloom's various observations on "Alastor" in *Yeats* (Oxford: Oxford University Press, 1970), a number of other studies are available. The first, and still valuable, investigation of allusions to Wordsworth in "Alastor" is the one by Paul Mueschke and Earl L. Griggs: "Wordsworth as the Prototype of the Poet in Shelley's *Alastor*," *Publications of the Modern Languages Association* 49 (March 1934): 229–45. Other essays that I have thought worthwhile (although I have found none that consider the "staging" of the relationship between the two poets) include: Yvonne M. Carothers' "*Alastor:* Shelley Corrects Wordsworth," *Modern Language Quarterly* 42:1 (March 1981): 21–47; Stuart Peterfreund's "Between Desire and Nostalgia: Intertextuality in Shelley's *Alastor* and Two Shorter Poems from the *Alastor* Volume," *Romanticism Past and Present* 9, no. 1 (winter 1985): 47–66; William Keach's "Obstinate Questionings: The Immortality Ode and *Alastor*," *The Wordsworth Circle* 12, no. 1 (winter 1981): 36–44; and Donald H. Reiman's "Wordsworth, Shelley, and the Romantic Inheritance," *Romanticism Past and Present* 5, no. 2 (1981): 3–22. Of these essays, I find Reiman's the most provocative and insightful, for he helpfully defines the difference between Wordsworth's "pastoral" relationship to the world (where parental figures are literally "pastors," or guardians) and Shelley's "Gothic sensibility," "a set of mind that caused him to see both the natural and the social world around him as essentially dangerous and hostile" (6).

36 Sedgwick's understanding of this scene (notably as Freud defines it in "A Child Is Being Beaten") and its central importance in poetic

empowerment is one of many contributions that she has made to efforts to revise the literary family romance. See "A Poem Is Being Written," *Tendencies* (Durham: Duke University Press, 1993).

37 Žižek in *Tarrying with the Negative: Kant, Hegel, and the Critique of Ideology* (Durham: Duke University Press, 1993) relates this distinction to what he calls "radical evil," a term to which I will later return. See especially his chapter "Cogito and the Sexual Difference."

38 In fearing that God may, indeed, inhabit the deep, both as a spirit who rescues and one who avenges, Shelley would be rereading not only Genesis (as a rival and threatened "creator" who perceives, in the place of a loving Father, a fearful vacancy), but also one of his favorite poems by Coleridge: *The Ancient Mariner.*

39 If the *objet petit a* is simply an object that signifies nothingness, so, Žižek suggests in *The Sublime Object of Ideology*, is the subject, which he describes as "the empty place opened in the big Other by the failure of . . . representation" (208). The sublimity of the one reproduces (or echoes or reflects) the sublimity of the other. The "Thing" is the nothingness that inhabits both object and subject *as* a "sublime" vacancy that represents "the very failure of representation to reach after the Thing" (203):

[T]he Sublime is no longer an (empirical) object indicating through its very inadequacy the dimension of a transcendent Thing-in-itself (Idea) but an object which occupies the place, replaces, fills out the empty place of the Thing as the void, as the pure Nothing of absolute negativity—the Sublime is an object whose positive body is just an embodiment of Nothing. . . .

. . . Herein lies the "last secret" of dialectical speculation: not in the dialectical mediation-sublimation of all contingent, empirical reality, not in the deduction of all reality from the mediating movement of absolute negativity, but in the fact that this very negativity, to attain its "being-for-itself," must embody itself again in some miserable, radically contingent corporeal leftover. (207)

40 Žižek, *Tarrying with the Negative,* p. 45.

41 Žižek describes this deprivation through the analogy of the cannibal, Hannibal Lecter, in "Silence of the Lambs." Further, he relates the obscene "want" of the superego in such acts of transference to the originary sacrifice required of the subject who *becomes* a subject by entering into the Symbolic Order. The death drive that characterizes the "*fort-da*" game enacted by the child who seeks to master loss haunts his movement into symbolic identification with the Law of the Father *not* as the loss of the "mother qua Thing" but rather as the loss of "part of the subject itself" (91), "the loss of my own substantial fullness of

being" (92), that is sacrificed to the Other's want in the very process of identification *with* that want.

42 Or, as Lacan would say, "barred."

4. Depression and Vocation in the 1805 *Prelude*

1 *The Letters of William and Dorothy Wordsworth,* ed. Ernest de Selin-court; 2d ed. revised by Chester L. Shaver (Oxford: Oxford University Press, 1967), 1:249–50.

2 All quotations from *The Prelude* are from the 1805 edition unless otherwise indicated. When derived from the 1799 *Prelude,* the citation will be preceded by the abbreviation TPP (Two-Part *Prelude*). The quotations are from *The Prelude: 1799, 1805, 1850,* ed. Jonathan Words-worth, M. H. Abrams, and Stephen Gill (New York: W. W. Norton, 1979). The citations, such as 10.325–26, refer to book number and line numbers.

3 Nicolas Abraham and Maria Torok, *The Shell and the Kernel: Renewals of Psychoanalysis,* vol. 1, ed. Nicholas T. Rand (Chicago: University of Chicago Press, 1994), p. 130. In *The Wolf-Man's Magic Word: A Cryptonomy,* trans. Nicholas T. Rand with a foreword by Jacques Derrida (Minneapolis: University of Minnesota Press, 1986), Torok and Abraham discovered the phenomenon they elaborated as "crypton-omy": the resourceful preservation of the dead whom the subject can neither surrender nor recognize in the unconscious, a burial site from which the still-living dead continue, "cryptically," to speak. This phenomenon was facilitated for the Wolf-man—who confused his father and sister (and would not give up either)—by his fluency in several languages, for this allowed for fortunate confusions, such as slips of the tongue, which enabled him both to reveal and to conceal his secret.

4 "Incorporation entails the fantasmic destruction of the act by means of which metaphors become possible: the act of putting the original oral void into words, in fine, the act of introjection" (*Shell and the Kernel,* p. 132).

5 While several studies, some scholarly and some not, remind Words-worth's readers of Dorothy's importance to his poetry, F. W. Bateson in *Wordsworth: A Re-Interpretation* (London: Longmans, Green, 1956) may be the only reader of Wordsworth's poetry who has made explicit Wordsworth's hunger for love, the ways in which Dorothy—having satisfied that need—is excluded from the poetry, and the presence of oral appetite in Wordsworth's growing poetic powers:

But it is the active appreciation of natural beauty that is the real theme of *The Prelude,* and this intimate cooperation between the human subject and the natural object is expressed in Wordsworth's poems of this period in images of eating and drinking. . . .

The Wordsworthian religion of nature seems to be implicit in these recurrent metaphors. Their primitive, infantile character, for one thing, shows how personal and subjective it was. In order to define his feelings in the presence of wild nature Wordsworth had to use some of the earliest and simplest sensations known to man. (182–83)

Bateson also suggests that Wordsworth's struggle after 1801 to understand the imagination's relationship to Nature and human community was a heroic effort both to recognize the power of his intimacy with Dorothy and to acquire something like "mental health": "The dilemma of his personal life was that solitude, even when mitigated by the company of one or two intimates, carried with it the potential threat of melancholia, the condition that Coleridge called Wordsworth's 'hypochondriacism,' while its opposite, the social life of a city, tended to smother and frustrate all that was most original and creative in him" (186). Wordsworth's "greatness," Bateson concludes, is his recognition of his profound psychic malaise, its roots in unappeasable and complex appetites, and his heroic (if failed) effort to acquire "health."

6 James Chandler in *Wordsworth's Second Nature* (Chicago: University of Chicago Press, 1984) makes a strong case that Wordsworth was in fact responding to the radical views of the French philosophes. See especially "An Ideology against 'Ideology,'" the chapter in which he proposes that ideology, while originally conceived by Destutt de Tracy as a "science of ideas," may be viewed "broadly" as "the politics of the French Enlightenment." To the explicit ideology of the philosophes Chandler opposes a covert "Burkean ideology that informs Wordsworth's poetry—'traditionalism' or 'the doctrine of second nature,'" which itself is then "an ideology against 'Ideology'" (218). As will become clear, my view of Wordsworthian Nature, and my own understanding of ideology (and my use of the term in reading poetry), differ from Chandler's, largely because I find it essential to bring to both terms an understanding of how ideology, *like* Wordsworth's "Nature," speaks most forcefully not through reason but through the unconscious. Burke clearly became important to Wordsworth, notably in the 1850 revisions of *The Prelude* that address Burke directly, but this is a complex issue that, like Wordsworth's growing "conservatism" generally after he had settled fully into life in the Lake District, I do not

address in this brief space. I do, however, find relatively consistent Wordsworth's portrayal of Nature from early texts to later ones.

7 See Mark Edmundson's "Vital Intimations: Wordsworth, Coleridge, and the Promise of Criticism" (*South Atlantic Quarterly* 91, no. 3 [summer 1992]: 739–64) for a related, but differently argued and directed, discussion of these matters. I particularly disagree with Edmundson's acceptance of an essential difference between philosophy and poetry, his dismissal of the unconscious as a viable resource for writers and critics, and his suggestion that an alternative to current critical practice might be an admiration that is moved to tearful silence. Nevertheless, I share Edmundson's concern that critics too readily indict both children *and* poets, and on similar (and contestable) grounds.

8 While clearly Wordsworth was troubled in the mid-nineties and later by the transformation of revolutionary ideals into Napoleon's imperial rule, I do not share Alan Liu's contention in *Wordsworth: The Sense of History* (Stanford: Stanford University Press, 1989) that key moments of *The Prelude* may be explained by Wordsworth's wish to identify with Napoleon. Neither am I persuaded by Douglas Wilson's endorsement of that reading in his psychoanalytic reconstruction of Wordsworth's "guilt" in the spots of time and on Mount Snowdon. Claiming that Wordsworth was "beguiled by power," Wilson argues that the poet "as Liu puts it, must atone for his excessive desires, for his betrayal by false imagination, for his seduction by the French Revolution that later succumbs to Napoleonic imperialism. . . . History, as Liu justly argues, not only explains the difficult crux of desire, but also prepares the crescendo of Wordsworth's ending" (*The Romantic Dream: Wordsworth and the Poetics of the Unconscious* [Lincoln: University of Nebraska Press, 1993], p. 165).

9 Harold Bloom, "Nature and Romanticism," *Romanticism and Consciousness: Essays in Criticism,* ed. Harold Bloom (New York: W. W. Norton, 1970), p. 9.

10 Geoffrey Hartman, "Romanticism and 'Anti-Self-Consciousness,' " *Romanticism and Consciousness,* p. 49.

11 M. H. Abrams, *Natural Supernaturalism: Tradition and Revolution in Romantic Literature* (New York: W. W. Norton, 1971), p. 94.

12 Wordsworth's crisis of the thinking self, emblematized in book 11 (lines 784–95) by the conflictual, awkward phrasing that conflates rather than distinguishes "mysteries of passion" and "reason" (and so leaves "one brotherhood" a helplessly dangling enterprise), could equally characterize the anxious abjection of much recent scholarship on Wordsworth. The onset of Romantic scholarship's own Wordsworthian "war

against the self" may be traced to a comparable disillusionment with poetic consciousness. In the aftermath of these strong and confident expressions of liberal and humanist beliefs just cited, a later generation of Romanticists has, with some justification (and perhaps with some Oedipal aggressiveness), indicted those beliefs as ideologically suspect, arguing that the allegedly private self, constructed from the unconscious misrecognitions of precisely such ideologies, can know with certainty neither the sources of that now-fictional self (or "consciousness") nor whatever may be designated as "material" reality, whether it is manifested as Nature, the body, and/or the mother. In fact, however, New Historicist and poststructuralist Wordsworthians, no less than their humanist predecessors, have misread Wordsworth's return to Nature as ineluctably reactionary and exploitative. While I will challenge more pointedly a few of these readings, particularly in the afterword, the wearying work of appraising them all belongs to another day and, perhaps, to someone else.

13 Gayatri Spivak, "Sex and History in *The Prelude*," *Texas Studies in Literature and Language* 23, no. 3 (fall 1981): 324–60; Mary Jacobus, *Romanticism, Writing, and Sexual Difference: Essays on "The Prelude"* (Oxford: Oxford University Press, 1989); Diane Long Hoeveler, *Romantic Androgyny: The Woman Within* (University Park: Pennsylvania State University Press, 1990); Rachel Crawford, "The Structure of the Sororal in Wordsworth's 'Nutting,'" *Studies in Romanticism* 31, no. 2 (summer 1992): 197–212.

14 Dorothy's presence is no more audible or active in the readings of some of Wordsworth's most influential male critics. In *William Wordsworth: A Life* (Oxford: Oxford University Press, 1989), Stephen Gill, for example, says of the siblings' months in Goslar: "In the absence of any evidence such as her later Grasmere journal provides, it is futile to speculate about what Dorothy's feelings were. Manuscript evidence does survive, however, to reveal how Wordsworth coped with the *isolation and silence* of that Goslar winter. He turned in, intensely, upon himself" (159; my emphasis).

15 Jean-Joseph Goux, *Symbolic Economies: After Marx and Freud,* trans. Jennifer Curtiss Gage (Ithaca: Cornell University Press, 1990).

16 These models offer a strong position from which to build upon the ecological readings of Wordsworth proposed in three recent investigations of the Romantics' interest in ecology. See Jonathan Bate's *Romantic Ecology: Wordsworth and the Environmental Tradition* (New York: Routledge, 1991), Nicholas Roe's *The Politics of Nature: Wordsworth and Some Contemporaries* (New York: St. Martin's Press, 1992), and Karl Kroeber's *Ecological Literary Criticism: Romantic Imagining and the Bi-*

ology of Mind (New York: Columbia University Press, 1994). As Kroeber argues, "The romantic poets are of special interest to those of us concerned to develop an ecologically oriented criticism exactly because they anticipate—sometimes shrewdly, sometimes absurdly—attitudes and conceptions that only in our century have been given either a solid scientific basis, or whose psychic grounding has only recently been persuasively analyzed" (19).

17 David Bohm, *Wholeness and the Implicate Order* (London: Routledge, 1994), p. 11.

18 M. H. Abrams, "The Design of *The Prelude:* Wordsworth's Long Journey Home," in *The Prelude: 1799, 1805, 1850,* p. 595.

19 The taskmaster behind that scholarly project had been from the beginning, of course, Coleridge, the "brother-poet" who was also in so many ways Wordsworth's intellectual father. In the letters that Coleridge sent to Wordsworth in Germany, he gently discouraged the versions of the *Prelude* and drafts of Lucy poems that William and Dorothy had sent to him, urging him to turn instead to philosophy. Coleridge describes the physical and mental discipline he expected of Wordsworth in a passage cited by Herbert Lindenberger: " 'Wordsworth should assume the station of a man in mental repose, one whose principles were made up, and so prepared to deliver upon authority a system of philosophy' " (*On Wordsworth's "Prelude"* [Princeton: Princeton University Press, 1963], p. 58). Work, not pleasure, is the means of such "repose."

20 Gill, *William Wordsworth,* p. 174.

21 In fact, a scholarship guided by the terms of the Oedipus complex itself returns—compulsively—to the gates of Eden, only to find its entry blocked. Neil Hertz in *The End of the Line: Essays on Psychoanalysis and the Sublime* (New York: Columbia University Press, 1985) has keenly analyzed such repetitive returns and inevitable blockages as a feature, particularly, of scholarly repudiations (or denials) of access to Eden. Hertz judges Thomas Weiskel's theorizations of the sublime in *The Romantic Sublime* as an irresistible movement toward, and a blindness before, the unspeakable and the unthinkable, a blindness that allows that moment's resolution into a reassuring identification with the Law that lies beyond the maternal sublime, an Oedipal injunction (the Law of the Father) that rescues reason, language, and phallic unity from the threat of pre-Oedipal regression:

We might even see in Weiskel's invocation of the (maternal) pre-Oedipal phases, in his interpretation of them as constituting the deep (hence primary) structure of the sublime and yet as still only a tributary of the Oedipal system into which it invariably flows, a more serious and argued version of Monk's joking about the woman not fit to be seen. The goal in each case is the Oedipal moment, that is, the goal is the sublime of conflict and structure. The scholar's *wish* is for the moment of blockage, when an indefinite and disarrayed sequence is resolved (at whatever sacrifice) into a one-to-one confrontation, when numerical excess can be converted into that supererogatory identification with the blocking agent that is the guarantor of the self's own integrity as an agent (53).

22 As we have learned from William Kerrigan, "home" is a word that resonates in similar ways for Milton, the poet whose ties to his own father and to God the Father carried the ambivalence of two very different sons—Jesus and Satan—and of another son (Samson), who, however flawed, redeemed himself in his father's (and Father's) eyes by challenging his heathen taskmasters. Samson finally finds a way to return home, to the (*two*) still-living father(s) whom he has refused to surrender as the price of entry into an alien culture. That home (in an interesting inversion of the elegy) now mourns the poet as sacrificed hero. See Kerrigan, *The Sacred Complex: On the Psychogenesis of "Paradise Lost"* (Cambridge: Harvard University Press, 1983).
23 Geoffrey Hartman, *Wordsworth's Poetry 1787–1814* (New Haven: Yale University Press, 1971).
24 Thomas Weiskel, *The Romantic Sublime: Studies in the Structure and Psychology of Transcendence* (Baltimore: Johns Hopkins University Press, 1986).
25 Paul Fry, in an original and authoritative investigation of poetic voices and the ode, reaches related conclusions that are, I would argue, similarly flawed by Oedipal premises. See especially his chapter on Wordsworth in *The Poet's Calling in the English Ode* (New Haven: Yale University Press, 1980) where he concludes that the Immortality Ode is an endorsement of the strategies of sublimation and denial that Peter Sacks has associated with the "healthy mourning" of the elegy: "Wordsworth's ode is more crucially a forgetting than an attempted reconstitution of any earlier self; it celebrates forgetting" (155); the poet's "sober coloring . . . consists in the discovery of personal strength through reverence for an absent father who can *only* be revered in strength when he is absent," a "moment of relieved self-conception that purifies the earthy nature of Aeneas's mother, Venus" (161).
26 Both interpretations are versions of the Kantian *Bestimmung* that Jacques Derrida discusses in "Economimesis" (*Diacritics* 11 [1981]: 3–25). As an alternative to Kant's theory of voice as inner hearing, Derrida, an appreciative reader of Abraham and Torok, proposes an image

of oral incorporation (and of oral rejection). For a fuller discussion of "Economimesis" and its relevance to poetic melancholia, see the introduction.

27 *Paradise Lost,* bk. 8, in *The Poems of John Milton,* ed. John Carey and Alastair Fowler (London: Longman, 1968).

28 See n. 22 for a fuller reference to Kerrigan's important work.

29 Richard Onorato, in *The Character of the Poet: Wordsworth in "The Prelude"* (Princeton: Princeton University Press, 1971) suggests that "breezes" are "metaphors of beginning" associated with the acquisition of language and the child's original incorporative relationship to the mother.

30 Two critics provide very different answers to this question. Mary Jacobus in *Romanticism, Writing, and Sexual Difference* presumes that Oedipal anxieties will lead to the poet's vocational failure, that is, to the poet's "unmaking" of his personal, lyric voice. These anxieties, she argues, are exacerbated by the dithyrambic form, a form that leads to a fear of drowning that leads, in turn, to a fear of Orphic "dismemberment," and that, ultimately, forecloses Wordsworth's hope that, through poetry, he might have (phallically) unified his voice and mastered his chosen form. She traces a process that Wordsworth enacts in the "glad preamble" that leads, she claims, from his (mistaken) effort to find through its dithyrambs an individual voice (a manic process that leads, to the poet's horror, not to one but to many voices, all of them threatening him with death), to his Oedipal recognition that, because he cannot "master" the sublime voices of the literary fathers that he has summoned unintentionally, he must drown his own, weak voice with the so-called harmonious voices of "oceanic" nature in a harmony that becomes, ultimately, the larger "voice of poetry" (171). Such a move— not coincidentally—drowns the fathers' voices as well. A sadder but wiser Wordsworth, Jacobus contends, comes to understand that the voice of poetry, at its best, "can produce 'A monument and arbitrary sign' for thought; and at worst, make only desultory sounds. This is the Eolian fantasy demystified, and along with it there collapses the entire Romantic fallacy of spontaneous lyric utterance, whether heard or overheard" (172). Poetry itself can only be saved from this flood, Jacobus continues, by a corresponding myth of the poetic voice as apocalypse, that is, the destruction of Nature and of the physical self. In "transcendentalizing" poetic voice into Logos or the Word, "Wordsworth uses silent reading to free poetry from the monumentality and arbitrary signs of death" that threaten him with castration or worse: "Disembodied sound—'The ghostly language of the ancient earth'— comes to be the archetype of poetry. In this light, the 'glad preamble' might be seen not only as a means of calling both poet and voice into being, but also as a way to fantasize their transcendence of material representation" (176). Jacobus, finally hearing only a disembodied (unheard) voice *as* the poetic vocation that Wordsworth constructed as a psychic defense, hints in her closing words that deafness might be preferable to hearing the ideological message of such poetry.

Addressing in a different manner Wordsworth's interest in the properties of water, Seamus Heaney, in "The Makings of a Music: Reflections on Wordsworth and Yeats" (*Preoccupations: Selected Prose, 1968–1978* [New York: Farrar, Straus & Giroux, 1980]), proposes that Wordsworth *succeeds* in hearing a voice that brings cheer to his melancholic mind. Wordsworth further succeeds, Heaney claims, in giving this voice a home *through* poetic form, a "making"—a process—that does *not* require his mastery either of self or of others. Rather, Heaney envisions Wordsworth as a poet for whom poetry belongs to a sequence of "physiological operations" that allow him to swim, *not* drown, "*with* the current of its form rather than against it" (61; my emphasis). Such a poetry, Heaney concludes, cannot be defined as work so much as "surrender" to an inner calling that all poets begin with (however differently such poets as Wordsworth and Yeats may *finish* the poetic process). In the first book of *The Prelude,* Heaney continues, "the tongue of the river . . . licked him into poetic shape" by endowing him with "the capacity of listening." To listen with the stillness of a tuning fork is a capacity that the poet learned in imitation of a river whose "passage flows, shifts through times and scenes, mixes, drifts and comes to rest with the child composed into a stilled consciousness, a living tuning fork planted between wood and hill" (70). Significantly, Heaney concludes, Wordsworth's is an auditory skill of "active quiet" that he learned not only in solitude with a paternal voice or, later, with his own internal echoes. Rather, Wordsworth's solitude, Heaney reminds us, was shared with Dorothy, whose presence brought further poetic rewards. Heaney cites Dorothy's journal entry of April 29, 1802, which is replete with references to water (as "falls"), voice, and death.

31 For the composing poet in Germany, who is himself finding transportation troubling between linguistic states, the name "Derwent" might well have provided a German-English, eponymous pun: "Derwent," "that went," or "*he* went." In this sense, perhaps, the river is indeed a lost—but recovered—father, even as his sister is a brook that intersects, and intervenes, at a critical point the poet's lonely narrative road.

32 *Selected Prose Writings,* ed. John O. Hayden (New York: Penguin, 1988), p. 324.

33 In this sense, Nature's voice assumes the inarticulate speech of the unconscious. Interpreting dreams, as Freud came to understand, typically requires "hearing" a message that the ego, even in dreams, has so censored that it sounds like the babble of a stream, of nonsense, or of an alien tongue. Derrida, in *Of Grammatology* (trans. Gayatri Spivak [Baltimore: Johns Hopkins University Press, 1974], p. 68), investigates those gaps in meaning, suggesting that in ordinary speech the unconscious, which language has repressed at the very "origin of signification," expresses itself as the "absent presence" of what he calls "dead time," a "spacing" (like Wordsworth's spots) that "articulates" "space and time, the becoming-space of time and the becoming-time of space." The repressed material of the unconscious may speak most forcefully in the gaps and halts of the Symbolic Order's deceptively real appearance. In these blank moments, in such spacings, where time itself ceases to flow, what Slavoj Žižek in works that I will cite fully later in this chapter designates (following Lacan) as the Real obtrudes as a failure of ordinary, seamless signification. The Real ultimately serves as an ominous reminder to those who inhabit the Symbolic Order that signification—which seems to generate its own "de-natured" immortality, its "always already-ness," simply by ceaselessly predicating being—can, itself, come to a halt in death. When we cease to find ourselves at home in signification, we are haunted by an unspecifiable feeling of mortality.

34 "Death is a displaced name for a linguistic predicament." See Paul de Man, "Autobiography as De-Facement," *The Rhetoric of Romanticism* (New York: Columbia University Press, 1984), p. 81.

35   There on the highest pinnacle he set
      The Son of God; and added thus in scorn:
         There stand, if thou wilt stand; to stand upright
      Will ask thee skill; I to thy Father's house
      Have brought thee, and highest placed, highest is best,
      Now show thy progeny; if not to stand,
      Cast thyself down; safely if Son of God . . .
      (*Paradise Regained*, 5.549–55)

36 Correspondences, one might add, that, in the wake of Paul de Man's critique of the organic metaphor in "Rhetoric of Temporality" have become, for many Romanticists, suspect. For hardworking and now-influential readings of book 5 that enact de Man's strategies as a hermeneutics of suspicion, see the issue of *Studies in Romanticism* (18, no. 4 [winter 1979]) that de Man edited.

37 Of the many readings of the Immortality Ode in relation to present

or absent, loving or threatening, *fathers,* Peter Manning's "Wordsworth's Intimations Ode and Its Epitaphs" (reprinted in *Reading Romantics* [New York: Oxford University Press, 1990]) is the one I have found most useful in developing my own understanding of Wordsworth's vexed recovery of this dead father *through* Nature. While I do not necessarily share Manning's conclusions about the altered, more sobering tone in the later revisions, I am indebted to his observations about the absent father in the poem and (as will become obvious later in this chapter) the son's metaphorical imitation of Nature's "self-begetting fertility" (75).

38 See also Cathy Caruth's exploration of this term in relation to Freud's use of "anaclisis" as a description of sexual development in *Empirical Truths and Critical Fictions: Locke, Wordsworth, Kant, Freud* (Baltimore: Johns Hopkins University Press, 1991), which follows from a different reading of Wordsworth's poetry, and of Freud, than my own.

39 Kristeva in *Tales of Love* (trans. Leon S. Roudiez [New York: Columbia University Press, 1987]) contributes a theory of voice and of hearing based on the earliest of separations in childhood, separations that are made possible and made less painful by the "loving father of individual prehistory." This paternal voice calls to the son from beyond the emptiness created by the son's incorporation (and melancholic encryption) of his first objects of desire—a nurturer that is not differentiated as either father or mother. (The space that has begun to open between the son's body and the world that had been, until now, entirely the nurturer's body is of course prerequisite for the acquisition of a language driven by loss, difference, and desire.) The paternal voice that calls from beyond that *vide* of loss, difference, and desire helps the son to begin to put words as well as (solid) food into his mouth. Without the opening of such a space between the parents and the child, which Kristeva defines as analogous to Narcissus looking into (but not falling into) a loving reflection, the son cannot "cathect" the ego that will become the self. Without that admiring gaze and loving voice, from beyond the new experience of emptiness, the son could not confidently acquire words. Were this the stern Father of the Law whose prohibition will later produce the superego, rather than the loving father who helps the son generate the first elements of an ego, the son in this narcissistic crisis might simply fall into the breach and (in Jacobus's judgment of failed poetry) *drown,* never to emerge as a subject.

40 Susan Wolfson, "The Illusion of Mastery: Wordsworth's Revisions of 'The Drowned Man of Esthwaite,' 1799, 1805, 1850," *PMLA* 99, no. 5 (October 1984): 917–35; Peter Manning, "Reading Wordsworth's Revision: Othello and the Drowned Man," *Reading Romantics,* pp. 87–114.

41 Wolfson details Wordsworth's "adjustments of biographical coordinates" in revisions of the poem. In fact, the drowning "happened on the first anniversary of her death—the poetry of the later death at once covering and subtly recovering the memory of the earlier one" (923). I do not share Wolfson's conclusion that Wordsworth's revisions express a need to "master" death by denying it.

42 Philip Kuberski in *Chaosmos: Literature, Science, and Theory* (Albany: State University of New York, 1994) explores the language of a Nature that itself refuses the binary operations of human thought. If we extend Kuberski's conclusions to *The Prelude*, Wordsworth glimpsed in the death of human constructs Nature's resistant but uncanny life. While Paul de Man dismisses the "organicism" of the poet who believes that poems, like flowers, may originate in a Nature that exists beyond the artifice of language, in "The Metaphor of the Shell" (*The Persistence of Memory* [Berkeley: University of California Press, 1992]) Kuberski, in his own reading of book 5, helps us to imagine, with Wordsworth, a Nature whose alien language of dead objects speaks with a yet-living voice to the poet from beyond the failures of metaphysics (or a narrowly defined reason) to represent, or to understand, either death or Nature. Fossils, shells, and stones, as Kuberski suggests, are figures or tropes for what the human mind recognizes (and commemorates) as death, even as they speak to us as manifestations of the otherness, the persistence, and the perfection of Nature's nonhuman memory, language, and history:

The literary, which is to say the unsettling, aspect of a shell or a skeleton is that it continues to exist after life has passed from it. Within the fleshy narrative of character and personality there is a plot like a stone, a pattern which links all men and women to the generic and the mortal. Thus even more uncanny is a seashell abandoned on the edge of the sea, and later found on a mountain miles above it. It was thus that Darwin, during his voyage on the *Beagle,* began to imagine the dynamic and ancient nature of the earth. While climbing in the Andes, some miles above the Pacific, he discovered the fossils of seashells. . . . Later he would imagine, like Wordsworth, the connection between the animate and the inanimate. (92)

43 This is perhaps the place to suggest how Kurt Heinzelman's understanding of Wordsworth's "work" differs from the representation of his vocation, and its place (or absence) in systems of exchange, that I have offered. While his reading of Wordsworth's concern to make poetry a matter of active exchange between laborer and consumer is more sympathetic than Liu's (*Wordsworth: The Sense of History*), nevertheless Heinzelman's paradigm does not do justice to Wordsworth's awareness

that meaning may be most significant when it lies buried, resistant to consumption. See Heinzelman, "Wordsworth's Labor Theory: An Economics of Compensation," in *The Economics of the Imagination* (Amherst: University of Massachusetts Press, 1980), pp. 196–233.

44 Hegel in *Phenomenology of Spirit* makes similar observations about the relationship between living being and inert skull. Indeed, he notes that the apparent antithesis of a skull or bone that continues to "be" when *Geist* is no longer its occupant leads Hegel, like Wordsworth, to note the limitations of a "final state of Reason" that "in its observational role is its worst; and that is why its reversal becomes a necessity" (206). From the translation of A. V. Miller (Oxford: Oxford University Press, 1977).

45 Interpretations of Wordsworth's repossession of this dream have a long history, including attribution of the original to Descartes, which may be traced in Richard Onorato's *The Character of the Poet*. Theresa M. Kelley, in "Spirit and Geometric Form: The Stone and the Shell in Wordsworth's Arab Dream" (*Studies in English Literature* 22 [1982]: 563–82) perceives the presence of the science of his day in Wordsworth's construction of a stone that "looks backward to traditional knowledge and its preservation" and the shell that "projects itself forward and seeks new options for self-preservation" (565).

46 Onorato in *The Character of the Poet* rightly reminds us that this dream would have been particularly compelling to an orphan, where "a death in the past" becomes "the impending revelation." I do not share his conviction, however, that book 5 is a response to "the pressure of regressive need in a continuing allegiance to the pleasure-principle" (375).

47 Indeed, when Wordsworth describes (implicitly to Coleridge) the pleasure of reading pastoral romances, the figure of his mother returns to him, almost as if unbidden. It is *The Prelude*'s only extended memorial to her.

48 Not only did Wordsworth grow up to become a preserver of frail shrines that speak, like the Arab to whom the dreamer sought to cleave, and to be tempted to follow the wandering Quixote who eschews family (as Wordsworth himself had done in 1795) for the sake of a "mad" romance with human ideals, but also, in imitation of the wandering peddlers he celebrates in other poems, to be attentive to "commerce." Yet Wordsworth, sophisticated in his understanding of how poetry moves backward as well as forward on its own feet, sought far more than prestige or financial gain in identifying with his peddlers. Like the learned packman whom the poet cites as one of two peddlers who were models for the figures in *The Ruined Cottage* and *The Pedlar* (poems, significantly, to which Wordsworth earnestly returned during the "dejection" year before his marriage), the wanderer serves in these poems as a figure for the reader whose book learning is confirmed by experience that is worldly and yet that is not conventionally familial. Wordsworth once said that had he sought a vocation other than poetry, he would have chosen the peddler's. The peddler literalizes with his feet the word "metaphor," bearing across distances stories and goods, dependent (as Wordsworth the poet would be) on his rhythmic "feet." All of the examples of wandering in book 5 are passages between words and things, and words and texts, in ways that accumulate, for the reader, adult experiences. And yet, paradoxically, they also resist exchange, notably the exchange of a child's lost (or dead) objects for their symbols only. The Arab, himself a literalization of desertion, would bury rather than carry meaning. Wordsworth is most like the Bedouin in his mastery of tempests that may redeem past time (*tempus*), even as they may induce fears of times to come.

49 Douglas Wilson in *The Romantic Dream* discusses in detail both the "dreamwork" of the spots and the ways in which they might be viewed as manifestations of the Freudian uncanny. What is missing from this very able account, no less (one might argue) than in Freud's own over-Oedipalized discussion of a home that is also not home, is the absence that in a sense may be foundational in "The Uncanny." If the emptiness or lack feared by the son leads him to fetishize the hidden feminine organs of pleasure and of generation, then he can only (as Julia Kristeva argues in *Black Sun*, trans. Leon Roudiez [New York: Columbia University Press, 1989], pp. 27–29), in turn, fear as "death-*bearing*" the mother/female whose lack he cannot *bear* (or bare) to "see." To this phenomenon one might well trace not only the blinded son's "sublime" encounters (that turn out to be his fearful recoveries of the "abyss" as a woman/Nature that he has himself incorporated and encrypted rather than as castrative father) but also, arguably, the history of skewed readings of *The Prelude* in which the poet is alleged to discover in Nature a masculine and Oedipal surpassal of Nature and identification with paternal (which is to say, human or even humanist) authority. See David Ellis's *Wordsworth, Freud, and the Spots of Time: Interpretation in "The Prelude"* (Cambridge: Cambridge University Press, 1985) for another, still Oedipal, approach.

50 Wolfson, "The Illusion of Mastery," p. 923.

51 It is in book 6 that Wordsworth describes this visit. Note the presence in this passage of the "naked pools," "bare fell," and—almost in echo of the "golden treasure" of books in book 5—"golden gleam":

> And o'er the Border Beacon and the waste
> Of naked pools and common crags that lay
> Exposed on the bare fell, was scattered love—
> A spirit of pleasure, and youth's golden gleam.
> (6.242–45)

Significantly, in this context the return to Penrith allows Wordsworth to productively misremember that Coleridge had shared in the experience. As he thinks of Coleridge's "melancholy lot" in the spring of 1804, preparing in London to embark for the Mediterranean, Wordsworth gives to this "spot," as he does to the actual spots of time, "A renovating virtue" by which, when depressed, "our minds / Are nourished and invisibly repaired":

> O friend, we had not seen thee at that time,
> And yet a power is on me and a strong
> Confusion, and I seem to plant thee there.
> Far art thou wandered now in search of health,
> And milder breezes—melancholy lot—
> But thou art with us, with us in the past,
> The present, with us in the times to come.
> There is no grief, no sorrow, no despair,
> No languor, no dejection, no dismay,
> No absence scarcely can there be for those
> Who love as we do. . . .
> (246–56)

52 In *Wordsworth and the Worth of Words* (Cambridge: Cambridge University Press, 1986), Hugh Sykes Davies helpfully discusses the ways in which Wordsworth effectively employs the repetition of key words in such passages as the spots of time.

53 Coleridge, as I suggest in n. 51 is also made a fellow traveler in the book 6 version of this return.

54 Snowdon is, of course, in many senses a refiguring of the poet's crossing of the Alps in book 6, where "Winds thwarting winds" are forlorn, "Black drizzling crags" "spake by the wayside / As if a voice were in them," and where Dorothy is herself metaphorically present as the brook that is a fellow traveler of the road "in this gloomy pass" (6.553–65). The narration of that crossing began with a memory of dejection, "A deep and genuine sadness" (491–92). It concludes with an image analogous to the "homeless waters": the "unfathered vapour" that Imagination is like, even as it approaches "athwart me." The lines that follow also anticipate Snowdon in that the poet, as he recognizes its "glory"

finds for the Imagination he is addressing *"our* home" (my emphasis), one that "Is with infinitude" (538–40). Such a mind, he concludes, seeks not visible authority but, rather because it is "blest in thoughts / That are their own perfection and reward" is "Strong in itself, and in the access of joy / Which hides it like the overflowing Nile" (545–48).

55 See previous n. 21 in which I discuss Hertz's feminization of the sublime. Slavoj Žižek, in an analysis of the sublime that also departs helpfully from the Kantian (and other Oedipal) configurations of it, defines the sublime object as whatever happens to stand in the place of the absent, and cathectic, Real. In this sense the sublime object represents both the impossibility of representing the Real within the constructs of the Symbolic Order and of the Real's ineffaceable presence in that very place. "Thus," Žižek concludes, "by means of the very failure of representation, we can have a presentiment of the true dimension of the Thing" (*The Sublime Object of Ideology* [London: Verso, 1989], p. 203). The Real intrudes, in other words, precisely in such blue chasms or breaches as Wordsworth encounters, through Nature's representation of the unrepresentable, on Snowdon. Lacan, in "God and the *Jouissance* of Woman" (*Feminine Sexuality: Jacques Lacan and the "École Freudienne"* [New York: W. W. Norton, 1982]) proposes that the Real is the domain of that which cannot exist: "God" and "Woman." Wordsworth's encounter of "The sense of God, or whatsoe'er is dim / Or vast in its own being" through a Nature whose pleasure is unrepresentable pleasure (and who, one might say, takes pleasure *in* the unrepresentable) may, according to both readings, suggest an encounter with the Real that is woman.

56 See previous note concerning God and the Real. Weiskel in *The Romantic Sublime* helpfully suggests that the experience of the sublime is precisely that of God's vacancy in a Protestant culture that expelled Him so quickly that the soul remains present but unoccupied.

57 The passages preceding that discussion concern, significantly, a "pinnace," a body of "dead still water" that echoes the solitary music of boy playing the flute, and the moon, his love for which was "analogous" to "patriotic and domestic love" (2.170–200).

58 In using the word "wand," Wordsworth resorts to the very tool of the wizards who in book 10 misled him into rationalism and who on the Plain of Sarum conduct both mysteries and human sacrifice.

59 Žižek represents this in particularly compelling language and diagrams in "Che Vuoi?" in *The Sublime Object of Ideology*. In *Tarrying with the Negative: Kant, Hegel, and the Critique of Ideology* (Durham: Duke University Press, 1993), he considers the ways in which reason itself depends upon our blind (and consecrating) faith in order for interpellation to persuade the self it has already occupied that the Symbolic Order or Law of the Father is (beyond all reason) eternal. It mimics, in other words, the infinity (the Real) that precedes (and, as both Žižek and Wordsworth know) will survive the death of human discourse and human history that excludes it: "Therein resides the ambiguous link between the Symbolic and death: by assuming a symbolic identity, i.e., by identifying myself with a symbol which is potentially my epitaph, I as it were 'outpass myself into death.' However, this precipitation toward death at the same time functions as its opposite; it is designed to forestall death, to assume my posthumous life in the symbolic tradition which will outlive my death—an obsessive strategy, if there ever was one: in an act of precipitous identification *I hasten to assume death in order to avoid it*" (76). So afraid are we of the nothingness we would experience in the Law's absence (that is, in its death) that we engage in "anticipatory identification" as a "kind of preemptive strike," Žižek claims, a "performative" speech act that allows the speaker to "elude and obliterate" the absence he fears "in the very kernel" of the Law. Althusser, Žižek concludes, "does justice to the moment of retroactivity" that makes the Symbolic Order seem so "real," "to the illusion of the 'always-already,' " yet Althusser "leaves out of consideration the anticipatory overtaking" that makes the interpellated subject repeatedly deny the Real—the nothingness, or the death— that haunts the "reality" of the Law.

60 My reading, while it is based on my own debts to poststructuralist theory (both psychoanalytic and Marxist), diverges sharply from interpretations of Snowdon offered by Mary Jacobus, Alan Liu, and (most recently) Douglas Wilson.

61 The cave of Yordas, no less than the cave in book 5, offers fascinating parallels to this one, for, as we may recall, it enables the poet to perceive, as a place of troubled but engaging "passage," the spectacles of slipping signifiers he encountered in the city.

62 Claudette Sartiliot, *Herbarium/Verbarium* (Lincoln: University of Nebraska Press, 1993).

63 "Scientists such as Ilya Prigogine and Eric Jantsch have argued that organic structures do indeed 'begin' with the spiral or turbulent movement in fluid media such as water or air, which either deepen into a vortex or rise into a cone. There is thus a passageway from the world of stars and seas, stones and water to the world of living creatures. . . . one discovers this startling complicity of life and geometry, of mathematical description and poetic forms: a seashell is both evidence and metaphor for this necessary relationship." Kuberski, *The Persistence of Memory*, p. 93.

Afterword

1 Harold Bloom, *The Anxiety of Influence: A Theory of Poetry* (Oxford: Oxford University Press, 1973), p. 31.

2 Harold Bloom, *Yeats* (Oxford: Oxford University Press, 1970), p. 5.

3 While the importance of distinguishing these three related terms is a central concern to Lacanian and Kristevan psychoanalysis, the urgency of our insistence on distinguishing the child's need and/or desire for the mother from its love for the father of individual prehistory is closely related to the distinction we insist exists between more "primitive" or "regressive" forms of internalization (incorporation) and the act that will eventually lead the child away from both mother and father: identification. Need continues to haunt our desire (as desire continues to haunt our love) for books no less than it does our more obviously human relations.

4 Jerome McGann, *The Romantic Ideology: A Critical Investigation* (Chicago: University of Chicago Press, 1983), p. 2.

5 Alan Liu, *Wordsworth: The Sense of History* (Stanford: Stanford University Press, 1989), pp. 392–93.

6 Cynthia Chase, "The Accidents of Disfiguration: Limits to Literal and Rhetorical Reading in Book V of *The Prelude*," *Studies in Romanticism* 18, no. 4 (winter 1979): 547–66. Citation is on p. 562.

7 "Like most readers, I had luxuriated in the language of 'St. Agnes,' conjured with the marked allusiveness of the text, and framed the poem by a number of allegorical systems. Always, however, there remained a felt abyss between discourse and meaning: always a clear impression of violence perpetrated. . . . Because the critical seemed at once overpowering and ineffectual, the pedagogical task felt distinctly guilty." Marjorie Levinson, *Keats's Life of Allegory: The Origins of a Style* (London: Basil Blackwell, 1988), p. 3.

8 Julia Kristeva in *Tales of Love* (trans. Leon S. Roudiez [New York: Columbia University Press, 1987]) elucidates the joint origins of language and love in the psyche as the child's tentative move from the maternal breast to the loving father of individual prehistory who mollifies but who also enables the leap from home into the world.

9 See Nicolas Abraham and Maria Torok, *The Wolf Man's Magic Word: A Cryptonymy,* trans. Nicholas T. Rand with a foreword by Jacques Derrida (Minneapolis: University of Minnesota Press, 1986).

10 Judith Butler, *Bodies That Matter: On the Discursive Limits of "Sex"* (New York: Routledge, 1993), p. 65.

11 Judith Butler, *Gender Trouble: Feminism and the Subversion of Identity* (New York: Routledge, 1990), p. 113.

12 From the two-volume edition of Wordsworth's *Poems,* ed. John O. Hayden (London: Penguin Books, 1977).

13 Wordsworth further confounds the difference between what Derrida in *Dissemination* (trans. Barbara Johnson [Chicago: University of Chicago Press, 1981]) calls the "nonviable seed" of writing, gathering the harvests of others while "wandering outside the domain of life" (152), and that of "living speech," which "makes its capital bear fruit and does not divert its seminal potency toward indulgence in pleasures without paternity" (152).

14 All quotations of poems by Keats are from *John Keats: Complete Poems,* ed. Jack Stillinger (Cambridge: Harvard University Press, 1982).

15 To call this a "family romance" would be insensitive, for Keats lost both of his parents before he turned for solace to books and to "bookishness." In *John Keats* (Cambridge: Harvard University Press, 1982), Walter Bate describes Keats's transformation from "normal" boisterousness to grieving scholarship:

Inevitably there was the momentary retreat that we all experience, and the strong but confused sense that a large responsibility had fallen on him. For he was now the oldest male in the family, and except for his grandmother the oldest person. The boy of fourteen who could plunge like a terrier against injustice now crept, said Edward Holmes, into a "nook under the master's desk" in the schoolroom at Enfield; and anyone who saw him, in this "impassioned and prolonged" sense of loss, felt the "liveliest pity & sympathy." In that desire to hide grief, that retreat of the small child beneath the desk of the kindly schoolmaster, John Clarke—there was no one else—we have a hint of the future. The home or refuge to which he gradually turns will have something to do with the sort of world John Clarke represented. (21)

16 I am grateful to Eve Kosofsky Sedgwick's pathbreaking studies of the discourse of addiction for much of the analysis that follows. "Jane Austen and the Masturbating Girl," "Epidemics of the Will," and "Privilege of Unknowing: Diderot's *The Nun,*" all reprinted in *Tendencies* (Durham: Duke University Press, 1993), especially illuminate the inescapable relationship between desire, reading, and discipline.

17 John Bayley, "Keats and Reality," *Read,* 21 March 1962.

18 Bate, *John Keats,* p. 448.

19 Ibid., p. 439.

20 Christopher Ricks, *Keats and Embarrassment* (Oxford: Oxford University Press, 1974), p. 94.

21 Earl Wasserman, "The Eve of St. Agnes," *The Finer Tone: Keats's Major Poems* (Baltimore: Johns Hopkins University Press, 1953), p. 109.

22 Jack Stillinger, "Skepticism in *The Eve of St. Agnes,*" *The Hoodwinking of Madeline* (Urbana: University of Illinois Press, 1971), p. 85.

23 Leon Waldoff, *Keats and the Silent Work of the Imagination* (Urbana: University of Illinois Press, 1985), pp. 63–64.

24 Ricks, *Keats and Embarrassment,* p. 165.

25 Tilottama Rajan, *Dark Interpreter: The Discourse of Romanticism* (Ithaca: Cornell University Press, 1980), p. 113.

26 Critical studies of *St. Agnes* typically cite the importance of Keats's experiences with love and death in the months preceding the poem's composition, yet one of the most powerful influences on this poem may well have been an encounter with gothic art and violence in Chichester. According to Bate, a day or two after January 21 (St. Agnes's Eve), when Keats probably began the poem, he and Brown walked to Bedhamptom. On January 25 they attended the dedication of the chapel of Stansted Park (just purchased by a wealthy man) to the mission of converting Jews to Christianity. Bate suggests that, beyond Gittings's observation of affinities between description in *The Eve of St. Mark* and this experience (see *Letters of John Keats,* ed. Robert Gittings [Oxford: Oxford University Press, 1970], p. 214), there exists a possible "connection between some of the detail in the windows and that in the casement stanza of the *Eve of St. Agnes.*" I believe the connection is not merely descriptive.

Following is Keats's recounting of the ceremony's (and the mission's) vulgarity, with "lambs" and "colors" and the frozen features of a parson, all of which suggest his own aesthetic distance from the objets d'art in *St. Agnes,* however great Keats's usual admiration for fine museum pieces: "This Chapel is built by a Mr Way a great Jew converter—who in that line has spent one hundred thousand Pounds—He maintains a great number of poor Jews—Of course his communion plate was stolen—he spoke to the Clerk about it—The Clerk said he was very sorry adding—'I dare Shay your honour its among ush' The Chapel is built in Mr Way's park—The Consecration was—not amusing—there were numbers of carriages, and his house crammed with Clergy—they sanctified the Chapel—and it being a wet day consecrated the burial ground through the vestry window. I begin to hate Parsons—" (February 14–May 3, 1819).

27 The revisions Keats made to this stanza (they were rejected by his friend and publisher) in fact make more explicit the suffused boundaries between text ("spell"), uninterrupted dream, and a sex that is both an identification with the object (being) and an incorporation (Porphyro encloses Madeline "heart to heart," while she—presumably—also takes him into a place yet more sheltered from the "dark winds" that threaten beyond the dream, the castle, and the poem). The boundary between innocence and experience, the hymen, may be violated or, like the spell (or her sleep), perhaps it is unbroken:

> See, while she speaks his arms encroaching slow,
> Have zoned her, heart to heart,—loud, loud the dark winds blow!

> For on the midnight came a tempest fell;
> More sooth, for that his quick rejoinder flows
> Into her burning ear: and still the spell
> Unbroken guards her in serene respose

Cited in Stillinger's commentary on *St. Agnes* in *John Keats: Complete Poems.*

28 In October 1997, while this chapter was in production at Duke University Press, Marjorie Levinson delivered a plenary talk at the North American Society for the Study of Romanticism, in Hamilton, Ontario. She took the occasion to discuss what she called her experience of "depression" in relationship to disappointments with Romanticism and with Marxism. In an effort to understand what she called the "negativism" of a "pattern of scholarly identification with Romanticism," she said that she had returned to her earliest memory of the scene of reading: sitting beside her mother, staring at an illustration in which a bunch of grapes covered the genitals. She has come to understand, she said, "learning to read as a defense against" such evidence, "a way of seeing absence and seeing more." She concluded her talk with a reading of Elizabeth Bishop's "In the Waiting Room," focusing on various tropes of incorporation that the poem includes and, she argued, withholds. She did not relate her conclusions concerning the connection between early childhood reading, psychoanalytic incorporation, and poetic or critical practice to work by Nicolas Abraham and Maria Torok, Judith Butler, and Julia Kristeva. My discussion of Levinson's reading of *The Eve of St. Agnes* was written three years before she delivered her 1997 NASSR talk.

29 Levinson, *Keats's Life of Allegory*, p. 9.

30 This judgment could be extended to Levinson's Marxist critique, itself dependent on her presumptions about what is natural or real. As Slavoj Žižek has argued, it is not in the "manifest content" but rather in the structure of dreams and in the forms of commodity fetishism that the "hard kernel of the real" may be understood.

31 Eve Kosofsky Sedgwick, "Privilege of Unknowing," p. 47.

Works Cited

Abraham, Nicolas, and Maria Torok. *The Shell and the Kernel: Renewals of Psychoanalysis.* Vol. 1. Edited by Nicholas T. Rand. Chicago: University of Chicago Press, 1994.
———. *The Wolf Man's Magic Word: A Cryptonymy.* Translated by Nicholas T. Rand with a foreword by Jacques Derrida. Minneapolis: University of Minnesota Press, 1986.
Abrams, M. H. "The Design of *The Prelude:* Wordsworth's Long Journey Home." In *The Prelude: 1799, 1805, 1850,* edited by Jonathan Wordsworth, M. H. Abrams, and Stephen Gill. New York: W. W. Norton, 1979.
———. *Natural Supernaturalism: Tradition and Revolution in Romantic Literature.* New York: W. W. Norton, 1971.
Aers, David. "Representations of Revolution: From *The French Revolution* to *The Four Zoas.*" In *Critical Paths: Blake and the Argument of Method,* edited by Dan Miller, Mark Bracher, and Donald Ault. Durham: Duke University Press, 1987.
Auden, W. H. *"Don Juan." The Dyer's Hand and Other Essays.* Selected by Edward Mendelson. New York: Vintage International, 1989.
Ault, Donald. *Narrative Unbound: Re-Visioning William Blake's "The Four Zoas."* Barrytown, N.Y.: Station Hill Press, 1987.
Bate, Jonathan. *Romantic Ecology: Wordsworth and the Environmental Tradition.* New York: Routledge, 1991.
Bate, Walter Jackson. *John Keats.* Cambridge: Harvard University Press, 1982.
Bateson, F. W. *Wordsworth: A Re-Interpretation.* London: Longmans, Green, 1956.
Baudrillard, Jean. *Symbolic Exchange and Death.* Translated by Iain Hamilton Grant. Original French publication, 1976. Thousand Oaks, Calif.: Sage Publications, 1993.
Bayley, John. "Keats and Reality." *Read.* 21 March 1962.
Blake, William. *The Complete Poetry and Prose of William Blake.* Edited by David V. Erdman. Commentary by Harold Bloom. Rev. ed. New York: Doubleday, 1988.
Bloom, Harold. *The Anxiety of Influence: A Theory of Poetry.* Oxford: Oxford University Press, 1973.
———. "Nature and Consciousness." In *Romanticism and Consciousness:*

Essays in Criticism, edited by Harold Bloom. New York: W. W. Norton, 1970. Pp. 1–2.

———. "The Unpastured Sea: An Introduction to Shelley." In *Romanticism and Consciousness: Essays in Criticism,* edited by Harold Bloom. New York: W. W. Norton, 1970. Pp. 374–401.

———. *Yeats.* Oxford: Oxford University Press, 1970.

Bohm, David. *Wholeness and the Implicate Order.* 1980. Paperback reprint, London: Routledge, 1994.

Bowlby, John. *Loss: Sadness and Depression.* Vol. 3 of the three-volume work *Attachment and Loss.* New York: Basic Books, 1980.

Bracher, Mark. "Rouzing the Faculties: Lacanian Psychoanalysis and the Marriage of Heaven and Hell in the Reader." In *Critical Paths: Blake and the Argument of Method,* edited by Dan Miller, Mark Bracher, and Donald Ault. Durham: Duke University Press, 1987. Pp. 166–203.

Brisman, Leslie. *Romantic Origins.* Ithaca: Cornell University Press, 1978.

Burton, Robert. *The Anatomy of Melancholy.* Philadelphia: J. W. Moore, 1855.

Butler, Judith. *Bodies That Matter: On the Discursive Limits of "Sex."* New York: Routledge, 1993.

———. *Gender Trouble: Feminism and the Subversion of Identity.* New York: Routledge, 1990.

Byron, George Gordon. *Byron's Don Juan: A Variorum Edition.* Edited by Truman Guy Steffan and Willis W. Pratt. Austin: University of Texas Press, 1957.

———. *Byron's Letters and Journals.* Edited by Leslie A. Marchand. London: John Murray, 1979.

———. *Don Juan.* Edited by T. G. Steffan, E. Steffan, and W. W. Pratt. New York: Penguin, 1982.

———. *The Poetical Works of Byron.* Edited by Robert F. Gleckner. Boston: Houghton Mifflin, 1975.

Carothers, Yvonne M. "*Alastor:* Shelley Corrects Wordsworth." *Modern Language Quarterly* 42, no. 1 (March 1981): 21–47.

Carr, Stephen Leo. "Illuminated Printing: Towards a Logic of Difference." In *Unnam'd Forms: Blake and Textuality,* edited by Nelson Hilton and Thomas A. Vogler. Berkeley: University of California Press, 1987. Pp. 177–96.

Caruth, Cathy. *Empirical Truths and Critical Fictions: Locke, Wordsworth, Kant, Freud.* Baltimore: Johns Hopkins University Press, 1991.

Chandler, James. *Wordsworth's Second Nature: A Study of the Poetry and Politics.* Chicago: University of Chicago Press, 1984.

Chase, Cynthia. "The Accidents of Disfiguration: Limits to Literal and Rhetorical Reading in Book V of *The Prelude.*" *Studies in Romanticism* 18, no. 4 (winter 1979): 547–66.

Chesser, Eustace, ed. *Shelley and Zastrozzi: Self-Revelation of a Neurotic.* London: Gregg Press, 1965.

Christensen, Jerome. *Lord Byron's Strength: Romantic Writing and Commercial Society.* Baltimore: Johns Hopkins University Press, 1993.

Claridge, Laura. *Romantic Potency: The Paradox of Desire.* Ithaca: Cornell University Press, 1992.

Clark, David L. " 'The Necessary Heritage of Darkness': Tropics of Negativity in Schelling, Derrida, and de Man." In *Intersections: Nineteenth-Century Philosophy and Contemporary Theory,* edited by Tilottama Rajan and David L. Clark. Albany: State University Press of New York, 1995.

Coleridge, Samuel Taylor. *Biographia Literaria. The Collected Works of Samuel Taylor Coleridge,* edited by James Engell and W. Jackson Bate. Princeton: Princeton University Press, 1983.

——. *Collected Letters of Samuel Taylor Coleridge.* Edited by Earl Leslie Griggs. Oxford: Oxford University Press, 1956.

Crawford, Rachel. "The Structure of the Sororal in Wordsworth's 'Nutting.'" *Studies in Romanticism* 31, no. 2 (summer 1992): 197–212.

Curran, Stuart. *Poetic Form and British Romanticism.* New York: Oxford University Press, 1986.

Davies, Hugh Sykes. *Wordsworth and the Worth of Words.* Cambridge: Cambridge University Press, 1986.

de Bolla, Peter. *The Discourse of the Sublime: Readings in History, Aesthetics, and the Subject.* Oxford: Basil Blackwell, 1989.

de Man, Paul. "Autobiography as De-Facement." *The Rhetoric of Romanticism.* New York: Columbia University Press, 1984.

——. "Intentional Structure of the Romantic Image." *The Rhetoric of Romanticism.* New York: Columbia University Press, 1984.

——. "Introduction." *Studies in Romanticism* (special issue: "Articles on the Rhetoric of Romanticism"): 18, no. 4 (winter 1979): 495–99.

Derrida, Jacques. *Aporias.* Translated by Thomas Dutoit. Stanford: Stanford University Press, 1993.

——. *Dissemination.* Translated by Barbara Johnson. Chicago: University of Chicago Press, 1981.

——. "Economimesis." *Diacritics* 11 (1981): 3–25.

——. *Of Grammatology.* Translated by Gayatri Spivak. Baltimore: Johns Hopkins University Press, 1974.

——. *Specters of Marx: The State of the Debt, the Work of Mourning, and the New International.* Translated by Peggy Kamuf. Introduction by Bernd Magnus and Stephen Cullenberg. Routledge: New York, 1994.

Eagleton, Terry. *The Ideology of the Aesthetic.* London: Basil Blackwell, 1990.

Edmundson, Mark. "Vital Intimations: Wordsworth, Coleridge, and the Promise of Criticism." *South Atlantic Quarterly* 91, no. 3 (summer 1992): 739–64.

Ellis, David. *Wordsworth, Freud, and the Spots of Time: Interpretation in "The Prelude."* Cambridge: Cambridge University Press, 1985.

Engell, James. *The Creative Imagination: Enlightenment to Romanticism.* Cambridge: Harvard University Press, 1981.

Erdman, David V. *Blake, Prophet against Empire.* Rev. ed. Garden City, N.J.: Anchor Books, 1969.

——, ed. *Blake and His Bibles.* West Cornwall, Conn.: Locust Hill Press, 1990.

Essick, Robert N. "*The Four Zoas:* Intention and Production." *Blake Illustrated Quarterly* 18 (spring 1985): 216–20.

——. *William Blake and the Language of Adam.* Oxford: Oxford University Press, 1989.

Ferenczi, Sandor. "Confusion of Tongues between Adults and the Child." In *The Assault on Truth,* edited by Jeffrey Moussaief Masson. New York: Farrar, Straus & Giroux, 1984. Pp. 283–95.

Foucault, Michel. *The History of Sexuality: Vol. 1.* Translated by Robert Hurley. New York: Vintage Books, 1980.

——. *Madness and Civilization: A History of Insanity in the Age of Reason.* Translated by Richard Howard. New York: Vintage Books, 1973.

Freud, Sigmund. *Beyond the Pleasure Principle.* Translated and edited by James Strachey. New York: W. W. Norton, 1990.

——. *Civilization and Its Discontents.* Translated and edited by James Strachey. New York: W. W. Norton, 1961.

——. *The Ego and the Id.* Translated by James Strachey. New York: W. W. Norton, 1962.

——. "Family Romances." *The Sexual Enlightenment of Children.* New York: Macmillan, 1963.

——. *The Future of an Illusion.* Translated by James Strachey. New York: W. W. Norton, 1982.

——. "Mourning and Melancholia." *General Psychological Theory.* New York: Macmillan, 1963.

——. "The 'Uncanny.'" In *On Creativity and the Unconscious,* edited by Benjamin Nelson. New York: Harper & Row, 1958.

Fry, Paul. *The Poet's Calling in the English Ode.* New Haven: Yale University Press, 1980.

Gelpi, Barbara Charlesworth. *Shelley's Goddess: Maternity, Language, Subjectivity.* New York: Oxford University Press, 1992.

Gill, Stephen. *William Wordsworth: A Life.* Oxford: Oxford University Press, 1989.

Gleckner, Robert F. *Blake and Spenser.* Baltimore: Johns Hopkins University Press, 1985.

——. *Byron and the Ruins of Paradise.* Baltimore: Johns Hopkins University Press, 1967.

——. "Most Holy Forms of Thought: Some Observations on Blake and Language." In *Essential Articles for the Study of William Blake, 1970–1984,* edited by Nelson Hilton. Hamden, Conn.: Archon Books, 1986. Pp. 91–117.

——. *The Piper and the Bard: A Study of William Blake.* Detroit: Wayne State University Press, 1959.

Godwin, William. *Things as They Are, or the Adventures of Caleb Williams.* Edited by Maurice Hindle. London: Penguin, 1988.

Goux, Jean-Joseph. *Symbolic Economies: After Marx and Freud.* Translated by Jennifer Curtiss Gage. Ithaca: Cornell University Press, 1990.

Grant, John E. "Jesus and the Powers That Be in Blake's Design for Young's *Night Thoughts.*" In *Blake and His Bibles,* edited by David V. Erdman. West Cornwall, Conn.: Locust Hill Press, 1990. Pp. 71–116.

Hartman, Geoffrey. "Romanticism and 'Anti-Self-Consciousness.'" In *Romanticism and Consciousness: Essays in Criticism,* edited by Harold Bloom. New York: W. W. Norton, 1970. Pp. 46–56.

——. *Wordsworth's Poetry 1787–1814.* 1964. Reprint, with "Retrospect 1971." New Haven: Yale University Press, 1971.

Heaney, Seamus. "The Makings of a Music: Reflections on Wordsworth and Yeats." *Preoccupations: Selected Prose, 1968–1978.* New York: Farrar, Straus & Giroux, 1980.

Hegel, G. W. F. *Phenomenology of Spirit.* Translated by A. V. Miller. Oxford: Oxford University Press, 1977.

Heinzelman, Kurt. "Byron's Poetry of Politics." *Texas Studies in Literature and Language* 23, no. 3 (fall 1981): 360–88.

——. *The Economics of the Imagination.* Amherst: University of Massachusetts Press, 1980.

Hertz, Neil. *The End of the Line: Essays on Psychoanalysis and the Sublime.* New York: Columbia University Press, 1985.

Hilton, Nelson. *Literal Imagination: Blake's Vision of Words.* Berkeley: University of California Press, 1983.

Hilton, Nelson, and Thomas A. Vogler, eds. *Unnam'd Forms: Blake and Textuality.* Berkeley: University of California Press, 1986.

Hoeveler, Diane Long. *Romantic Androgyny: The Woman Within.* University Park: Pennsylvania State University Press, 1990.

Hogle, Jerrold E. *Shelley's Process: Radical Transference and the Development of His Major Works.* New York: Oxford University Press, 1988.

Holmes, Richard. *Shelley: The Pursuit.* London: Penguin Books, 1987.

Irigaray, Luce. *Speculum of the Other Woman.* Translated by Gillian C. Gill. Ithaca: Cornell University Press, 1985.

Jacobson, Edith. "The Return of the Lost Parent." *Canadian Psychiatric Association Journal* 11 (1966): S259–S266.

Jacobus, Mary. *Romanticism, Writing, and Sexual Difference: Essays on "The Prelude."* Oxford: Oxford University Press, 1989.

Jameson, Fredric. *The Seeds of Time.* New York: Columbia University Press, 1994.

——. "The Vanishing Mediator; or, Max Weber as Storyteller." *The Ideologies of Theory: Essays 1971–1986,* Vol. 2. 1973. Reprint, Minneapolis: University of Minnesota Press, 1988.

Jamison, Kay Redfield. *Touched with Fire: Manic-Depressive Illness and the Artistic Temperament.* New York: Free Press, 1993.

Keach, William. "Obstinate Questionings: The Immortality Ode and *Alastor.*" *The Wordsworth Circle* 12, no. 1 (winter 1981): 36–44.

Keats, John. *Complete Poems.* Edited by Jack Stillinger. 1978. Reprint, Cambridge: Harvard University Press, 1982.

——. *Letters of John Keats.* Edited by Robert Gittings. Oxford: Oxford University Press, 1970.

Kelley, Theresa M. "Spirit and Geometric Form: The Stone and the Shell in Wordsworth's Arab Dream." *Studies in English Literature* 22 (1982): 563–82.

Kerrigan, William. *The Sacred Complex: On the Psychogenesis of "Paradise Lost."* Cambridge: Harvard University Press, 1983.

Kristeva, Julia. *Black Sun: Depression and Melancholia.* Translated by Leon S. Roudiez. New York: Columbia University Press, 1989.

——. *Powers of Horror: An Essay on Abjection.* Translated by Leon S. Roudiez. New York: Columbia University Press, 1982.

——. *Revolution in Poetic Language.* Translated by Margaret Waller. New York: Columbia University Press, 1984.

——. *Tales of Love.* Translated by Leon S. Roudiez. New York: Columbia University Press, 1987.

Kroeber, Karl. *Ecological Literary Criticism: Romantic Imagining and the Biology of Mind.* New York: Columbia University Press, 1994.

Kuberski, Philip. *Chaosmos: Literature, Science, and Theory.* Albany: State University of New York Press, 1994.

——. "The Metaphor of the Shell." *The Persistence of Memory.* Berkeley: University of California Press, 1992.

Kuhn, Reinhard. *The Demon at Noontide: Ennui in Western Literature.* Princeton: Princeton University Press, 1976.

Lacan, Jacques. *Feminine Sexuality: Jacques Lacan and the "École Freudienne."* New York: W. W. Norton, 1982.

Laplanche, Jean. *Life and Death in Psychoanalysis.* Translated by Jeffrey Mehlman. Baltimore: Johns Hopkins University Press, 1976.

Lepenies, Wolf. *Melancholy and Society.* Translated by Jeremy Gaines and Doris Jones. Cambridge: Harvard University Press, 1992.

Levinson, Marjorie. *Keats's Life of Allegory: The Origins of a Style.* London: Basil Blackwell, 1988.

Lindenberger, Herbert. *On Wordsworth's "Prelude."* Princeton: Princeton University Press, 1963.

Liu, Alan. *Wordsworth: The Sense of History.* Stanford: Stanford University Press, 1989.

Mann, Paul. "*The Book of Urizen* and the Horizon of the Book." In *Unnam'd Forms: Blake and Textuality,* edited by Nelson Hilton and Thomas A. Vogler. Berkeley: University of California Press, 1986. Pp. 49–68.

——. "The Final State of *The Four Zoas.*" *Blake Illustrated Quarterly* 18 (1985): 204–15.

Manning, Peter J. *Byron and His Fictions.* Detroit: Wayne State University Press, 1978.

——. *Reading Romantics: Texts and Contexts.* New York: Oxford University Press, 1990.

Marchand, Leslie. *Byron: A Portrait.* New York: Alfred A. Knopf, 1970.

Martindale, Colin. "Father's Absence, Psychopathology, and Poetic Eminence." *Psychological Reports* 31 (December 1972): 843–47.

Marx, Karl. *Marx's Capital: A Student Edition.* Edited by C. J. Arthur (London: Lawrence & Wishart, 1992).

McGann, Jerome. *The Romantic Ideology: A Critical Investigation.* Chicago: University of Chicago Press, 1983.

Milton, John. *Complete Poems and Major Prose.* Edited by Merritt Y. Hughes. New York: Macmillan, 1957.

——. *The Poems of John Milton.* Edited by John Carey and Alastair Fowler. London: Longman, 1968.

Mueschke, Paul, and Earl L. Griggs. "Wordsworth as the Prototype of the Poet in Shelley's *Alastor.*" *Publications of the Modern Language Association* 49 (March 1934): 229–45.

Muldoon, Paul. *Meeting the British.* Winston-Salem: Wake Forest University Press, 1987.

Onorato, Richard J. *The Character of the Poet: Wordsworth in "The Prelude."* Princeton: Princeton University Press, 1971.

Peacock, Thomas Love. "The Four Ages of Poetry." *Critical Theory since Plato.* Edited by Hazard Adams. New York: Harcourt Brace Jovanovich, 1971.

Peterfreund, Stuart. "Between Desire and Nostalgia: Intertextuality in Shelley's *Alastor* and Two Shorter Poems from the *Alastor* Volume." *Romanticism Past and Present* 9, no. 1 (winter 1985): 47–66.

Pynchon, Thomas. "Nearer, My Couch, to Thee." *New York Times Book Review,* 6 June 1993, 3.

Rajan, Tilottama. "Coleridge, Wordsworth, and the Textual Abject." *The Wordsworth Circle* 24, no. 2 (spring 1993): 61–68.

——. *Dark Interpreter: The Discourse of Romanticism.* Ithaca: Cornell University Press, 1980.

——. "Language, Music, and the Body: Nietzsche and Deconstruction." In *Intersections: Nineteenth-Century Philosophy and Contemporary Theory,* edited by Rajan and David L. Clark. Albany: State University of New York, 1995.

——. "Mary Shelley's *Mathilda:* Melancholy and the Political Economy of Romanticism." *Studies in the Novel* 26, no. 2 (summer 1994): pp. 43–68.

Reiman, Donald H. "Wordsworth, Shelley, and the Romantic Inheritance." *Romanticism Past and Present* 5, no. 2 (1981): 3–22.

Ricks, Christopher. *Keats and Embarrassment.* Oxford: Oxford University Press, 1974.

Roe, Nicholas. *The Politics of Nature: Wordsworth and Some Contemporaries.* New York: St. Martin's Press, 1992.

Sacks, Peter. *The English Elegy: Studies in the Genre from Spenser to Yeats.* Baltimore: Johns Hopkins University Press, 1985.

Sartiliot, Claudette. *Herbarium/Verbarium.* Lincoln: University of Nebraska Press, 1993.

Schiesari, Juliana. *The Gendering of Melancholia: Feminism, Psycho-*

analysis, and the Symbolics of Loss in Renaissance Literature. Ithaca: Cornell University Press, 1992.

Schiller, Friedrich von. *Naive and Sentimental Poetry and On the Sublime: Two Essays.* Translated with introduction and notes by Julius A. Elias. New York: Frederick Ungar, 1966.

Schor, Esther H. *Bearing the Dead: The British Culture of Mourning from the Enlightenment to Victoria.* Princeton: Princeton University Press, 1994.

Sedgwick, Eve Kosofsky. *Between Men: English Literature and Male Homosocial Desire.* New York: Columbia University Press, 1985.

——. *The Coherence of Gothic Conventions.* New York: Methuen, 1986.

——. "Epidemics of the Will." In *Tendencies.* Durham: Duke University Press, 1993. Pp. 130–42.

——. "Jane Austen and the Masturbating Girl." In *Tendencies,* pp. 109–29.

——. "A Poem Is Being Written." *Representations* 17 (winter 1987): 110–43. Reprinted in *Tendencies,* pp. 177–214.

——. "Privilege of Unknowing: Diderot's *The Nun.*" In *Tendencies,* pp. 23–51.

Shelley, Percy Bysshe. *The Complete Works of Percy Bysshe Shelley.* Edited by Thomas Hutchinson. Oxford: Oxford University Press, 1940.

——. "A Defense of Poetry." *Critical Theory since Plato.* Edited by Hazard Adams. New York: Harcourt Brace Jovanovich, 1971.

——. *Letters.* Edited by Frederick L. Jones. Oxford: Clarendon Press, 1964.

——. *The Poetical Works of Shelley.* Edited by Newell F. Ford. Boston: Houghton-Mifflin, 1974.

——. *Shelley's Literary and Philosophical Criticism.* Edited by John Shawcross. London: Humphrey Milford, 1923.

——. *Shelley's Poetry and Prose.* Edited by Donald H. Reiman and Sharon B. Powers. New York: W. W. Norton, 1977.

——. *Zastrozzi.* In *Shelley and Zastrozzi: Self-Revelation of a Neurotic,* edited by Eustace Chesser. London: Gregg Press, 1965.

Sickels, Eleanor M. *The Gloomy Egoist: Moods and Themes of Melancholy from Gray to Keats.* 1932. Reprint, New York: Octagon Books, 1969.

Simpson, David. "Reading Blake and Derrida." In *Unnam'd Forms: Blake and Textuality,* edited by Nelson Hilton and Thomas A. Vogler. Berkeley: University of California Press, 1986. Pp. 11–25.

Spivak, Gayatri. "Sex and History in *The Prelude.*" *Texas Studies in Literature and Language* 23, no. 3 (fall 1981): 324–60.

Steffan, Truman Guy. *Byron's "Don Juan": The Making of a Masterpiece.* Vol. 1 of *Byron's "Don Juan": A Variorum Edition,* edited by Steffan and Pratt. Austin: University of Texas Press, 1957.

Stillinger, Jack. "Skepticism in *The Eve of St. Agnes.*" *The Hoodwinking of Madeline.* Urbana: University of Illinois Press, 1971.

Stone, Lawrence. *The Family, Sex, and Marriage in England, 1500–1800.* New York: Harper & Row, 1977.

Thompson, E. P. *Witness Against the Beast: William Blake and the Moral Law.* New York: New Press, 1993.

Vogler, Thomas A. "Re: Naming MIL/TON." In *Unnam'd Forms: Blake and Textuality,* edited by Nelson Hilton and Thomas A. Vogler. Berkeley: University of California Press, 1986. Pp. 141–76.

Waldoff, Leon. *Keats and the Silent Work of the Imagination.* Urbana: University of Illinois Press, 1985.

Wasserman, Earl R. "The Eve of St. Agnes." *The Finer Tone: Keats's Major Poems.* Baltimore: Johns Hopkins University Press, 1953.

———. *Shelley: A Critical Reading.* Baltimore: Johns Hopkins University Press, 1971.

Weber, Max. *The Protestant Ethic and the Spirit of Capitalism.* Translated by Talcott Parsons. New York: Routledge, Chapman, and Hall, 1985.

Weiskel, Thomas. *The Romantic Sublime: Studies in the Structure and Psychology of Transcendence.* 1976. Paperback reprint, Baltimore: Johns Hopkins University Press, 1986.

Weissman, Judith. *Of Two Minds: Poets Who Hear Voices.* Hanover, N.H.: Wesleyan University Press, 1993.

West, Paul. *Byron and the Spoiler's Art.* New York: St. Martin's Press, 1960.

Wilson, Douglas B. *The Romantic Dream: Wordsworth and the Poetics of the Unconscious.* Lincoln: University of Nebraska Press, 1993.

Wolfson, Susan. "The Illusion of Mastery: Wordsworth's Revisions of 'The Drowned Man of Esthwaite,' 1799, 1805, 1850." *PMLA* 99, no. 5 (October 1984): 917–35.

Wordsworth, Jonathan. "The Two-Part *Prelude* of 1799." In *The Prelude: 1799, 1805, 1850,* edited by Jonathan Wordsworth, M. H. Abrams, and Stephen Gill. New York: W. W. Norton, 1979.

Wordsworth, William. *The Poems.* Vols. 1–2. Edited by John O. Hayden. London: Penguin, 1977.

———. *The Prelude: 1799, 1805, 1850.* Edited by Jonathan Wordsworth, M. H. Abrams, and Stephen Gill. New York: W. W. Norton, 1979.

———. *Selected Prose Writings.* Edited by John O. Hayden. New York: Penguin, 1988.

Wordsworth, William and Dorothy. *The Letters of William and Dorothy Wordsworth.* Edited by Ernest de Selincourt. 2d ed. revised by Chester L. Shaver. Vol. 1. Oxford: Oxford University Press, 1967.

Youngquist, Paul. *Madness and Blake's Myth.* University Park: Pennsylvania State University Press, 1989.

Žižek, Slavoj. *Enjoy Your Symptom! Jacques Lacan in Hollywood and Out.* London: Routledge, 1992.

———. *The Metastases of Enjoyment: Six Essays on Women and Causality.* London: Verso, 1994.

———. *The Sublime Object of Ideology.* London: Verso, 1989.

———. *Tarrying with the Negative: Kant, Hegel, and the Critique of Ideology.* Durham: Duke University Press, 1993.

Index

Guinn Batten is Assistant Professor of English
at Washington University in St. Louis, where she teaches
English Romanticism and modern Irish poetry. She has worked
as a newspaper writer and editor, taught yoga classes, earned
an MBA, and managed a small poetry press.

Library of Congress Cataloging-in-Publication Data
Batten, Guinn.
The orphaned imagination : melancholy and commodity culture in English
romanticism / Guinn Batten.
p.   cm.
Includes bibliographical references and index.
ISBN 0-8223-2205-6 (cloth : alk. paper). — ISBN 0-8223-2221-8
(pbk. : alk. paper)
1. English poetry—19th century—History and criticism.
2. Melancholy in literature.   3. Capitalism and literature—Great
Britain—History—19th century.   4. Commercial products—Great
Britain—History—19th century.   5. Poetry—Authorship—Economic
aspects—Great Britain.   6. Loss (Psychology) in literature.
7. Romanticism—Great Britain.   I. Title.
PR575.M34B38   1998
820.9'353—dc21   97-49691